Stock Investing For Canadians For Dummies

W9-CQI-531

The Ten Most Important Points about Stock Investing

1. You're not buying a stock; you're buying a company.

2. The only reason to buy a stock is because the company is making a profit and generating cash.

3. If you buy a stock that isn't making a profit and generating cash, then you're not investing — you're speculating.

4. A stock (or stocks in general) should never represent 100 percent of your assets.

5. In some cases (such as during a severe bear market), stocks are not a good investment at all.

6. A stock's price is dependent on the company, which in turn is dependent on its environment, which includes its customer base, its industry, the general economy, and geopolitics.

7. Your common sense and logic can be just as important in choosing a good stock as the advice of any investment expert.

8. Always have well-reasoned answers to questions such as "Why are you investing in stocks?" and "Why are you investing in a *particular* stock?"

9. If you are uncertain about the prospects of a company (and sometimes even if you are pretty sure), use stop-loss orders.

10. Even if your philosophy is "buy and hold for the long term," continue to monitor your stocks and consider selling them if they're not appreciating in value.

Important Things to Look at in a Company's Fundamentals

- **Earnings:** The bottom line should be higher than the year before.
- **Cash flow:** The company should be a cash generator.
- **Sales:** This "top line" number should be higher than the year before.
- **Debt:** The number should be lower than, or about the same as, the period before.
- **Equity:** The number should be higher than the year before.

Best Internet Tools for Canadian Investors

- Stock-screening tools available at Web sites such as www.smartmoney.com/tools
- Insider trading monitoring at Web sites such as www.marketwatch.com
- Earnings reports and estimates at www.firstcall.com
- Public document databases such as SEDAR at www.sedar.com
- Sources such as www.morningstar.ca that monitor analysts' views and provide stock strategy tips
- Great stock-investing books at www.chapters.indigo.ca or www.amazon.ca
- Resource for alternative views on the stock market (www.fallstreet.com)

For Dummies: Bestselling Book Series for Beginners

Stock Investing For Canadians For Dummies®

Cheat Sheet

The Best Financial Measures

- **Price to earnings ratio:** For large-cap stocks, the ratio should be under 20. For all stocks (including growth, small-cap, and speculative issues), it should not exceed 40.
- **Price-to-sales ratio:** This ratio should be as close to 1 as possible.
- **Return on equity (ROE):** ROE should be going up by at least 10 percent.
- **Earnings growth:** Earnings should be at least 10 percent higher than the year before. This rate should be maintained over several years.
- **Debt-to-asset ratio:** Debt should be 30 percent or less compared to assets.

Eight Events That Could Spell Trouble for Your Stock

- A bear market
- Heavy insider or institutional selling
- A lawsuit by the government or other stakeholder
- Excessive government taxation
- Excessive government regulation
- A securities commission or Attorney General investigation
- An economic slowdown or decline in the industry or sector
- National or international conflict (such as war or acts of terrorism)

Top Ten Web sites for Canadian Investors

- www.csi.ca
- www.tsx.com
- www.adviceforinvestors.com
- www.stockhouse.ca
- www.webfin.com
- cbs.marketwatch.com
- money.cnn.com
- finance.yahoo.com
- www.bloomberg.com
- www.multexinvestor.com

Recommended Reading List for Investors

- The company's annual report, including financial statements
- The reports that the company files with Canadian and U.S. securities regulators
- *Investor's Digest of Canada*
- *Investor's Business Daily*
- *The Globe and Mail* and *National Post*

WILEY

For Dummies: Bestselling Book Series for Beginners

Stock Investing
For Canadians

FOR DUMMIES®

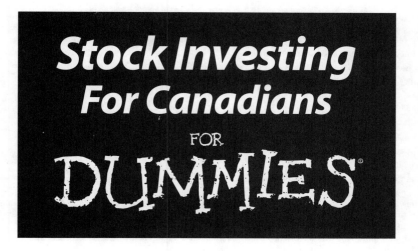

Stock Investing For Canadians

FOR

DUMMIES®

by Andrew Dagys
Paul Mladjenovic

WILEY

John Wiley & Sons Canada, Ltd.

Stock Investing For Canadians For Dummies®

Published by
John Wiley & Sons Canada, Ltd.
22 Worcester Road
Etobicoke, ON M9W 1L1
www.wiley.ca

National Library of Canada Cataloguing in Publication

Dagys, Andrew

Stock investing for Canadians for dummies / Andrew Dagys, Paul Mladjenovic.

Includes index.
ISBN: 0-470-83342-4

1. Stocks — Canada. 2. Investments — Canada. I. Mladjenovic, Paul J. II. Title.

HG5152.D23 2003   332.63'22'0971   C2003-904054-2

Printed in Canada

2 3 4 5 TRI 07 06 05

Distributed in Canada by John Wiley & Sons Canada, Ltd.

For general information on John Wiley & Sons Canada, Ltd., including all books published by Wiley Publishing, Inc., please call our warehouse, Tel 1-800-567-4797. For reseller information, including discounts and premium sales, please call our sales department, Tel 416-646-7992. For press review copies, author interviews, or other publicity information, please contact our marketing department, Tel: 416-646-4584, Fax 416-236-4448.

For authorization to photocopy items for corporate, personal, or educational use, please contact Cancopy, The Canadian Copyright Licensing Agency, One Yonge Street, Suite 1900, Toronto, ON, M5E 1E5 Tel 416-868-1620 Fax 416-868-1621; www.cancopy.com.

About the Authors

Andrew Dagys, CMA, is a best-selling author who has written and co-authored several books, including *Investing Online For Canadians For Dummies* (first and second editions), and *First-time Investing Online For Canadians — CliffsNotes, The Internet For Canadians For Dummies* Starter Kit (first and second editions), and *The Financial Planner for 50+*. Andrew contributes columns to *Forever Young, Canadian Living Magazine*, and other publications. He has appeared on Canada AM and several CBC broadcasts to offer his opinions on the Canadian and world investment landscape.

An avid investor, Andrew uses the Internet to advantage to identify compelling investment opportunities. His business, The Treetop Group, has helped match some of those opportunities with the financial needs of Canadian clients for years. Andrew also enjoys speaking to business and general audiences on the latest investment trends, and new developments in computer technology that can empower Canadians to help meet their personal objectives. He lives in Toronto with his wife Dawn-Ava, and three children — Brendan, Megan, and Jordan.

Andrew looks forward to your comments, and can be reached at aj-dagys@rogers.com.

Paul Mladjenovic is a certified financial planner, financial consultant, writer, and public speaker who has a Web site at www.mladjenovic.com. His business, PM Financial Services, has helped people with financial and business concerns since 1981. He achieved his CFP designation in 1985 and his BA degree from Seton Hall University in 1981. Since 1986, Paul has taught thousands of budding investors through popular national seminars such as "The $50 Wealthbuilder" and "Stock Investing Like a Pro." Paul has been quoted or referenced by many media outlets such as Bloomberg, CNBC, and many financial and business publications and Web sites. As an author, he has written the books *The Unofficial Guide to Picking Stocks* (Hungry Minds, 2000) and *Zero-Cost Marketing* (Todd Publications, 1995) and reports such as "1,001 Stocks with Dividend Reinvestment Plans." In addition, he has authored the software kit *Internet Wealth-Building Tools for Investors* and the forthcoming CD *The Financial Mega-Kit*. In recent years, he has achieved attention as a result of his economic forecasting. In 1999, he forecast the recent bear market.

Dedication

Andrew dedicates this book to his wife, Dawn-Ava, and their children — Brendan, Megan, and Jordan. He thanks God for them all. He commends those who have not lost the courage to invest wisely in the face of a challenging and changing world.

Paul dedicates this book to his beloved Fran, Adam, Joshua, and a loving, supportive family, and also thanks God for them. He also dedicates this book to the millions of people that deserve more knowledge and information to achieve lasting prosperity.

Authors' Acknowledgements

Andrew thanks Robert Harris, who continues to give him opportunities to write books about topics he is passionate about. He also thanks Melanie Rutledge, his editor for the last few years, who added tremendous value, insight, and a cheerful spirit to this work. In fact, she was a key champion of this title, and without her enthusiastic efforts a Canadian edition may not have materialized. Andrew appreciates the leadership and coordination of Joan Whitman, another talented Wiley team member he has had the longstanding pleasure of working with. He thanks Kelli Howey for her many contributions to the polishing of the title. Elizabeth McCurdy, and many others at John Wiley & Sons Canada deserve recognition for their part in shaping this book.

Paul, first and foremost, offers his appreciation and gratitude to the wonderful people at John Wiley & Sons. He finds it a pleasure to work with such a top-notch organization that works so hard to create products that offer readers tremendous value and information. He wishes all continued success. There are some notables there whom he wants to single out.

The first person is Marcia Johnson (his editor), a true publishing professional who has been extremely helpful, understanding, and patient. Those words are not enough to express his thanks for her fantastic guidance. He conveys a special (and he means very special) note of thanks to Cynthia Kitchel, another magnificent professional at John Wiley & Sons. Her forbearance and foresight at a critical juncture became instrumental in making this book a reality. Tina Sims is yet another John Wiley & Sons pro whom he is grateful to work with. She has been wonderful in helping shape his muddled prose into the type of writing that is worthy of the . . . *For Dummies* tradition.

He also wants to thank Kevin Thornton and Mark Butler, who championed this book from the beginning. Fran, Lipa Zyenska, helped make those late nights at the computer more tolerable, and helped him focus on the important things. Teamo and he thank God that they are by his side. With them and the rest of his loving family, he knows that the future will be bright.

His deepest thanks to Murray Sabrin, professor of finance at Ramapo College in New Jersey, who is also a fantastic author and writer. He offered expertise and feedback that have been very valuable and most appreciated.

Lastly, he acknowledges you, the reader. Over the years, you have made the . . . *For Dummies* books what they are today. Your devotion to these wonderful books created a foundation that played a big part in the creation of this volume and many more yet to come. He thanks you!

Publisher's Acknowledgements

We're proud of this book; please send us your comments at canadapt@wiley.com.

Some of the people who helped bring this book to market include the following:

Acquisitions and Editorial

Editor: Melanie Rutledge

Developmental and Copy Editor: Kelli Howey

Cover Photo: LWA-Dann Tardif/CORBIS

Production

Publishing Services Director: Karen Bryan

Project Manager: Elizabeth McCurdy

Project Coordinator: Abigail Brown

Layout and Graphics: Kim Monteforte, Heidy Lawrance Associates

Proofreader: Allyson Latta

Indexer: Belle Wong

John Wiley & Sons Canada, Ltd.

Bill Zerter, Chief Operating Officer

Robert Harris, Publisher, Professional and Trade Division

Publishing and Editorial for Consumer Dummies

Diane Graves Steele, Vice President and Publisher, Consumer Dummies

Joyce Pepple, Acquisitions Director, Consumer Dummies

Kristin A. Cocks, Product Development Director, Consumer Dummies

Michael Spring, Vice President and Publisher, Travel

Suzanne Jannetta, Editorial Director, Travel

Publishing for Technology Dummies

Andy Cummings, Acquisitions Director

Composition Services

Gerry Fahey, Executive Director of Production Services

Debbie Stailey, Director of Composition Services

Contents at a Glance

Introduction *1*

Part I: The Essentials of Stock Investing *7*
Chapter 1: It's Like Trading Hockey Cards! 9
Chapter 2: Taking Stock of Your Current Financial Situation and Goals 21
Chapter 3: Common Approaches to Stock Investing 35
Chapter 4: What Risk's Got to Do with It 49
Chapter 5: Say Cheese: Getting a Snapshot of the Market 69

Part II: Before You Get Started *83*
Chapter 6: Gathering Information 85
Chapter 7: Financial Planning for Stock Investors 103
Chapter 8: Going for Brokers 115
Chapter 9: Investing for Growth 135
Chapter 10: Investing for Income 149
Chapter 11: A Stock Investor's Guide to Value Investing 161

Part III: Picking Winners *171*
Chapter 12: Debunking the Company Annual Report 173
Chapter 13: Taking a Statement 185
Chapter 14: Recognizing Risk 205
Chapter 15: What the Statements Mean: Ratio Analysis 223
Chapter 16: Silly Income-Statement Tricks 239
Chapter 17: Silly Balance-Sheet Tricks 251

Part IV: Investment Strategies and Tactics *265*
Chapter 18: Taking the Bull (or Bear) by the Horns 267
Chapter 19: Analyzing Industries 277
Chapter 20: Stop! In the Name of Money 285
Chapter 21: 'Cause I'm the Tax Man 301

Part V: The Part of Tens *317*
Chapter 22: Ten Things to Think about Before You Invest 319
Chapter 23: Ten Things to Remember After You Invest 323
Chapter 24: Ten Warning Signs of a Stock's Decline 329

Appendix: Resources for Stock Investors *335*

Index *347*

Table of Contents

Introduction *1*

Why This Book? 2
How This Book Is Organized 3
    Part I: The Essentials of Stock Investing 3
    Part II: Before You Get Started 4
    Part III: Picking Winners 4
    Part IV: Investment Strategies and Tactics 5
    Part V: The Part of Tens 5
    Appendix 6
Icons Used in This Book 6

Part I: The Essentials of Stock Investing *7*

Chapter 1: It's Like Trading Hockey Cards! 9

A Piece of the Action 10
Why Companies Sell Stock 10
Going Public: It's No Secret 11
Canadian Regulators, and Toothless Tigers 12
Knowing the Product: Defining a Stock 14
    Your role as a shareholder 14
    Your rights as a shareholder 15
    Dividends 15
Spotting Stock Value 17
    How market capitalization affects stock value 17
    Sharpening your investment skills 19

Chapter 2: Taking Stock of Your Current Financial Situation and Goals 21

Establishing a Starting Point 22
    Step 1: List your assets in order of liquidity 22
    Step 2: List your liabilities 25
    Step 3: Calculate your net worth 27
    Step 4: Analyze your balance sheet 28
Funding Your Stock Program 29
    Step 1: Tally your income 30
    Step 2: Add up your outflow 31
    Step 3: Create a cash-flow statement 32
    Step 4: Analyze your cash flow 33
    Step 5: Find investment money in tax savings 34

Chapter 3: Common Approaches to Stock Investing **35**

   Investing by Time Frame 36
       Looking at the short term 36
       Considering intermediate-term goals 37
       Investing for the long term 38
   Investing by Style 38
       Growth investing 39
       Income investing 39
       Value investing 41
   Time Out: Other Investing Styles 43
       Conservative versus aggressive investing 43
       Fundamental investing 45
       Technical analysis–based investing 45
       Tell me a story 46
       Mo' money 47

Chapter 4: What Risk's Got to Do with It **49**

   Exploring Different Kinds of Risk 50
   Financial Risk 51
       Interest rates 52
       Liquidity 55
       Markets 55
       Inflation 57
       Currency 57
   Tax Risk 58
   Personal Risk 58
   Emotional Risk and Investor Psychology 59
       Paying the price for greed 60
       Recognizing the role of fear 60
       Looking for love in all the wrong places 60
   Minimizing Your Risk 61
       Gaining knowledge 61
       Getting your financial house in order 61
       Diversifying your investments: Markets, sectors,
           and companies 62
   Weighing Risk against Return 63

Chapter 5: Say Cheese: Getting a Snapshot of the Market **67**

   How Indexes Work 67
   The Dow Jones Industrial Average 68
   The TSX Exchanges 70
   Nasdaq 73
   Standard & Poor's 500 73
   Other U.S. Indexes 74
       Russell 3000 index 74
       Wilshire Total Market index 75

Over-the-Counter Stocks 75
    Over the Counter Bulletin Board (OTCBB) 75
    Pink Sheets 76
International Indexes 77
Investing in Indexes 78
    Exchange-traded funds (ETFs) 78
    Choices, choices 79

Part II: Before You Get Started.........................83

Chapter 6: Gathering Information ....**.85**

Figuring Out What You Need to Know 85
    Knowing where to look for answers 86
    Understanding stocks and the companies they represent 87
Staying on Top of Financial News and Trends 92
    Figuring out what a company's up to 92
    Discovering what's new with an industry 93
    Knowing what's happening with the economy 93
    Seeing what the politicians and government bureaucrats
        are doing 94
    Identifying trends in society, culture, and entertainment 95
Reading (and Understanding) Stock Tables 95
    52-week high 96
    52-week low 97
    Name and symbol 97
    Dividend 97
    Volume 98
    Yield 99
    P/E 100
    Day last 100
    Net change 100
Why Closing and Dividend Dates Matter 101
Evaluating (Avoiding?) Investment Tips 101
    Consider the source 102
    Get multiple views 102

Chapter 7: Financial Planning for Stock Investors **103**

How Financial Planning Works 103
    How financial planners differ from other advisers 104
    Financial planner services 104
    I don't need your advice...or do I? 105
    How your adviser charges you 106
    Kicking the tires: What you should look for 107
    Drilling deeper: Asking the right questions 108
ABC, XYZ, and Credibility 109
What a Good Financial Planner Will Do for You 110

A Training Run 111
    Search for and find a planner 111
    Get clarification of roles and responsibilities 112
    Gather your information 112
    Determine your goals and expectations 112
    Clarify your present financial situation and highlight
      any problem areas 113
    Get your financial plan 113
    Execute your financial plan 113
    Keep an eye on your financial plan 113

Chapter 8: Going for Brokers **115**
  Defining the Broker's Role 115
  Distinguishing between Full-Service and Discount Brokers 116
    Full-service brokers 117
    Discount brokers 118
  Choosing a Broker 120
    Self-regulatory organizations (SROs) in Canada 120
    Revisit your personal investing style 121
    Make your decision 122
  Online Brokerage Services 123
    Why online investing is popular 123
    Getting online trading services for less 123
    Trading online at a discount 124
  Checking Out Special Features 124
    How to open your online brokerage account 127
  Types of Brokerage Accounts 128
    Cash accounts 128
    Margin accounts 128
    Option accounts 129
  Evaluating Brokers' Recommendations 129
  Brokerage Reports: The Good, the Bad, and the Ugly 132
    The good 132
    The bad 132
    The ugly 133

Chapter 9: Investing for Growth **135**
  Understanding Growth Stocks 136
  Tips for Choosing Growth Stocks 137
    Checking out a company's fundamentals 137
    Deciding whether a company is a good value 138
    Looking for leaders and megatrends 140
    Considering a company with a strong niche 140
    Noticing who's buying and/or recommending the stock 141
    Learning investing lessons from history 142
    Evaluating the management of a company 142
    Figuring out whether a company will continue to do well 144
    Deciphering the key numbers of profitability 145

Exploring Small Caps and Speculative Stocks 145
Avoid IPOs, unless 146
If it's a small-cap stock, make sure it's making money 147
Investing in small-cap stocks requires analysis 147

Chapter 10: Investing for Income 149
Understanding Income Stocks 150
Advantages of income stocks 150
Disadvantages of income stocks 151
Analyzing Income Stocks 152
Tips for Selecting Income Stocks 154
Understanding your needs first 155
Checking the stock's payout ratio 156
Diversifying your stocks 156
Examining the company's bond rating 157
Examining Some Typical Income Stocks 158
Utilities 158
Real estate investment trusts (REITs) 159
Reasons REITs are right 159

Chapter 11: A Stock Investor's Guide to Value Investing 161
What Is Value Investing? 162
Buying a business 162
Making a conscious appraisal 163
Putting on the pinstripes? 164
Ignoring the market 164
Setting the value-investing style apart 165
AGAP: Assets and Growth at a Price 166
Figuring out what should determine a stock price 167
Going beyond AGAP 167
The Value Investing Style 169
No magic formula 169
Perform due diligence 170
Diversify? Are you sure? 170
Remember that it's not all or nothing 170

Part III: Picking Winners 171

Chapter 12: Debunking the Company Annual Report 173
About the Annual Report 173
Letter from the Chair — It Was the Economy's Fault! 175
What the Company Does 176
Financial Statements and Notes — The Beef 176
Financial statement items 177
Statements, messages, and more 178
Notes to financial statements 179
Summary of past financial figures 181

Auditor's Report — Watching the Watchdog 181
Management Discussion and Analysis (MD&A) of Operations 182
Where to Get This Stuff 183

Chapter 13: Taking a Statement 185

The Income Statement 185
    Revenues — The top line 186
    Cost of sales 186
    Grossed out on margins 187
    Selling, general, and administrative (SG&A) 187
    Research and development (R&D) 188
    Appreciating depreciation and amortization 188
    Reserves 188
    Interest-ed and taxed 189
    Income from continuing operations — we hope 190
    Extraordinary items 190
    They're such a special item: Impairments, investments,
        and other write-downs 191
    There you have it: Net income 192
The Balance Sheet 192
    Cash and cash equivalents 193
    Accounts receivable 194
    Inventory 195
    Fixed assets 196
    Investments: Companies are investors, too 197
    Intangible assets 197
    You can pay me now 198
    Long-term liabilities 199
    And now, meet the owners 199
Statement of Cash Flows 201
    Cash flow from operations 201
    Cash flow from investing activities 202
    "Free" cash flow 202
    Cash flow from financing activities 203

Chapter 14: Recognizing Risk 205

Corporate Governance Risk 206
    The role of the board of directors 206
    How the BOD manages risks 206
    Senior management's role in good governance: Rolling
        up the sleeves 207
    Management's role in controlling risk 207
    Back to the BOD 209
Ethical Risk 209
    Fraud 209
    Conflict of interest 210

Reputational Risk 210
Operational Risks 211
  Competition 211
  Obsolescence 212
  Outsourcing 212
  Reliance on few customers or suppliers 212
  Environmental risk 212
  Legal 213
  Other operational risks 213
Information and Technology Risks 214
  Piracy 214
  Privacy 214
Political Risk 215
  What is political risk? 215
  Ascertaining the political climate 216
  Roll down the top 216
Economic Risk 217
  Grossing you out with GDP 218
  Debt traps 218
  Raising confident consumers 219
  Lumping together the data with economic indexes ...219
  Key leading indicators 220

Chapter 15: What the Statements Mean: Ratio Analysis **223**
Ratio-nal Analysis 223
  Classes of ratios 224
  Knowing where to dial in 225
  Fine-tuning 225
Liquidity Ratios 226
  Current ratio 227
  Quick ratio 227
  Cash-flow ratios 228
Operating Ratios 229
  The return on equity (ROE) 229
  Return on assets (ROA) 230
  Return on sales (ROS) 230
  Receivables turnover 231
  Inventory turnover 231
  Fixed-asset turnover 232
  Total-asset turnover 232
  Non-financial operating productivity ratios 232
Leverage Ratios 233
  Debt-to-equity 233
  Times-interest-earned 233
  Working capital 234

Valuation Ratios 234
    Price to earnings 235
    Earnings to price 235
    Price to sales 235
    Price to book 236
Turn On, Tune In: Compare Ratios 236

Chapter 16: Silly Income-Statement Tricks **239**
How Did All This Start? 240
Revenue Manipulation 242
    Accelerating sales 242
    Mortgaging their souls 242
    Will that be cash, credit card, or stock? 243
    Creating revenue out of thin air 243
    Moving revenue in mysterious ways 244
    Stock investing for companies 244
Hiding Expenses: Capitalizing Costs 245
    Small fry 245
    Big fry 245
    Now that's a really, really big fry! 246
    Related-party transactions 246
Stock Options 246
    Option for what? 247
    What do the stakeholders say? 247
    So what options do we have? 247
Reserves 248
Tax Losses 249
Pro Forma Performance 249
    Picky, picky 249
    The good news is 250

Chapter 17: Silly Balance-Sheet Tricks **251**
Accounts-Receivable Allowances 252
    Message to auditor: It's the economy, stupid! 252
    Red flags and other signs 253
Inventories 253
    How it's done 253
Creative Acquisition Accounting 254
Special Charges and More Big Baths 255
    Where there's smoke 256
Hiding Liabilities: Off-Balance-Sheet Obligations 256
    Leasing transactions 257
    Securitization transactions 257
    Commitments and contingencies 258
    Creation of unconsolidated or special-purpose
        entities (SPEs) 258

Pension Plans 258
    Accounting impact, too 259
    Oh, and one more thing 260
Smoke and Mirrors 260
And Materiality Rabbits, Too 260
Buzzwords 261
Addressing Aggressive Accounting 261
Checklist for Accounting Manipulation 262

Part IV: Investment Strategies and Tactics 265

Chapter 18: Taking the Bull (or Bear) by the Horns 267
Bulling Up..268
    Recognizing the beast...268
    Toro! Approaching a bull market...270
Bearing Down..272
    Identifying the beast 273
    Heading into the woods: Approaching a bear market...............274
Straddling Bear and Bull: Uncertain Markets.............................275
    Pinpointing uncertainty is tough...275
    Sure you want to approach an uncertain market?.....................276

Chapter 19: Analyzing Industries 277
Badgering the Witness and Interrogating the Industries 278
    Is the industry growing?...278
    Are the industry's products or services in demand? 279
    What does the industry's growth rely on? 279
    Is this industry dependent on another industry? 280
    Who are the leading companies in the industry?.....................280
    Is the industry a target of government action? 280
    Which category does the industry fall into?.............................281
Don't Shoot the Messenger: Key Industries.................................283
    For sale 283
    Baby, you can drive my car...284
    Thanking Mr. Roboto 284
    Banking on it 284

Chapter 20: Stop! In the Name of Money 285
Call It a Day Order...286
Good-till-Cancelled (GTC) 286
    When you want to buy...287
    When you want to sell 288
Market Orders 288
Stop! I Order You! 289
    Trailing stops 290
    I beta you didn't know this...291

Limit Orders...292
    When you're buying 293
    When you're selling 293
Pass the Margin, Please..294
    Marginal outcomes 294
    Maintaining your balance 295
Going Short and Coming Out Ahead.........................296
    Setting up a short sale 297
    Oops! Going short when prices grow taller 298
    Watching out for ticks...299

Chapter 21: 'Cause I'm the Tax Man 301
Interest Income...302
Divident Income 303
    Grossed out 303
    Stock dividends and splits 304
Capital Gains and Losses 304
    Capital-gains deduction 305
    Superficial losses 305
    Reserves 305
Deferred-Income Tax Shelters and Plans 306
Registered Retirement Savings Plans (RRSPs) 306
    RRSP contribution limits 306
    Earned income limits 307
    Dollar limits..307
    Spousal Registered Retirement Savings Plans...........308
    Self-directed RRSPs 308
    Retirement allowances 309
    Locked-in RRSPs 309
Registered Retirement Income Funds (RRIFs)................310
A Recap..311
    Things to consider 312
    The great RRSP debate 312
Mutual Funds 313
The Tax-wise REIT...313
Labour-Sponsored Venture Capital Corporation (LSVCC)....................314
Oil, Gas, and Mineral Stock Investments......................315

Part V: The Part of Tens *317*

Chapter 22: Ten Things to Think about Before You Invest 319
Have Adequate Insurance 319
Update Your Career Skills 319
Take Care of Estate Planning 320
Establish an Emergency Fund 320

Set Up a Budget 320
Understand Basic Economics 320
Learn the Lingo 321
Read about Investing 321
Don't Follow the Herd 321
Discipline Yourself 322

Chapter 23: Ten Things to Remember After You Invest 323

Diversify Your Portfolio 323
Recognize that You're in for the Long Haul 324
Know the Business 324
Know the Industry 324
Plan for Taxes 325
Stay Informed 325
Know What's New with the Company 326
Compare and Profit 326
Employ Investing Techniques 327
Stay Focused 327

Chapter 24: Ten Warning Signs of a Stock's Decline 329

Earnings Slow Down or Head South 329
Sales Slow Down 330
Exuberant Analysts Despite Logic 330
Insider Selling 331
Dividend Cuts 331
Increased Negative Coverage 332
Industry Problems 332
Political Problems 332
Debt Is Too High or Unsustainable 332
Funny Accounting: No Laughing Here! 333

Appendix: Resources for Stock Investors 335

Basics of Investing 335
Financial-planning Sources 335
General Investor Supersites 336
Stock-investing Web Sites 337
Stock Exchanges 338
Periodicals and Magazines 339
Investor Associations and Organizations 339
Stock Screens 340
Company Research and Analyst Evaluations 340
Quotes 341
Charts 341
Earnings and Earnings Estimates 342
Industry Analysis 342

External Factors that Affect Market Value 343
Technical Analysis 343
Insider Trading 344
Taxes 344
Fraud 345
Investment News 345
Public Filings 346
Press Releases 346
IPOs 346

Index *347*

Introduction

● ●

*W*hat with today's woeful economic and investment climate, why would anyone want to invest in stocks? Shouldn't the horror show of the last few years be sending investors exiting stage left from the stock market?

To answer this question, it's important to turn to stock-investing history. While the past does not guarantee repeat performances, it's a strong indicator of future stock-market movement. From the mid-1950s, a bear market happened, on average, every five years. That's about ten bear markets. Before the most recent dreadful one, 1990 was our last bona fide bear market. We were way overdue! The average bear market was about ten months in duration, start to finish, and about 35 percent of bear markets have lasted 1.5 to 1.8 years. Yet, history shows that over the long term — bear markets and all — stocks outperformed bonds and money-market funds. Up close, stocks go up and down and on a chart may look like the teeth of a saw. But from afar, you'll see that the saw is pointing up. Over a period of decades, that's how the stock markets behaved. They went up.

Will the markets go up again? Okay, the hype-driven technology bubble was, for the most part, an aberration that is unlikely to recur anytime soon. Yet, stock markets can't seem to sit still — and that provides you with an investment opportunity! They're due to go up over the near term.

Many things cause stock markets to rebound and decline again, but perhaps the foremost of drivers are strong long-term underlying economic fundamentals, which stock markets mimic. While corporate scandals, bankruptcies, terrorism and war certainly contributed to recent market woes, they didn't start it. Stocks in North America were falling for about 18 months before Enron even unravelled. No, it was the bigger picture — the economy. Among many other things, this book seeks to help you anticipate economic rebounds and downturns.

When rebounds happen . . . wow. Things can get pretty exciting. That's because stocks tend to provide above-average returns during the early part of a recovery. We understand that from your perspective, and as long as economic woes persist, it's hard to imagine stock markets improving. You're tired of hearing about stocks, and want to rest. But consider the fact that Canadians felt most comfortable about buying stocks when they were soaring. Why? Money tends to follow money. Yet, that's when the potential for above-average future returns is minimal. It's when you want nothing to do with the market, or when the market has not peaked to overvalued levels, that you need to be in stocks to some extent.

This book will help you avoid the quagmire of investor "herd" psychology, providing a measured dose of facts, common sense, and discipline. So we advise the obvious — buy stocks when they're cheapest, during or soon after an economic downturn. Want proof, or something close to it? Consider the months after September 11, 2001. Millions of Canadians missed out on the S&P 500's subsequent 18.5-percent run (and the S&P/TSX's similar run) through mid-November. In fact, Nasdaq showed a 33.5-percent rise over that brief period. That was not a rally based on sound economic fundamentals, to be sure. However, at the time the market thought that things could not get any worse; most stocks went up sharply. Unfortunately, things did get worse — but not before we learned a valuable lesson about market recovery!

At the end of the day, you can be cautious in nature and still own stocks. The two are not mutually exclusive. And don't forget that not all stocks tumbled during this most recent bear market. Identifying and investing in stocks of companies with solid financial performance, strong management, and a great business plan can be very rewarding, and will minimize your risk. Keep that, and everything else we just discussed, in mind when you're thinking about investing. Welcome to this book — and welcome to the magical and exciting world of stocks!

Why This Book?

Even within the context of the stock-market environment we just described, this book will show you how to increase your effectiveness as an investor. One of the biggest reasons that investors lost so much money in the recent bear market was that they failed to *understand* and *act on* information in two key areas:

- ✔ Interpreting and reacting to readily available company financial statements and other basic financial information

- ✔ Identifying and being alert to common internal and external risks that companies face

Few stock-investing books ever delved into the above two areas, hence the value and uniqueness of this book. *Stock Investing For Canadians For Dummies* sets itself apart with major themes on the importance of financial information and the need for investors to assess risks. Learning how to use this easy-to-obtain information to your advantage will in turn set you apart from most other investors, and will help you build and preserve wealth.

This book provides you with most, if not all, of the core knowledge required to be an effective stock investor. Other books just discuss pieces of the whole. *Stock Investing For Canadians For Dummies* provides a bigger picture in organized and digestible bites.

✔ You'll learn about or revisit fundamental investing principles, and the recent changes that have happened in the Canadian equity landscape. We'll explore how you can get the most out of financial planners and brokers. You'll also learn about current and valuable investment information sources, as well as investment styles that may suit you best.

✔ A basic review of annual report information, including financial statements, will reveal how important it is to understand the language of business. We'll show you some of the tricks of the trade that companies use to make numbers look a lot better than they really are, and how you can spot them. We'll surprise you by revealing that risk comes in many stripes, and not just the ethical type that undid the Enrons and WorldComs of this world. In fact, there are scores of other risks investors can be exposed to and need to know about. These additional risks apply not only to volatile tech stocks, but also to established companies in sectors such as healthcare, financial services, resources, retail, and utilities. Information about risk is easy to get once you know where to look, and you'll learn how you can minimize investment risk by doing the right homework.

✔ To round things out, you'll learn how to spot crucial market and industry trends with the right information, and place stock orders in strategic ways to build and protect your wealth. We'll discuss how investment income is taxed, and what you can do to minimize taxes.

This book offers something for investors of all experience levels. Beginner investors get a crash course on stock investing. Veterans will gain even more core knowledge, like that described above. This book provides all this in an easy and humorous manner, instead of a stuffed-shirt or academic one. It is meant for everyday people (like the authors themselves).

How This Book Is Organized

The parts of *Stock Investing For Canadians For Dummies* progress with a straightforward, logical approach that makes it very easy to quickly find out what you need to know:

Part I: The Essentials of Stock Investing

This section is useful for everyone. Understanding the essentials of stock investing and investing in general can only help you, especially during these uncertain times. Stocks may even impact your finances in ways not readily apparent. For example, stocks aren't found only in individual accounts; they're also in mutual funds and pension plans.

An important point to remember is that stocks are really financial tools that are a means to an end. Investors should be able to answer the question "Why am I considering stocks at all?" Stocks are a great vehicle for wealth building, but only if investors realize what they can accomplish and how to use them.

One of the essentials of stock investing involves understanding risk. Too many investors are dismissive about it. The chapters on risk (another chapter is found in Part III) are some of the most important chapters that serious stock investors should read. While you can't avoid every type of risk out there, the lessons learned can help you recognize unacceptable risks and deal with them.

Part II: Before You Get Started

Once you're ready to embark on your sideline career as a stock investor, you'll need to use some resources to gather information about the stocks you're interested in. Fortunately, we live in the information age. We marvel at the hardships faced by investors from the 1920s era, who didn't have access to the superb resources available today. Today's investors are in an enviable position, and are empowered by some of the great nuggets of information available on the Internet. No longer do brokerage houses control all of the important investment information out there.

This part tells you where to find useful and reliable information and how to use it to be a more effective investor. We also explain that stocks can be used for growth, income, and value-investing purposes, and discuss the characteristics of each. To get a handle on your financial situation — and when you're ready to invest — you may wish to seek the advice of a financial planner and the services of a broker. There are several options with each, and we guide you through the selection process. Remember — the wrong broker could make you . . . uh . . . broker.

Part III: Picking Winners

Where do you turn to find specific information about a company's financial health? We show you the financial documents you should review to make a more informed decision. Once you find the information, you'll discover how to make sense of those data as well.

Looking through annual report information such as financial statements is critical, and we clarify what these statements really mean. One of the things investors failed to do during the bear market was to personally extract the story told by the financial statements. Instead, they relied on others to do this for them — others with different agendas or levels of financial knowledge. Even many analysts failed to see instances of aggressive accounting that so many companies seemed to espouse. The bottom line is if you want it done right, learn to do it yourself — read the valuable financial information! It doesn't take too long to learn, and even less time to apply. We promise!

In this part, you'll also reap the rewards from understanding the many forms of risk faced by companies you invest in. All companies are exposed to some risk and the best stock investors respect these risks.

Part IV: Investment Strategies and Tactics

Even the stocks of great companies can fall in a bad investing climate. This is where you should be aware of the "macro" environment, or big picture. You should monitor the stock-investing environment — this means tracking what's happening with the economy, and with the industry you are invested in. The big picture is the one area where all too many of the pros get it wrong. Fortunately, you have ready access to the right information needed to understand the investing environment! Once you understand stocks and the macro environment in which they operate, you can choose the strategy and the tactics to help steer you to wealth-building.

This part closes off with useful tips, strategies, and considerations that you shouldn't ignore in the areas of order-taking, taxes, and financial planning. Sound tax and financial planning is crucial for all Canadians. After all, taxes are the biggest expense in your lifetime.

Part V: The Part of Tens

We wrap up the book with a hallmark of . . . *For Dummies* books — the Part of Tens. These chapters give you a mini crash course in stock investing, including the ten things you should be aware of before you invest in your first stock.

What's that? You already bought stock? Then check out the chapter on what you should be aware of after you invest. You just might save a bundle. Learn the steps to take to avoid undue risk and fraud. To make this part complete, we offer some clues on how to recognize the warning signs of a stock that's poised to fall.

Appendix

Don't overlook the Appendix. It provides online resources to help you make informed investment decisions. Whether the topic is stock investing terminology, economics, or avoiding capital gains taxes, we include a treasure trove of resources to help you. The Appendix gives you some great places to turn to for help.

Icons Used in This Book

This icon flags a particular bit of advice that may give you an edge over other investors.

With this icon, we're reminding you about some information that you should always keep stashed in your memory, no matter whether you're new to investing or an old pro.

Pay special attention to this icon, because the advice here can prevent headaches, heartaches, and financial aches.

The text attached to this icon may not be crucial to your success as an investor, but it may enable you to talk shop with investing gurus and better understand the financial pages of your favourite business publication or Web site.

Part I

The Essentials of Stock Investing

The 5th Wave   By Rich Tennant

"WE TOOK A GAMBLE AND INVESTED ALL OUR MONEY IN A RACE HORSE. THEN IT RAN AWAY."

In this part . . .

You need to know some investing fundamentals before
you put your first dollar in the stock market. All too
many investors fail to tie their stock investing decisions
to their personal financial goals, and to their current
situation — it's essential to take this step so you will know
which stocks are suitable, and avoid undue risk. This part
will also provide you with an introduction to the many
different approaches to stock investing, so that you can
use the one that works best for you. You'll see that you can
even choose a combination of approaches. Several basic
risks that stock investors face are presented as well.
Identifying them at the outset will help you protect your
money. Finally, this part will introduce you to the major
stock indexes and exchanges — the places stocks call home.

Chapter 1

It's Like Trading Hockey Cards!

In This Chapter

▶ Understanding the difference between a stock and a company

▶ Considering why private companies go public

▶ Exploring initial public offerings (IPOs)

▶ Discovering different kinds of stocks

▶ Navigating your way to successful stock investing

*S*tock investing became all the rage during the late 1990s, when many Canadian investors watched their stock portfolios and mutual funds skyrocket in value as major North American markets experienced the fruits of an almost two-decades-long rising market (better known as a bull market).

Then came the dreaded bear market — complete with claws, sharp teeth, and three years of declining markets. Portfolios were mauled, chewed up, or worse. Investors with positive or even zero returns had downright bragging rights! Yet despite this recent roller coaster of a ride, about 40 percent of Canadians still invest in stocks today. Some of these Canadians hold stocks directly; others hold them indirectly in their mutual and pension funds. Canadians are a resilient bunch: while many of us got scared, we did not jump ship en masse!

Investment activity in Canada and the United States is a great example of the popularity that stocks experienced during that time period. Yet people really didn't know exactly what they were investing in, or the risks. If they had had a clear understanding of what a stock really represents, perhaps they could have avoided some expensive mistakes.

The purpose of this book is not only to tell you about the basics of stock investing, but also to let you in on some sharp strategies and tactics that can help you profit from the stock market. Before you invest your first dollar, you need to understand the basics of stock investing.

A Piece of the Action

The stock market is, well, a market of stocks. In essence, being in the market is like trading hockey cards. There is a buyer and a seller. The market is the schoolyard where buyers and sellers get together to trade cards. A sharp hockey-card trader (buyer) will try to guess which rookie player is the next Wayne Gretzky or Mario Lemieux. He or she will then try to obtain a future star player's rookie card and hope that that player scores a lot of goals, makes great saves, or is a solid defenceman. The card would almost certainly rise in value! The best price to pay is the lowest cash price, or the fewest cards traded away in return. The other trader and owner of the card (the seller) either will recognize greatness and ask a hefty price, or will fail to recognize talent and trade the card away for a song. In the hockey-card trading market (the schoolyard), you have kids who are buyers and kids who are sellers of cards. They may pay or get cash, and they may give up or get other cards.

The stock market is actually an established group of separate markets (many schoolyards in many countries) where Canadian investors can freely buy and sell millions of shares issued by thousands of Canadian and international companies. Like hockey-card traders, investors buy stocks because they seek gain in the form of appreciation (what happens when their stock, if held long enough, goes up in value — just like Wayne Gretzky's rookie card did), or income (some stocks pay income in the form of dividends), or both. (Sorry, no dividends are paid out by hockey players!) Those who already own stock may sell it to cash in and use the money for other purposes, like trading coins. Either way, investors pay or get cash, or give up or get more stock with the proceeds. A market is made!

Why Companies Sell Stock

Companies issue stock because they require money for a particular purpose. The first time a company sells stock to the public is known as an *initial public offering* (IPO), sometimes referred to as "going public." The most prominent new Canadian and U.S. stock IPOs are usually reported in the pages of financial publications, such as *The Globe and Mail*, the *National Post*, and *The Wall Street Journal*.

Generally, two types of companies go public by issuing stock:

- **An existing private company:** A company that is currently in operation as a private corporation but wants to expand.

- **A start-up company:** A company that is just starting up and decides to go public immediately to raise the capital necessary to establish itself.

Between the two, the safer situation for investors is the first type. That's because this kind of company has a proven track record — which hopefully includes growing sales, cash profits, and great ideas!

Why does a company go public? It goes public because it needs to raise the money necessary for its growth and financial success. More specifically, the money raised through a public offering of stock can be used for the following purposes:

- **To raise capital and finance expansion.** If ABC Corporation wants to increase its production capacity, it needs a new manufacturing facility. In order to raise the capital needed to build and operate the new facility, it may decide to sell stock to the public.

- **To invest in product (or service) research and development.** Many companies need money for research and development for a new invention or innovation.

- **To pay for the daily expenses of doing business.** Most companies have to pay for staff, benefits, utilities, and marketing efforts. Some companies may need additional operating capital until revenues from exciting new products and services catch up with and exceed expenses. (At least, that's the plan!)

- **To pay off debt.** The company may want to use the proceeds of a stock sale to pay off debt. Interest expense is the number-one financial anchor that causes companies to go bankrupt.

- **Miscellaneous reasons.** The company may need money for other reasons that are important for the health and growth of the enterprise, such as joint ventures and entry into brand-new lines of business.

Keep in mind that a stock offering doesn't always have to be in a first-time situation. Many companies issue stock in secondary offerings to gain the capital they need for expansion or other purposes.

Going Public: It's No Secret

When a private company wants to offer its stock to the public, it usually asks a stock underwriter to help. An *underwriter* is a financial company that acts as an intermediary between stock investors and public companies. The underwriter is usually an investment-banking company or the investment-banking division of a major brokerage firm. The underwriter may put together a group of several investment-banking companies and brokers. This group is also referred to as a *syndicate.* Usually the main underwriter is called the *primary underwriter,* and others in the group are referred to as *subsidiary underwriters.*

Before a company can sell stock to the public, a couple of things have to happen:

- ✔ The underwriter or syndicate agrees to pay the company a predetermined price for a minimum number of shares and then must resell those shares to buyers such as their own clients (which could be you or me), mutual funds, and other commercial brokerages. Each member of the syndicate agrees to resell a portion of the issued stock. The underwriters earn a fee for their underwriting services. CIBC World Markets is one example of an underwriting company. Its investment-banking business works with companies to help them raise capital, grow, and invest.

- ✔ The underwriter sets a time frame to start selling the issued stock (this is the window of time in which the primary market is taking place). The underwriter also helps the company prepare a preliminary prospectus that details the required financial and business information for investors, such as the amount of money being sought in the IPO, and who is seeking the money and why. (For details, see the section "Canadian Regulators, and Toothless Tigers" below.)

The preliminary prospectus is referred to as the "red herring" because it usually comes stamped with a warning in big red letters that identifies it as preliminary — a kind of disclaimer that warns you that the stock's price may or may not be changed from the original issue price indicated in the preliminary prospects.

The IPO stock usually isn't available directly to the public. Interested investors must purchase the initial shares through the underwriters authorized to sell the IPO shares during the primary market. After the primary market period — at the start of the secondary market — you can ask your own stockbroker to buy you shares of that stock. The *secondary market* is more familiar to the public and includes established, orderly public markets such as the TSX, the New York Stock Exchange, and the Nasdaq. (For more on the TSX, the new name for the Toronto Stock Exchange, see Chapter 5; we revisit IPOs in Chapter 9.)

Canadian Regulators, and Toothless Tigers

The market for IPOs and all public stocks is regulated reasonably well in the United States by the Securities and Exchange Commission (SEC). The SEC sets the standard for disclosure and governs the creation of the prospectus. The prospectus must contain information such as the description of the issuer's business, names and addresses of the key company officers, key information relating to the company's financial condition, and an explanation of how the proceeds from the stock offering will be used. (For more on what reports companies must file and how investors can benefit from this information, see Chapter 12.)

In Canada, provincial and territorial securities administrators — also known as securities commissions — oversee and govern the securities industry. They possess broad powers under provincial statutes called *securities acts*. Securities commissions don't pass judgment on the worthiness of an investment. Rather, they try to provide assurance that companies offering securities furnish investors with good and complete disclosure of all key and relevant facts. Companies provide this disclosure through a prospectus, and subsequently through updates such as annual reports and other statutory declarations.

Regulators promote integrity in the stock market and help provide a more level playing field. While the Canadian stock market regulatory system is established and efficient, it is nowhere near as effective as its U.S. counter-part. That's because it's a lot easier to get away with corporate malfeasance in Canada than it is in the U.S. (names like Bre-X, Livent, and YBM come immediately to mind). Even after the Canadian system reveals illegal and questionable acts by public companies, the system is toothless — it has a bark, but no bite. Relative to the U.S., very few corporate crooks in Canada wind up behind bars! Perhaps it's a lack of personnel, legislation, or political will that is at fault. At any rate, the road to full regulation in Canada remains long, and tougher measures are needed now.

Stock investors should know this so they can be proactive in identifying risks and in knowing their rights. It should also be noted that investment firms and their representatives must be registered with their respective provincial securities commission, either where they work or where they trade securities, and that they have to meet certain standards to become registered. Securities commissions can cancel the registrations of individuals or the firms they work for, to protect your interests. They are also empowered to investigate matters, prosecute persons, freeze funds, hear facts, take evidence, impose penalties, and/or seize documents for examination. However, securities commissions can't compel a company or individual to repay investors. All they can do is halt trading in a security and deny the violator the right to trade securities in the province.

Although there is no federal regulatory body in Canada as there is in the U.S., each provincial securities commission is a member of the umbrella organization Canadian Securities Administrators. CSA members work to standardize securities law.

The securities industry self-regulates through bodies such as the Investment Dealers Association (IDA) and the Mutual Fund Dealers Association (MFDA). Clearly, the Canadian stock investor is exposed to more investment risk than her U.S. counterparts. We revisit self-regulation in Chapter 8, where we discuss brokers.

Approval of the sale of stock by a provincial or territorial securities administrator doesn't mean that the administrator recommends the stock. Approval from an administrator means only that the sale of stock can go forward in accordance with provincial and federal laws. Approvals simply give some level of assurance that companies offering securities furnish investors with all the facts.

Knowing the Product: Defining a Stock

Stock represents ownership in a corporation (or company). Just like the owner of a car has a title that says he has ownership of a car, a stock certificate shows that you own a piece of a company. If a company issues stock of, say, 1 million shares and you own 100 shares, this means you have ownership equivalent to 1/10,000th of the company.

The physical evidence of ownership is a stock certificate, which shows what stock you own and how many shares. These days, investors rarely get the certificates in hand, direct from the company; instead, they simply trade through brokerage accounts (see Chapter 8 for lots of useful information on brokers) and shareholder service departments that hold the stock. Your brokerage statements tell you what you have — kind of like a bank statement. Such statements are sufficient today, when producing the actual stock certificate has become less necessary in our modern technological era than in the early days of stock investing.

There is a real distinction between the stock and the company. The company is what you invest in, and the stock is the means by which you invest. Some investors get confused and think that the company and its stock act as one entity.

Your role as a shareholder

When you own stock, you become a *shareholder* (also known as a *stockholder*). The benefit of owning stock in a corporation is that whenever the corporation profits, you profit as well. For example, if you buy stock in ATI Technologies Inc. and ATI comes out with an exciting new computer graphics product that the public wants in massive quantities, not only does the company succeed but so do you, depending on how much stock you own.

Just because you own a piece of that company, don't expect to go to the company's headquarters and say, "Hi! I'm a part owner. I'd like to pick up some office supplies since I'm running low. Thank you and keep up the good work." No, it's not quite like that.

As a regular shareholder, you generally do not have the privilege of intervening in the company's day-to-day operations. Instead, you participate in the company's overall performance at a distance.

As an owner, you participate in the overall success (or failure) of a given company along with the thousands or millions of others who are *co-owners* (other investors who own stock in the company). The flip side is that if the company is sued or gets on the wrong side of the law, you won't be in trouble — at least not directly. The company's stock value will be negatively affected and you'll most likely see a decline in the value of your stock, but you won't go to jail.

Your rights as a shareholder

A stock also gives you the right to make decisions that may influence the company, such as determining the share price. Each stock you own has a little bit of voting power, so the more shares of stock you own, the more decision-making power you have.

In order to vote you must attend an annual or special shareholders' meeting, or fill out a proxy ballot. The ballot contains a series of proposals that you may vote either for or against. Common questions concern who should be on the board of directors, whether to issue additional stock, and whether to acquire or be acquired by another company.

Dividends

Dividends are a type of reward that companies pay to shareholders. When a company is a cash generator because of good sales and cost control, it builds its cash war chest. Some of this cash is kept to finance further growth or is utilized for other business purposes. But many companies will also distribute cash directly to shareholders in the form of a cash dividend.

Who makes this decision? The people who run a publicly traded company are the ones who may choose to "declare" a cash dividend. Specifically, a company's board of directors is responsible for declaring it. Once declared, a "date of record" or "record date" is set. The record date means that shareholders on record on or before that date are entitled to the dividend. Anyone buying the stock subsequent to that date must wait until the next dividend declaration to be entitled to receive a dividend (on the payment date). There are usually several weeks between the dividend declaration date and the date of record.

Stocks will trade "ex-dividend" (or no dividend) from the second trading day (a weekday) before the record date. This is important, because if you trade shares near the dividend date you should expect the share price to drop by roughly the amount of the dividend.

The board of directors can also declare a "stock dividend." Companies that don't regularly pay cash dividends often opt instead to pay dividends in the form of their own stock. A 5-percent stock dividend means that for every 20 shares of stock you own, you obtain one new share as a dividend. You keep your same relative share of the book value of the company.

When a company declares a stock dividend, it keeps its accumulated cash. So, some companies prefer to issue a stock dividend to avoid paying out cash that they need to use elsewhere in their operations.

To recap, for typical Canadian dividends the events in Table 1-1 happen four times per year.

Table 1-1	The Life of the Quarterly Dividend	
Event	*Sample Date*	*Comments*
Date of declaration	January 15	The date that the quarterly dividend is declared by the company
Ex-dividend date	February 7	Starts the three-day period during which, if you buy the stock, you don't qualify for the dividend
Record date	February 10	The date by which you must be on the books of record to qualify for the dividend. All investors who are official shareholders on the record date will receive the dividend paid on the payment date regardless of whether they plan to sell the stock any time between the date of declaration and the date of record
Payment date	February 27	The date that payment is made (a dividend cheque is issued and mailed to shareholders who were on the books of record as of February 10)

We revisit dividends in Chapter 6 to show you where to find dividend information.

Spotting Stock Value

Imagine that you like soup, and you're willing to buy it by the can at the grocery store. In this example, the brands of soup available on the shelves are like companies, and their prices represent the prices that you would pay for the companies' stock. The grocery store is the stock market. What if two brands of soup are very similar, but one costs 70 cents while the other costs 95 cents? Which would you choose? Odds are that you would look at both brands, judge their quality, and, if they were indeed similar, you would take the cheaper soup. The soup at 95 cents is overpriced. It's the same with stocks. What if you compare two companies that are similar in every respect but have different share prices? All things being equal, the cheaper price has greater value for the investor. But there is another side to the soup example.

What if the quality of the two brands of soup is significantly different but their prices are the same? If one brand of soup is flavourless and poor quality and priced at 70 cents and the other brand is tasty and superior quality and also priced at 70 cents, which would you get? We'd take the good brand because it's better soup. Perhaps the lesser soup might make an acceptable purchase at, say, 30 cents. However, the inferior soup is definitely overpriced at 70 cents. The same example works with stocks. A badly run company isn't a good choice if a better company in the marketplace can be bought at the same — or a better — price.

Comparing the value of soup may seem overly simplistic, but doing so does cut to the heart of stock investing. Soup and soup prices can be as varied as companies and stock prices. As an investor, you must make it your job to find the best value for your investment dollars.

How market capitalization affects stock value

You can determine the value of a company (and thus the value of its stock) in many ways. The most basic way to measure this is to look at a company's market value, also known as market capitalization (or market cap). *Market capitalization* is simply the value you get when you multiply all the outstanding shares of a stock by the price of a single share.

Calculating the market cap is easy: it's the number of shares outstanding multiplied by the current share price. If the company has 1 million shares outstanding and its share price is $10, the market cap is $10 million.

Small cap, mid cap, and large cap aren't references to headgear; they're references to how large the company is, as measured by its market value. Here are the five basic stock categories of market capitalization:

- **Micro cap (under $250 million):** These are the smallest and hence the riskiest stocks available.

- **Small cap ($250 million to $1 billion):** These stocks fare better than the micro caps and still have plenty of growth potential. The key word here is *potential*.

- **Mid cap ($1 billion to $5 billion):** For many investors, this category offers a good compromise between small caps and large caps. These stocks have some of the safety of large caps while retaining some of the growth potential of small caps.

- **Large cap ($5 billion to $25 billion):** This category is usually best reserved for conservative stock investors who want steady appreciation with greater safety. Stocks in this category are frequently referred to as "blue chips."

- **Ultra cap (more than $25 billion):** These stocks are also called "mega caps" and obviously refer to companies that are the biggest of the big. Royal Bank and Exxon Mobil are examples.

From the point of view of safety, the company's size and market value do matter. All things being equal, large-cap stocks are considered safer than small-cap stocks. However, small-cap stocks have greater potential for growth. Compare these stocks to trees — which tree is sturdier, a giant California redwood or a small maple tree that is just a year old? In a great storm, the redwood would hold up well, while the smaller maple tree would have a rough time. But you also have to ask yourself which tree has more opportunity for growth. The redwood may not have much growth left, but the small maple tree has plenty of growth to look forward to.

For beginning investors, comparing market cap to trees is not so far-fetched. You want your money to branch out without becoming deadwood.

Although market capitalization is important to consider, don't invest (or not invest) because of it. It is just one measure of value. As a serious investor, you need to look at numerous factors that can help you determine whether any given stock is a good investment. Keep reading — this book is full of information to help you decide.

Sharpening your investment skills

Investors who analyze the company can better judge the value of the stock and profit from buying and selling it. Your greatest asset in stock investing is knowledge (and a little common sense). To succeed in the world of stock investing, keep in mind these key success factors:

- ✔ **Analyze yourself.** What do you want to accomplish with your stock investing? What are your investment goals? Chapter 2 can help you.

- ✔ **Know where to get information.** The decisions you make about your money and what stocks to invest in require quality information. If you want help with information sources, turn to Chapter 6.

- ✔ **Understand why you want to invest in stocks.** Are you seeking appreciation (capital gains), or income (dividends)? Look at Chapters 9 and 10 for information on this topic.

- ✔ **Do some research.** Look at the company whose stock you are considering to see whether it's a profitable company worthy of your investment dollars. Chapters 12 and 13 help you scrutinize the company.

- ✔ **Understand how the world affects your stock.** Stocks succeed or fail in large part due to the environment in which they operate. Economics and politics make up that world, so you should know something about them. Chapter 14 covers these topics.

- ✔ **Use investing strategies like the pros do.** In other words, how you go about investing can be just as important as what you invest in.

- ✔ **Keep more of the money you earn.** After all your great work in getting the right stocks and making the big bucks, you should know about keeping more of the fruits of your investing. We cover tax implications of stock investing in Chapter 21.

Actually, every chapter in the book offers you valuable guidance on some essential aspect of the fantastic world of stocks. The knowledge you pick up and apply from these pages has been tested over nearly a century of stock picking. The investment experience of the past — the good, the bad, and some of the ugly — is here for your benefit. Use this information to make a lot of money (and make us proud!).

Stock-market schizophrenia

Have you ever noticed a stock going up even though the company is reporting terrible results? How about seeing a stock nosedive despite the fact that the company is doing well? What gives? Well, judging the direction of a stock in a short-term period — over the next few days or weeks — is almost impossible.

Yes, in the short term stock investing is irrational. The price of a stock and the value of its company seem disconnected and almost schizophrenic. The key phrase to remember is *short term*. A stock's price and the company's value become more logical over an extended period of time. The longer a stock is in the public's view, the more rational the performance of the stock's price. In other words, a good company will continue to draw attention to itself; hence, more people will want its stock, and the share price will rise to better match the value of the company. Conversely, a bad company won't hold up to continued scrutiny over time. As more and more people see that it's not a good investment, the share price will fall. Over the long run, a stock's share price and the value of the company for the most part become equal.

Chapter 2

Taking Stock of Your Current Financial Situation and Goals

In This Chapter

▶ Preparing your personal balance sheet

▶ Developing your cash-flow statement

*Y*es, you want to make the big bucks. Yes, you want to succeed in the stock market and retire rich! But before you start shopping for that Caribbean island you're going to buy, you have to map out your action plan for getting there. Stocks can be a great component of most wealth-building programs, but you must first do some homework on a topic that you should be very familiar with — yourself. That's right. Understanding your current financial situation and clearly defining financial goals are the first steps in successful investing.

This chapter is undoubtedly one of the most important chapters in this book. It may at first seem to be a chapter more suitable for some general book on personal finance. Wrong! The greatest weakness of ineffective investors is not understanding their financial situation and how stocks fit in to that situation. More times than not, we have counselled people to stay out of the stock market because they were unprepared for the responsibilities of stock investing — they hadn't been regularly reviewing the company's financial statements or monitoring the company's operating risks.

Investing in stocks requires balance. Investors sometimes tie up too much money in stocks and therefore put themselves at risk of losing a significant portion of their wealth should the market plunge. That's exactly what happened to hundreds of thousands of Canadians during the recent bear market. On the flip side of things, more than half of Canadian adults place little or no money in stocks and therefore miss out on excellent opportunities to grow their wealth. Stocks should be a part of most investors' portfolios, but the operative word is *part*. Stocks should take up only a *portion* of your money. A disciplined investor also has money in bank accounts, bonds, mutual funds, REITs (real estate investment trusts), and other assets that offer growth or income opportunities. Diversification is a key to minimizing risk. (For more on risk, see Chapters 4 and 14.)

Establishing a Starting Point

The first step for budding investors is to know where you stand with your money right now. Whether you already own stocks or you're looking to get into stocks, you'll need the funds to do so. However, no matter what you hope to accomplish, you must establish where you stand with your current finances. To do this, the first thing you need to prepare and review is your personal balance sheet. A *balance sheet* is simply a list of your assets and your liabilities and what each item is currently worth at a specific time. I know that it sounds like accounting mumbo jumbo, but calculating your net worth is important to your future financial success, so just do it.

Composing your balance sheet is simple. Pull out a pencil and a piece of paper. For the computer-savvy, a spreadsheet software program accomplishes the same task. Gather up all your financial documents, such as bank and brokerage statements and other such paperwork — you need figures from these documents. Then follow the steps that we outline in the following sections. Update your balance sheet and income statement at least once a year to monitor your financial progress.

Your personal balance sheet is really no different from balance sheets that companies like Bombardier prepare. Most balance sheets have assets, obligations, and what's left over — positive or negative equity. (The main difference between your balance sheet and Bombardier's is a few zeros, but we help you work on that.) In fact, the more you find out about your own balance sheet, the easier it will be to understand the balance sheets of companies in which you're seeking to invest.

Step 1: List your assets in order of liquidity

Liquid assets aren't references to beer or cola (unless you're Molson, Labatt, or Sleeman Brewing & Malting Co.). No, *liquidity* in a financial context essentially means how quickly you can convert that particular asset (something you own that has value) into cash. Liquidity is important to your financial picture because ultimately you need cash for wants and needs that may present themselves. If you have to pay for a medical procedure or you find a good investment, having liquid assets can save the day.

Knowing the liquidity of an asset (such as an investment) is important for those moments when you need cash to buy some stock (or pay some bill). All too often, people have too little cash and too much wealth tied up in *illiquid investments* such as real estate, leading to what David Dodge, governor of the Bank of Canada, would call a "liquidity crisis." Being *illiquid* is just a fancy way of saying that you don't have the immediate cash to meet a pressing need. (Hey, we've all had those moments!) Review your assets and take measures to ensure that you have enough of both types of assets.

Listing your assets in order of liquidity gives you an immediate picture of which assets you can quickly convert to cash and which ones you can't. If you say, "I need money, and I need it now to pay X," you can see that cash-in-hand, your chequing account, and your savings account are at the top of the list. The items last in order of liquidity become obvious: they're things like real estate and other assets that could take a long time to convert to cash. Real estate, even in a seller's market, can take months to sell. Investors who don't have adequate liquid assets run the danger of selling assets quickly and possibly at a loss as they scramble to accumulate the cash necessary to meet their short-term financial obligations. For stock investors, it may mean prematurely selling stocks that were originally intended to be long-term investments.

The first asset on your list should be cash. You should have an amount equal to at least three to six months' worth of your gross living expenses. This time frame is important because it gives you a cushion during the most common forms of financial disruption in your life. A good example is the loss of your job. Finding a new job can take anywhere from three to six months (depending on the economy).

If your monthly expenses (or *outgo*) are $3,000, you should have at least $8,000, and probably closer to $15,000, in a secure, Canada Deposit Insurance Corporation (CDIC)–insured, interest-bearing bank account. Consider this an emergency fund and not an investment. Establish this amount in a bank account and leave it there. Don't use it to buy stocks.

Too many Canadians don't have an emergency fund, meaning that they put themselves at risk. Walking across a busy street while wearing a blindfold is a great example of putting yourself at risk, and in recent years many investors have done the financial equivalent. They piled on tremendous debt, put too much into investments (such as stocks) that they didn't understand, and had little or no savings. Being unaware of financial pitfalls such as these certainly creates more risk of financial problems.

Resist the urge to start thinking of your investment in stocks as a savings account generating more than 20 percent per year. This is dangerous thinking! If your investments tank, or if you lose your job, you certainly will have your own "liquidity crisis."

Table 2-1 shows a typical listing of assets. Use it as a guide for making your own asset list.

Table 2-1	John Q. Investor: Personal Assets as of December 31, 2003	
Asset Item	*Market Value*	*Annual Growth Rate %*
Current Assets		
Cash on hand and in chequing	$150	0
Bank savings accounts and guaranteed investment certificates	$500	2%
Stocks	$2,000	11%
Mutual funds	$2,400	9%
Other financial assets	$240	
Total current assets	**$5,290**	
Long-term assets		
Auto	$1,800	−10%
Residence	$150,000	5%
Real estate investment	$125,000	6%
Personal stuff (such as jewellery)	$4,000	
Total long-term assets	**$280,800**	
Total assets	**$286,090**	

The first column of Table 2-1 describes the asset (a *current asset* means that you can quickly and conveniently convert it to cash).

The second column gives the most current market value for that item. Keep in mind that this is not the purchase or original amount; it reflects the amount you would realistically get if you were to sell it in the current market.

The third column tells you how well that investment did from one year ago. If the percentage rate is 5 percent, that means that item increased in value by 5 percent from a year ago. You need to know how well *all* your assets are doing.

Figuring out the annual growth rate (in the third column) as a percentage is not difficult. Say that you bought 100 shares of the stock Gro-A-Lot Corp.

(GAL) and its market value on December 31, 2002, was $50 per share, for a total market value of $5,000 (100 shares × $50 per share). When you checked its value on December 31, 2003, you found out it was at $60 per share. (Make believe that no dividends were paid during the year.) The annual growth rate is 20 percent. You calculate this by taking the amount of the gain ($60 – $50 = $10) and dividing it by the value at the beginning of the time period ($5,000). In this case, you get 20 percent, or $1,000 divided by $5,000.

What if GAL also generated a dividend of $2 per share during that period? In that case, GAL would have generated a total return of 24 percent. Total return would take both the appreciation ($10 per share) and the dividend income ($2 per share) and divide the total return ($10 + $2, or $12) by the value at the beginning of the year ($50 per share). This works out as a total of $1,200 ($1,000 of appreciation and $200 total dividends), or 24 percent ($1,200 ÷ $5,000).

Long-term assets are basically items that aren't very liquid. They certainly have value, but you can't necessarily convert them to cash quickly. Notice that the Auto category has a negative percentage in the third column. This reflects the fact that an automobile is generally a depreciating asset and should be reflected as such. You need to know which of your assets are going down in value as well as which ones are going up.

The last line lists the total for all the assets and their current market value. The third column answers the question "How well did your total assets grow from a year ago?"

Step 2: List your liabilities

Liabilities are simply the bills that you're obligated to pay. Whether it's a credit card bill or a mortgage payment, it's an amount of money you have to pay back eventually (with interest). If you don't keep track of your liabilities, you may end up thinking that you have more money than you really do.

Table 2-2 lists some common liabilities. Use it as a model when you list your own.

Table 2-2	Listing Personal Liabilities	
Liabilities	*Amount*	*Paying Rate %*
Credit cards	$4,000	15%
Personal loans	$13,000	10%
Mortgage	$100,000	8%
Total liabilities	$117,000	

The first column in Table 2-2 names the type of debt. Don't forget to include student loans and auto loans if you have any of these. Never avoid listing a liability because you're embarrassed to see how much you really owe. Be honest with yourself — doing so will help you improve your financial health.

The second column shows the current value (or current balance) of your liabilities. You should list the most current balance to see where you stand with your creditors. If you compare your liabilities and your personal assets, you may find opportunities to reduce the amount you pay in interest. Say, for example, that you pay 15 percent on a credit card balance of $4,000 but also have as a personal asset $5,000 in a bank savings account earning 2 percent in interest. In that case, you may want to consider taking $4,000 out of the savings account and paying off the credit card balance. Doing so would save you $520; the $4,000 in the bank was earning only $80 (2 percent of $4,000), while you were paying $600 on the credit card balance (15 percent of $4,000).

The third column reflects how much interest you're paying for carrying that debt. This information should be an important reminder to you about how debt can be a wealth zapper. Credit card debt can have an interest rate of 16 percent or more. To add insult to injury, Canada Customs and Revenue Agency (CCRA) doesn't even make it tax-deductible. Using a credit card to make even a small purchase can cost you if you maintain a balance. A $50 sweater at 18 percent can end up costing $59 when you add in the potential interest you would pay.

If you can't pay off high-interest debt, at least look for ways to minimize the cost of carrying the debt. The most obvious ways include the following:

- **Replacing high-interest cards with low-interest cards.** Many companies offer incentives to consumers to sign up with favourable rates that can be used to pay off high-interest cards.

- **Replacing unsecured debt with secured debt.** Credit cards and personal loans are *unsecured* (meaning that there's no collateral or other asset to secure the debt); therefore, they have higher interest rates because this type of debt is considered riskier for the credit card company. Sources of secured debt (such as home-equity-line accounts and brokerage accounts) provide you with a means to replace your high-interest debt with lower-interest debt. Secured debt has lower interest rates because it's less risky for the creditor — the debt is backed up by collateral (your home or your stocks).

In 1989, Bankruptcy Canada reported that there were about 30,000 personal bankruptcies and 9,000 business bankruptcies. At the end of 2001, the figures were about 79,000 and 10,000, respectively. While Canadian businesses showed a measure of fiscal discipline, Canada's personal insolvencies set a record high in 2001! The consumer bankruptcy story improved only marginally in

Robbing Peter to pay Paul

In recent years, there has been tremendous activity in the world of home equity financing and mortgage refinancing. Millions of people have borrowed more and more money secured by the rising equity in their homes. People are using this money both for good reasons (to pay off high-interest debt) and for not-so-good reasons (to finance an extravagant lifestyle or to speculate in risky investments).

2002 and 2003. (In the U.S., the personal bankruptcy figure has hovered around the 1-million mark over the past seven years.) Clearly, many Canadians need to make a 180-degree turn with respect to their spendthrift ways. Every Canadian should make a diligent effort to control and reduce any personal debt, or risk their personal wealth being wiped out during periods of economic decline. Those who do not will probably have to sell off their stocks just to stay solvent. Remember, Murphy's Law states that you *will* sell your stock at the worst possible moment. Don't go there!

Step 3: Calculate your net worth

Your *net worth* is an indication of your total wealth. The basic equation for calculating net worth is total assets (Table 2-1) less total liabilities (Table 2-2) equals net worth (net assets).

Table 2-3 shows this equation in action with a net worth of $169,000 — a very respectable number. For many investors, just *having* a net worth is great news. Use Table 2-3 as a model to analyze your own financial situation. Your mission (if you choose to accept it — and you should) is to ensure that your net worth increases from year to year as you progress toward your financial goal.

Table 2-3	Figuring Out Your Personal Net Worth	
Totals	*Amounts ($)*	*Increase from Year Before*
Total assets (from Table 2-1)	$286,090	+5%
Total liabilities (from Table 2-2)	$117,000	–2%
Net worth (total assets less total liabilities)	$169,090	+3%

Step 4: Analyze your balance sheet

Create a balance sheet to illustrate your current finances. Take a close look at it and try to identify any changes you can make to increase your wealth. Sometimes reaching your financial goals can be as simple as refocusing the items on your balance sheet. Here are some brief points to consider:

- For the items that constitute your emergency (or rainy-day) fund, is the money sitting in an ultra-safe account and earning the highest interest available? Bank money market accounts or money market funds are recommended. The safest type of account is a Canadian or U.S. treasury money market fund.

- Can you replace depreciating assets with appreciating assets? Say that you have two home-theatre stereo systems. Why not sell one and invest the proceeds? You may say, "But I bought that unit two years ago for $500, and if I sell it now, I'll only get $300." That's your choice. You need to decide what will help your financial situation more — a $500 item that keeps shrinking in value (a *depreciating asset*), or $300 that can grow in value when invested (an *appreciating asset*).

- Can you replace low-yield investments with high-yield investments? Maybe you have $5,000 in a bank guaranteed investment certificate (GIC) earning 3 percent. You can certainly shop around for a better rate at another bank, but you can also seek alternatives that offer a higher yield, such as Canada Savings Bonds or short-term bond funds.

- Can you pay off any high-interest debt with funds from low-interest assets? If, for example, you have $5,000 earning 2 percent in a taxable bank account and you maintain $2,500 in a credit card account on which you pay 18 percent (nondeductible), you may as well pay off the credit card balance and save on the interest.

- If you're carrying debt, is that money being used to give you an investment return that is greater than the interest you're paying? Carrying a loan with an interest rate of 8 percent is acceptable if that borrowed money is yielding more than 8 percent elsewhere. Suppose that you have $6,000 in cash in a brokerage account. If you qualify, you can actually make a stock purchase greater than $6,000 by using margin (essentially a loan from the broker). You can buy $12,000 of stock using your $6,000 in cash, with the remainder financed by the broker. Of course, you pay interest on that margin loan. But what if the interest rate is 6 percent and the stock you're about to invest in has a dividend that yields 9 percent? In that case, the dividend can help you pay off the margin loan, and you keep the additional income. (For more on buying on margin, see Chapter 20.)

✔ Can you sell any personal stuff for cash? Garage sales and auction Web sites like eBay.ca can help you replace unproductive assets with investable cash.

✔ Can you use your home equity to pay off consumer debt? Borrowing against your home has more favourable interest rates, and this interest is still tax-deductible.

Paying off consumer debt by using funds borrowed against your home is a great way to wipe the slate clean. What a relief to get rid of your credit card balances! Just don't be the type of borrower who runs up the consumer debt again. You could become overburdened and experience financial ruin (not to mention homelessness). Not a pretty picture.

The important point to remember is that you can take control of your finances with discipline (and with the advice we offer in this book).

Funding Your Stock Program

If you're going to invest money in stocks, the first thing you need is . . . money! Where is that money going to come from? If you're waiting for that inheritance to come through, you may have to wait a long time, considering all the advances being made in healthcare lately. What's that? You were going to invest in healthcare stocks? How ironic. Yet, the challenge still comes down to how to fund your stock-investing program.

For many investors, reallocating investments and assets does the trick. *Reallocating* simply means selling some investments or other assets and reinvesting that money into stocks. It boils down to deciding what investment or asset you should sell or liquidate. Generally, you probably want to consider those investments and assets that give you a low return on your money (or no return at all). If you have a complicated mix of investments and assets, you may want to consider reviewing your options with a financial planner. (We talk about financial planners in Chapter 7.) Reallocation is just one part of the answer; your cash flow is the other part.

Ever wonder why there's so much month left at the end of the money? Consider your cash flow. Your *cash flow* refers to what money is coming in (income) and what money is being spent or disbursed (outgo). The net result is either a positive cash flow or a negative cash flow, depending on your cash-management skills. Maintaining a positive cash flow (more money coming in than going out) helps you to increase your net worth (mo' money, mo' money, mo' money!). A negative cash flow ultimately depletes your wealth and wipes out your net worth if you don't turn it around immediately. The following sections show you how to analyze your cash flow. The first step is to do a cash-flow statement.

Dot-com-and-go

If there were to be a book about negative cash flow, any one of a hundred dot-com companies that flew sky-high in 1999 and crashed in 2000 and 2001 would be qualified to write it. Companies such as eToys.com, Pets.com, and DrKoop.com were given millions, yet they couldn't turn a profit and eventually closed for business. You may as well call them "dot-com-and-go." You can learn from their mistakes. (Actually, they could have learned from you.) In the same way that profit is the most essential single element in a business, a positive cash flow is important for your finances in general and for funding your stock investment program in particular.

Don't confuse a cash-flow statement with an income statement (also called a "profit and loss statement" or an "income and expense statement"). A cash-flow statement is simple to calculate because you can easily track what goes in and what goes out.

With a cash-flow statement (see Table 2-6), you ask yourself three questions:

- What money is coming in? In your cash-flow statement, jot down all sources of income. Calculate it for the month and then for the year. Include everything — salary, wages, interest, dividends, and so on. Add them all up and get your grand total for income.

- What is your outgo? Jot down all the things that you spend money on. List all your expenses. If possible, categorize them into essential and nonessential. You should have an idea of all the expenses that you could reduce without affecting your lifestyle. But before you do that, make as complete a list as possible of what you spend your money on.

- What's left? If your income is greater than your outgo, then you should have money ready and available for stock investing. No matter how small an amount it may seem, it will definitely help. Fortunes have been built when people started to diligently invest as little as $25 to $50 per week or per month. If your outgo is greater than your income, then you better sharpen your pencil. Cut down on nonessential spending and/or increase your income. If your budget is a little tight, hold off on your stock investing until your cash flow improves.

Step 1: Tally your income

Using Table 2-4 as a worksheet, list and calculate the money you have coming in. The first column describes the source of the money, the second column indicates the monthly amount from each respective source, and the last column indicates the amount projected for a full year. Include all income, such as wages, business income, dividends, interest income, and so on. Then project these amounts for a year (multiply by 12) and enter those amounts in the third column.

Table 2-4	Listing Your Income	
Item	*Monthly $ Amount*	*Yearly $ Amount*
Salary and wages		
Interest income and dividends		
Business net (after taxes income)		
Other income		
Total income		

This is the amount of money you have to work with. To ensure your financial health, don't spend more than this. Always be aware of and carefully manage your income.

Step 2: Add up your outflow

Using Table 2-5 as a worksheet, list and calculate the money that's going out. What are you spending, and on what? The first column describes the source of the expense, the second column indicates the monthly amount, and the third column shows the amount projected for a full year. Include all the money you spend, including credit card and other debt payments; household expenses such as food, utility bills, and medical expenses; and money spent for non-essential expenses such as video games and elephant-foot umbrella stands.

Table 2-5	Listing Your Expenses (Outflow)	
Item	*Monthly $ Amount*	*Yearly $ Amount*
Payroll taxes		
Rent or mortgage		
Utilities		
Food		
Clothing		
Insurance (medical, auto, homeowners, and so on)		

(continued)

Table 2-5 *(continued)*

Item	Monthly $ Amount	Yearly $ Amount
Telephone		
Real estate taxes		
Auto expenses		
Charity		
Recreation		
Credit card payments		
Loan payments		
Other		
Total Outflow		

Payroll taxes is just a category in which to lump all the various taxes that are taken out of your paycheque. Feel free to put each individual tax on its own line if you prefer. The important thing is that you create a comprehensive list that is meaningful to you. You may notice that the outgo doesn't include items such as payments to an RRSP and other savings vehicles. Yes, these do impact your cash flow, but they're not expenses; the amounts that you invest (or have invested for you by your employer) are essentially an asset that benefits your financial situation versus an expense that doesn't have value but helps you build wealth.

Step 3: Create a cash-flow statement

Okay, you're almost at the end. The last step is creating a cash-flow statement so that you can see (at a glance) how your money moves — how much comes in and how much goes out and where it goes.

Plug the amount of your total income (from Table 2-4) and the amount of your total expenses (from Table 2-5) into the Table 2-6 worksheet to see your *cash flow.* Is it positive or negative?

Table 2-6	Looking at Your Cash Flow	
Item	*Monthly $ Amount*	*Yearly $ Amount*
Total income (from Table 2-4)		
Total outgo (from Table 2-5)		
Net inflow/outflow		

The bottom line for you is this: Is your cash flow good or not? Do you generate positive cash flow — more coming in than going out — so that you can start investing in stocks (or other investments), or are expenses overwhelming your income? Doing a cash-flow analysis isn't just about finding money in your financial war chest to fund your stock-investing program. First and foremost, it's about your financial well-being. Are you managing your finances well or not?

Recall our earlier warning that Canada's personal insolvencies hit a record high recently and the U.S. also has suffered recent record numbers of personal bankruptcies — in these cases, personal debt and expenses far exceeded whatever income was generated. This should serve as another reminder to all Canadians to watch their cash flow: keep income growing, and expenses and debt as low as possible.

Step 4: Analyze your cash flow

Use your cash-flow statement to identify sources of funds for your investment program. The more you can increase your income and the more you can decrease your outgo, the better. Scrutinize your data. Where can you improve the results? Here are some questions to ask yourself:

✔ How can you augment your income? Do you have hobbies, interests, or skills that can generate extra cash for you?

✔ Can you get more paid overtime at work? How about a promotion or a job change?

✔ Where can you cut expenses?

✔ Have you categorized your expenses as either "necessary" or "nonessential"?

✔ Can you lower your debt payments by refinancing or consolidating loans and credit card balances?

✔ Have you shopped around for lower insurance or telephone rates?

✔ Have you analyzed your taxes to see whether you can lower the amount withheld from your pay?

Step 5: Find investment money in tax savings

According to the Canadian and U.S. tax foundations, the average Canadian and American citizen pays more in taxes than in food, clothing, and housing combined. Sit down with your tax adviser and try to find ways to reduce your taxes. A home-based business, for example, is a great way to gain new income and increase your tax deductions, resulting in a lower tax burden. Your tax adviser or accountant can make recommendations that will work for you.

One tax strategy to consider is doing your stock investing in a tax-sheltered account, such as an open or locked-in self-directed RRSP. Again, check with your tax adviser for deductions and strategies available to you. For more on the tax implications of stock investing, see Chapter 21.

Chapter 3

Common Approaches to Stock Investing

In This Chapter

▶ Deciding whether long-term or short-term investments are right for you

▶ Looking at your objectives for investing

▶ Determining your investing style

*B*efore investing in stocks, ask yourself, "When do I want to reach my financial goals?" Stocks are a means to an end. Your job is to figure out what that end is — or, really, *when* it is. Are you seeking to retire in ten years, or next year? Are you paying for your kid's university education next year, or 18 years from now? The length of time you have before you need the money that you hope to earn from stock investing is one important factor that determines what stocks you should buy. Table 3-1 gives you some guidelines for choosing the kind of stock that's best suited for your goals.

Table 3-1	Matching Stock Types to Financial Goals and Investor Types	
Type of Investor	*Time Frame for Your Financial Goal*	*Type of Stock Most Suitable*
Conservative (worries about risk)	Long-term (more than five years)	Large-cap stocks and mid-cap stocks
Aggressive (high tolerance to risk)	Long-term (more than five years)	Small-cap stocks and mid-cap stocks
Conservative (worries about risk)	Intermediate-term (two to five years)	Large-cap stocks, preferably with dividends
Aggressive (high tolerance to risk)	Intermediate-term (two to five years)	Small-cap stocks and mid-cap stocks
Short term	One to two years	Don't even think about stock investment!

Table 3-1 gives general guidelines, but keep in mind that not everyone can neatly fit into a particular profile. Every Canadian investor has a different personal situation, set of goals, and level of risk tolerance. Remember that *large cap, mid cap,* and *small cap* just refer to the size (or market capitalization, also known as market cap) of the company. All things being equal, large companies are safer (less risky) than small companies. For more on market caps, see the section "Investing by Style" later in this chapter.

Investing by Time Frame

Are your goals long term or short term? Answering this question is important, because individual stocks can be either great or horrible choices depending on the term you're looking at. Generally, the term can be short, intermediate, or long. The following sections outline what kinds of stocks are most appropriate for each term length.

Investing in stocks becomes less risky as the necessary time frame lengthens. Stock prices tend to fluctuate on a daily basis, but they do have a tendency to trend up or down over an extended period. Even if you invest in a stock that goes down in the short term, you're likely to see it rise and even go above your investment if you have the discipline to wait it out and let the stock price appreciate.

Looking at the short term

Short term generally means one year or less, although some people say that short term means two years or less. You get the point.

All of us have short-term goals. Some are modest, such as setting aside money for a vacation next month or buying some furniture for the den. Other short-term goals are more ambitious, such as accruing funds for a down payment for a new home purchase within six months. Whatever the expense or purchase, you need a predictable accumulation of cash soon. If this sounds like your situation, stay away from the stock market!

Because stocks can be so unpredictable in the short term, they're a bad choice for short-term purposes. We continue to marvel in disbelief whenever we hear market analysts saying things like "At $20 a share, XYZ is a solid investment, and we feel that its stock should hit our target price of $35 within six to nine months." You just know that someone will hear that and say, "Gee, why bother with 3 percent at the bank when this stock will rise by more than

50 percent? I better call my broker." The stock may indeed hit that target amount (and may even surpass that price), or it may not. Most of the time, however, the target price is not reached, and the investor is disappointed. The stock could even go down! But what if the money invested was meant to be used for an important short-term need? Remember, short-term stock investing is very unpredictable, and your short-term goals are better served with stable, interest-bearing investments (like GICs) instead.

During the raging bull market of the late 1990s, investors watched as some high-profile stocks went up 20 to 50 percent in a matter of months. Hey, who needs a savings account earning a measly 4 percent interest when stocks grow like that! Of course, when the bear market hit in 2000 and those same stocks fell 50 to 70 percent, suddenly a savings account earning a measly 4 percent interest rate didn't seem so bad after all.

Stocks, even the best ones, will fluctuate in the short term. No one can really predict the price movement accurately (unless they have some inside information), so stocks are definitely not appropriate for any financial goal that you need to reach within one year.

Considering intermediate-term goals

Intermediate-term refers to your financial goals that need to be reached within five years. If, for example, you need to accumulate funds to put money down for investment real estate property four years from now, some growth-oriented investments may be suitable.

Although *some* stocks *may* be appropriate for a two- or three-year period, not all stocks are good intermediate-term investments. There are different types and categories of stocks. Some stocks are fairly stable and hold their value well, such as the stock of much larger or established companies. Other stocks have prices that go all over the place, such as the stocks of untested companies that are just starting out and haven't been in existence long enough to develop a consistent track record.

If you plan to invest in the stock market to meet intermediate-term goals, large established companies or dividend-paying companies in much-needed industries (like food and beverage or electric utilities, for instance) are good choices for you. *Dividends* are payments made to an owner (unlike *interest*, which is payment to a creditor). Dividends are a great form of income, and companies that issue dividends tend to have more stable share prices as well. For more information on dividend-paying stocks, see Chapter 9.

Investing for the long term

Stock investing is best suited for making money over a long period. When you measure stocks against other investments in terms of five or (preferably) ten or more years, they excel. Even investors who bought stocks in the depths of the Great Depression saw profitable growth in their stock portfolios over a ten-year period.

In fact, if you take any ten-year period over the past 75 years, you'll see that stocks beat out other financial investments (such as bonds or bank investments) in every single ten-year period when measured by total return (taking into account reinvesting and compounding of capital gains and dividends)! As you can see, the long term is where stocks shine most. Of course, it doesn't stop there. You still have to do your homework and choose stocks wisely — because, even in good times, you can lose money if you invest in companies that go out of business. The chapters in Parts III and IV show you, among other things, how to pick winners by evaluating specific companies and industries, and alert you to factors in the general economy that can affect stock behaviour.

Because there are many different types and categories of stocks, virtually any investor with a long-term perspective should add stocks to his investment portfolio. Whether you're saving for a young child's university fund or for your own retirement, carefully selected stocks have proven to be a superior long-term investment.

Investing by Style

When a lady was asked why she bungee-jumped off the bridge that spanned a massive ravine, she answered, "Because it's fun!" When someone asked the fellow why he went in a pool that was chock full of alligators and snakes, he responded, "Because someone pushed me." Your investment in stocks should not happen for any other reason except a purpose that you understand and buy into. That purpose should then translate into a corresponding investment style. If your purpose is to preserve your savings, then a conservative investment style is appropriate. Even if you invest because some adviser told you to, be sure that you get an explanation of how that stock choice fits your investment purpose and style.

We know a very nice, elderly lady who had a portfolio brimming with aggressive-growth stocks because she had an overbearing stockbroker. Her purpose, and style (which should be driven by her purpose), should have been conservative. She ought to have chosen investments to preserve her wealth rather than to grow it aggressively. Obviously, the broker's own purpose got in the way.

Stocks are just a means to an end. Determine your desired outcomes and then match your style to those outcomes. A detailed comparison of conservative versus aggressive investing is provided later in this chapter. Following is a discussion of some classic and common investing styles.

Growth investing

When investors want their money to grow, they're looking for investments that appreciate in value. *Appreciate* is just another way of saying "grow." If you have a stock that you bought for $8 per share and now it's $30 per share, your investment has grown by $22 per share — that's appreciation. We know we would appreciate it!

Appreciation (also known as *growth* or *capital gain*) is probably the primary reason that people invest in stocks. Few investments have the potential to grow your wealth as conveniently as stocks. If you're looking to the stock market to make lots of money relatively quickly (and assuming you're not averse to assuming some risk), then Chapter 9 will provide loads of discussion about investing for growth. In fact, the chapter is devoted to it!

Stocks are a great way to grow your wealth, but they're not the only way. Many investors seek alternative ways to make money, but many of them are more aggressive and carry significantly more risk. You've probably heard about people who made a quick fortune in areas such as commodities (like wheat, pork bellies, or precious metals), options, and other more sophisticated investment vehicles. Keep in mind that you should limit risky investments to only a portion of your portfolio, such as 10 percent of your investable funds. Experienced investors, however, can go as high as 20 percent.

Income investing

Not all investors want to make a killing. Some people just want to invest in the stock market as a means of providing themselves with a steady income — they don't need stock values to go through the ceiling. Instead, they need stocks that perform well consistently. They want to preserve their existing level of wealth.

If your purpose for investing in stocks is to provide yourself with stable income, you need to choose stocks that pay dividends. Dividends are paid quarterly to shareholders on record, and are described in detail in Chapter 1.

Distinguishing between dividends and interest

A word of caution is called for here. Don't confuse dividends (which we discussed in Chapter 1) with interest. Most people are familiar with interest because that's how their money has grown for years in the bank. The important difference between the two is that *interest* is paid to creditors, while *dividends* are paid to owners. (Shareholders are owners — if you hold stock you're an owner, because stocks represent shares in a publicly traded company.)

When you buy stock, you're buying a piece of that company. When you put money in a bank (or when you buy bonds), you're really loaning your money. You become a creditor, and the bank or bond issuer is the debtor — as such, it must eventually pay your money back to you with interest.

Recognizing the importance of an income stock's yield

Investing for income means that you have to consider that investment's yield. If you're seeking income from a stock investment, you must compare the yield from that particular stock with alternatives. Looking at the yield is a way to compare the income you would receive from one investment with that from others. Table 3-2 shows some comparative yields.

Table 3-2	Comparing the Yields of Various Investments				
Investment	*Type*	*Amount*	*Pay Type*	*Payout*	*Yield*
Smith Co.	Stock	$50/share	Dividend	$2.50	5%
Jones Co.	Stock	$100/share	Dividend	$4	4%
Acme Bank	Bank GIC	$500	Interest	$25	5%
Acme Bank	Bank GIC	$2,500	Interest	$131.25	5.25%
Acme Bank	Bank GIC	$5,000	Interest	$287.50	5.75%
Brown Co.	Bond	$5,000	Interest	$300	6%

To understand how to calculate yield, you need the following formula:

Yield = Payout ÷ Investment amount

Yield enables you to compare how much income you would get for a prospective investment compared with the income you would get from other investments.

Jones Co. and Smith Co. are both typical dividend-paying stocks (in this example, presume that both companies are similar in most respects). But these two stocks have different dividends. How can you tell whether a $50 stock with a $2.50 annual dividend is better (or worse) than a $100 stock with a $4 dividend? The yield tells you.

Even though Jones Co. pays a higher dividend ($4), Smith Co. has a higher yield (5 percent). Therefore, if we had to choose between those two stocks as an income investor, we would choose Smith Co. Of course, if we truly wanted to maximize our income and didn't really need our investment to appreciate a lot, we would probably choose Brown Co.'s bond, because it offers a yield of 6 percent.

Dividend-paying stocks do have the ability to increase in value. They may not have the same growth potential as growth stocks, but at the very least they have a greater potential for capital gain than bank GICs or bonds.

We explore income investing in full detail in Chapter 10.

Value investing

The great bear market of the first part of this decade appears to have played itself out. To say that it left a lasting impression on most Canadian investors would be an understatement. As a result of the bear market, we observed a decided shift in what most investors seek. Momentum investing — where investors follow a herd of other investors after the next big thing — is passe. In fact, at the moment there really is no "next best thing," only a smattering of smaller "interesting" things! We briefly describe momentum investing later in this chapter, and explain why it was big in years past.

Value investing is, on the other hand, a fundamental investing style that focuses on the strengths of an individual stock and the underlying company. Value investing is buying stocks as if you were buying the business itself. Value investors emphasize the intrinsic value of assets and current and future profits, and pay a price equal to or less than that value. This style of investing is one of the key themes of this book; it is covered in more depth in Chapter 11 and in other chapters where appropriate. A brief overview here will help introduce you to its basic principles.

The ultimate question about value investing is this: "What am I buying — and what am I paying for it?" Canadians who recognize the importance of that fundamental investing question typically adopt, or are amenable to, a value-investing style. It's different from growth investing, and different from income investing, yet value investing has elements of both. Tremendous value may be found in an income stock at its current price. Value can also be indicated in a growth stock, as long as the price is right relative to its higher risk. Value can be measured in at least three basic ways.

Book value per share

The first way to determine value is to measure a stock's book value per share. Book value is the amount that one share of a company's common stock would be worth if the powers-that-be were to liquidate the company, pay the amounts owed, and divide the remaining cash among the shareholders. (This assumes that the book value determined by accountants is roughly the same as the street value of assets held, and the real current value of liabilities owed.)

Over the past few years, it has been typical to see Canadian stocks average about 5:1. This means that shares of Canadian companies are currently priced at an average of about five times a company's worth. This is a high level, in our opinion, so you want to look for stocks that are reasonably priced relative to this benchmark.

Price–earnings ratio

The second way to measure a stock's value is by using the price–earnings ratio. This is the multiple a stock trades at as compared to its annual earnings. If a company earned $1 per share last year and its stock is currently selling for $10, its price–earnings ratio is 10:1, or 10.

In the S&P 500 index (we discuss stock indexes in Chapter 5), the average P/E ratio over the past few years has been about 23, based on the most recent actual earnings of companies that make up that index. While this is not its highest level in history, it's still pretty close!

Keep in mind that you should consider the P/E ratio in the context of the growth prospects of the company you're considering for investment. A company that sells at a P/E of 10 — below market averages — may not be desirable if it has exhibited annual growth in earnings of only 3 percent. Yet, a stock boasting a higher current P/E multiple of 20 might be still be considered desirable if it's demonstrating a great trend of annual earnings growth of 35 percent per year or more! Also consider a stock's P/E ratio in the context of the stock's industry group. A stock selling at a P/E of 12 will be attractive if the average P/E among other stocks in its industry is hovering at 19.

Dividend value

A third way to measure a stock's value is the stock's dividend. You may do well if you can find stocks that meet the prior two criteria and also pay dividends. That would be the icing on the cake! Consider past or expected future increases in the stock's dividend payout.

You don't have to use the value-investing approach for *all* of your investments. Depending on your goals, it's okay to mix investing styles.

Are dividends important?

The role and value of dividends is an ongoing debate among value investors and commentators. Is it better for companies to keep it all, or to return some or all of it to you? The keep-it-all school maintains that the company has better ways to invest it than you do (after all, if this is not the case the company probably isn't a good value investment in the first place). The give-it-back school wants some of their returns back as cash to keep management honest, and because they're confident that they themselves, as talented value investors, will find good ways to invest the return.

Take this advice from Warren Buffett: "For some reason, people take their cues from price action rather than from values. What doesn't work is when you start doing things that you don't understand or because they worked last week for somebody else. The dumbest reason in the world to buy a stock is because it is going up."

Oh, and one other thing. How can you spot the value investor at a cocktail party? Easy. He's the only one talking about an actual company while all the other guests stand around discussing the stock market.

Time Out: Other Investing Styles

At this stage, we want to introduce you to some additional investing styles and concepts other than the core styles of growth, income, and value investing (each of which has an entire chapter devoted to it in this book). There's a lot of confusing terminology out there, so some clarification is in order. These new terms to follow are often just more ways of referring to growth, income, value investing, a combination of the three — or none of the above.

Conservative versus aggressive investing

Conservative investing isn't necessarily a reference to growth, income, or value. It's not even a reference to the type of investor you are, although the type of investment you make does generally describe your objectives. Conservative investing means that you are averse to excessive risk — you put your money in something proven, tried, and true, such as banks and government-backed securities. It can also mean investing in a cash-rich, well-run, and stable growth company. At best, the definition of "conservative investing" can be a bit of a moving target. It tends to mean different things to different stock investors.

Conservative investing

To inject some clarity into this debate, it may be fair to say that conservative stock investors want to invest their money in companies that have exhibited some of the following qualities:

- **Proven performance:** Conservative investors want companies that have, year after year, shown increasing sales and earnings. They don't demand anything spectacular, just a strong and steady performance.

- **Market size:** Companies should be large cap (short for "large capitalization"). In other words, companies should have a market value exceeding $10 billion in size. Conservative investors surmise that bigger is safer.

- **Market leadership:** Companies should be leaders in their industries.

- **Perceived staying power:** Conservative investors want companies with the financial clout and market position to weather uncertain market and economic conditions, no matter what happens in the economy or which prime minister gets elected.

Conservative investors don't mind if their share prices jump (who would?), but they're more concerned with growth over the long term.

Aggressive investing

Aggressive stock investors can be in for the long term or the intermediate term, but in any case they want stocks that are jackrabbits — those that have the potential to break out of the pack.

Aggressive investors want to put their money in companies that have exhibited some of the following qualities:

- **Great potential:** The company must have goods, service, ideas, or ways of doing business that are better than the competition.

- **Capital-gains possibility:** Aggressive investors don't prioritize dividends. If anything, aggressive investors don't really care about dividends. They believe that the money that would have been dispensed as dividends is better reinvested in the company. This, in turn, can spur greater growth.

- **Innovation:** Companies should have technologies, ideas, or innovative methods that make them stand out.

Aggressive investors usually seek out small-capitalization stocks, known as *small caps,* because they have plenty of potential for growth. The growth potential stems from the fact that many of these newer companies have fresh ideas that sell, are aggressive in their quest to grow their business operations, and strive to become future market leaders. So why invest in stodgy, big companies when you can invest in smaller enterprises that could become tomorrow's leaders? Aggressive investors have no problem investing in obscure companies, because they hope that such companies will become another JDS Uniphase or Home Depot.

The value investor looks for consistency in an attempt to minimize risk and provide a margin of safety for his or her investment. This is not to say the value investor *won't* invest in a risky enterprise; it's just to say that the price paid for earnings potential must correctly reflect the risk. Consistency need not be absolute, but predictable performance is important.

Fundamental investing

Fundamental investors look at the fundamentals of a business — assets, revenue, growth, cash profits, dividends, productivity, gross margins, and so on. In that light, it's easy to see how a value investor can also be considered to be a fundamental investor, except that a value investor also looks for a great bargain! Even a growth investor can be considered to be a fundamental investor, because growth is one of several things that fundamental investors look for.

As you can see, the definition of fundamental investing is broad; it seems to encompass a lot of investing styles. On the other hand, it properly reflects the holistic approach necessary to be a successful investor today. In other words, you can't rely on just one measure of company performance. Looking only at company growth, or only at the extent of dividends paid, is not enough to base an investment decision on. The fundamental investor looks at several fundamental measures of a company's financial condition to get the big picture.

Despite its sketchy definition, fundamental investing ultimately requires that investors look at the intrinsic value of a business and the value that the business is likely to deliver to the shareholder in the future. It's a sharp contrast to the investing style that we'll discuss next.

Technical analysis–based investing

A technical analyst, like a fundamental analyst, deals in numbers. In fact, *technical analysis*, also known as TA, is all about numbers. The technical analysis style of investing applies statistical models and patterns to stock price movement with little (if any) regard to the underlying fundamentals of the company. For a pure TA investor, the stock — not the company — tells the only story he wants to hear.

The TA practitioner studies price and volume charts and statistically determined buy and sell signals all day long. In a sense, a TA technician is a student of market and industry behaviour rather than company-specific performance. The price patterns observed are really the collective decisions, attitudes, behaviours, and psyche of the public. The TA technician studies the price behaviour that results from these collective decisions and believes that the market, and stock behaviour, can be anticipated.

As a very basic example, one TA term that is used quite often to describe a stock is *head and shoulders*. In this pattern, the stock will peak and then sell off as the first wave of profit takers emerges and — you guessed it — takes profits! The stock price then peaks again at the next level, and sells off more sharply. Finally, it peaks at a third and lower level, as those missing the first two peaks try to capitalize on a suspected opportunity. However, the stock then reverses lower as the whole pattern runs out of steam.

Since we're all human, certain patterns of behaviour do tend to repeat themselves more often than not. Markets are not driven by random number generators. There is a rhyme and reason to the market. Therefore, there is merit to the TA approach (and there's merit in the myriad software packages and literature that support it). But TA investing is a far cry from value investing. Done in isolation, TA investing can lead to ruin. However, when done in tandem with and as a support for other investing styles, it can give you a real investor's edge!

Day traders are the biggest proponents of the TA investing style. A day trader makes her living by buying and selling stocks back and forth. The day trader hopes to make a profit on a continuous series of individual transactions, usually with various stocks. The objective of the day trader is to make a profit on very small fluctuations in the stock price. The typical day trader takes all of her money off the table by the end of the trading day. Loads of software, most of it TA-oriented, is available for day traders.

While day traders generally adopt the TA style, most ignore the principles behind value, growth, and income investing. That is perfectly fine, because the TA investing style fits the day trader's very short-term and focused objectives — namely, to make a series of quick and small profits in a short period of time.

Tell me a story

Story stock investing, also known as *concept stock investing*, subscribes to an irrational, albeit sometimes effective, approach. It strives to benefit from the very real herd mentality that sometimes exists in the stock market. Money tends to follow money, and people seem to be more comfortable investing in a stock after they see others investing in it too. This is often true even if it means paying a higher price! The best example of story and concept investing is a recent one — the late 1990s technology stock mania.

Any company whose name ended in *.com*, *Networks*, or *Communications* was a concept stock. These stocks all had a story that was associated with a larger story — that the Internet and personal computing would change the way we all live. Any companies that were participants in this wave of the future were bound to become hugely successful. Unfortunately for many Canadians, except perhaps value investors, many of these companies were spendthrifts, or could not repay their colossal debt loads when the appetite for technology spending was satisfied. Yet, if you look at a company's "good news" story (and the extent of its media coverage), the public exposure can benefit your investment greatly. There are all too many value stocks out there that do not see the light of day simply because no one — neither stock analysts nor the media — follows them. A balance between value and concept investing styles can serve you well.

Mo' money

Momentum investing, yet another investing style, is a combination of TA and story stock investing. The momentum investor piles on to stocks that are already making a directional move, perhaps even because they are story stocks. Cool, sexy stocks with a driven chart pattern, and much media and analyst coverage, can really catch fire as far as price movement is concerned. The technology stock boom epitomized momentum investing, especially within the Internet sector of the high-tech industry.

Momentum investing can be great for agile investors. It's no place for the value investor. Remember, value investors invest with regard to price only as it relates to value. Value investors don't invest because of price movement.

Chapter 4

What Risk's Got to Do with It

In This Chapter

▶ Considering the types of risk

▶ Taking steps to reduce your risk

▶ Spreading your money around

▶ Balancing risk against return

*I*nvestors face many risks, most of which we cover in this chapter. The simplest definition of risk for investors is "the possibility that your investment will lose some (or all) of its value." Yet risk is not something to fear but something to understand and plan for. You need to get familiar with the concept of risk. You must understand the oldest equation in the world of investing: risk versus return. This equation states the following:

> If you want a greater return on your money, you need to tolerate more risk. If you don't want to tolerate more risk, you must tolerate a lower rate of return.

This point about risk is best illustrated by a moment from an investment seminar. An attendee explained that he had his money in the bank, but was dissatisfied with the rate of return. "The yield on my money is pitiful! I want to put my money someplace where it can grow." When the seminar leader suggested investing in common stocks or growth mutual funds — which offer a solid, long-term growth track record — he responded, "Stocks? I don't want to put my money there. It's too risky!" Okay, then. If you don't want to tolerate more risk, then don't complain about earning less on your money. Risk (in all its forms) has a bearing on all your money concerns and goals. That's why it's so important that you understand risk before you invest.

This man — like all of us — needs to remember that risk is not a four-letter word. Well, it does have four letters, but you know what we mean. Risk is present no matter where you put your money. Even if you simply stick your money in your mattress, risk is involved — several kinds of risk, in fact. There is the risk of fire. What if your house burns down? There is the risk of theft. What if burglars find your stash of cash? There is also relative risk. In other words, what if your relatives find it?

Be aware of the different kinds of risk, and you can easily plan around them to keep your money growing.

Exploring Different Kinds of Risk

Think about all the ways that an investment can lose money. You can list all sorts of possibilities. It might make you think, "Holy cow! Why invest at all?"

Don't let risk frighten you. After all, life itself is risky. Just make sure that you understand the different kinds of risk before you start navigating the investment world. Be mindful of risk and find out about the possible effects of risk on your investments and personal financial goals.

Hundreds of thousands of Canadians recently witnessed their personal investment account balances shrivel. One of the biggest reasons for the decline in portfolio balances was that these investors, or the persons they entrusted their capital to, underestimated the importance of the risk side of the investment equation. They remembered that stocks had a potential for great returns, but forgot that risk came in all shapes and sizes.

Companies without ethical management and good governance practices had all kinds of skeletons march out of their closets and into the media spotlight. They scared investors, who took their money and ran away from the stock. In turn, the stock price fell. This scenario, as we now know, replayed itself like a broken record, especially in 2001 and 2002. (We discuss ethical risk in more detail in Chapter 14.)

Geopolitical risk, equally unpredictable, is not company-specific. In other words, when geopolitical risk such as the Iraq war rears its head, entire markets suffer. Virtually every investor, not just investors in specific troubled companies, exits from the equity market. This causes a snowball effect, where everyone follows the herd of investors selling out their equities. That behaviour can potentially lead to severe market corrections (steep drops in market indexes, which are explained in Chapter 5) or even crashes. It is interesting to note that before almost every war over the past 40 years markets fell significantly in the short term. But once the war actually started, markets commenced an almost immediate rebound. A savvy investor may spot such trends and try to capitalize on the favourable odds of such a quick rebound happening again. (We also discuss geopolitical risk in Chapter 14.)

There are all too many risks to track. However, we introduce some of the most significant risks that can harm you financially as an investor. The risks that follow are the most common, easy to track, and manageable risks that you should be aware of.

Financial Risk

The financial risk of stock investing is that you can lose your money if the company whose stock you purchase loses money or goes belly up. This type of risk is the most obvious, because companies do go bankrupt.

You can greatly enhance the chances that your financial risk will pay off by doing an adequate amount of research and choosing your stocks carefully (which this book helps you do). Financial risk is a real concern even when the economy is doing well. Some diligent research, a little planning, and a dose of common sense will help you reduce your financial risk.

In the stock-investing mania of the late 1990s, millions of investors (along with many pundits and commentators in the media) ignored some financial risks that were obvious problems with many popular stocks. Investors blindly plunked their money into stocks that were bad choices. Consider investors who put their money into DrKoop.com, a health information Web site, in 1999 and held on during 2000. Despite the fact that DrKoop.com never earned a penny of profit, it hit a high of $45 a share as the great rush toward Internet stocks became a bloated, speculative investment bubble. But the bubble popped in 2000. DrKoop.com needed life support as its mounting losses pushed the stock to below $2!

Similarly, investors saw their money in eToys.com vanish as its losses and excessive debt drove it into the ground. The eToys stock, which flew higher than a kite in 1999, eventually went the way of Cabbage Patch dolls as the company filed for bankruptcy in early 2001. The stock fell from $85 in late 1999 to literally zero in March 2001. Although eToys re-emerged from the ashes as a new company under new ownership, the damage to investors had already been done. Time will tell whether these types of innovative business models work, but as of late 2003, don't even consider such investments; they are best suited for risk-loving speculators! (*Now* you're talking risk!)

Investors who did their homework regarding the financial conditions of these companies discovered the hallmarks of financial risk — high debt and low (or no) earnings, and plenty of competition. They steered clear, avoiding tremendous financial loss. Investors who didn't do their homework were lured by the status of these companies — the poster children of booming Internet fortunes — and lost their shirts.

We don't believe that the individual investors who lost money by investing in these trendy, high-profile companies deserve all the responsibility for their tremendous financial losses; some high-profile analysts and media sources also should have known better. The late 1990s are a case study of how euphoria and the herd mentality rather than good, old-fashioned research and common sense won the day (temporarily). The excitement of making potential fortunes can get the best of people sometimes, and they throw caution to the wind. Historians will look back at those days and say, "What *were* they thinking?" Achieving true wealth takes diligent work and careful analysis.

In terms of financial risk, the bottom line is . . . well . . . the bottom line! A healthy bottom line means that a company is making money. And if a company is making money, then you can make money by investing in its stock. However, if a company isn't making money, neither will you if you invest in it. Profit is the lifeblood of any company. (Are you listening, Dr. Koop?)

Interest rates

Interest-rate risk may sound like an odd type of risk. In fact, interest-rate risk is a common consideration for investors. This refers to the fact that interest rates change on a regular basis, causing some challenging moments. Interest rates are set by banks, and the primary institution that people watch closely is the U.S. Federal Reserve (the Fed), which is, in effect, the country's central bank. The Fed raises or lowers interest rates, actions that in turn cause banks to raise or lower interest rates accordingly. Interest-rate changes affect consumers, businesses, and, of course, investors.

The scenario outlined in the following paragraphs gives you a generic introduction to the way fluctuating-interest-rate risk can affect investors in general.

Suppose that you buy a long-term, high-quality corporate bond and get a yield of 6 percent. Your money is safe, and your return is locked in at 6 percent. Whew! That's a guaranteed 6 percent. Not bad, huh? But what happens if, after you commit your money, interest rates increase to 8 percent? You lose the opportunity to get that extra 2 percent interest. The only way to get out of your 6-percent bond is to sell it at current market values and use the money to reinvest at the higher rate.

The only problem with this scenario is that the 6-percent bond is likely to drop in value because interest rates rose. Why? Say that the investor is Bob and the bond yielding 6 percent is a corporate bond issued by Lucin-Muny (LM). According to the bond agreement, LM must pay 6 percent (called the "face rate," or "nominal rate") during the life of the bond and then, upon maturity, pay the principal. If Bob buys $10,000 of LM bonds on the day they are issued, he gets $600 (of interest) every year for as long as he holds the bonds. If he holds on until maturity, he'll get back his $10,000 (the principal). So far so good, right? The plot thickens, however.

Say that he decides to sell the bond long before maturity and that, at the time of the sale, interest rates in the market rise to 8 percent. Now what? The reality is that no one would want his 6-percent bond if the market is offering bonds at 8 percent. What's Bob to do? He can't change the face rate of 6 percent, and he can't change the fact that only $600 will be paid each year for the life of the bond. What will have to change so that current investors get the *equivalent* yield of 8 percent? If you said, "The bond's value will have to go down" . . . bingo! In this example, the bond's market value needs to drop to $7,500 so that investors buying the bond would get an equivalent yield of 8 percent. Here's how that figures:

New investors would still get $600 annually. However, $600 is equal to 8 percent of $7,500. Therefore, even though investors would get the face rate of 6 percent, it equals a yield of 8 percent because the actual investment amount is $7,500. In this example there is no financial risk, but it illustrates how interest-rate risk can present itself. Bob finds out that you can have a good company with a good bond yet still lose $2,500 because of the change in the interest rate. Of course, if Bob doesn't sell, he won't realize that loss.

The lesson in all of this is that you can still lose money even in an apparently sound investment because of something sounding as harmless as "interest rates have changed."

Rising and falling interest rates offer a special risk to stock investors. Historically, rising interest rates have had an adverse effect on stock prices. There are several reasons for this, and we outline them for you in the following sections.

Hurting a company's financial condition

Rising interest rates have a negative impact on companies that carry a large current debt load or that need to take on more debt, because when interest rates rise, the cost of borrowing money rises, too. This ultimately reduces the company's profitability and its ability to grow. When a company's profits (or earnings) drop, its stock becomes less desirable, and its stock price will fall.

Affecting a company's customers

Every company succeeds when it sells its products or services. But what happens if its customers (specifically, other companies that buy from it) are negatively impacted by increased interest rates? The financial health of its customers will directly affect the company's ability to grow sales and earnings.

For a good example of this situation, consider what happened to Cisco Systems in 2000. Because a huge part of its sales went to the telecommunications industry, the health of that entire industry was vital to Cisco's profitability. The telecom industry's debt ballooned to $700 billion. This debt became the telecom industry's financial Achilles heel, which in turn became a pain in the neck to Cisco. As telecom companies bought less (especially from Cisco), Cisco's profits shrank. From March 2000 to March 2001, Cisco's stock fell by nearly 70 percent! As of September 2001, Cisco's stock price continued to decline because the companies that were Cisco's customers were hurting financially.

Affecting investors' decision-making considerations

When interest rates rise, investors start to rethink their investment strategies. This can result in one of two outcomes:

- ✔ Investors may sell any shares in interest-sensitive stocks that they hold. Interest-sensitive industries include electric utilities, real estate, and the financial sector. Although increased interest rates can hurt these sectors, the reverse is also generally true: Falling interest rates boost the same industries. Keep in mind that interest-rate changes affect some industries more than others.

- ✔ Investors who favour increased current income (versus waiting for the investment to grow in value to sell for a gain later on) are definitely attracted to investment vehicles that offer a higher rate of return. Higher interest rates can cause investors to switch from stocks to bonds or GICs.

Hurting stock prices indirectly

High or rising interest rates can have a negative impact on any investor's total financial picture. What happens when an investor struggles with burdensome debt, such as a second mortgage, credit card debt, or *margin debt* (debt you incur from borrowing against stock in a brokerage account)? He may sell some stock in order to pay off some of his high-interest debt. Selling stock to service debt is a common practice that, when taken collectively, can hurt stock prices.

The late 1990s economy saw a tremendous explosion of personal, mortgage, and corporate debt. These record-setting levels of debt subsequently resulted in record levels of personal bankruptcies and loan defaults for both consumers and corporations. Many investors sold their stock to pay for their debt. This action in turn forced stocks to fall further. Debt considerations played an instrumental role in the decline of stock prices during 2000.

Because of the effects of interest rates on stock portfolios, both direct and indirect, investors should regularly monitor interest rates in both the general economy and in their personal situations. Although stocks have proven to be a superior long-term investment (the longer the term, the better), every investor should maintain a balanced portfolio that includes other investment vehicles, such as money market funds, savings bonds, and/or bank investments.

A diversified investor should have some money in vehicles that do well when interest rates rise. These include such things as money market funds, Canada Savings Bonds, and other variable-rate investments whose interest rates rise when market rates rise. These types of investments add a measure of safety from interest-rate risk to your stock portfolio.

Liquidity

Liquidity risk is the risk that cash will not be available to meet all cash-related obligations as they come due. This risk may arise because of an undesired selling off of assets in order to meet short-term cash commitments. Selling assets off too soon may result in your getting a less than ideal price, or being unable to hold on to that asset for strategic or operational purposes.

Liquidity risk can also be explained as what happens when a company's current assets (those that can be readily liquidated in one year or less) fall short of current liabilities (those that are due within one year). Current assets include things like cash in the bank, marketable securities in other companies, accounts receivable from customers, and inventory. Current liabilities include things like accounts payable, and the current portion of longer-term debt that is due in the current year. When the payment of current obligations that exceed current assets can't be delayed any longer, a company enters into a liquidity crisis. In some cases, the company in financial distress will go to the bank to try to get bridge financing in the form of a line of credit, or bank demand loan (that is, one that has to be paid whenever the bank demands). But quite often, lenders will shy away from throwing good money at bad companies — those that don't have their fiscal house in order. The lesson here is that the investor should likewise steer clear of any company that is financially distressed, insolvent, and appearing to be heading into bankruptcy.

Markets

When people talk about *the market* and how it goes up or down, it sounds like a monolithic entity instead of what it really is — a group of millions of individuals making daily decisions to buy or sell stock. No matter how modern our society and economic system, you can't escape the laws of supply and demand. When masses of people want to buy a particular stock, it becomes in demand and its value rises. That value rises higher if the supply is limited. Conversely, if no one's interested in buying a stock, its value falls. This is the nature of market risk. The value of your stock can rise and fall on the fickle whim of market demand.

Millions of investors buying and selling each minute of every trading day affect the share price of your stock. This fact makes it impossible to judge which way your stock will move tomorrow or next week. This unpredictability is why stocks aren't appropriate for short-term financial growth.

In April 2001, a news program reported that in 2000 a fellow with $80,000 in the bank decided to invest it in the stock market. Because he was getting married in 2001, he wanted his money to grow faster and higher so that he could afford a nice wedding and a down payment on the couple's future home. What happened? His money shrank to $11,000, and he had to change his plans.

Reduced cash flow is only one headache you face when you lose money this way — the idea of postponing a joyful event, such as a wedding or a home purchase, just adds to the pain. The gent in the preceding story could have easily minimized his losses with some knowledge and discipline.

Markets are by their nature volatile; they go up and down, and investments need time to grow. This poor guy (literally, now) should have been aware of the fact that stocks in general aren't suitable for short-term (one year or less) goals. Despite the fact that the companies he invested in may have been fundamentally sound, all stock prices are subject to the gyrations of the marketplace and need time to trend upward.

Investing requires diligent work and research before you put your money in quality investments with a long-term perspective. *Speculating* is making a relatively quick profit by monitoring the short-term price movements of a particular investment. Investors seek to minimize risk, whereas speculators don't mind risk, because it can also magnify profits. There is a clear difference between speculating and investing, and investors frequently become speculators and ultimately put themselves and their wealth at risk. Don't go there!

Consider the married couple nearing retirement who decided to play with their money to see about making their pending retirement more comfortable. They borrowed a sizable sum by tapping into their home equity to invest in the stock market. (Their home, which they had paid off, had enough equity to qualify for this loan.) What did they do with these funds? You guessed it; they invested in the high-flying stocks of the day, which were high-tech and Internet stocks. Within eight months, they lost almost all their money.

Understanding market risk is especially important for people who are tempted to put their nest eggs or emergency funds into volatile investments such as growth stocks (or mutual funds that invest in growth stocks or similar aggressive investment vehicles). Remember, you can lose everything.

Inflation

Inflation is the artificial expansion of the quantity of money so that too much money is used in exchange for goods and services. To consumers, inflation shows up in the form of higher prices for goods and services. Inflation risk is also commonly referred to as "purchasing-power risk." This just means that your money doesn't buy as much as it used to. For example, a dollar that bought you a sandwich in 1980 can barely buy you a chocolate bar a few years later. For you, the Canadian investor, this means that the value of your investment (a stock, for example) may not keep up with inflation.

Say that you have money in a bank savings account currently earning 4 percent. This account has flexibility in that if the market interest rate goes up, the rate you earn in your account goes up. Your account is safe from both financial risk and interest-rate risk. But what if inflation is running at 5 percent?

In an inflationary economy, 4-percent inflation means that if your money is earning 3 percent, you're actually losing money. The purchasing power of your money decreases, so that you end up buying less instead of more with the same amount of money. While inflation is not a big risk to Canadians today, it may be in the future. It's good to keep the reality of inflation risk in the back of your mind, especially if you invest within a long-term time frame.

Currency

Foreign-exchange risk for a company is the risk of losing money from movements in foreign-exchange rates when that company's assets are not currency-matched to its liabilities. Simply stated, it is the risk that the value of a business operation, or stock, will be affected by changes in exchange rates.

This means that if you, the Canadian investor, invest in foreign stocks, or in a stock equity mutual fund company that invests in foreign companies, you are exposed to a certain measure of currency risk. If you have lots of investments in U.S. stocks, and the Canadian currency rises relative to the U.S. dollar, you will experience an immediate paper loss, or an actual loss when you sell that stock. On the other hand, if the U.S. dollar goes up relative to the Canadian dollar, you have a gain. Whenever your Canadian dollars have to be converted into a different currency to make a certain investment, changes in the value of the currency relative to the Canadian dollar will affect the total loss or gain on the investment when the money is converted back.

To reduce the risk of foreign-exchange losses, equity mutual fund managers use a variety of techniques known as "currency hedging." As an individual stock investor, however, your best bet at reducing your exposure to currency risk is to invest in jurisdictions with a stable economy, currency, and political system. The currency of the U.S. is one example of a currency that is stable relative to the Canadian dollar. Sure, it fluctuates. But it does not exhibit anywhere near the type of wild gyrations that you may have seen in some South American currencies in the late 1990s.

Tax Risk

Taxes (such as income tax or capital gains tax) don't affect your stock investment directly, but they can affect how much of your money you get to keep. Because the entire point of stock investing is to build wealth, you need to understand that taxes take away a portion of the wealth that you're trying to build. Taxes can be risky because, if you make the wrong move with your stocks (selling them at the wrong time, for example), you can end up paying higher taxes than you need to. Because Canadian tax laws change so frequently, tax risk is part of the risk-versus-return equation, as well.

Many investors set up their wealth in tax-advantaged RRSP vehicles such as self-directed and locked-in RRSPs. However, some investments, like money-losing stocks or tax-deferred real estate investment trusts (REITs), may be better kept outside of tax shelters such as an RRSP or registered retirement income fund (RRIF). (In the year you turn 69, you must collapse your RRSP. Your options are to cash in the entire amount and be taxed at the highest rate for your tax bracket; purchase an annuity for a predictable income stream; or convert the RRSP into a RRIF, which is like an RRSP except that it forces you to take a minimum amount out each year.)

Because of the complexities involved with the Canadian tax system, you ought to work closely with your qualified tax adviser to ensure that the tax impact of your investing strategy is considered. Seeking tax advice tailored to your personal objectives can save you thousands of tax dollars. (We introduce you to some investment-related tax principles and rules that you should remember in Chapter 21.)

Personal Risk

Frequently, the risk involved with investing in the stock market may not be directly involved with the investment or factors directly related to the investment; sometimes the risk is with the investor's circumstances.

Suppose that investor Jim Canuck puts $15,000 into a portfolio of common stocks. Imagine that the market experiences a drop in prices that week and Jim's stocks drop to a market value of $14,000.

Because stocks are good for the long term, this type of decrease is usually not an alarming incident. Odds are that this dip is temporary, especially if Jim carefully chose high-quality companies. (Incidentally, if a portfolio of high-quality stocks *does* experience a temporary drop in price, it can be a great opportunity to get more shares at a good price.)

Over the long term, Jim would probably see the value of his investment grow substantially. But what if Jim experiences financial difficulty and needs quick cash during a period when his stocks are declining? He may have to sell his stock to get some money.

This problem occurs frequently for investors who don't have an emergency fund or a rainy-day fund to handle large, sudden expenses. You never know when your company may lay you off or when your basement may flood leaving you with a huge repair bill. Car accidents, medical emergencies, and other unforeseen events are part of life's bag of surprises — for anyone. Be sure to set money aside for sudden expenses before you buy stocks. Then you won't be forced to prematurely liquidate your stock investments to pay emergency bills.

You probably won't get much comfort from knowing that stock losses are tax deductible — a loss is a loss. However, you can avoid the kind of loss that results from prematurely having to sell your stocks if you maintain an emergency cash fund. A good place for your emergency cash fund is in either a bank savings account or a money market fund.

Emotional Risk and Investor Psychology

Huh? What does emotional risk have to do with stocks? Emotions are important risk considerations because the main decision makers are human beings. Logic and discipline are critical factors in investment success, but even the best investor can let emotions take over the reins of money management and cause loss. For stock investing, the main emotions that can sidetrack you are fear and greed. You need to understand your emotions and what kinds of risk they can expose you to.

Paying the price for greed

In the 1998–2000 period, millions of investors threw caution to the wind and chased highly dubious, risky dot-com stocks. The dollar signs popped up in their eyes (just like slot machines) when they saw that easy street was lined with dot-com stocks that were doubling and tripling in a very short time. Who cares about price–earnings (P/E) ratios when you can just buy stock, make a fortune, and get out with millions? (Of course, *you* care about making money with stocks, so you can flip to Chapters 3 and 11 to find out more about P/E ratios.)

Unfortunately, the lure of the easy buck can easily turn healthy attitudes about growing wealth into unhealthy greed that blinds investors to common sense.

Recognizing the role of fear

Greed can be a problem, but fear is the other extreme. People who are fearful of loss frequently avoid suitable investments and end up settling for a low rate of return. If you have to succumb to one of these emotions, at least fear exposes you to less loss.

Looking for love in all the wrong places

Tina Turner might ask, "What's love got to do with it?" Stocks are dispassionate, inanimate vehicles, but people can look for love in the strangest places. Emotional risk occurs when investors fall in love with a stock and refuse to sell it even when the stock is plummeting and shows all the symptoms of getting worse. Emotional risk also occurs when investors are drawn to bad investment choices just because they sound good, are popular, or are touted by family or friends.

You can just see the promo for a television talk show: "Investors and their stocks: Has romance shrunk to codependency?" Or you can imagine Dr. Phil's next guest: "My XYZ stock is dissatisfying, yet I can't let go!" Ugh. People have lost tonnes of money because of an unhealthy attachment to an investment.

Love and attachment are great in relationships with people but are horrible with investments. Keep in mind that stocks (as with any investment) are tools for building wealth to improve your life. No more, no less. If the stock isn't performing, get rid of it. Try not to fall in love with a stock!

Minimizing Your Risk

Now, before you go crazy thinking that stock investing carries so much risk that you may as well not get out of bed, take a breath. Minimizing your risk in stock investing is easier than you think. Although wealth building through the stock market doesn't take place without some amount of risk, you can take steps to maximize your profits and still keep your money secure.

Gaining knowledge

The more familiar you are with the stock market — how it works, factors that affect stock value, and so on — the better you can navigate around its pitfalls and maximize your profits. Diminishing risk starts with gaining knowledge. You've probably heard the cliché "The more you know, you more you grow." The same knowledge that enables you to grow your wealth also enables you to minimize your risk. Before you put your money anywhere, you want to know as much as you can. (This book is a great place to start.)

Lack of knowledge constitutes the greatest risk of all to new investors. But it's a needless risk, because if you take the time and trouble to educate yourself about stock investing you can avoid the biggest — and most expensive — mistakes. Check out Chapter 6 for a rundown of the kinds of information you should know before you buy stocks, as well as the resources that can give you the information you need to invest successfully.

Oddly enough, some people spend more time analyzing a restaurant menu to buy a $10 meal than researching where to put their next $5,000. In the past few years, millions of investors lost trillions of dollars simply because they didn't know what they were getting into. We met an investor who lost a lot of money on an Internet stock. We got blank stares when we asked him simple questions about the stock, such as "How much money does the company make?" and "What is the company's price/earnings ratio?"

In this book, we squeeze as much information as possible between the covers in order to steer you in the right direction, but the responsibility rests with you to stay on top of changes and developments.

Getting your financial house in order

Believe it or not, some people out there have $13,987 in consumer debt and $1.38 in their bank account and barely make ends meet, yet they think, "Gee, the stock market could make me rich!" Many such people have no business investing in stocks.

Before you buy your first stock, do the following things to get your finances in order:

- ✔ Have a cushion of money somewhere safe, such as in a bank account or treasury money market fund, in case you suddenly need cash for an emergency. A minimum amount to set aside when times seem good is at least three months' worth of your gross living expenses. If the times are uncertain, you should have at least four or five months' worth.

- ✔ Reduce your debt. Overindulging in debt was the worst personal economic problem for many Canadians in the late 1990s. Consumer spending along with job layoffs and speculative investment choices recently drove the bankruptcy rate in Canada to new highs.

- ✔ Make sure that your job is as secure as you can make it. Are you keeping your skills up to date? Is the company you work for strong and growing? Is the industry that you work in strong and growing?

- ✔ Make sure that you have adequate insurance to cover you and your family's needs in case of illness, death, disability, and so on.

We don't want to get into a long laundry list of tips here. Advice on what to do before you invest could be a whole book in itself. The bottom line is that you want to make sure that you are, first and foremost, financially secure before you take the plunge into the stock market. If you're not sure about your financial security, look over your situation with a financial planner. (You can find out more about financial planners in Chapter 7.)

Diversifying your investments: Markets, sectors, and companies

When you talk to any astute financial adviser about risk in the stock market, the first piece of advice you're likely to hear is, "You can reduce your risk with proper diversification." Fair enough. But what does that mean?

Diversification is a strategy for reducing risk by spreading your money across different investments. Some investors even diversify not so much their investments, but rather their investment styles. It's a fancy way of saying, "Don't put all your eggs in one basket." For most people, that advice is generally true. Having a little bit in this investment and a little bit in that investment means never having to say, "I lost all my money!" But how do you go about divvying up your money and distributing it among different investments? The easiest way to understand proper diversification may be to look at what you should *not* do:

✔ **Don't put all your money in just one stock.** Sure, if you choose wisely and select a hot stock, you may make a bundle, but the odds are tremendously against you. Unless you're a real expert on that particular company, it behooves you to have only a small portion of your money in any one stock. As a general rule, the money you tie up in a single stock should be money you can do without.

✔ **Don't put all your money in one industry.** I know people who own several stocks, but the stocks are all in the same industry. Again, if you're an expert in that particular industry, it could work out. But just understand that you're not properly diversified. If a problem hits an entire industry, you'll get hurt.

✔ **Don't put all your money in just one type of investment.** Stocks may be a great investment, but you should have money elsewhere. Bonds, mutual funds, bank accounts, treasury securities, REITs, and precious metals are perennial alternatives to complement your stock portfolio.

Okay, now that you know what you *shouldn't* do, what *should* you do? Until you become more knowledgeable, follow this advice:

✔ **Don't put any more than 25 percent of your investment capital directly into stocks.**

✔ **Invest in four or five different stocks that are in different industries.** Which industries? Choose industries that offer products and services that have shown strong, growing demand. To make this decision, use your common sense (which isn't as common as it used to be). Think about the industries that people will need no matter what happens in the general economy, such as food, energy, and other consumer necessities. Then pick the market-leading company in that industry. Market leadership is a critical thing to look for in a stock. Of course, the stock would have to be priced just right — if it's not, the runner-up may do just fine. See Chapter 19 for more information about analyzing industries.

Weighing Risk against Return

How much risk is appropriate for you, and how do you handle it? Before you try to figure out what risks accompany your investment choices (or opportunities), you should first analyze the one topic you should be an expert on — yourself. What are you all about? What are you trying to accomplish? What are your goals? What is your investor profile? Are you comfortable taking chances with your money, or are you very concerned about risk? Here are some points to keep in mind when weighing risk versus return in your situation:

✔ **Your financial goal:** In five minutes with a financial calculator, you can easily see how much money you're going to need to become financially independent (presuming that this is your goal). Say that you need $500,000 in ten years for a worry-free retirement and that your financial assets (such as stocks, bonds, and so on) are currently worth $400,000. In this scenario, your assets would need to grow by only 2.5 percent to hit your target. Getting investments that grow by 2.5 percent safely is easy to do because that is a relatively low rate of return.

The important point is that you don't have to knock yourself out trying to double your money with risky, high-flying investments; some run-of-the-mill bank investments will do just fine. All too often, investors take on more risk than is necessary. Figure out what your financial goal is so that you know what kind of return you realistically need.

✔ **Your investor profile:** Are you nearing retirement, or are you fresh out of university? Your life situation matters when it comes to looking at risk versus return. If you're just beginning your working years, you can certainly tolerate greater risk than someone facing retirement. This is true because even if you lose big time, you still have a long time horizon in which to recoup your money and get back on track. However, if you're approaching retirement, risky or aggressive investments will do much more harm than good. If you lose money, you don't have as much time to recoup your investment, and the odds are that you'll need the investment money (and its income-generating capacity) to cover your living expenses once you are no longer employed.

✔ **Asset allocation:** We never advise retirees to put a large portion of their retirement money into a high-tech stock or other volatile investment. But if they still want to speculate, we don't see a problem with that as long as they limit such investments to 5 percent of their total assets. As long as the bulk of their money is safe and sound in secure investments (such as treasury bonds), we know we can sleep well (knowing that *they* can sleep well!).

Asset allocation beckons back to diversification. For people in their 20s and 30s, having 75 percent of their money in a diversified portfolio of growth stocks (such as mid-cap and small-cap stocks) is acceptable. For people in their 60s and 70s, it's not acceptable. They may, instead, consider investing no more than 20 percent of their money in stocks (mid caps and large caps are preferable). Check with your financial adviser to find the right mix for your particular situation.

Better luck next time

A little knowledge can be very risky. Consider the true story of one "lucky" fellow who played the lottery in 1987. He discovered that he had a winning ticket, with the first prize of $412,000. He immediately ordered a Porsche, booked a lavish trip to Hawaii for his family, and treated his wife and friends to a champagne dinner at a posh restaurant. When he finally went to collect his prize, he found out that he had to share first prize with more than 9,000 other lottery players who also had the same winning numbers. His share of the prize was actually only $45! Hopefully, he invested that tidy sum based on his increased knowledge about risk.

Chapter 5

Say Cheese: Getting a Snapshot of the Market

In This Chapter

▶ Defining indexes

▶ Understanding the Dow Jones industrial average

▶ Exploring Canadian exchanges

▶ Looking at Nasdaq and other indexes

"*H*ow's the market doing today?" is the most common question that interested parties ask about the stock market. "What did the TSX (formerly the Toronto Stock Exchange) do?" "How about the Dow and Nasdaq?" Invariably, people asking those questions are expecting the performance number of an index. "Well, the TSX fell 47 points to 7,500, while Nasdaq was unchanged at 1,482." Indexes can be useful, general gauges of stock market activity. They give the investor a basic idea of how well (or how poorly) the overall market is doing.

An *index* is a statistical measure that represents the value of a batch of stocks. This measure is used like a barometer to track the overall progress of the market (or a segment of it). There are indexes for all sorts of markets, but in this chapter we focus our attention on stock market indexes.

How Indexes Work

The oldest stock market index is the Dow Jones industrial average. It was created in 1896 by Charles Dow and covered only 12 stocks (the number increased to 30 stocks in 1928, and it has remained the same to this day). Because this was long before the age of computers, calculating a stock market index was kept simple and was done arithmetically by hand. Dow would add up the stock prices of the 12 companies and then divide it by 12. Technically, this was an *average* and not an index. Nowadays, the number gets tweaked to also account for things such as stock splits.

However, indexes get calculated differently. The primary difference between an "index" and an "average" is the concept of weighting. *Weighting* refers to the relative importance of the items when they are computed within the index. There are several kinds of indexes:

- ✔ **Price-weighted index:** This index tracks changes based on the change in the individual stock's price per share.

  To give you an example of this, suppose that you own two stocks: Stock A, worth $20 per share, and Stock B, worth $40 per share. In a price-weighted index, the stock at $40 is allocated a greater proportion of the index than the one at $20. However, the market-value weighted index calculates the market capitalization (total shares times the share price).

- ✔ **Market-value weighted index:** This index tracks the proportion of a stock based on its market capitalization (or market value).

  Say that in your portfolio the $20 stock (Stock A) has 10 million shares and the $40 stock (Stock B) has only 1 million shares. Stock A's market cap is $200 million, while Stock B's market cap is $40 million. Therefore, in a market-value weighted index, Stock A represents 83 percent of the index's value because of its much larger market cap.

  This sample portfolio shows only two stocks — obviously not a good representative index. Most investing professionals (especially money managers and mutual-fund firms) use a broad-based index as a benchmark to compare their progress. A *broad-based index* is an index that represents the performance of the entire market, such as the S&P 500. (See the section "Standard & Poor's 500" later in this chapter.)

- ✔ **Composite index:** This is an index or average that is a combination of several indexes or averages. An example is the S&P/TSX composite or the New York Stock Exchange (NYSE) composite index, which tracks the entire exchange by combining all the stocks and indexes that are included in it.

Indexes give the investor an instant snapshot of how well the market is doing. They offer a quick way to compare the performance of one investor's stock portfolio or mutual funds with the rest of the market. If the Dow goes up 10 percent in a year and your portfolio shows a cumulative gain of 12 percent, then you know that you're doing well. The Appendix in the back of this book lists resources to help you keep up with various indexes.

The Dow Jones Industrial Average

The most famous stock market barometer is our first example — the Dow Jones industrial average (DJIA). The DJIA (simply referred to as "the Dow") is most frequently the index quoted when someone asks how the market is doing. The Dow is price-weighted and tracks a "basket" of 30 of the largest and most influential public companies in the stock market. The following list shows the current roster of 30 stocks tracked on the DJIA.

3M Co. (MMM)

Alcoa Inc. (AA)

Altria Group Inc. (MO)

Amber Intl. Group (AIG)

American Express (AXP)

Boeing Co. (BA)

Caterpillar Inc. (CAT)

Citigroup Inc. (C)

Coca-Cola Co. (KO)

Disney (Walt) Co. (DIS)

Du Pont (EI) (DD)

Exxon Mobil Corp (XOM)

General Electric (GE)

General Motors (GM)

Hewlett-Packard (HPQ)

Home Depot Inc. (HD)

Honeywell Intl. (HON)

IBM (IBM)

Intel Corp. (INTC)

Johnson & Johnson (JNJ)

JPMorgan Chase (JPM)

McDonalds Corp. (MCD)

Merck & Co. (MRK)

Microsoft Corp. (MSFT)

Pfizer Inc. (PFE)

Procter & Gamble (PG)

SBC Comm. (SBC)

United Tech. Corp. (UTX)

Verizon Comm. (VZ)

Walmart Stores (WMT)

The roster of the Dow has changed many times during the 100-plus years of its existence. The only original company from 1896 is General Electric. Most of the changes on the Dow have occurred for reasons such as mergers and bankruptcy. However, some changes were done to simply reflect the changing times. Microsoft, for example, isn't an "industrial" company in the truest sense of the word, but it was added to the DJIA in 1999, while companies such as Union Carbide were dropped.

The Dow isn't a pure gauge of industrial activity, because it also includes a hodgepodge of nonindustrial issues such as J.P. Morgan Chase and Citigroup (banks), Home Depot (retailing), and Nortel (telecommunications). Because of these changes, it doesn't adequately reflect industrial activity. During the late 1990s and right up to 2001, true industrial sectors such as manufacturing had difficult times, yet the Dow rose to record levels.

Serious investors are better served by looking at the following:

- **Broad-based indexes:** For U.S. stocks, indexes such as the S&P 500 and the Wilshire 5000 are more realistic gauges of the stock market's performance. In Canada, look at the S&P/TSX composite index.

- **Industry or sector indexes:** These are better gauges of the growth (or lack of growth) of specific industries and sectors. If you buy a gold stock, then you should track the index for the precious-metals industry.

Dow Jones has several averages, including the Dow Jones transportation average (DJTA) and the Dow Jones utilities average (DJUA). Both of these are more strictly managed than the Dow. The DJUA sticks to utilities, so it tends to be an accurate barometer of the market it represents. (The same goes for the DJTA.)

The TSX Exchanges

In April 2002, the Toronto Stock Exchange re-branded its organization and adopted the acronym TSX. TSX are the initials attached to the core operating businesses of the TSX Group: the TSX (also still known as the Toronto Stock Exchange), TSX Venture Exchange, and TSX Markets. The TSX Group collectively manages all aspects of Canada's senior and junior stock markets, and is based in Toronto. It also has offices in Montreal, Winnipeg, Calgary, and Vancouver, and is itself publicly listed on the TSX. Dizzy yet?

The TSX is now Canada's sole exchange for the trading of senior equities. The Montreal Exchange assumes responsibility for the trading of derivatives. The recently merged Vancouver and Alberta stock exchanges (previously named the CDNX Exchange) were subsequently purchased by the TSX, and the new exchange is now called the TSX Venture Exchange. As a subsidiary of the TSX, all support functions of the former CDNX exchange (legal, finance, human resources, and technology) were centralized at the TSX. The TSX Venture Exchange continues to perform corporate-finance functions for the junior venture capital marketplace, remains a separate marketplace, and uses existing technology at the TSX. If you understood all this on the first read, proceed to the head of the class. The teacher wants to give _you_ an apple!

The S&P/TSX 60 index includes 60 large-capitalization stocks for Canadian equity markets. The index is market-capitalization weighted, weight-adjusted for things like share float (shares readily available to the general public), and balanced across ten industry sectors (see Table 5-1).

Table 5-1	**S&P/TSX 60 Industry Sectors**	
Sector	_Weight (%)_	_Number of Companies_
Consumer discretionary	6.81	7
Consumer staples	3.29	4
Energy	16.14	9
Financials	35.74	9
Healthcare	2.08	2
Industrials	6.01	6
Information technology	4.13	5
Materials	14.57	13
Telecom services	6.70	2
Utilities	4.53	3

The S&P/TSX 60 constituents are selected for inclusion using Standard & Poor's guidelines concerning company capitalization, liquidity, and fundamentals. The following list shows the current lineup of 60 stocks tracked on the S&P/TSX 60.

Abitibi-Consolidated Inc. (A)

Alcan Inc. (AL)

Bank of Montreal (BMO)

Barrick Gold Corp. (ABX)

Biovail Corp. (BVF)

Brascan Corp. (BNN.LV.A)

Canadian Imperial Bank of Commerce (CM)

Agrium Inc. (AGU)

ATI Technologies Inc. (ATY)

Bank of Nova Scotia, The (BNS)

BCE Inc. (BCE)

Bombardier Inc. (BBD.SV.B)

Cameco Corp. (CCO)

Canadian National Railway Co. (CNR)

Canadian Natural Resources Ltd. (CNQ)	Canadian Pacific Railway Ltd. (CP)
Canadian Tire Corp. Ltd. (CTR.NV)	Celestica Inc. (CLS.SV)
Cognos Inc. (CSN)	Cott Corp. (BCB)
CP Ships Ltd. (TEU)	Dofasco Inc. (DFS)
Domtar Inc. (DTC)	Enbridge Inc. (ENB)
EnCana Corp. (ECA)	Fairmont Hotels & Resorts Inc. (FHR)
Falconbridge Ltd. (FAL.LV)	George Weston Ltd. (WN)
Husky Energy Inc. (HSE)	Imperial Oil Ltd. (IMO)
Inco Ltd. (N)	Kinross Gold Corp. (K)
Loblaw Companies Ltd. (L)	Magna International Inc. (MG.SV.A)
Manulife Financial Corp. (MFC)	MDS Inc. (MDS)
National Bank of Canada (NA)	Nexen Inc. (NXY)
Nortel Networks Ltd. (NT)	NOVA Chemicals Corp. (NCX)
Novelis Inc. (NVL)	Petro-Canada Inc. (PCA)
Placer Dome Inc. (PDG)	Potash Corporation of Saskatchewan Inc. (POT)
Precision Drilling Corp. (PD)	Quebecor World Inc. (IQW.SV)
Research In Motion Ltd. (RIM)	Rogers Communications Inc. (RCI.NV.B)
Royal Bank of Canada (RY)	Shaw Communications Inc. (SJR.NV.B)
Shoppers Drug Mart Corp. (SC)	Sun Life Financial Inc. (SLF)
Suncor Energy Inc. (SU)	Talisman Energy Inc. (TLM)
Teck Cominco Ltd. (TEK.SV.B)	TELUS Corp. (T)
Thomson Corp., The (TOC)	Toronto-Dominion Bank, The (TD)
TransAlta Corp. (TA)	TransCanada Corporation (TRP)

The S&P/TSX 60 serves as the benchmark for related products such as
exchange-traded funds and index options (discussed later in this chapter).
Approximately $6 billion in index products is indexed to the S&P/TSX 60 index.
The S&P/TSX 60 is part of the S&P Global 1200, a world equity index that
covers 29 countries.

The Dow and the S&P/TSX 60 index both represent key gauges of stock market
activity. However, both have one major drawback: They track fewer than 70
companies. Regardless of their status in the market, the companies in the
Dow represent a limited number, so they don't communicate the true pulse of
the market. For example, when the Dow and S&P/TSX composite (formerly the
TSE composite) surpassed the record 10,000 milestone during 1999 and 2000,

the majority of (non-index) companies showed lacklustre or declining stock price movement.

Nasdaq

Nasdaq became a formalized U.S. market in 1971. The name used to stand for National Association of Securities Dealers Automated Quote system, but now it is simply "Nasdaq" (as if it were a name, like Peter or Eddie). Nasdaq indexes are similar to other indexes in style and structure. The only difference is that, well, it covers Nasdaq. The Nasdaq has two indexes (both reported in the financial pages):

- **Nasdaq composite index:** Most frequently quoted on the news, the Nasdaq composite index covers the more than 5,000 companies that trade on Nasdaq. The companies encompass a variety of industries, but the index's concentration has primarily been technology, telecom, and Internet industries.

  Because of the hypergrowth that these industries experienced during the late 1990s, the Nasdaq composite surpassed even the Dow briefly in popularity. Because the Nasdaq composite index is market-value weighted, it soared to its all-time high of 5,048 in March 2000.

- **Nasdaq 100 index:** The Nasdaq 100 tracks the 100 largest companies in Nasdaq. This index is for investors who want to concentrate on the largest companies, which tend to be especially weighted in technology issues.

In either case, the point that investors have to remember is that although these indexes track growth-oriented companies, these issues are also very volatile and carry commensurate risk. The indexes themselves bear this out; in the bear market of 2000 to 2002 (and even extending into 2003), they fell more than 60 percent.

Standard & Poor's 500

The Standard & Poor's 500 (S&P 500) is an index that tracks the 500 largest (measured by market value) publicly traded companies. It was created by the publishing firm Standard & Poor's (we bet you could have guessed that). Because it contains 500 companies, the Standard & Poor's 500 is more representative of the overall market's performance than the DJIA's 30, or the S&P/TSX 60's (you guessed it) 60 companies. Money managers and financial advisers actually watch the Standard & Poor's 500-stock index more closely than the DJIA. Mutual funds in both Canada and the U.S. especially like to measure their performance against the S&P 500 rather than against any other index.

The S&P 500 doesn't attempt to cover the 500 "biggest" companies. It instead includes companies that are widely held and widely followed. The companies are also industry leaders in a variety of industries, including energy, technology, healthcare, and finance. It is a market-value weighted index (which we explain in the section "How Indexes Work" earlier in this chapter).

Although it is a reliable indicator of the market's overall status, the S&P 500 also has some limitations. Despite the fact that it tracks 500 companies, the top 50 companies encompass 50 percent of the index's market value. This situation can be a drawback because those 50 companies have a greater influence on the S&P 500 index's price movement than any other segment of companies. In other words, 10 percent of the companies have an equal impact to 90 percent of the companies on the same index. Therefore, the index may not offer an accurate representation of the general market.

These 500 companies are not set in stone. They can be added or removed as market conditions change. A company can be removed if it is not doing well or goes bankrupt. A company in the index can be replaced by another company that is doing better.

Other U.S. Indexes

Although the Dow, Nasdaq, and S&P 500 are the stars of the Canadian and U.S. financial press, other indexes are equally important to follow because they cover other important facets of the market, such as small-cap and mid-cap stocks. The Russell 2000 and the Wilshire 5000 are useful because they cover a much broader range of publicly traded companies.

There are other, less sexy indexes that cover specific sectors and industries. If you're investing in an Internet stock, you should also check the Internet Stock Index to compare what your stock is doing as measured against the index. You can find indexes that cover industries such as transportation, brokerage firms, retailers, computer companies, and real estate firms. For a comprehensive list of specialty and other indexes, go to www.djindexes.com (a Dow Jones & Co. Web site).

Russell 3000 index

The Russell 3000 index is mentioned here as a great example of an index that seeks more comprehensive inclusion of U.S. companies. It includes the 3,000 largest publicly traded companies (nearly 98 percent of publicly traded stocks). The Russell 3000 is important because it includes many mid-cap and small-cap stocks. Most companies covered in the Russell 3000 have an average market value of a billion dollars or less.

The Russell 3000 index was created by the Frank Russell Company, which actually computes a series of indexes such as the Russell 1000 and the Russell 2000. The Russell 2000, for example, contains the smallest 2,000 companies from the Russell 3000, while the Russell 1000 contains the largest 1,000 companies. The Russell indexes do not cover micro-cap stocks (companies with a market capitalization under $250 million).

Wilshire Total Market index

The Wilshire 5000 index, often referred to as the Wilshire Total Market index, is probably the largest stock index in the world. Created in 1980 by Wilshire Associates, it started out tracking 5,000 stocks and has ballooned to cover more than 7,500 stocks. The advantage of the Wilshire 5000 is that it's very comprehensive, covering nearly the entire market. (At the very least, the stocks tracked are the largest publicly traded stocks.) It includes all the stocks that are on the major stock exchanges (such as the NYSE) and the largest issues on smaller exchanges like Nasdaq. By default, it also includes all the stocks covered by the S&P 500. The Wilshire 5000 is a market-value weighted index, which we discuss in the section "How Indexes Work" earlier in this chapter.

Over-the-Counter Stocks

Willingly or unwittingly, thousands of Canadian investors in U.S. stocks have been pushed into a little known and loosely regulated area of the financial markets: over-the-counter (OTC) stocks. (An OTC security is one that is not traded on a stock exchange, due primarily to an inability to meet listing requirements on senior or junior exchanges. However, financial intermediaries called "market makers" help investors with stock brokerage accounts to buy and sell securities "over-the-counter," in other words "behind the scenes," on an independent electronic trading platform.)

How could this turn of events happen? If you still own Enron, Worldcom, Kmart, or Global Crossing, former high-flying stocks, then you already know that they were dropped by the major exchanges. The result is that investors are now forced to buy and sell these shares over the counter.

Over the Counter Bulletin Board (OTCBB)

The Over the Counter Bulletin Board, or OTCBB, was created in the early 1990s and is owned and run by Nasdaq. It's essentially an online marketplace available for investors for stock quotes of small-cap, micro-cap, and speculative companies. The OTCBB is technically not a stock exchange, but rather an electronic bulletin board system used by market makers to quote stock prices.

Market makers

A market maker is a brokerage operation that keeps a firm bid and ask price in a given security by standing ready, willing, and able to buy or sell at publicly quoted prices (referred to as "making a market"). While the nuts and bolts of the market-making process are beyond the scope of this book, market makers essentially show bid and offer prices for specific numbers of selected securities. If these prices are met, they will immediately buy for, or sell from, their own accounts. Market makers are most commonly used in the OTC bulletin board stock venue.

Market makers are critical for maintaining liquidity and efficiency for the particular securities that they make markets in. At most firms, there is a tight separation of the market-making side of the business and the brokerage side. Otherwise, there would be a clear and unethical incentive for brokers to recommend securities simply because the firm makes a market in that stock.

BBX system

Recently, the BBX system has been proposed to replace the OTC Bulletin Board. The BBX will suit much of the same companies that are currently quoted on the OTCBB, but will be a higher-quality market. Enhancements and other changes to the BBX will include higher listing standards, no minimum share price or market capitalization, and no shareholder-equity requirements. The BBX will have an automated digital trading system to permit swift order negotiation and execution. The new system will also improve the overall transparency of the marketplace, where you'll be able to see the nitty-gritty behind a stock quote more easily.

Pink Sheets

The term *Pink Sheets* comes from the pink paper that was used to quote stock prices before the system was automated in 2000. In fact, the Pink Sheets is a nearly-century-old stock quote service providing another venue for OTC stocks. Pink Sheets was there way before there was even a Nasdaq. Like the OTCBB, the Pink Sheets is technically not an exchange, but rather an electronic bulletin board system for market makers to quote stock prices. Pink Sheets– and OTCBB–listed companies are both OTC.

In 2000, the Pink Sheets system finally went electronic to meet growing demand. Pink Sheets stocks are purchased and sold in the same manner that OTCBB stocks are — through your broker. The two systems are now essentially the same, and will be even after the introduction of the new BBX system. Both will dynamically update with real-time quotes and provide a fast stream

Facts about the Pink Sheets

The Pink Sheets is home to about 3,500 stocks. Not all are troubled companies that were given the boot by Nasdaq or the New York Stock Exchange (NYSE). About $100 million a day trades through the Pink Sheets. That's a drop in the bucket compared to the $440 billion average daily trade amount on the NYSE. However, it's home to the foreign company Nestlé, which prefers the Pink Sheets listing so that it can avoid the administration involved in meeting some of the more labour-intensive U.S. reporting requirements — it's just a business decision that the company has made. Another stock — Anderson-Tully — trades at US$175,000 per share! You can find some great values on the Pink Sheets. Many companies listed there trade at eight times earnings or a small fraction of book value, pay great dividends, and have competent and experienced management.

of updated information to a market maker. Although the Pink Sheets used to (and to a certain extent still does) have a bad reputation because of its history, these measures should make the system better.

However, it's sometimes very difficult to buy a Pink Sheets stock at your price — or to unload it, especially when volumes are low. Low volumes can be a nasty attribute with Pink Sheets, and are a risk that should be watched. Also, there are no reporting requirements for Pink Sheets companies (and, up until four years ago, the OTCBB had no reporting requirements either). For example, Pink Sheets companies don't have to submit statutory filings, such as quarterly financial statements. Regardless, many Pink Sheets companies still elect to fully report key information. To the extent that there is reporting, the Pink Sheets system is almost the equivalent of OTCBB stocks.

While you shouldn't avoid a stock just because it is listed over the counter, do an additional measure of research to identify and monitor the risks.

International Indexes

Investors need to remember that the whole world is a vast marketplace that interacts with and exerts tremendous influence on individual national economies and markets. Whether you have one stock or a mutual fund, keep tabs on how your portfolio is affected by world markets. The best way to get a snapshot of international markets is, of course, with indexes. Here are some of the more widely followed international indexes:

✔ **Nikkei (Japan):** This is considered Japan's version of the Dow. If you're invested in Japanese stocks or in stocks that do business with Japan, you want to know what's up with the Nikkei.

 ✔ **FTSE-100 (Great Britain):** Usually referred to as the "footsie," this is a market-value weighted index of the top 100 public companies in the United Kingdom.

 ✔ **CAC-40 (France):** This index tracks the 40 public stocks that trade on the Paris Stock Exchange.

 ✔ **DAX (Germany):** This index tracks the 30 largest and most active stocks that trade on the Frankfurt Exchange.

You can track these international indexes (among others) at major financial Web sites, such as www.bloomberg.com and www.marketwatch.com.

Failing to keep a watchful eye on the international market can cost you. What if you had stock in a company that had most of its customers in Argentina, for example? The years 2001 and 2002 were especially terrible for Argentina's weak economy and its markets. If you had understood the interconnectedness of world markets, you could have sold your stock (or placed stop losses on it, as described in Chapter 8) before it got clobbered because of Argentina's economic woes.

Investing in Indexes

Is it possible to invest directly in indexes? If the market is doing well and your specific stock is not, why not find a way to invest in the index itself? With investments based on indexes, you can invest in the general market or a particular industry.

Say that you want to invest in the DJIA. To have a portfolio that mirrors the DJIA, is it practical to buy shares in each of the 30 stocks that make up this index? This approach sounds too expensive for the average investor, but there are practical alternatives. You may immediately think that the answer is a mutual fund, but in this case you're only partially right. Although some great mutual funds are out there, this book is, after all, about stocks. A more appropriate vehicle for stock investors is an exchange-traded fund (ETF).

Exchange-traded funds (ETFs)

ETFs are essentially index investments — hybrids between a stock and an index. They represent, and provide you with the approximate return of, a target stock index. That's an ETF.

ETFs can be traded on a stock exchange such as the TSX or the NYSE. While you transact with a bank or mutual fund company to obtain an index mutual fund, you obtain an ETF just like you would a stock — cite the ticker symbol, indicate the number of shares you want, and voila, your order is filled! Through a discount broker such as TD Waterhouse, you can get just about any ETF out there for as low as $40. You don't need to be concerned about minimum board lots of 100, since you can get as little as one ETF unit if you wish. (A board lot is an arbitrary unit of measure used by stock exchanges to express share quantities or share "bunches" available for purchase and sale at a point in time.) With ETFs dividends can be paid to shareholders, and shares can be bought on margin. You have the ability to buy an entire portfolio of stocks as easily as you'd buy a single stock.

Scores of Canadian, U.S., and other foreign global stock indexes are tracked by ETFs. They can track indexes such as the Dow Jones industrial average or the S&P/TSX 60. Even other international stock markets — such as the German DAX or the Japanese Nikkei indexes — can be mimicked. Within an index, ETFs can also be fine-tuned to include only sectors such as healthcare or technology. Many indexes are available through ETFs — which does present a bit of a problem.

Choices, choices

There are so many ETFs to choose from. Perhaps too many. Cherry-picking through the choices can be confusing and time-consuming. While Canadian ETFs are not as plentiful as American ETFs, many new ETF products are coming our way in the near future. To help you select one, consider the ETF's management-expense ratio (MER). The lower the MER, the higher your return.

Consider also the index being tracked. ETFs often allow you to choose several differently structured indexes (S&P/TSX 60, S&P/TSX Canadian energy index, and so on) that track the same general market (Canadian companies on the TSE). Also, ensure that the ETF is liquid, because some funds may go a whole week without being traded once.

ETFs in Canada

One of the larger groups of ETFs in Canada is the iUnits — Canadian members of the global family of exchange-traded funds from Barclays. You can look over their ETF offerings at www.iunits.com/english/iunitsfunds/fundvalues.cfm. These include ETFs connected to the S&P/TSX 60 and those that track Canadian financial services and gold-producing companies.

Another ETF is available through State Street Global Advisors (SSgA). The SSgA Dow Jones 40 Fund buys shares in the 40 companies that make up the Dow Jones Canada 40 index — typically liquid and large-capitalization companies that encompass all industry sectors in Canada.

Most Canadian ETFs are RRSP-eligible, and Canadians with RRSP savings can also get American S&P 500–based ETFs that are without foreign-content restrictions when placed inside an RRSP. ETFs are also tax-smart in other ways. Because they change their portfolio mixes only a few times to reflect changes in their mimicked index, this translates into fewer taxable distributions of potential taxable gains.

Check out the www.exchangetradedfunds.com Web site for more information about Canadian and global ETFs.

Diamonds are forever

Another major example of an ETF is Diamonds — Dow Jones Industrial Average Depository Receipts — which is assigned the stock symbol DIA. When you buy DIA, it's like buying a piece of the portfolio of stocks that comprise the DJIA. Because it's like a stock, you can actually buy as little as one share.

When investing in DIAs (and most ETFs), here are some important points to keep in mind:

- ✔ You can buy them through your broker. Like any stock, the purchase or sale is easy, no matter whether you call up the broker or do the transaction at the broker's Web site.

- ✔ You can purchase ETFs on margin. Again, just as with other stock, ETFs are marginable securities.

- ✔ ETFs are inexpensive to buy. Most ETFs can be purchased by as little as one share. Some types must be purchased in a round lot (100 shares or more). Find out from the exchange that lists them or through your broker.

- ✔ Expect to pay management fees. The institutions that package and sell the ETFs do charge fees for doing so. These charges are usually embedded in the cost structure of the ETF, so you don't pay them directly. The only fees that you may notice are the commissions that your broker charges you to buy and sell them. Keep in mind that all fees affect the return on your investment.

- ✔ There will be tax implications. A lower incidence of capital gains makes ETFs more tax efficient. In addition, dividends may be issued; these are taxed by Canada Customs and Revenue Agency (CCRA) differently than other sources of income.

✔ You still need to diversify. This point should be obvious, but it is important to mention here. Diversification is always an important issue for investors (especially small investors). ETFs are obviously more diversified than a single stock and have inherently less risk. However, ETFs will go up and down based on the stocks that are in the ETF. If the real estate sector is having difficulties, an ETF specializing in real estate will go down in value.

✔ The valuation is not precise. An ETF strives to mirror the index as much as possible, but it may not always be 100-percent accurate. However, the difference is usually inconsequential.

Qubes, Spiders, and Holders

Some other noteworthy ETFs that are very popular and worth some further investigation include the following:

✔ **QQQ:** This ETF mirrors the Nasdaq 100. It's one of the most popular and widely-traded ETFs, and perhaps most risky. Called "the Qube," it lets you invest directly in the Nasdaq 100 index of the largest non-financial stocks listed on the Nasdaq National Market.

✔ **SPDRs:** SPDRs, or Spiders, is the street name for Standard & Poor's Depository Receipts. There are a batch of these. The main SPDR tracks the S&P 500, but you can also invest in SPDRs that cover specific sectors, such as healthcare, energy, and other major segments of the S&P 500.

✔ **HOLDRS:** These are ETFs that are issued by Merrill Lynch and traded on the American Stock Exchange (AMEX). HOLDRS (for **Hol**ding Company **D**epositary **R**eceipt**s**) give stock investors the ability to buy a portfolio of stocks in a single stock that covers a specific sector, such as energy or healthcare.

You can get updated information on ETFs through the Web sites of major exchanges. You can also check out www.spdrindex.com and www.holdrs.com.

ETFs generally have the same characteristics as the indexes themselves. Whether they move up or down, they give the investor the opportunity to do just as well as the market itself.

Part II
Before You Get Started

The 5th Wave — By Rich Tennant

BILL and Irwin discover The Land of Lost Files

MY GOD! THIS IS A BUDGET AND ANALYSIS REPORT FOR THE MARKETING DEPT. OF A FORTUNE 500 COMPANY. MUST HAVE KILLED THE POOR FOOL TO LOSE THIS.

In this part . . .

Now that you have the theory of stock investing down, it's time to roll up your sleeves and lay some groundwork — you'll find out where you can get some key information about stocks and the companies they represent. You'll learn what to look for if you seek the advice of a financial planner. This part will also show you what products and services to expect from the many different stockbrokers that are out there. The balance of this part will show you in some detail how to invest in stocks to achieve growth, income, and value.

Chapter 6

Gathering Information

· ·

In This Chapter

▶ Exploring financial issues important to a well-informed investor

▶ Interpreting stock tables

▶ Revisiting dividend news

▶ Recognizing good (and bad) information

· ·

Knowledge and information are two critical success factors in stock investing. (Isn't that true about most things in life?) People who plunge headlong into stock investing without sufficient knowledge of the market, types of risks, and current information in particular quickly learn the lesson of the speeding skier who didn't find out ahead of time that the ski run he was on was actually closed due to rock hazards (ouch!). In their haste to avoid missing so-called golden investment opportunities, investors too often end up losing money.

There's no such thing as a single (and fleeting) magical moment, so don't feel that if you let an opportunity pass you by you'll always regret that you missed your one big chance. The stock market is an entity that opens and closes every day. Tomorrow's opportunities may not even be imaginable today. Resist the urge to jump at what seem to be golden investment opportunities unless you really know what you're doing. Don't chase stocks that are having an upward price run but lack solid fundamentals. A better approach is to first build your knowledge by finding quality information. Then buy stocks and make your fortune more assuredly. Where do you start and what kind of information should you acquire? Keep reading.

Figuring Out What You Need to Know

If you're just beginning to study the stock market and you still can't tell the difference between stock in your investment portfolio and stock in a warehouse, take the time to find out all you can. Beginners need to start with the fundamentals. Before you buy stock, you need to know that the company you're investing in is all of the following:

✔ Financially sound, growing revenues, and generating cash

✔ Offering a variety of products and services (not a one-trick pony) that are in demand by consumers

✔ In a strong and growing industry that is not too cyclical

✔ Thriving in a strong and growing general economy

Knowing where to look for answers

The adage "You've got to learn to walk before you can run" applies to stock investing as well. Before you invest in stocks, you need to be completely familiar with the basics of stock investing. At its most fundamental level, stock investing is about using your money to buy a piece of a company that will provide you rewards in the form of appreciation in stock value, or dividend income. Fortunately, many resources are available to help you find out about stock investing. Some of our favourite places are the stock exchanges themselves.

TSX educational resources

Who knows better about the mechanics of stock investing in Canada than the country's largest stock exchange? As we discuss in Chapter 1, stock exchanges are organized marketplaces for the buying and selling of stocks (and other securities). The TSX has lots of investor education resources — online and off. If you live in Toronto or are visiting, you can check out the TSX's Stock Market Place in the heart of downtown, where special education programs provide the public with a free hands-on learning experience that explores capital markets in Canada. Stock Market Place also has snazzy multimedia digital displays that track global exchange performance in live, real-time fashion. Quite often, investment professionals are on hand to give free public seminars on various investment topics. It's pretty cool and definitely worth a visit if you want to learn more about investing.

Resources from the king of the hill

As the world's premier stock exchange, the New York Stock Exchange (NYSE) provides a venue for stock buyers and sellers to execute their trading transactions. The NYSE makes money not only from a piece of every transaction but also from fees charged to companies and brokers that are members of their exchanges. The main exchanges for most stock investors are the NYSE, the American Stock Exchange (AMEX), and Nasdaq. All three of these exchanges encourage and inform people about stock investing. They usually offer free tutorials at their Web sites and free investor publications for anyone who asks. Here's where to find that information:

✔ TSX: www.tsx.ca

✔ New York Stock Exchange: www.nyse.com

✔ American Stock Exchange: www.amex.com

✔ Nasdaq: www.nasdaq.com

They don't offer free information because they're so benevolent. Don't get us wrong — they are upstanding institutions — but their main interest is to see to it that stock investing grows in its acceptance and activity. After all, that's how they make money. Still, they provide terrific information resources for investors.

Understanding stocks and the companies they represent

Stocks represent ownership in companies. Before you buy individual stocks, you should understand the companies whose stock you're considering and find out about their operations. It may sound like a daunting task, but the point is easier to digest when you realize that companies work very similarly to how you work — they make decisions on a day-to-day basis just as you do.

Think about how you grow and prosper as an individual or as a family, and you see the same issues with companies and how they grow or prosper. Low earnings or high debt are examples of financial difficulties that can affect both people and companies. Understanding companies' finances is easier when you take some time to pick up information in two basic disciplines: accounting and economics. These two disciplines play a significant role in understanding the performance of a company's stock.

Accounting for taste and a whole lot more

Accounting. Ugh! But face it: Accounting is the language of business, and believe it or not you're already familiar with the most important accounting concepts! Just look at the following three essential principles:

✔ **Assets minus liabilities equals net worth.** In other words, take what you own (your assets), subtract what you owe (your liabilities), and the rest is yours (net worth)! Your own personal finances work the same way as Imperial Oil's (except with fewer zeros).

A company's balance sheet shows you its net worth at a specific point in time (such as December 31). The net worth of a company is the bottom line of its asset and liability picture, and tells you whether the company is *solvent* (that is, it has the ability to pay its debts without going out of business). The net worth should be regularly growing; compare it to the same point a year earlier. A company that has a $5-million net worth on December 31, 2002, and a $6-million net worth on December 31, 2003, is doing well; its net worth has gone up 20 percent ($1 million) in one year.

✔ **Income minus expenses equals net income.** In other words, take what you make (your income), subtract what you spend (your expenses), and the remainder is your net income (or net profit or net earnings) — your gain.

A company's net income is the whole point of investing in stock. As it profits, the company becomes more valuable, and in turn its stock price will become more valuable. To discover a company's net income, look at its income statement. Try to determine whether the company uses its gains wisely, including reinvesting it for continued growth or paying down debt.

✔ **Do a comparative financial analysis.** That's a mouthful, but it's just a fancy way of saying how a company is doing now compared with something else (like a prior period or a similar company).

If you know that a company you're looking at had a net income of $50,000 for the year, you might ask "Is that good or bad?" Obviously, making a net profit is good, but you also need to know whether it's good compared to something else. If last year the net profit was $40,000, then you know that the company's doing better than before. But if a similar company has a net profit of $100,000 for the same period, you might wonder what's wrong with the company you're looking at (and steer clear of its stock).

Accounting *can* be this simple. If you understand these three basic points, you'll be ahead of the curve (in stock investing as well as in your personal finances). For more insights on how to use a company's financial information to pick good stocks, see Chapters 12 and 13.

Economics is dismal only if you don't understand it

Economics. Double ugh! No, no one is asking you to understand "the inelasticity of demand aggregates" (thank heavens!) or "marginal utility" (say what?). But a working knowledge of basic economics is crucial (and I mean crucial) to your success and proficiency as a stock investor. The stock market and the economy are joined at the hip. The good (or bad) things that happen to one have a direct effect on the other.

Alas, economics is lost on many investors (and some so-called experts on TV, too). Understanding basic economics helps us (and will help you) filter the financial news to separate relevant information from the irrelevant and make better investment decisions. Here are a few important economic concepts to be aware of:

✔ **Supply and demand:** How can anyone possibly think about economics without thinking of the ageless and timeless concept of supply and demand? Supply and demand is, simply stated, the relationship between what's available (the supply) and what people want and are willing to pay for (the demand). This equation is the main engine of economic activity and is extremely important for your stock-investing analysis and decision-making process. I mean, would you really buy stock in a company that makes elephant-foot umbrella stands if you found out that there was an oversupply and nobody wants them anyway?

✔ **Cause and effect:** If you were to pick up a prominent news report and read, "Companies in the table industry are expecting plummeting sales," would you rush out and invest in companies that sell chairs or manufacture tablecloths? Considering cause and effect is an exercise in logical thinking — and believe you me, logic is a major component of sound economic thought.

When you read business news, play it out in your mind. What good (or bad) can logically be expected given a certain event or situation? If you're looking for an effect ("I want a stock price that keeps increasing"), then you should understand the cause. Here are some typical events that could cause a stock's price to rise:

- **Positive news reports about a company:** The news may report that a company is enjoying success with increased sales or a new product.

- **Positive news reports about a company's industry:** The media may be highlighting that the industry is poised to do well.

- **Positive news reports about a company's customers:** Maybe your company is in industry A, but its customers are in industry B. If you see good news about industry B, that could be good news for your stock.

- **Negative news reports about a company's competitors:** If it is in trouble, its customers may seek alternatives to buy from, including your company.

- **Economic effects from government actions:** Political and governmental actions have economic consequences. As a matter of fact, nothing (and I mean nothing!) has a greater effect on investing and economics than government. Government actions usually manifest themselves as taxes, laws, or regulations. They also can take on a more ominous appearance, such as war or the threat of war. Government can wilfully (or even accidentally) cause a company to go bankrupt, disrupt an entire industry, or even cause deflation. It controls the money supply, credit, and all public securities markets. A single government action can have a far-reaching and systemic effect that can have a direct (or indirect) economic impact on your stock investments.

What would happen to the elephant-foot umbrella stand industry if a 50-percent sales tax were passed for that industry? Such a sales tax would certainly make the product uneconomical and would encourage consumers to seek alternatives to elephant-foot umbrella stands. It may even boost sales for the wastepaper basket industry!

The opposite can be true as well. What if a Canadian tax credit were passed that encourages the use of solar power in homes and businesses? That would obviously have a positive impact on industries that manufacture or sell solar power devices. (Just don't ask me what would happen to solar-powered elephant-foot umbrella stands.)

Is the topic of government appropriate in a chapter about economics? Actually, we don't see how you can understand one without being aware of the other. It's like trying to understand boats without understanding the sea. It's that relevant.

Because most investors ignored some basic observations about economics in the late 1990s, they subsequently lost trillions in their stock portfolios. In the late 1990s, the United States experienced the greatest expansion of debt in history, coupled with a record expansion of the money supply. (Both are controlled by the Federal Reserve, the U.S. government's central bank, usually referred to just as "the Fed.") This growth of debt and money supply resulted in more consumer (and corporate) borrowing, spending, and investing. This activity hyperstimulated the stock market and caused stocks to rise 25 percent per year for five straight years. In Canada, much the same scenario played itself out (rising debt and money supply), but on a much lesser scale.

Of course, you should always be happy to earn 25 percent per year with your investments, but such a return can't be sustained and encourages speculation. This artificial stimulation by the Fed resulted in the following:

- More people depleted their savings. After all, why settle for 3 percent in the bank if you can get 25 percent in the stock market?

- More people bought on credit. If the economy is booming, why not buy now and pay later? Consumer credit hit record highs.

- More people borrowed against their homes. Why not borrow and get rich now? I can pay off my debt later.

- More companies sold more goods as consumers took more vacations and bought SUVs, electronics, and so on. Companies then borrowed to finance expansion, open new stores, and so on.

- More companies went public and offered stock to take advantage of more money that was flowing to the markets from banks and other financial institutions.

In the end, spending started to slow down as consumers and businesses became too indebted. This slowdown in turn caused the sales of goods and services to taper off. However, companies had too much overhead, capacity, and debt as they expanded too eagerly. At this point, companies like Nortel and JDS Uniphase were caught in a financial bind. Too much debt and too many expenses in a slowing economy mean one thing: Profits shrink or disappear.

Know thyself

If you're reading this book, you're probably doing so because you want to become a successful investor. Granted, to be a successful investor you have to select great stocks, but having a realistic understanding of your own financial situation and goals is equally important. We recall one investor who lost $10,000 in a speculative stock. The loss wasn't devastating to him because he had most of his money safely tucked away elsewhere. He also understood that his overall financial situa-tion was secure and that the money he lost was "play" money, the loss of which wouldn't have a drastic effect on his life. But many investors lose even more money, and the loss does have a major, negative effect on their lives. You may not be like the investor who could afford to lose $10,000. Take time to understand yourself, your own financial picture, and your personal invest-ment goals before you decide to buy stocks.

To stay in business, companies had to do the logical thing — cut expenses. What is usually the biggest expense for companies? People! To stay in business, many companies started laying off employees. As a result, consumer spending dropped further as more people either were laid off or had second thoughts about their own job security.

As people had little in the way of savings and too much in the way of debt, they had to sell their stock to pay their bills. This was a major reason that stocks started to fall in 2000. Earnings started to drop because of shrinking sales from a sputtering economy. As earnings fell, stock prices also fell.

The lessons from the 1990s are important ones for investors today:

✔ Stocks are not a replacement for savings accounts. Always have some money in the bank.

✔ Stocks should never occupy 100 percent of your investment funds.

✔ When anyone (including experts) tells you that the economy will keep growing indefinitely, be skeptical and read diverse sources of information.

✔ If stocks do well in your portfolio, consider protecting your shares (both your original investment and any gains) with stop-loss orders. (See Chapter 20 for more on these strategies.)

✔ Keep personal debt and expenses to a minimum.

✔ Remember that if the economy is booming, a decline is sure to follow as the ebb and flow of the economy's business cycle continues.

In an issue of *The Economist*, a writer joked "How many investors does it take to change a light bulb? None — the market has already discounted the change." The underlying message behind this joke is that stock markets respond to economics, in a big and fast way.

Staying on Top of Financial News and Trends

Reading the financial news can help you decide where (or where not) to invest. Many newspapers, magazines, and Web sites offer great coverage of the Canadian and world financial scene. Obviously, the more informed you are the better, but you don't have to read everything that's written. The information explosion in recent years has gone beyond overload, and you could easily spend so much time reading that you have little time left for the process of investing.

The most obvious publications of interest to stock investors are the two Canadian national dailies — the *National Post* (www.nationalpost.com) and *The Globe and Mail* (www.globeandmail.com). Other useful publications include the *Wall Street Journal* and *Investor's Business Daily,* U.S. newspapers that also cover world financial news. These leading publications report the news and stock data as of the day before.

Some other leading Web sites are CBS's MarketWatch (www.marketwatch.com) and Bloomberg (www.bloomberg.com), which include Canadian company news and information. For mostly Canadian content, take a look at Adviceforinvestors.com (www.adviceforinvestors.com). It has research, advice, and daily press releases from Canadian companies. These Web sites can also give you news and stock data within 15 to 20 minutes of a transaction.

The Appendix at the back of this book provides more information on these resources, along with a treasure trove of some of the best publications, resources, and Web sites to assist you.

The following sections suggest some topics that stock investors should be on the lookout for when considering the purchase of individual stocks.

Figuring out what a company's up to

Before you invest, you need to know what's going on with a company. When you read about a company, either from the company's literature (its annual report, for example) or from media sources, be sure to get answers to some pertinent questions:

- **Is the company making more net income than it did the prior year?** You want to invest in a company that is growing.

- **Are the company's sales greater than the year before?** Remember, you won't make money if the company isn't making money.

> ✔ **Is the company issuing press releases on new products, services, inventions, or business deals?** All of these achievements indicate a strong, vital company.

Knowing how the company is doing, no matter what is happening with the general economy, is obviously important. To better understand how companies tick, see Chapters 12 and 13.

Discovering what's new with an industry

As you consider investing in a stock, make it a point to know what's going on in that company's industry. If the industry is doing well, your stock will likely do well, too. But then again, the reverse is also true.

Yes, I have seen investors pick successful stocks in a failing industry, but those are exceptional cases. By and large, succeeding with a stock is easier when the entire industry is doing well. As you're watching the news, reading the financial pages, or viewing financial Web sites, check out the industry to see that it's strong and dynamic. See Chapter 19 for information on analyzing industries.

Knowing what's happening with the economy

No matter how well or how poorly the overall economy is performing, you should stay informed about its general progress. It's easier for the value of stock to keep going up when the economy is stable or growing. The reverse is also true; if the economy is contracting or declining, the stock will have a tougher time keeping its value. Some basic items you should keep tabs on include the following:

> ✔ **Gross domestic product (GDP):** This is roughly the total value of output for a particular nation, measured in the dollar amount of goods and services. In Canada and the U.S., GDP is reported quarterly. Rising GDP bodes well for your stock. When the GDP is rising 3 percent or more on an annual basis, that is solid growth. When the GDP rises less than 3 percent that is less than stellar (or mediocre) growth. GDP under zero (or negative) means that the economy is shrinking. As a general rule, two consecutive quarters of negative growth indicate a recession. Persistent and steep shrinkage in the economy over a large number of quarters may indicate a depression.

✔ **The index of leading economic indicators (LEI):** The LEI is a snapshot of a set of economic statistics covering activity that precedes what's happening in the economy. Each statistic helps you understand the economy in much the same way that barometers (and windows!) help you understand what's happening with the weather. Economists don't just look at an individual statistic; they look at a set of statistics to get a more complete picture of what's happening with the economy. Certain indicators lead the economy, some coincide with the economy, and others lag behind the economy.

Housing starts (the number of houses that have been contracted to be built), for example, is a leading economic indicator. If more houses are being built, other sectors, such as building supplies and home services, get more business. Because stock investors usually look to the future, any clues about the general direction of the economy are valuable as a guide to the public's investment decision-making process. Chapter 15 goes into some detail on ways the economy affects stock prices.

Seeing what the politicians and government bureaucrats are doing

Being informed about what public officials are doing is vital to your success as a stock investor. Because literally thousands of laws are passed every year by federal, provincial, and local governments, monitoring the political landscape is critical to your success. The news media report what the prime minister and Parliament are doing, so always ask yourself "How will this new law or event affect my stock investment?" Also monitor the U.S. political scene, as decisions made there not only affect any U.S. stock holdings you may have but also invariably creep up to impact Canada.

When taxes are increased or decreased, some people and organizations benefit and others don't. When laws and regulations get passed, usually someone wins and someone loses. Constantly ask yourself, "In this particular situation, who will win and who will lose? Will the company I bought stock in win or lose?" Be aware of ways that the political environment can affect the value of your stocks.

Rarely do changes in taxes, laws, and regulations affect merely one company. Usually, an entire industry or even the entire economy feels the effects of change. So, if a company that you're considering investing in appears to be affected by a new law or regulation, you can probably assume that the company's stock will also be affected.

Identifying trends in society, culture, and entertainment

As odd as it sounds, trends in society, popular culture, and entertainment affect your investments, directly or indirectly. For example, headlines such as "The greying of Canada — more people than ever before become senior citizens" give you some important information that can make or break your stock portfolio. With that particular headline, you know that as more and more people age, companies that are well positioned to cater to this growing market's wants and needs may mean a successful stock for you.

Keep your eyes open to emerging trends in society at large. What trends are evident now? What wants and needs can be anticipated for tomorrow's society? Being alert, staying a step ahead of the public, and choosing stock appropriately gives you a profitable edge over other investors. If you own stock in a solid company with growing sales and earnings, other investors will eventually notice. As more investors buy up your company's stocks, you will be rewarded as the share price increases.

Reading (and Understanding) Stock Tables

The stock tables in major business publications, such as the _National Post_ and _The Globe and Mail,_ are loaded with information that can help you become a savvy investor — _if_ you know how to interpret them. You need the information in the stock tables for more than selecting promising investment opportunities. You also need to consult the tables after you invest, to monitor how your stocks are doing. If you bought HokySmoky common stock last year at $12 per share and you want to know what it's worth today, check out the stock tables.

If you look at the stock tables without knowing what you're looking at or why, it's the equivalent of reading _War and Peace_ backward through a kaleidoscope. Nothing makes sense. But we can help you make sense of it all (well, at least the stock tables!). Table 6-1 shows a sample stock table for you to refer to as you read the sections that follow.

Table 6-1		Deciphering Stock Tables						
52-Wk High	52-Wk Low	Name (Symbol)	Div	Vol	Yld	P/E	Day Last	Net Chg
21.50	8.00	SkyHighCorp (SHC)	3143	76			21.25	+.25
47.00	31.75	LowDownInc (LDI)	2.35	2735	5.7	18	41.00	−.50
25.00	21.00	ValueNowInc (VNI)	1.00	1894	4.5	12	22.00	+.10
83.00	33.00	DoinBadlyCorp (DBC)		7601			33.50	−.75

Every newspaper's financial tables are a little different, but they give you basically the same information. However, even though it is updated daily, this section is not the place to start your search for a good stock; actually, it should be where it ends. The stock tables are the place to look when you know what you want to buy — or you already own a particular stock — and you're just checking to see the most recent price.

Each item gives you some clues about the current state of affairs for that particular company. The sections that follow describe each column to help you understand what you're looking at.

52-week high

The column labelled "52-Wk High" (refer to Table 6-1) gives you the highest price that a particular stock has reached in the most recent 52-week period. The value in knowing this is that you can gauge where the stock is now versus where it has been recently. SkyHighCorp's (SHC) stock has been as high as $21.50, while its last (most recent) price was $21.25, the number listed in the "Day Last" column. (Flip to the "Day Last" section for more on understanding this information.) SkyHighCorp's stock is trading very high right now, because it's hovering right near its overall 52-week-high figure.

Now, take a look at the DoinBadlyCorp's (DBC) stock price. It seems to have tumbled big-time. Its stock price has had a high in the past 52 weeks of $83, but it's currently trading at $33.50. Something just doesn't seem right here. During the past 52 weeks, DBC's stock price fell dramatically. If you're thinking about investing in DBC, find out why the price fell. If the company is a strong one, it may be a good opportunity to buy it at a lower stock price. If the company is having tough times, avoid it. In any case, research the company and find out why its stock has declined.

52-week low

The column labelled "52-Wk Low" gives you the lowest price that particular stock has reached in the most recent 52-week period. Again, this information is crucial to your ability to analyze a stock over a period of time. Looking at DBC in Table 6-1, you can see that its current trading price of $33.50 is right about where its 52-week low is. So far, DBC doesn't look like a real catch.

Keep in mind that the high and the low prices just give you a range for how far that particular stock's price has moved within the past 52 weeks. They could alert you that a stock has problems, or they could tell you that a stock's price has fallen enough to make it a bargain. Simply reading the 52-week high and 52-week low columns isn't enough to determine which of those two things is happening. They basically tell you to get more information before you commit your money.

Name and symbol

This is the simplest column. It tells you the company name (usually abbreviated) and the stock symbol assigned to the company. Once you have your eye on a stock for potential purchase, get familiar with its symbol. Knowing the symbol makes it easier to find it in the financial tables, which list stocks in alphabetical order by symbol. Stock symbols are the language of stock investing, and you need to use them in all stock communications, from getting a quote at your broker's office (even by touch-tone, using only your phone's buttons and no voice) to buying stock over the Internet.

Dividend

A bird's-eye view of dividends is presented to you in Chapter 1, where we essentially define them as payments to owners (shareholders). On a more nitty-gritty level, we now show you how dividend information appears in stock tables (shown under the "Div" column in Table 6-1), and what you should look for.

If — and this can be a big if — a company pays a dividend, it's shown in the dividend column. The amount you see is the annual dividend quoted as though you owned one share of that stock. If you look at LowDownInc (LDI) in Table 6-1, you can see that you would get $2.35 as an annual dividend for each share of stock that you own. The dividend is usually paid quarterly. If we own 100 shares of LDI, the company would pay us a dividend of $58.75 each quarter ($235 total per year).

A healthy company strives to maintain or upgrade the dividend for share-holders from year to year. In any case, the dividend distribution is very important if you're a stock investor who also seeks income. For more about investing for income, see Chapter 10. Companies that don't pay dividends are bought by investors primarily for growth. For more information on growth stocks, see Chapter 9.

Volume

Normally, when you hear the word *volume* on the news, it refers to how much stock is bought and sold for the entire market. ("Well, stocks were very active today. Trading volume at the TSX was 270 million shares, and the NYSE hit 2 billion shares.") Volume is certainly important to watch, because the stocks that you're investing in are somewhere in that activity. For our purposes here, though, the volume (the "Vol" column in Table 6-1) refers to the individual stock.

Volume tells you how many shares of that particular stock were traded that day. If only 100 shares are traded in a day, then the trading volume is 100. SHC had 3,143 shares change hands on the trading day represented in Table 6-1. Is that good or bad? Neither, really. Usually volume for a particular stock is mentioned in the business news media when it is unusually large. If a stock normally has volume in the 5,000 to 10,000 range and all of a sudden has a trading volume of 87,000, then it's time to sit up and take notice.

Keep in mind that a low trading volume for one stock may be a high trading volume for another stock. You can't necessarily compare one stock's volume against that of any other company. The large-cap stocks like Nortel or Home Depot typically have trading volumes in the millions of shares almost every day, while less active, smaller stocks may have average trading volumes that are far, far lower.

The main point to remember is that trading volume that is far in excess of that stock's normal range is a sign that something is going on with that stock. It may be negative or positive, but something newsworthy is happening with that company. If the news is positive, the increased volume is a result of more people buying the stock. If the news is negative, the increased volume is probably a result of more people selling the stock. What are typical events that cause increased trading volume? Some positive reasons include the following:

> ✔ **Good earnings reports:** A company announces good (or better than expected) earnings.

✔ **A new business deal:** A company announces a significant and favourable business deal, such as a joint venture, or lands a big client.

✔ **A new product or service:** A company's research and development department creates a potentially profitable new product.

✔ **Indirect benefits:** A company may benefit from a new development in the economy or from a new law passed by Parliament.

Some negative reasons for an unusually large fluctuation in trading volume for a particular stock may include the following:

✔ **Bad earnings reports:** Profit is the lifeblood of a company. If a company's profits fall or disappear, you'll see more volume.

✔ **Governmental problems:** The stock is being targeted by government action (such as a lawsuit or Ontario Securities Commission probe).

✔ **Liability issues:** The media report that a company has issued a recall notice concerning a defective product, or has a similar problem.

✔ **Financial problems:** Independent analysts report that a company's financial health is deteriorating.

The bottom line is to check out what's happening when you hear about heavier than usual volume (especially if you already own the stock).

Yield

In general, yield is a return on the money you invest. However, in the stock tables, *yield* ("Yld" in Table 6-1) is a reference to what percentage that particular dividend is to the stock price. Yield is most important to income investors. It is calculated by dividing the annual dividend by the current stock price. In Table 6-1, you can see that the yield du jour of ValueNowInc. (VNI) is 4.5 percent (a dividend of $1 divided by the company's stock price of $22). Notice that many companies have no yield reported; because they have no dividends, yield cannot be calculated.

Keep in mind that the yield reported in the financial pages changes daily as the stock price changes. Yield is always reported as if you're buying the stock that day. If you bought VNI on the day represented in Table 6-1, your yield would be 4.5 percent. But what if VNI's stock price rose to $30 the following day? Investors who bought stock at $30 per share would obtain a yield of just 3.3 percent. (The dividend of $1 would then be divided by the new stock price, $30.) Of course, because you bought the stock at $22, you essentially locked in the prior yield of 4.5 percent. Lucky you. Pat yourself on the back.

P/E

The P/E ratio indicates the ratio between the price of the stock and the company's earnings. P/E ratios are widely followed and important barometers of value in the world of stock investing. The P/E ratio (also called the "earnings multiple," or just "multiple") is frequently used to determine whether a stock is expensive (a good value). Value investors find P/E ratios to be essential to analyzing a stock as a potential investment. As a general rule, the P/E should preferably be 10 to 20 for large-cap or income stocks. For growth stocks, a P/E no greater than 30 to 40 is preferable.

In the P/E ratios reported in stock tables, *price* refers to the cost of a single share of stock. *Earnings* refers to the company's reported earnings per share as of the most recent four quarters. The P/E ratio is the price divided by the earnings. In Table 6-1, VNI has a reported P/E of 12, which is considered a low P/E. Notice how SHC has a relatively high P/E (76). This stock is considered too pricey, as you're paying a price equivalent to 76 times earnings. Also notice that the stock DBC has no available P/E ratio. Usually this lack of a P/E ratio indicates that the company reported a loss in the most recent four quarters.

Day last

The "Day Last" (or "Close") column tells you how trading ended for a particular stock on the day represented by the table. In the stock table in Table 6-1 earlier in this chapter, the stock LDC ended the most recent day of trading at 41. Some newspapers report the high and low for that day in addition to the stock's ending or closing price for the day.

Net change

The information in the net-change column ("Net Chg" in Table 6-1) answers the question "How did the stock price end today compared with its trading price at the end of the prior trading day?" Table 6-1 shows that SHC stock ended the trading day up 25 cents (at $21.25). This tells you that SHC ended the prior day at $21. On a day when VNI ends the day at $22 (up 10 cents), you can tell that the prior day it ended the trading day at $21.90. You get the idea.

Why Closing and Dividend Dates Matter

Reading and understanding the news about dividends is essential if you're an *income investor* (someone who invests in stocks as a means of generating regular income). Paying particular attention to important dividend dates helps you benefit as an investor.

To begin, you should be aware of the fact that there are three business days between the date of execution of a trade and the "closing" or "settlement" date. The closing or settlement date is the date on which the trade is finalized, usually three business days after execution. Similar in concept to a real estate closing, it's the official date on which you are the proud new owner (or happy seller) of the stock.

As we discuss in Chapter 1, there are also three business days between the ex-dividend date and the date of record. This information is important to know if you want to qualify to receive an upcoming dividend. Timing is important, and the following example is the best way to explain it.

Say that you want to buy Value Now, Inc. (VNI) in time to qualify for the quarterly dividend of 25 cents per share. Assume that the date of record (the date by which you have to be an official owner of the stock) is February 10. You have to execute the trade (buy the stock) no later than February 7 to be assured of the dividend. If you execute the trade right on February 7, the closing date would occur three days later, on February 10 — just in time for the date of record.

But what if you execute the trade on February 8, a day later? Well, the trade's closing date would be February 11, which would occur *after* the date of record. Because you wouldn't be on the books as an official shareholder on the date of record, you wouldn't get that quarterly dividend. In this example, the February 7–10 period is called the *ex-dividend period*.

Evaluating (Avoiding?) Investment Tips

Psssst. Have I got a stock tip for you! Come closer. You know what it is? Research! What we're trying to tell you is that you should never automatically invest just because you get a hot tip from someone. Good investment selection means looking at several sources before you decide on a stock. There's no shortcut. That said, getting opinions from others never hurts — just be sure to carefully analyze the information you get. The following sections present some important points to bear in mind as you evaluate tips and advice from others.

Consider the source

Frequently, people buy stock based on the views of some market strategist or market analyst. People may see an analyst being interviewed on a television financial show and take that person's opinions and advice as valid and good. The danger here is that the analyst could easily be biased because of some relationship that isn't disclosed on the show.

It happens on TV all too often. The show's host interviews analyst U.R. Kiddingme from the investment firm Foolum & Sellum. The analyst says, "Implosion Corp. is a good buy with solid, long-term, upside potential." You later find out that the analyst's employer gets investment-banking fees from Implosion Corp. Do you really think that analyst would ever issue a negative report on a company that's helping to pay the bills? It's not likely. Being suspicious can keep you from being a sucker.

Get multiple views

One source isn't enough to base your investment decisions on unless you have the best reasons in the world for thinking that a particular, single source is outstanding and extremely accurate and prescient. A better approach is to scour current issues of independent financial publications, such as *Barron's, Canadian Business, SmartMoney,* and other publications listed in this book's Appendix. Search the Internet for information, too. The Appendix lists lots of informative Web sites for you to check out.

Chapter 7

Financial Planning for Stock Investors

....

In This Chapter

▶ Finding out what financial planners do

▶ Deciphering the industry's designations

▶ Spotting solid financial planners

▶ Knowing what to expect when you meet with your financial planner

....

*W*hat is financial planning, other than a reason to break out into a cold sweat? Just about everyone's heard of the concept, but few can really explain it. Perhaps a simple approach is called for here. Here it goes: Financial planning is the method of meeting your personal objectives through the proper management of your finances. Your goals could be short-term, medium-term, long-term, or a combination of the above.

Managing your finances means a lot more than it sounds like. It's about making the right investments, paying down debts, generating different types of income, getting insured properly, making tax-smart financial decisions, budgeting, planning your estate, and more! The issue of financial planning obviously needs to be taken seriously. By understanding financial planning as a whole, you will better understand the impact of your stock investing decisions on your financial plan.

How Financial Planning Works

Life is full of choices, and the choices that you make are often driven by your personal goals. So goal-setting is an important process in the context of building your wealth. Saving for your child's education, buying an Acura, getting a cottage, or planning for retirement are examples of defined and clearly set goals, each having varied time frames. A well-crafted and clear financial plan helps you tremendously to reach set goals by clarifying where you are now relative to where you want to be in the future. It provides a road map and checkpoint for all your financial decisions. Turn here, and you'll get dinged with this much tax. Turn there, and you'll save that many dollars. Do nothing, and you'll miss out on the next bull run. Each decision made or not made has a financial impact. By being prepared and empowered with a financial plan, you'll see the forest *and* the trees. Financial planning, if done well, will assist you in adapting better to life's choices and changes thrown your way. It will help you stay on track to your goals and objectives.

How financial planners differ from other advisers

Many Canadians wonder how the work of a financial planner distinguishes itself from the work of other advisers playing in the arena of finance. How do they differ from brokers and investment advisers (discussed in Chapter 8)? From others? Let's once again simplify things by saying that financial planners are individuals who understand how to utilize the financial planning process, or in other words know how to help you meet your goals through good financial management. They use a big-picture and integrated approach — how an estate-planning decision will impact current year's taxes, or how an income-based investing approach will impact your retirement cash flow in 2014. Advisers who are not financial planners will likely *not* see your goals through a big-picture, integrated lens. They may maximize investment returns, or minimize taxes, but they may also fail to point out — or just not be focused on — the fact that investment returns and taxes are very interrelated!

Financial planners examine all your requirements and help you with your financial needs — namely investing, debt reduction, insurance, tax planning, budgeting, estate and retirement planning, and so on. They may work on a single financial issue today, but will invariably do so in the framework of your overall goals and objectives. They *do* use the big-picture and integrated approach. They will ultimately discuss stock investing with you.

Financial planner services

There are many products and services offered by financial planners. Life insurance, segregated funds, estate planning, and tax services are just a small array of things offered. Yet, whenever you meet a person who tells you that he can do all this by himself, it should sound alarm bells. At best, a true financial planner is part of a group of partners that tackles your financial situation as a team. Just knowing about taxes alone takes years of education.

Investment savvy takes years, even decades, to build. This should be the first acid test about financial planning for a reasonably complex financial situation. For simpler financial planning engagements, perhaps one person can in fact provide a great plan. That's fine — just be sure that the planner has been there and done that before. More specific things to look for and ask about follow later in this chapter.

One important thing to note in the context of the investment industry is that, in addition to giving advice on a variety of topics, most financial planners are licensed by provincial overseers to sell one or more types of financial products or services. What they do, and can do, hinges on their credentials (discussed later) and the company they work for. Some provide only financial planning advice. Others specialize in offering advice in specific areas such as taxation or budgeting. Still others sell only financial products. A bona fide planner will plan your financial affairs within a big-picture context. This can be done by one person (for a simple plan) or a team of financial planners (for more complex client profiles). The key is that true financial planners know the larger picture about you. Okay, we agree that we may sound like a broken record, but the message is definitely worth repeating — it's your money at stake!

I don't need your advice...or do I?

How do you really know if you require professional financial planning assistance? Can't you wing it yourself? Again, the best financial planners have spent years in training and have loads of experience. Can you really match that? Financial issues are complicated. If you are unsure about your ability to build personal wealth, or can't get a clear reading on what finances you'll have in the future, consider the advice of a professional. Personal risk assessments, retirement objective-setting, budgeting, debt reduction, and inheritance management are but a few of the many areas in which a professional financial planner could help you. Even if you are confident about your financial planning prowess, you may not have the time or inclination to invest weeks in assessing your financial matters.

As you can see, there are many reasons to consult a financial professional, all of them valid. When it comes to your financial affairs, it's usually worthwhile to take this view: When in doubt, ask an expert! If you're puzzled about conflicting advice from various sources, find it hard to meet payments, believe you are overtaxed, and can't seem to save money, consider seeking the advice of a qualified financial planner. A good financial planner will help you grow your savings and help you meet some of your non-financial objectives as well. A bad planner will only plan his own finances by overcharging you for bad advice!

The times they are a changin'

Decades ago, registered retirement savings plans were simple — put money in, and take it out in retirement. Then rules were added to ensure that you took out a bit of cash at a time after you retired (which is why registered retirement income funds, discussed in Chapter 21, were created).

These days the financial landscape is complicated and confusing. The federal government introduced even more rules about RRSPs as a way to help you meet a set of personal goals including first-time home ownership and putting your kids through university or college. Only recently, the 2003 federal budget raised RRSP limits.

Government rules seem to change all the time!

Changes in your lifestyle also impact your financial planning. If you want to build lots of wealth, you'll have to take more risk with a more aggressive investment style. A new member in your family, loss of a loved one, career change, job loss, or inheritance could put your financial plans into a different gear. Change is everything, and everywhere. Your financial plan will get more complex and fluid as the years go by. It gets buffeted by anticipated and unanticipated changes. Your plan is never set in stone.

A financial adviser can play a valuable role by keeping a second set of eyes on changes in your life. She will keep track of personal and regulatory changes and understand your needs. For you, she will be an agent of change.

How your adviser charges you

Financial planners can be paid in many ways. Some make commissions on the sale of products, like a car salesperson. Others draw a salary if they work for a company. Many work on a fee-for-service or hourly-rate basis. Still others charge flat rates for services provided, or are paid a fee based on a percentage of income or assets under administration. The manner by which you pay for financial planning services should be discussed at the very beginning of the first client–adviser meeting. It's possible that the planner will offer you a choice of how she might be paid. Whatever the potential arrangement, it is key that you get the payment structure in writing.

How much will you be charged? Well, we hate to use weasel words but — it depends. (Okay, you can throw the tomatoes at us now.) The amount you pay the planner depends on your financial and even non-financial objectives and needs. It is also driven by the financial planner's experience and credentials. Nevertheless, you should be able to get a ballpark figure of possible costs based on the work desired.

Kicking the tires: What you should look for

In selecting a financial planner, seek first someone you can trust. This is easier said than done. There are too many people who call themselves financial planners and advisers but who may not be qualified to give you the professional level of service that you paid for. To help you along, the following guidelines are things to look for and do when choosing a financial planner:

- ✔ **Know your goals and objectives.** Identify both your financial goals and your non-financial goals that depend on finances. Examples include desired insurance coverage, estate-planning expectations, investment goals, educational aspirations, and so on.

- ✔ **Look for credentials and knowledge.** Many degrees and designations can be held by financial planners. Choose a licensed pro who has met rigorous standards in the financial-planning domain, and who is bound by and follows a code of professional ethics.

- ✔ **Ask for references and talk to others.** Determine whether the financial planner works alongside other professionals such as accountants, investment advisers, insurance brokers, and lawyers. Get references from all planning team members. As a minimum, get a verifiable biography of these individuals. Also get referrals from other advisers, work colleagues, and trusted friends.

- ✔ **Meet with several planner candidates.** Enquire about their education, work experience, and professional specialties. Also ask about the size and duration of their practice, and how they stay in touch with clients. Direct client contact is a good sign that your adviser cares about your finances.

- ✔ **Do a background check.** If it is feasible to do this, call their professional associations or the local Better Business Bureau to check on any complaint record and to determine whether they remain in good standing.

- ✔ **Know what to expect.** Ask for a document detailing the proposed method of compensation and disclosing any conflicts of interest, business associations, and personal credentials.

The more complex your situation, the more of these guidelines you should implement.

Drilling deeper: Asking the right questions

Based on the above preliminary research, you're ready to meet face-to-face again with the two or three advisers you feel most comfortable with. This is an opportunity to ask specific questions and assess the reactions to those questions. Finding the financial planner that's right for your needs takes legwork and some tough questions. But if this stage of the process is done properly, you'll be rewarded with good service and value-for-money over the long term.

There are several questions you can ask a prospective financial adviser before engaging him. Don't shy away from asking these questions, either on the telephone or during a personal visit. Don't permit yourself to be hurried — the financial-planning process is a comprehensive and complicated one. Expect to spend at least one hour on the first interview. Also expect that your adviser will ask you questions, too.

First, confirm some of your preliminary research: enquire about credentials (most professional designations require financial-planning courses), expertise (very few advisers are Jacks or Jills of all trades), and experience (very important in today's turbulent and complex market). Your prospective adviser should be at the ready to talk about financial issues such as budgeting, insurance, investing, and tax strategies. She should also have close working relationships with professionals specializing in accounting, law, and insurance.

On a more specific level, ask whether the adviser charges on a fee, fee-and-commission, or commission-only basis. Can the adviser provide you with an estimate of the overall cost of service over a certain time frame? Does the adviser specialize in a certain type of client or investing style? Quite often, advisers have niches in certain income, age, or vocational groups. Also confirm professional affiliations. If the adviser does not belong to any professional organization, ask for the reasons. Talk about his independence and objectivity to discern whether the adviser is limited or favourable only to his employer's own financial products and services. Find out how the prospective adviser will structure your investment portfolio. Will he execute the trades (riskier due to a lack of oversight on your part), or only tell you what trades you ought to execute? Does she perform independent analyses, or depend on the research and analysis of others?

Also ask whether the adviser will contact you directly or whether an associate or assistant will do the talking for him. How much of the actual work is the adviser doing? All of it? Half of it? Only a quick review of what others have done on your behalf? If your financial affairs will be delegated to others, set up a date to meet the assistant to ensure proper qualifications, personal style, and fit. Determine as well how many times you can expect to meet with the adviser to review your financial affairs. Also, will he take you out to a ball game? (Just kidding, of course!)

After all is said and done, review everything you have learned, and select your adviser. Get everything in writing. Ask for a written contract to document the nature and scope of services to be provided by the financial planner — this includes compensation agreements. Once the stage is set, re-evaluate the client–adviser relationship on a regular basis. Business relationships tend to be long-term, so make sure that your planner tracks changes in your life and makes appropriate adjustments to your financial plan as warranted. We agree that this is a somewhat tedious process. Yet, it's obviously very important.

ABC, XYZ, and Credibility

How can you tell if a financial planning professional is qualified? One way is to see if your financial planner is a member of a professional body related to financial planning. At a minimum, it demonstrates that the planner is committed to professional development. That's a good thing. One thing to remember is that there is no one "best" designation. The value of the designation is measured by the quality of the person holding it. An experienced financial planner with an "easier to get" designation may be a better fit than the geek with no interpersonal skills who aced his exams but who never bothers — or is too shy — to find out about any changes in your life that may critically impact your financial plan. So we don't make assumptions here. We simply list the options for you. It's up to you to use your judgment in finding the right balance between technical know-how and experience and savvy. The following list of financial-planning designations attests to the fact that there are all too many letters representing credentials:

- ✔ **Canadian Investment Manager (CIM):** Individual who specializes in portfolio and wealth management. The title is granted by the Canadian Securities Institute (CSI).

- ✔ **Certified Financial Planner (CFP):** Administered and overseen by the Financial Planners Standards Council (FPSC). CFP licensees must meet the Council's standards in education, experience, examination, and ethics. Continuing education is required.

- ✔ **Certified General Accountant (CGA):** An accounting designation granted to individuals who have fulfilled the educational and experience requirements of their provincial governing body. CGAs are trained in tax, accounting, and financial management. They are required to abide by a code of conduct and participate in a mandatory continuing education program.

- ✔ **Certified Management Accountant (CMA):** Person who passed the requirements of his or her provincial society of management accountants. CMAs are financial-management professionals who combine accounting and strategic business management skills.

- **Chartered Accountant (CA):** Someone who has passed the national Uniform Final Exam. CAs have extensive training in tax and other areas of financial management and must adhere to a code of conduct.

- **Chartered Financial Analyst (CFA):** A person who passed exams administered by the U.S.–based Association for Investment Management and Research (AIMR). Money and fund managers and stock analysts typically sport this designation.

- **Chartered Financial Consultant (CH.F.C.):** Person who passed a course of study in financial planning and wealth accumulation. It is granted by the Canadian Association of Insurance and Financial Advisors (CAIFA).

- **Chartered Financial Planner:** Person who earned a general financial-planning designation granted by the Canadian Institute of Financial Planning. The program is now phased out.

- **Fellow of the Canadian Securities Institute (FCSI):** Designation is awarded by the CSI. To obtain this designation, students require a minimum of five years' experience in the financial services industry. They also have to obtain an additional array of other CSI designations, and complete several CSI courses of study and seminars.

- **Financial Management Advisor (FMA):** Another designation awarded by the CSI. The FMA educational route delivers extensive financial planning skills to serve high-net-worth individuals who seek complex financial strategies to meet their objectives. The designation is achieved by completion of several other CSI courses.

- **Personal Financial Planner (PFP):** Granted by the Institute of Canadian Bankers, this title is earned upon successful completion of the Personal Financial Planning Program and the Institute's Designation Qualification Process.

- **Registered Financial Planner (R.F.P.):** Awarded by the Canadian Association of Financial Planners (CAFP) to its qualifying members. The program is now phased out.

What a Good Financial Planner Will Do for You

Most business relationships with financial planners are long-term, spanning one or more decades in many cases. It only makes sense for you to enter into this business relationship with certain expectations.

Consider several issues and what you expect from your financial planner. Were you provided with written documentation itemizing professional qualifications, industry experience, compensation methods, business affiliations, and any potential conflicts of interest? Were all of your financial concerns understood and factored into the financial plan? Was the assessment of your investment philosophy and risk tolerance correct?

Any new information about your life situation ought to be included in your financial plan. If your stock portfolio was down over the past few years, your financial planner ought to have discussed new possible strategies with you. The financial plan itself should be realistic in the context of achieving your objectives. Budgets should include implementation details specifying dates, amounts, and activities.

After one or two years have passed, evaluate whether, and how well, your financial planner reviewed your plan to see that the overall planning strategy is on track to meet your personal objectives. If your portfolio involves stock and other forms of equity investing, your financial planner ought to be providing you with periodic updates on the performance of your investment portfolio. He or she should be in regular contact with you, even if it's just a quick and cheesy e-card to say hello.

A Training Run

You may be wondering what the typical financial planning process looks like. Essentially, the process consists of eight phases (discussed next) for a financial plan that's a bit involved and complex. Knowing the phases of the financial planning process will give you a framework against which you can evaluate the financial planner, as well as the financial plan itself. It's like going to the doctor already armed with basic information about what ails you. You're better prepared to ask the right questions about alternatives, expected outcomes, and chances of success! Understanding the financial planning process will help you get maximum value out of it. While the process differs slightly from planner to planner, and engagement to engagement, the following discussion represents a rough sketch of the key milestones you should expect to see.

Search for and find a planner

We discuss this earlier in the chapter. This phase requires you to

- Be prepared with some financial knowledge
- Know your financial objectives
- Look for proper credentials, and assess the level of expertise and experience of a planner
- Ask for references
- Meet with several candidates

✔ Perform a background check on candidates

✔ Get documentation about compensation, conflicts of interest, and business associations

✔ Meet face-to-face again with the two or three advisers you feel best about

✔ Ask very specific questions about the planner's proposed approach with you

✔ Assess the planner's use of professionals specializing in accounting, law, and insurance

✔ Get an estimate of the overall cost of service

Get clarification of roles and responsibilities

Make the terms of the engagement very clear regarding services to be provided and your responsibilities as a client (for example, keeping the financial planner updated about any significant and relevant changes in your life). Itemize and document the planner's responsibilities. Understand how the planner will be compensated. Have a discussion about the scope of the engagement, and reach an agreement as to how outcomes and financial plans will be determined (for example, plans can be developed and reassessed annually or every two years).

Gather your information

Garbage in, garbage out. Your planner depends on accurate, complete, relevant, and timely information to even begin crafting a good financial plan. Information required may include a list of your assets and liabilities, current insurance coverage, upcoming family obligations such as nursing home payments, and so on. Expect to receive a questionnaire to help you along.

Determine your goals and expectations

An additional interview between you, your planner, and his or her associates (such as lawyers or estate-planning specialists) should help you define your personal and financial goals and top priorities. Before the interview that includes this discussion, prepare yourself by thinking in advance about your preferences, values, financial philosophy, and expected outcomes as they relate to your financial goals.

Clarify your present financial situation and highlight any problem areas

Expect your planner to analyze your personal information to evaluate your current financial condition. This includes a look at your net worth, cash flow, and tax-bracket information. At this stage, the planner will home in specifically on areas such as cash flow, insurance needs and coverage, cash requirements for special projects, current investment portfolio, employer benefits available, estate-planning objectives, and other needs (such as continuing education or medical expenses).

Get your financial plan

Once your planner provides you with a financial plan tailored to meet your personal objectives and presents the plan to you, you and your planner should work in tandem to ensure that the plan actually meets your personal objectives. Also check to see whether the projections, and the assumptions behind those projections, appear realistic and plausible. Make sure as well that the planner's recommendations are practical and have reasonable timelines attached.

Execute your financial plan

Your planner will offer to help you carry out the recommendations in the financial plan, if you have chosen to take this route. This may include coordinating contacts with other professional associates such as lawyers, accountants, and insurance brokers or agents. If you feel that you can carry out the recommendations by yourself, fine. If not, then pay the extra amount required to see the plan to fruition. Recommendations, without actions to see them through, lack value.

Keep an eye on your financial plan

Reach an understanding with your financial planner on who will be responsible for monitoring your plan in terms of how it is helping you move toward your objectives. If your planner is doing this, she should be in periodic contact with you to go over the progress of the plan. This is the part of the financial planning process where adjustments to recommendations or assumptions driving those recommendations can be made. If adjustments are not made as required, then your financial plan will become obsolete very quickly. Yet, you will continue to pay your adviser. Not a good deal!

This last part of the process will likely include a discussion about changes in your personal circumstances, for example, major life events such as divorce, death, birth, illness, marriage, and retirement and how they might affect your objectives. The impact of new tax legislation and circumstances in the Canadian economy will be considered as well.

Chapter 8

Going for Brokers

In This Chapter

▶ Finding out what brokers do

▶ Telling the difference between full-service and discount brokers

▶ Selecting a broker

▶ Learning about online brokers

▶ Exploring the types of brokerage services and accounts

▶ Figuring out what brokers' recommendations mean

▶ Examining brokerage reports

*W*hen you're ready to dive in and start investing in stocks, you first have to choose a broker. It's kind of like buying a car: You can do all the research in the world and know exactly what kind of car you want to buy; still, you have to buy it through a car dealer. Similarly, when you want to buy stock, your task is to do all the research you can to select the company you want to invest in. Still, you need a broker to actually buy the stock, whether you buy in person or online. In this chapter, we set out to introduce you to the intricacies of the investor–broker relationship.

For information on various types of orders you can place with a broker, such as market orders, stop-loss orders, and so on, flip to Chapter 20.

Defining the Broker's Role

The broker is the intermediary between you and the world of stock investing. The broker's primary role is to serve as the vehicle through which you either buy or sell stock. When we talk about brokers, we're referring to organizations such as TD Waterhouse, E*Trade Canada, Merrill Lynch HSBC Canada, and many others that can buy stock on your behalf. Brokers can also be individuals who work for such firms. Although you can buy some stocks directly from the company that issues them, to purchase most stocks you still need a broker.

The primary task of brokers is the buying and selling of stocks, but they can perform other tasks for you, including the following:

- ✔ **Providing advisory services:** Investors pay brokers a fee for investment advice.

- ✔ **Offering limited banking services:** Brokers can offer features such as interest-bearing accounts and cheque writing.

- ✔ **Brokering other securities:** Brokers can also buy bonds, mutual funds, and other investments on your behalf. Keep in mind that the word *securities* refers to the world of financial (or paper) investments and that stocks are only a small part of that world.

Personal stockbrokers make their money from individual investors like you and me through various fees, including the following:

- ✔ **Brokerage commissions:** This is a fee for buying and/or selling stocks and other securities.

- ✔ **Margin interest charges:** This is interest charged to investors for borrowing against their brokerage account for investment purposes.

- ✔ **Service charges:** These are charges for performing administrative tasks and other functions. Brokers charge fees to investors for RRSPs, for mailing stocks in certificate form, and other special services.

There is a distinction between personal stockbrokers and institutional stockbrokers. Institutional brokers make money from institutions and companies through investment banking and securities placement fees (such as initial public offerings and secondary offerings), advisory services, and other broker services. Personal stockbrokers generally offer the same services to individuals and small businesses.

Distinguishing between Full-Service and Discount Brokers

There are two basic categories of stockbrokers: full-service and discount. The type you choose really depends on what type of investor you are. In a nutshell, full-service brokers are suitable for investors who need some guidance, while discount brokers are better for those who are sufficiently confident and knowledgeable about stock investing to manage with minimal help.

Full-service brokers

Full-service brokers are just what the name indicates. They try to provide as many services as possible for investors who open accounts with them. When you open an account at a brokerage firm, a representative is assigned to your account. This representative is usually called an *account executive,* a *registered rep,* or a *financial consultant* by the brokerage firm. This person usually has a Canadian securities licence and is knowledgeable about stocks in particular and investing in general.

What they can do for you

Your account executive is responsible for assisting you, answering questions about your account and the securities in your portfolio, and transacting your buy and sell orders. Here are some things that full-service brokers can do for you:

- ✔ **Offer guidance and advice.** The greatest distinction between full-service brokers and discount brokers is the personal attention you receive from your account rep. You operate on a first-name basis, and you disclose much information about your finances and financial goals. The rep is there to make recommendations about stocks and funds that are hopefully suitable for you.

- ✔ **Provide access to research.** Full-service brokers can give you access to their investment research department, where you can get in-depth information and analysis on a particular company. This information can be very valuable, but be aware of the pitfalls. (See the section "Evaluating Brokers' Recommendations" later in this chapter.)

- ✔ **Help you achieve your investment objectives.** Beyond advice on specific investments, a good rep gets to know you and your investment goals and *then* offers advice and answers your questions about how specific investments and strategies can help you accomplish your wealth-building goals.

- ✔ **Make investment decisions on your behalf.** Many investors don't want to be bothered when it comes to investment decisions. Full-service brokers can actually make decisions for your account with your authorization. This service is fine, but be sure to require them to explain their choices to you.

What to watch out for

Although the full-service brokers, with their seemingly limitless assistance, can make life easy for an investor, you need to remember some important points to avoid problems:

- Brokers and account reps are still salespeople. Most are honest; some are complete shills. No matter how well they treat you, they're still compensated based on their ability to produce revenue for the brokerage firm. They generate commissions and fees from you on behalf of the company. (In other words, they're paid to sell you things.)

- Whenever your rep makes a suggestion or recommendation, be sure to ask why and request a complete answer that includes the reasoning behind the recommendation. A good adviser should be able to clearly explain the rationale behind every suggestion. If you don't fully understand and agree with the advice, don't take it.

- Know that working with a full-service broker costs a bit more than a discount broker. Discount brokers are paid simply for performing the act of buying or selling stocks for you. Full-service brokers do that and more. Additionally, they provide advice and guidance. Because of that, full-service brokers are more expensive (through higher brokerage commissions and advisory fees). Also, most full-service brokers expect you to invest at least $5,000 to $10,000 just to open an account. Grrrr.

- Handing over decision-making authority to your rep can be a possible negative because letting others make financial decisions for you is always dicey — especially when they're using *your* money. If they make poor investment choices that lose you money, you may not have any recourse, because you authorized them to act on your behalf.

- Some brokers engage in an activity called churning. *Churning* is basically buying and selling stocks for the sole purpose of generating commissions. Churning is great for brokers but bad for customers. Sometimes a broker may do a lot of trading in the account. The account may show little in terms of investment success but cost you dearly in commissions. Churning generates a lot of activity for the primary purpose of making more money for the broker (not for you!).

Some of Canada's full-service brokers include Merrill Lynch HSBC Canada, RBC Dominion Securities, and TD Waterhouse Investment Advice. Of course, all brokers now have full-featured Web sites to give you further information about their services. Get as informed as possible before you open your full-service account. A full-service broker should be there to help you build wealth, not make you . . . uh . . . broker.

Discount brokers

Perhaps you don't need any hand-holding from a broker. You know what you want, and you can make your own investment decisions. All you want is someone to transact your buy/sell orders. In that case, go with a discount broker. Discount brokers, as the name implies, are cheaper to engage than full-service brokers. They don't offer advice or premium services, though — just the basics required to perform your stock transactions.

If you choose to work with a discount broker, you must know as much as possible about your personal goals and needs. You have a greater responsibility for conducting adequate research to make good stock selections, and you must be prepared to accept the outcome, whatever that may be. Because you're advising yourself, you can save on costs that you would have incurred had you paid for a full-service broker.

You should also note that most Canadian discount (and full-service) brokers are also online (Internet) brokers. (We discuss online brokers in detail later in this chapter.) Conventional discount brokers (such as TD Waterhouse and Scotia McLeod Direct Investing) have offices throughout Canada that you can walk into and speak to customer service staff face-to-face. You can transact in person, over the phone, or through the Internet. That's the sort of thing that makes them conventional. Pure online discount brokerage firms (like E*Trade Canada) have essentially the same services, but without the walk-in offices and automated telephone trading. They're a little unconventional, and that's just the way they like it!

What they can do for you

Conventional discount brokers share many of the same primary advantages over full-service brokers, including the following:

- ✔ **Lower cost:** This lower cost is usually the result of lower commissions.

- ✔ **Unbiased service:** Because discount brokers offer you the ability to transact your buys and sells only without advice, they have no vested interest in trying to sell you any particular stock.

- ✔ **Access to information:** Established discount brokers offer extensive educational and research resources at their offices or on their Web sites.

What to watch out for

Of course, doing business with discount brokers also has its downside:

- ✔ **No guidance:** Because you've chosen a discount broker, you *know* not to expect guidance, but the broker should make this clear to you anyway. If you're a knowledgeable investor, the lack of advice is considered a positive thing — no interference.

- ✔ **Hidden fees:** Discount brokers may shout about their lower commissions, but commissions aren't their only way of making money. Many discount brokers charge extra for services that you may think are included, such as issuing a stock certificate or mailing a statement. Ask whether they charge annual fees for maintaining RRSPs, or fees for transfering stocks and other securities (such as bonds) in or out of your account. Find out what interest rates they charge for borrowing through brokerage accounts.

- ✔ **Minimal customer service:** If you deal with an Internet brokerage firm, find out about its customer service capability. If you can't transact business at its Web site, find out where you can call for assistance with your order.

Choosing a Broker

There are a few other issues to resolve before choosing a broker. The first issue is the broker's hair colour. Okay, okay, we'll stop the cheap jokes. Really, once you have decided whether to go the full-service or discount broker route, you have to make sure that you select a brokerage firm that's a member in good standing of one of Canada's self-regulatory organizations, or SROs. With big-name brokerages that you recognize, this is no big problem — all are probably in good standing. But with smaller brokerages you need to check this out, and we'll show you where to go to do this. Another thing to do before choosing a broker is to assess and revisit your personal investing style, something we help you do in Chapter 3. We discuss both issues next.

Self-regulatory organizations (SROs) in Canada

Canadian stock exchanges and the Investment Dealers Association of Canada (IDA) represent Canada's SROs for the investment industry. An SRO has been provided with legislated authority and the responsibility to regulate its member firms. They ensure that SRO members meet standards governing stocks and other securities. SROs regulate markets and trading, as well as firms that are members, their employees, and their business practices. They do this by establishing rules regulating how stock markets must operate. They monitor and visit brokers and other investment dealers on a periodic basis to ensure that mandated rules of operation (such as those concerning solvency) are followed. SROs investigate suspected infractions by sending out investigators and compliance officers to review things in more depth when necessary.

As indicated in Chapter 1, the provincial securities commissions have a national group that works toward making securities regulations consistent and standardized across Canada. This group is called the Canadian Securities Administrators (CSA). It's useful, but offers nowhere near the power wielded by the more independent regulators of U.S. stock markets. As a result, options and remedies to the Canadian individual stock investor are limited. You should note that although the IDA is an SRO, it regulates member firms operating mostly in the bond and money markets, not the equity markets that stocks are part of.

To find out if a firm is a member of an SRO, check out the Web sites (under Member Firms) of the Investment Dealers Association (www.ida.ca), or TSX (www.tsx.ca). (We discuss stock exchanges in Chapter 5.) You can also contact these organizations the good old-fashioned way — by phone!

Revisit your personal investing style

Before you choose a broker, you need to analyze and re-assess your personal investing style. Once you know yourself and the way you invest, then you can proceed to finding the kind of broker that fits your needs. It's almost like choosing shoes; if you don't know your size, you can't get a proper fit. (And if you get it wrong you can be in for a really uncomfortable future.)

Consider Bob and Ed. Both men are knowledgeable, confident, and competent investors, so they each choose a discount broker — makes sense. Bob likes to trade stocks very frequently. Ed is a buy-and-hold type, but he likes to use margin. *Trading on margin* means using the stocks and other securities in your brokerage account as collateral to purchase more shares. (See Chapter 20 for more on margin.) Which discount broker is suitable for which investor?

Say that there are two discount brokers, JumpCo and StayCo. JumpCo charges $9 per trade, while StayCo charges $25. However, when it comes to margin trading, JumpCo charges 10 percent, while StayCo usually charges a full percentage point lower.

In this example, JumpCo is better suited to Bob's style of investing, while StayCo is better for Ed. Because Bob likes to trade frequently, the commission charge makes it more economical. Ed will pay a higher commission, but he'll eventually make his money back through lower margin-interest costs.

This example clearly illustrates how different investors can benefit by analyzing themselves and then choosing an appropriate broker.

Interviewing individual brokers

Ask about the individual broker's education and experience. If he has successfully completed an appropriate course of study, it points to a certain degree of skill and knowledge required for the job. (The Canadian Securities Institute, introduced in Chapter 7, administers several advanced courses dealing with advanced wealth-management and investment-portfolio management techniques.) Good investment decisions are most likely made by qualified brokers.

Enquire about the broker's typical client profile. Are clients growth or income investors? Are they young professionals or persons entering retirement? Brokers with profiles consistent with your own needs will be better tuned to your investment objectives. It's always reassuring to realize that your broker has other clients that are much like you.

Also discuss expected outcomes. Outcomes include the type of services you are seeking, types of research and recommendations to expect, and desired returns.

Make your decision

When it's time to choose a broker, keep the following points in mind:

- ✔ Match your investment style with an SRO-member brokerage firm that charges the least amount of money for the services you're likely to use most frequently.

- ✔ Compare all the costs of buying, selling, and holding stocks and other securities through a broker. Don't look only at commissions; compare other costs, too, such as margin interest and other service charges.

- ✔ Contact a few firms before making your selection. Ask them if they are currently seeking accounts like yours. Ask for and call a few references to find out about the broker's strengths and weaknesses.

- ✔ If you selected the full-service-firm route, ask for a recommendation of one or more brokers at the brokerage who would be appropriate to handle your account, and interview them.

- ✔ Read articles that compare brokers in publications and newspapers such as *Canadian Business* and the *National Post*.

Your broker will influence your finances in a big way, so take the time to get to know her and decide whether she is the adviser for you.

Finding brokers is easy. They're listed in the Yellow Pages as well as in many investment publications and on financial Web sites. Start your search by using the sources in the Appendix at the back of this book, which includes a list of the major brokerage firms.

The Canadian Investor Protection Fund (CIPF) is overseen by the Canadian investment industry and provides coverage for Canadians making investments through its members. It insures brokerage accounts similar to the way the Canada Deposit Insurance Corporation (CDIC) insures bank accounts. CIPF limits coverage losses up to $1,000,000, and covers losses of securities, cash balances, and certain other investments. However, the losses can only result from the insolvency of a CIPF member firm. CIPF doesn't cover losses from unsuitable investments, an issuer of securities that is insolvent, or a market correction! Check out the CIPF Web site (www.cipf.ca) for full and detailed information. By the way — you aren't covered if the market corrects!

Investing is no more than the allocation of capital for use by an enterprise with the idea of achieving a suitable return. He or she who allocates capital best wins!

Online Brokerage Services

Investing online through the Internet has flourished for several reasons. Online investing, via an online brokerage service, lets you buy and sell stocks and other financial instruments using your personal computer and an Internet connection. As mentioned before, most online broker services are provided by traditional full-service and discount brokers. Several factors contribute to the rapid growth of online investing.

Why online investing is popular

First, the Internet provides quick and easy access to raw investment information (such as a stock quote) as well as refined information (such as a broker's analysis of a company, or other information services previously available only to investment professionals). Second, by eliminating the need for actual brokers or advisers, online brokers can offer commission rates that are lower than offline brokers charge. For example, buying 500 shares of Bombardier through a traditional full-service broker could cost you about $100 in commissions. Online, the cost is about $35. Easy account access is another reason for the popularity of online investing. Online brokers conveniently provide you with access to your account and the ability to place orders anytime and anywhere in Canada (or abroad) as long as you have an Internet connection. Finally, control of the investment process appeals to many investors. You can research a company, buy shares in it, monitor its progress, and chat with other shareholders in that company to hear their opinions.

Getting online trading services for less

As you may have guessed, no two online brokerage services are alike. Furthermore, individual brokerages may change their services and fees to keep pace with their competitors. To find the online broker that best meets your needs, you must investigate the prices, services, and features that various brokers offer.

Make certain that your brokerage doesn't charge you for services that are free elsewhere, or are hidden. Some hidden fees may include:

- Higher fees for accepting odd-lot orders (orders that include increments of less than 100 shares)
- Fees for sending out certificates (some firms charge $50 per certificate)
- Fees to close your account
- Fees to withdraw funds from your trading account

Trading online at a discount

You can't measure broker service with a formula. You have to look at both financial and non-financial criteria.

Cost is one factor, as we just found out. Definitely look at how much each broker charges in commission at different volumes of trades. Also assess the quality of online trade execution by talking to others who use a service you are considering. Are real-time quotes available? Is research material available? What is the overall ease of use of the service? Does the broker provide online screening tools?

Product selection is another important factor. You want to be able to trade things like guaranteed investment certificates, gold and silver certificates, municipal bonds, futures, Canadian and foreign equities, and so on. A list of investment products to consider is provided later in this chapter.

Response time should be quick. Some online brokers boast trade execution times of less than nine seconds! Phone each firm to see how long it takes for the broker to respond. E-mail each broker under consideration with a few questions; ask for an application to be sent by mail. Again, evaluate the response time.

Table 8-1 on page 125 lists several discount brokerage services in Canada.

Checking Out Special Features

Commission structures range widely from firm to firm because some Internet brokers include special or added features. When deciding which broker is best for you, factor in some or all of the features that we list in this section. First, consider whether each broker offers the following in your cash account:

- ✔ Low minimum amount required to open an account
- ✔ Low monthly fees with minimum equity balance
- ✔ No additional charges for postage and handling
- ✔ A summary of cash balances
- ✔ A summary of order status
- ✔ A summary of your portfolio's value
- ✔ Confirmation of trades (via e-mail, phone, or Canada Post)
- ✔ A historical review of your trading activities

Table 8-1	You Can Trade at a Discount		
	Minimum Online Trade Fee	*Minimum Automated Telephone Trade Fee*	*Minimum Broker - Assisted Trade Fee*
BMO InvestorLine 1-800-387-7800 www.bmoinvestorline.com	$25 for up to 1,000 shares	$25 for up to 1,000 shares	$40 minimum price per trade
CIBC Investor's Edge 1-800-567-3343 www.investorsedge.cibc	$25 for up to 1,000 shares	$25 for up to 1,000 shares	$43 minimum price per trade
Disnat 1-800-268-8471 www.disnat.com	$29 for up to 1,000 shares	Not available	$42 on orders of up to $2,000
E*Trade Canada 1-888-872-3388 www.canada.etrade.com	$26.99 minimum	Not available	Online trade fee plus $35
Merrill Lynch HSBC Canada 1-866-865-4722 www.mlhsbc.ca	$29 for up to 1,000 shares	Not available	$40 minimum per trade
National Bank Discount Brokerage 1-800-363-3511 www.nbc.com	$24.95 for up to 1,000 shares	$24.95 for up to 1,000 shares	$40.95 minimum per trade
Royal Bank Action Direct Brokerage 1-800-769-2560 www.actiondirect.com	$29.95 for up to 1,000 shares	$35 for up to 1,000 shares	$43 minimum per trade
Scotia McLeod Direct Investing 1-800-263-3430 www.scotiabank.com	$25.95 for up to 1,000 shares	$25.95 for up to 1,000 shares	$34.95 minimum per trade
Sun Life Securities 1-800-835-0812 www.sunsecurities.com	$29 for up to 1,000 shares	Not available	$43 minimum per trade
TD Waterhouse 1-800-465-5463 www.tdwaterhouse.ca	$29 for up to 1,000 shares	$29 (TalkBroker or Web Broker or Wireless) $35 (Telemax) for up to 1,000 shares	$43 minimum per trade

The broker eNorthern (at www.enorthern.com or 1-888-829-7929) is another option to consider, but requires that you have Explorer 5.5+ or Navigator 6.0+, or better. Also take note that Charles Schwab Canada recently merged into Scotia McLeod Direct Investing.

✔ No charges for RRSP account maintenance

✔ Consolidation of your money market, investments, and chequing and savings accounts

Second, consider whether each broker offers the following account features:

✔ Unlimited cheque-writing privileges

✔ Dividend collection and reinvestment

✔ Debit cards for ATM access

✔ Interest earned on cash balances

✔ Wire transfers accepted

✔ No RRSP account inactivity fees or surcharges

Third, find out which of the following types of investments the broker enables you to trade:

✔ Stocks (foreign or domestic)

✔ Options

✔ Canada and provincial savings bonds

✔ Government of Canada and U.S. government treasury bills

✔ Bankers' acceptances

✔ Commercial paper

✔ Mortgage-backed securities

✔ Bonds (corporate or agency)

✔ Bonds (municipal)

✔ Treasury notes

✔ Zero-coupon bonds

✔ Guaranteed investment certificates (GICs)

✔ Precious metals

✔ Mutual funds

✔ Investment trusts

Finally, determine whether the brokerage offers the following analytical and research features:

- ✔ Real-time online quotes
- ✔ Reports on insider trading
- ✔ Economic forecasts
- ✔ Company profiles and breaking news
- ✔ Earnings forecasts
- ✔ End-of-day prices automatically sent to you

How to open your online brokerage account

Internet brokerage firms are basically cash-and-carry enterprises. They all require investors to open an account before trading — a process that takes from two to three weeks to complete. Minimum account balances are becoming a rarity these days, but a few online brokerages still require that the book value of cash and securities you own at any given time exceeds a minimum amount. Since most Canadian brokerages do not require minimum account balances, you can open an account with a nominal deposit. However, there are only so many shares of Alcan that you can buy economically with $300 in your account!

When you place an order, your Internet broker withdraws money from your cash account to cover your trade. If you sell stock or receive a dividend, the Internet broker adds money to your cash account. If you develop a good history, your Internet broker may allow you to place trades without funds in your cash account if you settle within three days. All Internet brokers require that you complete an application form (which you can download online by following the instructions given at the Web site) that includes your name, address, and social insurance number; your work history; and a personal cheque, certified cheque, or money order for the minimum amount (if any) needed to open an account. Some brokers accept wire transfers or securities of equal value. Canadian law requires all brokerages to have your signature on file.

To speed up the process, you can complete application forms online or fax them to the Internet broker. You must then follow up by sending the completed, written, and signed forms via Canada Post within a pre-set (usually two-week) time frame, or the account is cancelled. The Internet broker then verifies all the information on the form and opens your account. Investors are sent a personal identification number (PIN) by mail. After you receive your PIN, you're ready to begin trading.

Types of Brokerage Accounts

Once you start investing in the stock market, you have to somehow actually *pay* for the stocks you buy. Most brokerage firms offer investors several different types of accounts, each serving a different purpose. We present three of the most common types in the following sections. The basic difference boils down to how particular brokers view your creditworthiness when it comes to buying and selling securities. If your credit isn't great, your only choice is a cash account. If your credit is good, you can open either a cash account or a margin account.

To open an account, you'll have to fill out an application and submit a cheque or money order for the minimum amount required.

Cash accounts

A *cash account* is just what you think it is. To begin trading, you must deposit a sum of money along with the new account application. The amount of your initial deposit varies from broker to broker. Some brokers have a $10,000 minimum, while others will let you open an account for as little as $75. Use the resources in the Appendix to help you shop around.

With a cash account, your money has to be deposited in the account before the closing (or "settlement") date for any trade you make. The closing occurs three business days after the date you make the trade (date of execution).

In other words, if you call your broker on Monday, October 10 and order 50 shares of CashLess Corp. at $20 per share, then on Thursday, October 13 you'd better have $1,000 in cash sitting in your account (plus commission). Otherwise, you'll be charged interest at rates as high as 19 percent, and your next trade will be blocked by the credit department!

If you have cash in a brokerage account (remember, all accounts are brokerage accounts, and "cash" and "margin" are simply types of brokerage accounts), see whether the broker will pay you interest on it and how much. Some offer a service in which uninvested money earns money market rates.

Margin accounts

A *margin account* gives you the ability to borrow money against the securities in the account to buy more stock. Once you're approved, your brokerage firm gives you credit. A margin account has all the benefits of a cash account plus this ability of buying on margin (which you can read more about in Chapter 20).

For stock trading, the margin limit is 50 percent. In other words, if you plan to buy $10,000 worth of stock on margin, you need at least $5,000 in cash (or securities owned) sitting in your account. The interest rate that you pay varies depending on the broker, but most brokers generally charge a rate that is several points higher than their own borrowing rate.

Why use margin? Margin is to stocks what mortgage is to buying real estate. You can buy real estate with all cash, but many times using borrowed funds makes sense.

Option accounts

An *option account* gives you all the capabilities of a margin account (which in turn also gives you the capabilities of a cash account) plus the ability to trade stock and index options. When you open an options account, the broker usually asks you to sign a statement that you are knowledgeable about options and are familiar with the risks associated with them.

Although options can be an effective addition to a stock investor's array of investing tools, the topic goes beyond the scope of this book.

Evaluating Brokers' Recommendations

In recent years, Canadians have become enamoured of a new sport: the rating of stocks by analysts on TV financial shows. Frequently these shows feature a dapper market strategist talking up a particular stock. Some stocks have been known to jump significantly right after an influential analyst (who is sometimes barely 20 years old) issues a buy recommendation. Analysts' speculation and opinions make for great fun, and many people take their views very seriously. However, most investors should be wary when analysts make a recommendation — especially the glib and glitzy ones who love the sound of their own voice. It's often just showbiz.

Brokerage houses, through their blue-suited armies of analysts, issue their recommendations (advice) as a general indicator of how much regard they have for a particular stock. The following list presents the basic recommendations (or ratings) and what they mean to you:

✔ **Strong buy and buy:** Hot diggity dog! This is the one to get. The analyst loves this pick, and you would be very wise to get a bunch of shares. The thing to keep in mind, however, is that *buy* recommendations are about as common as snow in Alberta.

✔ **Accumulate and market perform:** An analyst who issues these types of recommendations is positive, yet unexcited, about the pick. This is akin to asking a friend if he likes your new suit and getting the one-word response "nice" in a monotone voice. It's a polite reply, but you wish the opinion had been more enthusiastic.

✔ **Hold or neutral:** Analysts use this language when their back is to the wall but they still won't say, "Sell that loser!" This is like when your mother told you to be nice and either say something positive or keep your mouth shut. In this case, it is the analyst's way of keeping his mouth shut.

✔ **Sell:** Many analysts should have issued this recommendation during 2000 and 2001, but few actually uttered it. What a shame. So many investors lost money because some analysts were either too nice or just afraid to be honest and sound the alarm to urge people to sell.

✔ **Avoid like the plague:** We're just kidding about this one, but we wish that this recommendation were available. We've seen plenty of stocks that we thought were dreadful investments — stocks of companies that made no money and were in terrible financial condition, which should never have been considered at all. Yet investors gobbled up billions of dollars' worth of stocks that eventually became worthless.

Don't get us wrong — an analyst's recommendation is certainly a better tip than what you might get from your barber or your sister-in-law's neighbour, but you should view it with a healthy dose of reality. Analysts have biases because their employment depends on the very companies that are being presented. What investors should listen to when a broker talks up a stock is the reasoning behind the recommendation. In other words, why is the broker making this recommendation? What is she focusing on?

Keep in mind that analysts' recommendations can play a useful role in your personal stock-investing research. If you find a great stock and *then* you hear analysts give glowing reports on the same stock, you're on the right track! Here are some points to keep in mind:

✔ **How does the analyst arrive at a rating?** The analyst's approach to evaluating a stock can help you round out your research as you consult other sources, such as newsletters and independent advisory services.

✔ **What type of approach does this analyst use?** Some use *fundamental analysis* (looking at the company's financial condition and factors related to its success, such as its standing within the industry and the overall market). Other analysts use *technical analysis* (looking at the company's share-price history and judging past share-price movements to derive some insight regarding the stock's future price movement).

Many analysts may use a combination of the two methods. Is this analyst's approach similar to your approach, or to those of sources that you respect or admire?

✔ **What is the analyst's track record?** Has the analyst had a consistently good record through both bull and bear markets? Major financial publications such as *Barron's* in the U.S. and *Investor's Digest of Canada* (in 2002 named the World's Best Financial Advisory by NEPA, the Newsletter and Electronic Publisher's Association), and Web sites such as MarketWatch.com and Webfin.com (a Canoe site), regularly track recommendations from well-known analysts and stock pickers.

✔ **How does the analyst treat important aspects of the company's performance, such as sales and earnings?** How about the company's balance sheet? Industry? The essence of a healthy company is growing sales and earnings coupled with strong assets and low debt.

✔ **Is the industry that the company is in doing well?** Do the analysts give you insight on this important information? A strong company in a weak industry can't stay strong for long.

✔ **What research sources does the analyst cite?** Does the analyst quote the federal or provincial government or industry trade groups to support her thesis? These sources are important because they help to give a more complete picture regarding the company's prospects for success. Imagine that you decide on the stock of a strong company. But what if the provincial government (through agencies such as the Ontario Securities Commission) is penalizing the company for fraudulent activity? Or what if the company's industry is shrinking or has ceased to grow (making it tougher for the company to continue growing)? The astute investor looks at a variety of sources before buying shares.

✔ **If the analyst cites a target price for the stock ("We think the stock will hit $100 per share within 12 months"), does she present a rational model, such as basing the share price on a projected price–earnings ratio?** The analyst must be able to provide a logical scenario about why the stock has a good chance of achieving the cited target price within the time frame mentioned. You may not necessarily agree with the analyst's conclusion, but the explanation should help you decide whether the stock choice was well thought-out.

✔ **Does the company that is being recommended have any ties to the analyst or the analyst's firm?** During 2000 and 2001, the financial industry got bad publicity because many analysts gave positive recommendations on stocks of companies that were doing business with the very firms that employed those analysts. This was probably the biggest reason that analysts were so wrong in their recommendations. Ask your broker to disclose any possible conflict of interest.

Brokerage Reports: The Good, the Bad, and the Ugly

Clint Eastwood, where are you? Traditionally, brokerage reports have been a good source of information for investors seeking informed opinions about stocks. And they still are, but some brokerage reports have gotten bad press in recent years — and deservedly so.

The good

Research departments at brokerage firms provide stock reports and make them available for their clients and investment publications. The firms' analysts and market strategists generally prepare these reports. Good research is critical, and brokerage reports can be very valuable. What better source of guidance than full-time experts backed up by million-dollar research departments? Brokerage reports have some strong points:

- The analysts are professionals who should understand the value of a company and its stock. They analyze and compare company data every day.

- They have at their disposal tremendous information and historical data that they can sift through to make informed decisions.

- If you have an account with the firm, you can usually access some of the information free.

During the late 1990s, some of these analysts gained celebrity status as the public fervour over stock investing turned it into a national pastime. Analysts said, "X is a great stock. Buy it." Millions bought. Stocks soared. Brokerage firms made tonnes of money. Analysts got million-dollar bonuses. Common investors became wealthier. And they lived happily ever after! (Don't stop here. Keep reading. . . .)

The bad

Well, brokerage reports may not be bad in every case, but at their worst they're quite bad. Brokers make their money from commissions and investment-banking fees (nothing bad here). However, they can find themselves in the awkward position of issuing brokerage reports on companies that are (or could be) customers for the brokerage firm that employs them (hmm — could be bad). Frequently, this relationship can result in a brokerage report that paints an overly positive picture of a company that's a poor investment (yup, that's bad).

Sometimes, good research can be compromised by conflicts of interest.

During 1998–2000, a very large number of brokerage reports issued glowing praise of companies that were either mediocre or dubious. Investors bought up stocks such as tech stocks and Internet stocks. The sheer demand pushed up stock prices, which gave the appearance of genius to analysts' forecasts, yet they rose essentially as a self-fulfilling prophecy. The stocks were very overvalued and were flying on a wing and a prayer. Analysts and investors were feeling lucky.

The ugly

Investors lost a tonne of money (oooh, ugly). Money that was painstakingly accumulated over many years of work vanished in a matter of months as the bear market of 2000 hit (uglier). Retirees who had trusted some smooth-talking but slippery analysts saw nest eggs lose 40 to 70 percent in value (yikes, very ugly). In total, Canadian investors lost billions during 2000 and 2001, much of it needlessly.

A record number of lawsuits and complaints were filed against Canadian and U.S. brokerage firms. For Bay Street and Main Street, some tough lessons were learned. Regarding research reports from brokerage firms, the following points can help you avoid getting a bad case of the uglies:

- Always ask yourself "Is the provider of the report a biased source?" In other words, is the broker getting business in any way from the company that is being recommended?

- Never, never, NEVER rely on just one source of information, especially if it is the same source that is selling you the stock or other investment.

- Do your research before you rely on a brokerage report.

- Undertake your due diligence before you buy stocks anyway. Look at the chapters in Part I and Part II to understand your need for diversification, risk tolerance, and so on.

- Verify the information provided with a trip to the library, or from Web sites (see the Appendix).

Chapter 9

Investing for Growth

In This Chapter

▶ Defining growth stocks

▶ Figuring out how to choose growth stocks

▶ Looking at small caps and other speculative investments

Growth — actually watching your money grow — is the primary reason that investors choose stocks for their wealth-building portfolio. Keep in mind that growth stocks are a little riskier than average, but their potential for . . . um . . . growth is greater, too. If you're the type of investor who has enough time to let somewhat risky stocks trend upward, or enough money so that a loss won't devastate you financially, then growth stocks are definitely for you. The challenge is to figure out which stocks will make you richer quicker.

Short of starting your own successful business, stock investing is the best way to profit from a business venture. We want to re-emphasize that to make money in stocks consistently over the long haul, you must remember that you're investing in a company; buying the stock is just a means for you to participate in the company's success (or failure).

Why does it matter that you think of stock investing as buying a *company* versus buying a *stock?* Invest in a stock only if you are just as excited about it as if you were the CEO and in charge of running the company. If you were the sole owner of the company, would you act differently than if you were one of a legion of obscure shareholders? Of course you would. As the owner of the company, you would have a greater interest in the company. You would have a strong desire to know how the enterprise is doing. As you invest in stocks, make believe that you're the owner and take an active interest in the company's products, services, sales, earnings, and so on. This attitude and discipline will enhance your goals as a stock investor. This approach is especially important if your investment goal is growth. It can be fun to be involved!

Understanding Growth Stocks

A stock is considered a *growth stock* when it's growing faster and higher than stocks of other companies with similar sales and earnings figures. We say *higher than other companies* because you have to measure growth against something. Usually, you compare the growth of a company with growth from other companies in the same industry, or compare it with the stock market in general. In practical terms, when you measure the growth of a stock against the stock market, you're actually comparing it against a generally accepted benchmark, such as a specific S&P/TSX index, or the broader Standard & Poor's 500 (S&P 500). We discuss indexes in Chapter 5.

If a company has earnings growth of 15 percent per year over three years or more and the industry's average growth rate over the same time frame is 10 percent, then this stock qualifies as a growth stock. A growth stock is called that not only because the company is growing but also because the company is performing well with some consistency. Just because your Canadian company's earnings did great versus the S&P/TSX composite index's average in a single year doesn't cut it. Growth must be consistently accomplished.

Although comparison is a valuable tool for evaluating a stock's potential, you don't want to pick growth stocks on the basis of comparison alone. You should also scrutinize the stock's internal fundamentals to make sure that it has other things going for it to improve your chance of success. (See the next section, "Tips for Choosing Growth Stocks," for examples.)

We have asked people in investing seminars and classes, "What is Yahoo!?" Usually the answer we get is "It's a search engine," or "It's a Web site directory." Actually, Yahoo! is an advertising company. Yes, it does have a great search engine, but we label Yahoo! an advertising company because that's how it makes most of its money.

When choosing growth stocks, you should consider investing in a company only *if* it makes a profit and *if* you understand *how* it makes that profit. We know people who invested in Yahoo! and other companies in the Internet sector simply because they were excited about the potential of the Internet. Perhaps they just got caught up in the media hype. Then, from 2000 to 2003, most Internet companies started to crash and burn. Some died with a bang; others with a whimper. As Internet companies failed, Yahoo!'s revenue fell as well, because most of its money came from . . . Internet companies! So even though Yahoo! made money during some bad years, its sales and profits shrank in that time frame, and its stock fell 80 percent!

Unfortunately, many investors who bought Yahoo! shares didn't know *how* Yahoo! made money, so they couldn't have predicted that Yahoo!'s revenues would fall as sharply as they did. You need to know such information so that you can monitor the industry and more accurately predict whether the company you choose to invest in will continue to make money based on the likelihood that its customers, in turn, will be making money. For more on how industry success affects individual stocks, see Chapter 19.

Tips for Choosing Growth Stocks

Although the information in the previous section can help you shrink your stock choices from thousands of stocks to maybe a few dozen or a few hundred (depending on how well the general stock market is doing), the purpose of this section is to help you cull the so-so growth stocks to unearth the go-go ones. It's time to dig deeper for the biggest potential winners. Keep in mind that you probably won't find a stock to satisfy all the criteria presented here. Just make sure that your selection meets as many as realistically possible. But hey, if you do find a stock that meets all of the criteria cited, *buy as much as you can!*

Checking out a company's fundamentals

When you hear the word *fundamentals* in the world of stock investing, it refers to the company's financial condition and related data. When investors do *fundamental analysis,* they look at the company's fundamentals — its balance sheet, income statement, cash flow, and other operational data, along with external factors such as the company's market position, industry, and economic prospects. Essentially, the fundamentals should indicate to you that the company is in strong financial condition. Fundamentals are essentially the *vital signs* of a company — the things absolutely required to stay healthy and growing. A fundamentally sound company has consistently solid earnings, low debt, and a commanding position in the marketplace.

Chapter 15 goes into greater detail about analyzing a company's financial aspects. Here are several reasons to buy stock in companies that are in healthy financial condition:

- **Greater survivability during bad times:** Companies that have good earnings and sales and low debt are in stronger shape than companies that don't (duh!). When flash-in-the-pan growth stocks hit bad times, they wither and die. In 2001, many stocks that were once hot properties beloved by analysts and the talking heads on financial shows ended up filing for bankruptcy (the most obvious examples being Enron and WorldCom).

✔ **Takeover money to build strength:** A strong financial position gives a company the ability to make purchases that can further the company's strength. A purchase can be something as simple as an equipment upgrade or as complex as the acquisition of another company.

✔ **Marketing opportunities to ensure continued success:** A company's strong finances can help launch new products or pay for new ways of selling existing goods and services.

The companies that weathered the recent bear market the best and had somewhat stable, if not growing, share prices were those that prospered during tough times, exploited opportunities to buy out competitors or companies providing synergies, and stayed focused on their goals and strategies.

Deciding whether a company is a good value

You already know that a *growth stock* is the stock of a company that is performing better than its peers in categories such as sales and earnings. *Value stocks* are stocks that are priced lower than the value of the company and its assets. You can identify a value stock by analyzing the company's fundamentals and looking at some key financial ratios, such as the price to earnings ratio. (For more on that topic, see Chapter 15.) If the stock's price is lower than the company's fundamentals indicate it should be (in other words, it's undervalued), then it's a good buy — a bargain — and the stock is considered a great value.

Comparing growth and value stocks

Over the years, a debate has quietly raged in the financial community about growth versus value investing. Some people believe that growth and value are mutually exclusive. They maintain that large numbers of people buying stock with growth as the expectation tend to drive up the stock price relative to the company's current value. Growth investors, for example, are not put off by price to earnings (P/E) ratios of 30 or 40 or higher. Value investors, meanwhile, would be too nervous buying a stock at those P/E ratio levels. Which investing philosophy is right?

Believe it or not, incorporating both when possible is the best approach. A value-oriented approach to growth investing will serve you best. Long-term growth stock investors spend time analyzing the company's fundamentals to make sure that the company's growth prospects lie on a solid foundation. But what if you had to choose between a growth stock and a value stock? Which would you choose? Growth stocks tend to have better prospects for growth for the immediate future (from one to four years), but value stocks tend to have less risk and more steady growth over a longer term.

Evaluating your values

Value can be defined in many, many ways. Kind of like *pleasure*, the term probably means something different to each one of us. Investors of all feathers attach different meanings — a day trader can look at a small uptick and call a stock a value at a current price. Even among value investors, the definition of the word might vary. Not to settle the issue here (we can't), but we thought additional perspective might be in order. Timothy Vick, in his book *Wall Street on Sale* (McGraw-Hill, 1999), provides a few definitions of value that are recognized by U.S. civil law:

✔ *Fair market value* is whatever someone will be willing to pay for a similar asset — it's also called market value.

✔ *Book value* is a company's net worth on an *accounting* basis, which may differ from true financial value because of accounting rules, timing, and so on.

✔ *Liquidation value* (which is very subjective and hard to predict) is what a company would be worth if all its assets were sold.

✔ *Intrinsic value* is "what an appraiser could conclude a business is worth after undertaking an analysis of the company's financial position," based on assets, income, and potential growth. The value investor looks to establish intrinsic value. Only in some situations will the value investor take book or liquidation value into account.

The bottom line is that growth is much easier to achieve when you seek solid, value-oriented companies in growing industries. To better understand industries and how they affect stock value, see Chapter 19.

Learning from successful value-oriented-growth investors

Value-oriented-growth investing probably has the longest history of success versus most other stock investing philosophies. The track record for those who use value-oriented-growth investing is enviable. Warren Buffett, John Templeton, and Peter Lynch are a few of the more well-known practitioners. Each may have his own spin on the concepts, but all have successfully applied the basic principles of value-oriented-growth investing over many years.

What also made them stand out from the crowd is that they were truly disciplined, long-term investors; they didn't speculate or constantly jump in and out. Investors, especially in recent years, have become impatient, short-term–oriented, and lacking in discipline. They were all too easily buffeted by the trade winds of the day.

Appraising the value, relating the value to the price, and looking for a good bargain capture the essence of the value approach.

Looking for leaders and megatrends

A strong company in a growing industry is a common recipe for success. If you look at the history of stock investing, this point comes up constantly. Investors should be on the alert for megatrends because they also help to ensure your success.

What is a megatrend? A *megatrend* is a major development that has huge implications for most (if not all) of society and for a long time to come. Good examples are the advent of the Internet and the aging of Canada. Take the Internet, for example. Its potential for economic application is still being developed. Millions are flocking to it for many reasons. And Statistics Canada and other studies tell us that Canadians over age 55 will be the fastest growing segment of our population during the next decade. How does the stock investor take advantage of a megatrend?

Many people thought that the road to Internet riches was paved with dot-com businesses. Investors lost millions rushing into Internet stocks before they found out how these companies actually made money. The Internet is a very useful technology, and its business and economic impact will become more and more evident in the months and years to come. However, investors should understand how people and businesses can actually profit from the Internet. For example, when people ask what stocks would profit from the Internet, we say delivery and fulfillment services, online security firms, and other companies that are "plumbers" of the Internet. They look quizzically at us. "Huh? Why not invest in AMillionBucksRightNow.com?"

The serious investor says, "Hmm. Where is the money *really* being made on the Internet?" As hundreds of the dot-coms spend tons of money to establish their businesses, who is getting *their* money? That's right . . . delivery and fulfillment services, online security firms, and those that service Internet activity. Great examples of companies that service the Internet are Nortel Networks, Cisco Systems, and VeriSign. During the late 1990s, when the Internet megatrend was being established, Nortel was a phenomenal growth stock that turned many patient, alert investors into millionaires. What industries and megatrends seem promising right now? Think about this question as you look for potential growth stocks.

Considering a company with a strong niche

Companies that have established a strong niche are consistently profitable. Look for a company with one or more of the following characteristics:

- ✔ **A strong brand:** Companies such as McCain, Coca-Cola, and Microsoft come to mind. Yes, other companies out there can make French fries, soda, or software, but a business needs a lot more to overtake companies that have established an almost irrevocable identity with the public.

✔ **High barriers to entry:** Rogers Communications and Petro-Canada have set up tremendous distribution and delivery channels that competitors can't easily duplicate. High barriers to entry offer an important edge to companies that are already established.

✔ **Research and development (R&D):** Companies such as Biovail and Merck spend a lot of money researching and developing new pharmaceutical products. This investment becomes a new product with millions of consumers who become loyal purchasers, so the company's going to grow.

Noticing who's buying and/or recommending the stock

You can invest in a great company and still see its stock go nowhere. Why? Because what makes the stock go up is demand — there needs to be more buyers than sellers of the stock. If you pick a stock for all the right reasons and the market notices the stock as well, that attention will cause the stock price to climb. The things to watch for include the following:

✔ **Institutional buying:** Are mutual funds and pension plans buying up the stock you're looking at? If so, this type of buying power can exert tremendous upward pressure on the stock's price. Some resources and publications track institutional buying and how that will affect any particular stock. (You can find these in the Appendix.) Frequently, when a mutual fund buys a stock, others soon follow. In spite of all the talk about independent research, a herd mentality still exists. Money follows money!

✔ **Analysts' attention:** Are analysts talking about the stock on the financial shows? As much as you should be skeptical about an analyst's recommendation (given the recent stock market debacles), it offers some positive reinforcement for your stock. Don't ever buy a stock solely on the basis of an analyst's recommendation. Just know that if you buy a stock based on your own research and analysts subsequently rave about it, it bodes well for the stock price. A single recommendation by an influential and reputable analyst can still be enough to send a stock skyward.

✔ **Newsletter recommendations:** Newsletters are usually published by independent researchers (or so we hope). If influential newsletters are touting your choice, that praise is also good for your stock. Although some great newsletters are out there (you can find them within some of the Web sites listed in the Appendix) and they offer information that's as good or better than the research departments of some brokerage firms, don't base your investment decision on a single tip. (But it should make you feel good if the newsletters tout a stock that you've already chosen!)

✔ **Consumer publications:** No, you won't find investment advice here. This one seems to come out of left field, but it is a source that you should notice. Publications such as *Consumer Reports* regularly look at products and services and rate them for consumer satisfaction. If a company's offerings are well received by consumers, that's a strong positive for the company. This kind of attention will ultimately have a positive effect on that company's stock.

Learning investing lessons from history

A growth stock is not a creature like the Loch Ness monster — always talked about but rarely seen. Growth stocks have been part of the financial scene for nearly a century. Examples abound that offer rich information that you can apply to today's stock market environment. Look at past market winners, especially those of the 1970s and 1980s, and ask yourself, "What made them profitable stocks?" We mention these two decades because they offer a stark contrast to one another. The '70s were a tough, bearish decade for stocks, while the '80s were bullish times. Being aware and acting logically is as vital to successful stock investing as it is to any other pursuit. Over and over again, history gives you the formula for successful stock investing:

✔ Pick a company that has strong fundamentals, including signs such as rising sales and earnings and low debt. (See Chapters 13 and 15.)

✔ Make sure that the company is in a growing industry. (See Chapter 19.)

✔ Be fully invested in stocks during a bull market, when prices are rising in the stock market and in the general economy. (See Chapter 18.)

✔ During a bear market, switch more of your money out of growth stocks (such as technology) and into defensive stocks (such as utilities).

✔ Monitor your stocks. Hold on to stocks that continue to grow, and sell those stocks that are declining. (See Chapter 24 for some warning signals to watch out for.)

Evaluating the management of a company

The management of a company is crucial to its success. Before you buy stock in a company, you want to know that the company's management is doing a great job. But how do you determine that? If you call up a company and ask, it may not even return your phone call. How would you know whether management is running the company properly? The best way is to check the numbers. The following sections tell you the numbers you need to check. You will see that if the company's management is running the business well, the result is a rising stock price.

Return on equity

Although you can measure how well management is doing in several ways, you can take a quick snapshot of a management team's competence by checking the company's return on equity (ROE). ROE is a neat way to see whether the company is using its equity (or net assets) efficiently and profitably. The ROE is best expressed in the following table illustrating the balance sheet for Grobaby, Inc. (See Chapter 13 for more details on balance sheets.) The balance sheet is a simple financial statement that illustrates total assets minus total liabilities equals net assets (or "net equity"). For public stock companies, the net assets are called "shareholders' equity" or simply "equity."

	Balance Sheet	*Balance Sheet*
Grobaby, Inc.	December 1, 2002	December 1, 2003
Total assets (TA)	$55,000	$65,000
Total liabilities (TL)	–$20,000	–$25,000
Equity (TA less TL)	$35,000	$40,000

As you can see, this table provides a simple summary of the company's balance sheet — the formula of assets minus liabilities. Look at the balance sheet to discover the company's equity to help calculate the ROE.

Then there's the income statement. (Chapter 13 also goes into detail about it.) The *income statement* is a simple financial statement that expresses the equation sales less expenses equals net earnings (or net income or net equity). You want to look at a company's equity and relate it to the company's earnings.

	Income Statement	*Income Statement*
Grobaby, Inc.	Year 2002	Year 2003
Sales	$82,000	$90,000
Expenses	–$75,000	–$78,000
Net earnings	$7,000	$12,000

In the first table, you can see that Grobaby, Inc., increased the equity from $35,000 to $40,000 in one year. The second table shows that its earnings went from $7,000 to $12,000. The ROE for the year 2000 is 20 percent ($7,000 in earnings divided by $35,000 in equity), which is a solid number. The following year, the ROE was 30 percent ($12,000 in earnings divided by $40,000 in equity). For ROE, the higher the number the better. Any number higher than 10 percent is great, and Grobaby, Inc.'s management is sprouting some great numbers.

Equity and earnings growth

Two additional barometers of success are a company's growth of equity and growth in earnings. In the first table, Grobaby, Inc.'s equity grew by $5,000 (from $35,000 to $40,000), or 14 percent, which is very good. Also, look at the growth in earnings (in the second table). The earnings grew from $7,000 to $12,000, or a percentage increase of 71 percent ($12,000 less $7,000 equals $5,000, and $5,000 divided by $7,000 is 71 percent), which is excellent — management is doing good things here.

Insider buying

Watching management as it manages the business is important, but another indicator of how well the company is doing is whether management is buying shares in the company as well. If a company is poised for growth, who better to know than management? And if it is buying up the company's stock en masse, then that's a great indicator of the stock's potential. See Chapter 14 for more details on insider trading.

Figuring out whether a company will continue to do well

One of us met a senior credit officer at a bank who indicated that he never made a bad business loan in the 30 years that he was at his position. Never! He made some loans that went bad later, but he never made a bad loan. What's the secret of his success? He made loan decisions by looking at the company applying for the loan. If the company looked good, the loan was approved. But circumstances do change. The credit officer's experience is a very telling point that stock investors should be aware of.

The point of the preceding story is that a company's financial situation does change and that a diligent investor continues to look at the numbers for as long as the stock is in her portfolio. You may have chosen a great stock from a great company with great numbers in 2001, but chances are pretty good that the numbers have changed since then.

Great stocks don't always stay that way. A great selection that you're drawn to today may become tomorrow's pariah. Information, both good and bad, moves like lightning. In late 2000, Nortel was considered a cream-of-the-crop stock. Analysts fell over themselves extolling its virtues. Yet Nortel shocked investors as, quarter after quarter, it reported a series of massive losses. In late 2002 it was near bankruptcy — its stock price fell from a split-adjusted $250 in December 2000 to a staggering 67 cents a share in October 2002! All too many Canadians witnessed their equity portfolios dwindle. What's an investor to do?

Deciphering the key numbers of profitability

A great stock should continue to be great (or at least good), otherwise why hold it? This is where you look at the underlying company's fundamentals. Are they holding up well? The main numbers you should look at include the following:

- ✔ **Sales:** Are the company's sales this year surpassing last year's? As a decent benchmark, sales of a growth company should be at least 10 percent higher than last year.

- ✔ **Earnings:** Are earnings at least 10 percent higher than last year? Earnings should grow in tandem with sales (or, hopefully, better).

- ✔ **Debt:** Is the company's total debt equal to or lower than that of the prior year? The death knell of many a company has been excessive debt.

There's more to a company's financial condition than what we mention here, but these are the most important numbers. We also realize that using the 10-percent figure may seem an oversimplification, but one doesn't need to complicate matters unnecessarily. We know someone's computerized financial model will come out to 9.675 or maybe 11.07, but we keep it simple for now.

Exploring Small Caps and Speculative Stocks

Everyone wants to get in early on a hot new stock. Why not? You buy Shlobotky, Inc., at $1 per share and hope it zooms to $98 before lunchtime. Who wouldn't want to buy a stock that could become the next Biovail or Microsoft? This is why investors are attracted to small-cap stocks.

Small cap (or small capitalization) is a reference to the company's market size. _Small-cap stocks_ are stocks that have a market value under $1 billion. Investors may face more risk with small caps, but at least they also have the chance for greater gains.

Out of all the types of stocks, small-cap stocks continue to exhibit the greatest amount of growth. In the same way that a tree planted last year will have more opportunity for growth than a mature 100-year-old maple or oak, small caps have greater growth potential than established large-cap stocks. Of course, a small cap will not exhibit spectacular growth just because it's small. It will grow when it does the right things, such as increasing sales and earnings by producing goods and services that customers want.

Keep in mind that for every small company that becomes a Fortune 500 firm, hundreds of other companies fail to grow at all or go out of business. When you try to pick the next great stock before any evidence of growth, you're not investing; you're speculating. Have you heard that one before? Of course you have, and you'll hear it again. Don't get us wrong — there's nothing wrong with speculating. The important point is that you should know it when you're doing it. If you're going to speculate in small stocks hoping for the next Cisco Systems, then use the guidelines we present in the following sections to increase your chances of success.

Avoid IPOs, unless . . .

As we see in Chapter 1, initial public offerings (IPOs) are the birthplace of public stocks. This is the proverbial ground floor. The IPO is the first offering to the public of a company's stock. The IPO is also referred to as "going public." Because a company's going public is frequently an unproven enterprise, investing in an IPO can be risky.

Do you remember an IPO by the company Lipschitz & Farquar? No? We didn't think so. It was among the majority of IPOs that did not succeed. In recent years, investors have also lost a lot of money by investing in brand-new companies offering growth opportunities in high-tech and Internet businesses. Bid.com in Canada and eToys.com in the U.S. are two of many examples of Internet start-ups that ceased to exist within a few years of going public.

Yet, every great stock started as a small company going public. We can all recount the tales of Research in Motion, Biovail, Dell, Home Depot, and hundreds of other great success stories. Investors also found more assured opportunities for growth in well-established enterprises that went public. One example is Canadian National Railway. It was a stable and established enterprise when it was owned many years ago by the federal government. It proved increasingly profitable and innovative after it went public through an IPO. Sales and its stock price generally continued to grow from the time it was publicly offered. Today, CN is a dominant force in the North American railway system.

For investors, the lesson is clear: Wait until a track record appears, before you invest in a newly public company. If you don't, you're simply rolling the dice. Oh, one more thing ... at the moment, there aren't many IPOs to choose from. Battle-scarred investors now remember all too well that new companies are very risky investments. As a result, the IPO market has shrivelled to a shadow of its former high-flying self.

If it's a small-cap stock, make sure it's making money

You may recall that we emphasize two points when investing in stocks:

- ✔ Make sure that a company is established. (Being in business for at least three years is a good minimum.)
- ✔ Make sure that a company is profitable.

These points are especially important for investors in small stocks. Plenty of start-up ventures lose money but hope to make a fortune down the road. A good example is a company in the biotechnology industry. Biotech is an exciting area, but it's esoteric, and at this early stage companies are finding it difficult to use the technology in profitable ways. You may say, "But shouldn't I jump in now in anticipation of future profits?" You may get lucky, but understand that when you invest in small-cap stocks, you're speculating.

Investing in small-cap stocks requires analysis

The only difference between a small-cap stock and a large-cap stock is a few zeros in their numbers and the fact that you need to do more research with small caps. By sheer dint of size, small caps are riskier than large caps, so you offset the risk by accruing more information on yourself and the stock in question. Plenty of information is available on large-cap stocks because they're widely followed. Small-cap stocks don't get as much press, and fewer analysts issue reports on them. Here are a few points to keep in mind:

- ✔ **Understand your investment style.** Small-cap stocks may have more potential rewards, but they also carry more risk. No investor should devote a large portion of his capital to small-cap stocks. If you're considering retirement money, you're better off investing in large-cap stocks, bonds, bank accounts, and mutual funds. For example, retirement money should be in investments that are either very safe or that have proven track records of steady growth over an extended period of time (five years or longer).

- ✔ **Check with SEDAR or FreeEDGAR.** Get the financial reports of Canadian public companies through SEDAR (System for Electronic Document Analysis and Retrieval) at www.sedar.com. U.S. public companies must file their reports with the SEC (Securities and Exchange Commission) and you can access the reports through FreeEDGAR (Electronic Data Gathering, Analysis, and Retrieval) at www.freeedgar.com. (FreeEDGAR is free, but you have to register.) The reports you can access offer more complete information on the company's key activities and finances. You can also check to see whether any significant lawsuits have been filed against the company.

✔ **Check other sources.** See whether the stock is followed by brokers and independent research services, such as Value Line. If two or more different sources like the stock, it's worth further investigation. Check the resources in the Appendix for further sources of information before you invest.

Chapter 10

Investing for Income

In This Chapter

▶ Defining income stocks

▶ Selecting income stocks

▶ Looking at some typical income stocks

Investing for income means investing in stocks that will provide you with regular money payments (dividends). Income stocks may not offer stellar growth, but they're good for a steady infusion of money. What type of person is best suited to income stocks? Income stocks can be appropriate for many investors, but they are especially well suited for the following Canadians:

✔ **Conservative and novice investors:** These investors like to see a slow-but-steady approach to growing their money while getting regular dividend cheques. Novice investors who want to start slowly and avoid excessive risk also benefit from income stocks.

✔ **Retirees:** Growth investing is best suited for long-term needs, while income investing is best suited to current needs. Retirees may want some growth in their portfolios, but they're more concerned with regular current income that can keep pace with inflation.

✔ **Investors waiting out a bear market:** An aggressive investor in speculative and other growth stocks may recognize an impending bear market (we discuss bear-market signals in Chapter 18) and decide to shift temporarily to a more conservative strategy. These investors may still wish to be in stocks, but now see the usefulness of defensive stock sectors like utilities. Utility stock prices may not grow in leaps and bounds, but they're somewhat stable and pay dividends. (We discuss defensive income stocks in the next section of this chapter.)

If you have a low tolerance for risk, your investment goal is anything less than long term, and you're not averse to shifting stock investing strategies, income stocks may be your best bet.

Understanding Income Stocks

When we talk about generating recurring income from stocks, we're usually talking about *dividends*. As we indicate in Chapter 1 where we discuss dividends, a dividend is nothing more than money paid out to the owner of stock. A good income stock is a stock that has a higher-than-average dividend (typically 4 percent or higher) and is purchased primarily for income — not for spectacular growth potential.

A dividend is quoted as an annual number but is usually paid on a quarterly, pro-rata basis. In other words, if the stock is paying a dividend of $4, you would probably be paid $1 every quarter. If, in this example, you had 200 shares, you would be paid $800 every year (if the dividend isn't changed during that period), or $200 per quarter. Getting that regular dividend cheque every three months (for as long as you hold the stock) can be a nice perk.

Dividend rates are not guaranteed — they can go up or down, or, in some extreme cases, the dividend can be discontinued. Fortunately, most companies that issue dividends continue them indefinitely and actually increase dividend payments from time to time. Historically, dividend increases have equaled (or exceeded) the rate of inflation.

Advantages of income stocks

Income stocks tend to be among the least volatile of all stocks, and many investors view them as defensive stocks. *Defensive stocks* are stocks of companies that sell goods and services that are generally needed no matter what shape the economy is in. (Don't confuse defensive stocks with *defence stocks,* which specialize in goods and equipment for the military.) Food, beverage, and utility companies are great examples of defensive stocks. We need the products and services they provide. Even if the economy is experiencing tough times, people still need to eat, drink, and turn the lights on. Companies that offer relatively high dividends are also typically very large, established firms in stable or highly regulated industries.

The share price of income stocks may not rise as high or as fast as growth stocks, but they do have the ability to rise, which increases your potential to grow your wealth, in addition to the dividend the stock pays you. That's a potential bonus!

Some industries in particular are known for high-dividend stocks. Utilities (such as electricity, gas, and water) and real estate investment trusts (REITs) are areas where you definitely find income stocks. (Canadian REIT shares are technically referred to as *units*, and not shares. But they have a lot of similarities with income stocks since they have growth and income distribution potential.) Yes, you can find high-dividend stocks in other industries, but you will find the highest concentration of them in these two. For more details, see the sections highlighting some of these industries later in this chapter.

Disadvantages of income stocks

Before you say, "Income stocks are great! I'll get my chequebook and buy a batch right now," take a look at some potential disadvantages (ugh!). Income stocks do come with some fine print.

What goes up . . .

Income stocks can go down as well as up, just as any stock does. Obviously, you won't mind your income stock going up in value, but it can go down just as easily. The factors that affect stocks in general — politics, economic trends, industry changes, and so on — affect income stocks, too. Fortunately, income stocks don't get hit as hard as other stocks when the market is declining. This is because high dividends tend to act as a support to the stock price. Therefore, income stocks' prices usually fall less dramatically than the prices of other stocks in a declining market.

Interest-rate sensitivity

Income stocks can be sensitive to rising interest rates. When interest rates go up, other investments (such as corporate bonds, Canadian or U.S. treasury securities, and bank guaranteed investment certificates) are more attractive relative to income stocks. If your income stock is yielding 4 percent and interest rates are going to 5 percent, 6 percent, or higher, it can make you think, "Hmm. Why settle for a 4-percent yield when I can get a guaranteed 5 percent or better elsewhere?" As more and more investors sell their low-yield stock, the prices for those stocks fall.

Another point to remember is that rising interest rates may hurt the company's financial strength. If the company has to pay more interest, that may affect the company's earnings, which in turn may affect the dividend.

Dividend-paying companies that are experiencing falling revenues tend to cut dividends.

Inflation eats into dividends

Although many companies raise their dividends on a regular basis, some don't. Or, if they do raise their dividends, the increases may be small. If income is your primary consideration, you want to be aware of this. If you're getting the same dividend year after year and this income is important to you, rising inflation will be a problem. Say that you have XYZ stock at $10 per share with an annual dividend of 30 cents (the yield is 30 cents divided by $10, or 3 percent). If the yield were 3 percent last year and again this year, how would you feel if inflation were 5 percent last year and 6 percent this year? Because inflation means that your costs are rising, inflation shrinks the value of the dividend income you receive.

As you can see, even conservative-income investors can be confronted with different types of risk (Chapter 4 and Chapter 14 cover the topic of risk in greater detail). Fortunately, the rest of this chapter helps you carefully choose income stocks so that you can minimize these potential disadvantages.

Don't forget CCRA

Another downside of income stocks is that the dividends paid by stocks are taxable as income, subject to the Canadian dividend tax credit. This means that you have to report the money you receive in dividends as income to Canada Customs and Revenue Agency (CCRA).

Dividend income is taxed at a higher level (especially for investors in the highest tax bracket) than the taxes attributable to capital gains, where only one half of a capital gain is included in taxable income. For more information on the taxation of investment income, including capital gains, see Chapter 21.

Analyzing Income Stocks

You should look at income stocks in the same way that you do growth stocks when assessing the financial strength of a company. Getting nice dividends can come to a screeching halt if the company can't afford to pay them. If your budget depends on dividend income, then monitoring the company's financial strength is that much more important.

Minding your dividends and interest

Dividends are sometimes confused with interest. However, *dividends* are payouts to owners, while *interest* is a payment to a creditor. A stock investor is considered a part owner and is enti-tled to dividends when they are issued. When you get interest at the bank, the bank is pay-ing you this money because it borrowed the money from you and you're the creditor.

When comparing stocks that pay dividends, how do you know which one will give you the highest income? What if your hunt for income stocks boils down to two stocks, and Stock A pays an annual dividend of $5 while Stock B pays $4? Do you take Stock A with the higher dividend? Well, if both companies are similar and their stock prices are the same, then yes. But it's rarely that simple. Usually you have different stock prices to figure into the equation.

How do you decide which stocks will pay the most money? The main thing to look for in choosing income stocks is *yield* (the percentage rate of return paid on a stock in the form of dividends). Looking at a stock's dividend yield is the quickest way to find out how much money you'll earn from a particular income stock versus other dividend-paying stocks (or even other investments such as a bank account). Table 10-1 illustrates this point. Dividend yield is calculated in the following way:

Dividend yield = Dividend income ÷ Stock investment

Use the information in Table 10-1 to compare the yields from different investments and to see how evaluating yield can help you choose the stock that will earn you the most money.

Table 10-1		Comparing Yields		
Investment	*Type*	*Investment Amount*	*Annual Investment Income (Dividend)*	*Yield (Annual Investment Income ÷ Investment Amount)*
Smith Co.	Common stock	$20 per share	$1.00 per share	5%
Jones Co.	Common stock	$30 per share	$1.50 per share	5%
Wilson Bank	Savings account	$1,000 deposit	$40	4%

Most people have no problem understanding yield when it comes to bank accounts. If someone tells you that their GIC has an annual yield of 3.5 percent, you can easily figure out that if they deposit $1,000 in that GIC account, a year later they will have $1,035. The GIC's market value in this example is the same as the deposit amount — $1,000. That makes it easy to calculate.

How about stocks? When you see a stock listed in the financial pages, the dividend yield is provided along with the stock's price and annual dividend. The dividend yield in the financial pages is always calculated as if you bought the stock on that given day. Just keep in mind that, based on supply and demand, stock prices change virtually every day (every minute!) that the market is open. Therefore, the yield will change as well.

What if you bought stock in Skateco a month ago at $20 per share? With an annual dividend of $1, you know that your yield is 5 percent. But what if today Skateco is selling for $40 per share? If you look in the financial pages, the yield quoted would be 2.5 percent. Gasp! Did the dividend get cut in half?! No, not really. You're still getting 5 percent because you bought the stock at $20 instead of the current $40; the quoted yield is for investors who purchase Skateco today. Investors who buy Skateco stock today would pay $40 and get the $1 dividend, but the yield has changed to 2.5 percent, which is the yield that they lock into. So, while Skateco may have been a good income investment for you a month ago, it's not such a hot pick today because the price of the stock doubled, cutting the yield in half. Even though the dividend hasn't changed, the yield has changed dramatically because of the stock price change.

Another way to look at yield is by considering the amount of investment, using Skateco as the example. The investor who bought, say, 100 shares of Skateco when it was $20 per share would have paid only $2,000 (100 shares times $20 — leave out commissions to make the example simple). If the same stock were purchased later at $40 per share, the total investment amount would be $4,000 (100 shares times $40). In either case, the investor would get a total dividend income of $100 (100 shares times $1 dividend per share). From a yield perspective, which investment is yielding more — the $2,000 investment or the $4,000 investment? Of course, it's better to get the income ($100 in this case) with the smaller investment (a 5-percent yield is better than a 2.5-percent yield).

A final point about income stocks in general is that you don't stop scrutinizing them after you acquire them. You may have made a great choice that gives you a great dividend, but that doesn't mean that it will be that way indefinitely. Monitor the company's progress for as long as it is in your portfolio. Use resources such as finance.yahoo.com and www.stockhouse.ca (see the Appendix for more resources) to track your stock and to monitor how well that particular company is continuing to perform.

Tips for Selecting Income Stocks

Income stocks may be less volatile and less risky than growth stocks, but you still must do your homework when selecting them. The following sections introduce some important points to keep in mind before you choose an income stock.

Understanding your needs first

You choose income stocks primarily because you want or need income now. As a secondary point, income stocks have the potential for steady, long-term appreciation. So if you're investing for retirement needs that won't occur until 20 years from now, maybe income stocks aren't suitable for you — better to invest in growth stocks, because they're more likely to grow your money faster over your stated lengthy investment term.

If you're certain that you want income stocks, do a rough calculation to figure out how big a portion of your portfolio income stocks should occupy. Suppose that you need $25,000 in investment income to satisfy your current financial needs. If you have bonds that give you $20,000 interest income and you want the rest to be dividends from income stocks, you need to choose stocks that will pay you $5,000 in annual dividends. To obtain that $5,000 income if the investment amount that you have remaining to allocate is $80,000, you know that you need a portfolio of income stocks that provide $5,000 in dividend income or a yield of 6.25 percent ($5,000 divided by $80,000 equals a yield of 6.25 percent).

Use the following table as a general guideline for understanding your need for income:

Item	*Sample amounts*	*Your amounts*
A. How much annual income do you need?		$10,000
B. The Value of your portfolio (or money available for investment)		$150,000
C. Yield necessary to achieve income (divide item A by item B)		6.7%

With this simple table, you know that if you have $150,000 in income stocks yielding 6.7 percent, you would receive income of $10,000 to meet your financial needs. You may ask, "Why not just buy $150,000 of bonds (for instance) that yield at least 6.7 percent?" Well, if that $10,000 is sufficient for you and inflation for the foreseeable future is zero, then you would have a point. Unfortunately, inflation will probably be with us for a long time. This is where the feature of steady growth that income stocks may provide will benefit you.

The most sensible portfolio for income investors is obviously a mix of both dividend-paying stocks and bonds, so that you can have some measure of diversification. Even something as simple as a mix of 50 percent dividend-paying stocks and 50 percent bonds provides a balance of income and some growth potential (as well as reduced risk as an added bonus).

Obviously, the points in this section serve merely as illustrations for the uses of income stocks. Every Canadian investor is different. If you're not sure about your current or future needs, your best choice is to consult with a financial planner.

Checking the stock's payout ratio

The payout ratio tells you what percentage of the company's earnings are being paid out in the form of dividends. Keep in mind that companies pay dividends from their net earnings. Therefore, the company's earnings should always be higher than the dividends the company pays out.

Say that the company Urn More Corp. (UMC) has annual earnings of $1 million. (Remember that earnings are what you get when you subtract expenses from sales.) Total dividends to be paid out are $500,000, and the company has 1 million outstanding shares. Using those numbers, you know that UMC has earnings per share (EPS) of $1 ($1 million in earnings divided by 1 million shares) and that it pays an annual dividend of 50 cents per share ($500,000 divided by 1 million shares). The dividend payout ratio is 50 percent (the 50 cents dividend is 50 percent of the $1 EPS). This is a healthy dividend payout ratio because even if the company's earnings were to fall by 10 percent or 20 percent, it would still have plenty of room to pay dividends. People concerned about the safety of their dividend income should regularly watch the payout ratio.

When a company suffers significant financial difficulties, its ability to pay dividends is compromised. So if you need dividend income to help you pay your bills, you better be aware of the dividend payout ratio. Generally, a dividend payout ratio of 60 percent or less is safe. Obviously, the lower the percentage, the safer the dividend.

Diversifying your stocks

If most of your dividend income comes from stock in a single company or from a single industry, consider reallocating your investment to avoid having all your eggs in one basket. The same concerns for diversification you may have for a portfolio of growth stocks apply to income stocks as well. If all of your income stocks are in the electric utility industry, then any problems in the electric utility industry will be potential problems for your portfolio too.

Before you choose an income stock, look at the other stocks you currently have to make sure that they're not exposed to similar concentration risks, and select a new one from a different industry. For example, tobacco stocks usually have a nice dividend, but the tobacco industry has been experiencing legal and political challenges that offer special risks to the companies (and their dividends).

Examining the company's bond rating

Bond rating? Huh? What's that got to do with dividend-paying stocks? Well, corporate bonds are like government bonds, except that they come with slightly better yields than government bonds. BCE, Air Canada, and EnCana Corporation are examples of Canadian issuers of corporate bonds. Corporate bonds must provide better yields because they are riskier than the government variety. Companies may go out of business; governments generally do not. The services of bond rating agencies are needed to help assess this credit risk.

Bond rating agencies, such as the Dominion Bond Rating Service (www.dbrs.com), and Standard & Poor's (www2.standardandpoors.com), which includes the former Canada Bond Rating Service, are there to help. Both have similar rating schemes. Ratings of AAA, AA, and A are considered "investment grade" or of high quality. Bs and Cs indicate poor, speculative, or default grades. Anything lower than that is considered very risky (these bonds are referred to as "junk bonds"). Both assess, among other things, whether a company will have enough money to pay its interest obligations, and the full principal amounts at maturity.

The company's bond rating is very important to income-stock investors. The bond rating offers insight into the company's financial strength. To fully understand why this is important, consider the following:

- ✓ If the bond rating is good, that means the company is strong enough to pay its obligations. These obligations include expenses, payments on debts, and dividends. If a bond rating agency gives the company a high rating (or if it raises the rating), that's a great sign for anyone holding the company's debt or receiving dividends.

- ✓ If a bond rating agency lowers the rating of a bond, that means that the company's financial strength is deteriorating — a red flag for anyone who owns the company's bonds or its stock. A lower bond rating today may mean trouble for the dividend later on.

- ✓ If the bond rating is not good, that means that the company is having difficulty paying its obligations. If the company can't pay all of its obligations, then it will have to choose which ones to pay. More times than not, a financially troubled company chooses to cut dividends — or (in a worst-case scenario) not pay dividends at all.

Examining Some Typical Income Stocks

Although every industry has stocks that pay dividends, some industries have a greater number. You won't find too many dividend-paying income stocks in the high-tech or biotech industry; odds are that you won't even find one! The reason is that these types of companies need a lot of money to finance expensive research and development (R&D) projects to create new products. Without R&D, the company can't create new products to fuel sales, growth, and future earnings. High-tech, biotech, and other innovative industries tend to be industries of choice for growth investors.

Income stocks tend to be in established industries with established cash flows and less emphasis on financing or creating new products and services. When you're ready to start your search for a great income stock, start looking at utilities and real estate investment trusts — established industries with good track records — for high-dividend vehicles.

Utilities

Utilities generate a large cash flow. (If you don't believe me, look at your gas and electric bills!) Cash flow includes money from income (sales of products and/or services) and other items (such as the selling of equipment, for example). This cash flow is needed to cover things such as expenses, including dividends. Utilities are considered the most common type of income stocks, and many investors have at least one in their portfolio. Investing in your own local utility isn't a bad idea. You know that when you pay your energy bill, you're helping out at least one investor. Before you invest in a utility company, consider the following:

- ✔ **The utility company's financial condition:** Is the company making money, and are its sales and earnings growing from year to year? Make sure that the utility's bonds are rated A or higher for further assurance regarding the company's financial strength. Most Canadian utilities are owned by provincial and municipal governments, and are rated to reflect that. The risk is lower than for U.S. utilities, which are run mostly by the private sector.

- ✔ **The company's dividend payout ratio:** Because utilities tend to have a good cash flow, don't be too concerned if the ratio reaches 70 percent. Again, from a safety point of view, however, the lower the rate the better. See the "Checking the stock's payout ratio" section earlier in this chapter for more on payout ratios.

- ✔ **The company's geographic location:** If the utility covers an area that is doing well and offers an increasing population base and business expansion, that bodes well for your stock.

Real estate investment trusts (REITs)

A REIT is a "company." Although legally structured as a closed-end investment trust that owns, maintains, and manages real estate, most REITs boast enterprising, internal management running a truly sophisticated organization. Most Canadian and U.S. REITs are publicly traded on major Canadian and U.S. stock exchanges. These public REITs have their own ticker symbols and trade the same way as common stocks do. The vast majority of REITs are still American.

In North America, there are well over 200 publicly traded REITs to choose from (and over 20 in Canada). And in the same way that a mutual fund can provide you with a basket of publicly traded companies, a REIT lets you hold virtually any form of commercial real estate out there: office towers, malls, apartments, hotels, storage facilities, and even prisons! REITs buy real estate, manage it, develop it on their own (to a limited degree), or do a combination of these things.

Reasons REITs are right

During the recent bear market, investors flocked to REITs as a defensive haven of sorts. REITs also remain popular because they

- Provide generally positive returns over the long term
- Expose investors to lower risk and provide higher stability relative to stocks
- Provide generous dividend yields when compared to like income-generating instruments
- Offer capital appreciation potential
- Possess distinct tax advantages (deferred tax payments and reduced tax rates)
- Trade quickly and easily on major exchanges
- Represent a creative way to hold small chunks of real estate
- Benefit from good management in most cases
- Combine the best features of real estate, stocks, and mutual funds
- Are considered mainstream and proven by Canadian and U.S. investors

REITs versus real estate corporations

The key focus of Canadian REITs today is to provide *unitholders* with a reliable income stream from steady distributions. On the other hand, the returns from real estate corporation shares come mainly from capital gains related to the growth of cash flow or value of properties. Dividends from real estate corporations may be few and far between.

For a REIT, the upside potential to asset value is somewhat limited by the impact of both a high-percentage distribution payout ratio and limited debt (financial leverage) levels. In other words, there is a bit less cash flow left over to finance growth and to qualify for more debt to finance expansion.

The tax-wise REIT

REITs have some very special and significant tax benefits to the unitholder. A portion of distributions from a REIT will not be immediately included in your current year's taxable income. However, in the current year you are required to reduce your units' tax cost base by the amount paid or payable to you by a REIT. You will realize a higher capital gain (on a lower ACB) when the unit is sold at a future date. Depending on the REIT's structure and circumstances, up to 100 percent of the cash distribution can be received in this tax-deferred manner. This deferral represents one of the key tax benefits associated with REITs. A second benefit is that when you do sell your REIT units, only 50 percent of the capital gain is included in your taxable income. (We revisit the taxation of REITs in Chapter 21.)

Of course, REITs have disadvantages, too, including the following:

- ✔ **Real estate risks:** Owning shares in a REIT carries the same investment risks as any real estate investment. If the property owned by the REIT is in trouble, so is the REIT.

- ✔ **Less profit than direct real estate investing:** That's the trade-off. Because REITs offer less risk than buying real estate on your own, they also offer a lower return on your investment.

When you're looking for a REIT to invest in, analyze it the way you would analyze a property. Look at the location and type of the property. If shopping malls are booming in Vancouver and your REIT buys and sells shopping malls in Vancouver, then you'll do well. However, if your REIT invests in office buildings across the country and the Canadian office building market is overbuilt and having tough times, so will you.

Investing for income is an alternative to consider if you're a conservative or beginner investor. It's also great if you're a retiree who counts on stable income that keeps pace with inflation. Or, even if you're a wildly speculative investor, you can benefit from the shelter that income stocks provide during the dreary days of a bear market. Sometimes, when the stock markets get cold, windy, and dark, it's best to follow the lead of the bear, instead of standing in its weighty way. Follow it into hibernation for a few months. This approach can save you a bundle!

Chapter 11

A Stock Investor's Guide to Value Investing

In This Chapter

▶ Defining value investing

▶ Getting to know AGAP

▶ Understanding the value investing style

So you wonder . . . what happened? You look at the numbers, the charts, the graphs. The euphoria of the '90s bull market is just a memory. You were once flying high, checking your portfolio daily to see what had grown that day and by how much. JDS +4, NT +3.5, EMC +3. You totalled everything up monthly, quarterly, and yearly. You could rattle off the doubles, triples, home runs, and 10-baggers. You once bragged to your friends about how your stocks made more money than you did. You had a can't-miss attitude toward your stock selections, and you couldn't wait to tell your friends at the water cooler (well, the espresso machine) about your latest stock, your latest success.

But now you're just hanging on. Hoping, as if in an airplane passing through turbulence, that the pilot indeed has control of the plane and that eventually you will level off and perhaps even climb to a comfortable cruising altitude once again. Wouldn't it be great just to be flying level, not caring about the bumps or low altitude? You wonder if maybe, blinded by success and the euphoria of the moment, you missed something obvious in your investing practices. You wonder . . .

"Did I get caught up in a frenzy, like so many others have in history? Am I another Dutch tulip bulb trader? Another Florida land speculator? Another 1929 stock speculator? Was I really better than everyone else, a breed apart, or was I just part of the frenzy, part of the times?

"Were my stocks, my portfolio, my investing strategy really a breed apart? Should I have paid $35 for Certicom, $78 for Research in Motion, $85 for Amazon? With no earnings and few-to-no assets (except the cash already invested by others 'in the know')? Should I have believed those who were touting the New Economy in every newspaper and magazine, on every TV show — guests and brokerage analysts on Newsworld Business, pontificating that earnings don't matter, interest rates don't matter, that seemingly all the old investing yardsticks had been thrown in the trash heap, and that things really are different this time?

"Did prices get away from value? Should I have been thinking about my investments differently?"

If this sounds like you, you may be an ideal candidate to take up value investing. Or at least learn a little more about it. You're hardly alone — thousands of investors are self-assessing their investing styles, and many more-experienced investors have gone through this ritual before. If you've seldom or never invested before, you are also an ideal candidate for a value investing approach will make you less likely to experience the opening scenario. You know what they say about an ounce of prevention.

So what *is* value investing? It's a subject we revisit throughout this book. In this chapter, we try to fully define value investing, explain the value investing approach, and write a little about the traits of a good value investor. This chapter alone won't make you an expert, but it will at least enable you to know what others in the office are talking about when the topic of value investing comes up.

What Is Value Investing?

You were hoping for a simple, straightforward answer to this one. Learn a couple of formulas and go beat the markets once again. Well, partly right. Value investing goes beyond formulas. It's an approach, a style of investing. It doesn't provide a panacea or a quick fix to all of your investing problems. Rather, as an approach or style it provides the basis for you, the prudent investor, to apply your skills toward selecting better investments in a more rational, less speculative market.

Buying a business

Here's a definition:

Value investing is buying stocks as if you were buying the business itself. Value investors emphasize the intrinsic value of assets and current and future profits and pay a price equal to or less than that value.

Okay, sounds good so far. That's what you always did, right? Looked at the profile, looked at the industry, industry position growth rates, analyst ratings, yadda, yadda, yadda. But how closely did you look at the balance sheet? Income statement? Cash flows? Did you fully understand what you saw? Did you compare what you saw to other companies in the industry? Did you try to evaluate what the company was worth? Or did you merely rely on analyst projections of sales growth and income growth rates? Something else? How did you pick that company, anyway?

Moreover, what about the price? If you tried to value the company, did you _then_ check to see whether the price was below that value? Anywhere near it? Or did you look at the price first, noting its trend, relative strength over the last three months, volume, and steady up-and-to-the-right pattern? Did that pattern excite you? Did it cause you to jump on board, hoping that the train wouldn't leave the station without you? If you're in this latter camp, you weren't taking a value approach. And if you were listening to people in chat rooms and to investment "advice" from your room-service personnel, you were far removed from the confines of the value-investing world. It's not that these habits are necessarily wrong; they simply indicate something other than a value approach.

Making a conscious appraisal

If you were interested in buying a business for yourself and thought the corner hardware store looked attractive, how much would you be willing to pay for it? You would likely be influenced by the sale price of other hardware stores and by opinions shared by neighbours and other customers. But you would still centre your attention on the intrinsic economic value — the worth and profit-generation potential — of that business, and a determination of whether that worth and profit justified the price, before you committed your hard-earned dough.

Value investors like to refer to this as an _appraisal_ of the business. They appraise it just as one would appraise a piece of property or a prized antique. In fact, a business appraisal is deeper and more systematic than either of those two examples, as value is assigned to property or antiques mainly by looking at the market and seeing what other houses or vases of similar quality sold for. In the investing arena, there's so much more to go on. There are real facts and figures, all publicly available, upon which the investor can base a true numbers appraisal, an appraisal of _intrinsic_ value.

Appraising the value, relating the value to the price, and looking for a good bargain capture the essence of the value approach.

Putting on the pinstripes?

You've heard of the analysts. Those guys (and gals) who raise and lower earnings estimates and offer buy, hold, and sell recommendations. Those guys and gals who occasionally dress their recommendations up as *near-term neutral, long-term accumulate, market outperform,* or some other clever euphemism meaning buy, hold, or sell. They often get it right, but you would be surprised at the number of times the experts get it wrong, either making calls on horses already out of the barn or just blindly following the herd wherever it might wander. Our point here is not to blame the analysts — as fun as that may be — but to point out that in some sense, at least in normal times, they perform a task akin to value investing. They take a close look at the numbers and the company in their analytical process, but often they're influenced by their peers, their firms, and investor sentiment when making their calls. Whether or not you use or leverage their work is entirely up to you.

The point: Adopting the value-investing approach — and in fact just about any investing approach — requires you to *become your own investment analyst.* The pay can be good, but isn't guaranteed. One thing for certain: You'll never have to buy or dry clean a Harry Rosen suit!

Ignoring the market

In a recent letter to shareholders by Warren Buffett, he wrote that "Our managers concentrate solely on maximizing the long-term value of the *businesses* that they own." The bird of a value-investing feather is easily spotted. Focusing on the company itself, *not* on the market, is a consistent value-investing attribute. As a general rule, value investors ignore the market and could care less what the S&P/TSX, Dow, or Nasdaq do on a particular day. They tune out the analysts, brokers, commentators, chat-roomers, and friends (insofar as their investment advice is concerned, anyway). In his 2002 letter, Buffett mused about his fund managers, saying that "we now have six managers over 75 . . . our rationale: 'It's hard to teach a new dog old tricks.'" Old dogs won't follow trendy but risky investing fads.

Value investors have a long-term focus. And if they've done their homework right, what the market does to their stocks on a daily basis is irrelevant. If the company has value but the stock went down on Tuesday, a value investor feels that it's probably a result of the market misreading the company's value.

Now, to be sure, extrinsic factors can affect stock prices. Interest rates, in particular, can affect not only stock prices but also the true intrinsic value of companies, as the cost of capital rises and falls and the value of alternative investments increases. So while it makes sense to pay some attention to the markets, especially in the long term, daily fluctuations — particularly when they are *just* that — should be ignored. The value investor waits a few years to forever for their investments to mature (we bet *that's* a concept some of you haven't thought about in a while). The value investor looks for a good price with respect to value, but doesn't try to time the market. If the value is there and the price is right, it will probably be right tomorrow, too.

Setting the value-investing style apart

In Chapter 3, we briefly introduce other investing styles to you. You hear lots of talk about these other styles in the media. Terms like *fundamental and technical analysis, momentum investing, day trading, growth and income investing,* and *speculating* are all common to hear. Now, we'd like to compare the *value-investing* approach to these other styles. Specifically, we ask this question: Is a certain investing style also value investing?

All investing styles make money some of the time, but no one style makes money all of the time. Each style suggests a different approach to stock markets, the valuation of companies, and the valuation of stocks. As a teaching tool, explaining other investing styles is one of the best ways to illustrate what value investing is and is not.

Table 11-1 recaps the differences among the various investing styles introduced and discussed in Chapter 3.

Table 11-1	Comparing Investing Styles			
Investing Style	*Stock Price Driven By*	*Relationship between Price and Value*	*Buy Based On*	*Is It Value Investing?*
Fundamental	Financials, earnings, dividends	Price will *eventually* equal value	Positive or improving fundamentals	Yes Value investors look at fundamentals, then price
Growth	Earnings growth, growth prospects	Value will eventually equal price	Sustained or improving growth prospects	Yes Growth is part of the value equation
Income	Cash yield vs. alternatives	Price should equal value	Yield vs. alternatives, risk profile	Sometimes Income can be part of the value equation

(continued)

Table 11-1 *(continued)*

Investing Style	Stock Price Driven By	Relationship between Price and Value	Buy Based On	Is It Value Investing?
Momentum	Price trend, trend strength	Not related	Trend strength, relative strength	No
Speculation	Events, probability of occurrence	Usually none	Reward vs. risk	No
Story	Company story, market psychology	Not related	Timeliness	Can be part of intangibles of value investing
Technical	Patterns, trends, market psychology	Not related	Buy signals	No
Value	Intrinsic value	Price should be at or below value	Value obtained for price	Of course

AGAP: Assets and Growth at a Price

To help you remember what value investing is all about (and with so much to remember these days, a little help is probably a good thing), we would like to furnish you with an acronymic handle for the value investing approach: AGAP. This is the equivalent of tying a string to investors' fingers, to help them remember an important investing principle.

The value-investing approach is to apply AGAP principles. When examining a company for the first time (or when examining one of those dogs or puppies already lurking in your portfolio), you want to look through the AGAP lens:

- ✔ **Assets.** Does this company have the assets or the worth (deducting liabilities) to prosper in its business?
- ✔ **Growth.** Are there profits, and are profits on a growth path?
- ✔ **Price.** Finally, considering both assets and growth, is the price right? Is it a *bargain?*

Using an AGAP approach, you will be able to recognize and value assets and growth, and will gain the ability to assess whether the price is right. Consider AGAP as you make your investing decisions going forward, and you may save yourself some mouse-finger mistakes in the form of impulsive price- or market-driven investments. Even if you're not a value investor by definition, the AGAP criteria provide you with a good reality check.

Figuring out what should determine a stock price

Nobody knows what really does determine a stock price. If anyone did, you'd be reading his or her book, not ours. It makes sense at this juncture to add a little financial theory, but only a very little. You see, financial theory, with all its fancy equations and statistical constructs, hasn't really explained much. But we think it's useful to at least be aware of the fundamental basis of a stock price.

Financial scholars suggest that a stock price should be equal to the sum of all cash flows likely to be returned from that investment over the indefinite future, translated to an equivalent present value (a dollar 30 years from now will be worth less than a dollar today).

In the short term, this cash flow usually occurs in the form of dividends. In the long term, this cash flow is made up of dividends, but also includes proceeds from divesting assets to shareholders or proceeds if the company is acquired for cash or securities by another company. These cash flows are virtually impossible to estimate precisely, as they depend not only on the company's performance over a long time but also on management's policy toward payout. Nevertheless, this long-term view of value should be kept in the back of our minds. Enough theory for now.

Going beyond AGAP

We're going to go just a bit deeper, beyond AGAP, to add a little context. In our experience, relying on numbers alone is a bit dangerous. If you were a Nortel investor back in 1999 (and as widely held as Nortel was, that's somewhat likely), you probably felt pretty good about things. Strong brand, strong income growth, balance sheet looked okay, snazzy commercials — everyone was saying positive things about Nortel. But here was a company that made overly aggressive financial forecasts, was too far ahead of the curve on the latest but highly expensive optical technology, and whose biggest customers were already in trouble and slipping daily. The point is that it's important to examine the fundamentals and basics, but it's also important to understand the business context in which a company operates.

Expanding on AGAP, a company that has the "right stuff" will also perform *consistently* and possess the right *intangibles*.

Consistency

How steady is the business, how steady is the market that the business is in, how steady are the profits, and how steady is the growth? Going back to the hardware-store example from earlier in the chapter, before agreeing to buy the store you would want to know that the customer base is stable and that income flows are steady *or at least predictable*. If that's not the case, you would need to have a certain amount of additional capital to absorb the variations and perhaps a reserve for more advertising or promotion to bolster the customer base.

In short, there would be a certain uncertainty (oops, sorry about that!) in the business, which, from the owner's point of view, translates to *risk*. The presence of risk requires additional capital and causes greater doubt about the success of the investment for you or any other investors in the business. As a result, the potential return required to accept this risk and make you, the investor, look the other way is greater.

Intangibles

To be a good value investor, or any kind of investor who looks beyond ticker symbols, you must see behind the pure numbers. Looking at the market or markets in which the company operates is important. Looking at products, market position, brand, public and customer perception, leadership, opinions and actions of the investment community, and a host of others factors is also important. Intangibles — assets that are non-physical in nature but have value to a company — are one of these other factors. Intangibles include things like goodwill and patents. We look at these and other intangibles in Chapter 13 and Chapter 17. Here, we provide just the basics.

So now we're back to the example of Nortel, a company with lots of intangible assets. Nortel's statements looked okay, but there were problems with its intangibles such as a saturated market and customer solvency problems. Despite the seemingly high value of tangible and intangible assets on the balance sheet, difficulties were emerging with consistency and performance. There was a resultant lingering concern about price, which at 40 to 50 times earnings was rich and certainly demanded perfection. From a value standpoint, were investors in for a fall? You bet.

Take stock or not: Types of value investments

When you think about investments, you probably first think of stocks. Not a bad place to start, and for sure there are literally hundreds, probably thousands, of stocks that could be considered as value stocks. This book focuses primarily on assessing value in companies and investing in their stocks.

But other valid and occasionally exotic ways exist to play the value game. Most bonds are considered value investments for the income-oriented value investor. There are convertible bonds (bonds that offer a base income level with the added benefit of growth participation, as they are convertible to common stocks at a certain price). Value-oriented mutual funds are everywhere. And if true value can be represented to you only by something you can stand on and that they ain't making any more of, there's real estate and real estate investment trust (REIT) vehicles that can land you in value territory. (We introduced and discussed REITs in Chapter 10.)

The Value Investing Style

We've stated it before: Value investing is a style of investing. It's an approach to investing. You, as an investor, might adopt some of the principles presented here, but not all of them. You need to develop the style and system that works for you, and the knowledge available in the rest of this book will contribute to your style.

No magic formula

Some people buy and read investing books looking for a magic formula that guarantees success. Value investing isn't quite that simple. There are so many elements and nuances that go into a company's business that you can't know them all, let alone figure out how to weight them in your model. So, rather than having a recipe for success, you will instead have a list of ingredients that should be in every dish. But the art of cooking it to create a suitable value investment is up to you.

Like all other investing approaches, value investing is both art and science. It is more scientific and methodical than some approaches, but it is by no means completely formulaic. Why, if it were, everyone would use the same formula, and there would be no reason for a market! Stock prices would simply equal formulaic value. Wouldn't that be boring?

Perform due diligence

We can't say it enough: The value investor must do the numbers and work to understand a company's value. Although there are information sources and services that do some of the number crunching, you're not relieved of the duty of looking at, interpreting, and understanding the results. Diligent value investors review the facts and don't act until they're confident in their understanding of the company, its value, and the relation between value and price.

Nipping closely at the heels of diligence is *discipline.* The value investor does the work, applies sound judgment, and patiently waits for the right price. That is what has separated the masters like Buffett from the rest.

Diversify? Are you sure?

You've probably heard that the key to investing success is to diversify. It's mentioned on every talk show, and it's written about in every investing magazine. Diversification provides safety in numbers and avoids the eggs-in-one-basket syndrome, so it protects the value of a portfolio.

Well, yes, there's a certain truth to that. But again, borrowing from the masters we find that diversification serves only to dilute returns. That's right — it dilutes your returns! If you're doing the value-investing thing right, *you are picking the right stocks at the right price*, so there's no need to provide this artificial insurance.

But, golly gee whiz, maybe diversification isn't such a bad idea until you first prove yourself to be a *good* value investor. But remember, diversification is not a value-investing technique, and too many stocks will likely dilute returns. You can read more about this in Chapter 4.

Remember that it's not all or nothing

If you decide that you like the value investing approach, it doesn't have to be an all-or-nothing commitment. It's reasonable to mix investing styles. The value-investing approach should serve you well if you use it for, say, 80 percent or 90 percent of your portfolio. Be diligent, select the stocks, and sock them away for the long term as a portfolio foundation. But that shouldn't exclude the possibility of trying to hit a few home runs through more aggressive short-term tactics. These tactics can make you a lot of money a lot faster than traditional value investments, which may require years for the fruits to ripen. Of course, this doesn't mean taking unnecessary or silly risks; rather, it means that sometimes investments can perform well based on something other than intrinsic value. It doesn't hurt to try to capitalize on that, so long as you understand the risks and are willing to face losses.

Part III
Picking Winners

The 5th Wave   By Rich Tennant

"I opened with a big sale on 'CLOSED' signs, and no one came in. I decided to add some 'KEEP OUT' signs but still no one came in. But now I'm gonna invest in some 'BIO-HAZARD' signs – throw 'em in the window and see what happens."

In this part . . .

Now you know the basic stock investing theories, who to turn to for advice and stock brokerage services, and which style (or styles) of investing suits you best. You're probably itching to pick some stocks. When you have your choices narrowed, you want to look at specific financial information available about each company. This part shows you what the numbers in financial statements and other information in annual reports mean. You'll learn about more risks to be alert to, and how to further decode financial statements with straightforward ratio analysis. Then you'll get down into the mud pit and learn about the dirty tricks some companies like to play with their financial statements to make things look a lot better than they really are. Armed with the lessons in this part, you'll be ahead of the pack and poised to pick winning stocks.

Chapter 12

Debunking the Company Annual Report

· ·

In This Chapter

▶ Perusing an annual report

▶ Understanding what auditors can do

▶ Knowing where to find annual reports

· ·

*J*ust the thought of wading through financial documents probably makes your eyes glaze over. We know you'd rather wait for the movie. But this task isn't as bad as you think, and you really need to get familiar with corporate financial documents — because your financial success is on the line. Why? One of the key reasons that so many investors suffered losses in the stock market over the period covered by the recent bear market is that they did not understand the language of business — accounting. Specifically, they did not fully understand the message provided by financial statements and other financial information. (Another key reason for losses suffered was a blatant disregard for very real risks, which is covered in Chapters 4 and 14. We don't want to put all the scary stuff in just one chapter!)

In this chapter, we discuss the basic documents that you will come across (or should come across) most often in your investing life. How else will you know how well (or how poorly) a company is doing? There is some essential financial information that all Canadian investors need to know, not only at the time of the initial investment decision, but also for as long as that stock remains in their portfolio. This chapter will show you some basic but critical information in a clear light.

About the Annual Report

Once you're a regular shareholder, the company will send you its annual report. If you're not already a shareholder, contact the company's investor relations department for a copy. Also, more and more companies allow you to download their annual report from their Web site. A company's annual report (also referred to as the "shareholders' report") can help you keep track of the company's progress. This is a critical document, although it also doubles as a public relations tool for management's purpose. It is your job, as the investor, to *ooh* and *aah* at the nice graphics and carefully crafted prose while seeking out the critical nuggets of information regarding your stock and its potential future. It's also important to distinguish the gold nuggets from the gravel.

Before we get to the components of the annual report, we want to give you some convincing reasons to take the time to carefully analyze an annual report:

- ✔ **You want to know how well the company is doing.** Are earnings higher, lower, or the same as the year before? How are sales doing? These numbers should be clearly presented in the financial section of the annual report.

- ✔ **You want to find out whether the company is making more money than it's spending.** How does the balance sheet look? Are assets higher or lower than the year before? Is debt growing, shrinking, or about the same as the year before?

- ✔ **You want to get an idea of management's strategic plan for the coming year.** How will management build on the company's success? This is usually covered in the beginning of the annual report — frequently in the letter from the chairperson of the board.

Your task boils down to figuring out where the company has been, where it is now, and where it's going. As an investor, you don't need to read the annual report like a novel — from cover to cover. Instead, approach it like a newspaper and jump around to the relevant sections; get the answers you need to decide whether or not you should buy or hold on to the stock. Focus on the annual reports of companies you're heavily invested in.

If you plan to hold the stock for the long haul, reading the annual report and other reports covered in this chapter will be very helpful to you. If you intend to get rid of the stock soon or plan to hold it only for the short term, then reading these reports diligently isn't quite as critical.

Not every annual report is put together in exactly the same way — the style of presentation varies. Some annual reports have gorgeous graphics or actual coupons for the company's products, while others are in a standard black-and-white typeface with no cosmetic frills at all. But every annual report does include core basic content, such as the income statement and the balance sheet. The following sections present typical components of an average annual report. Keep in mind that every annual report may not have the sections in the same order.

Letter from the Chair — It Was the Economy's Fault!

The first thing you see is usually the letter from the chairperson of the board. It is the "Dear Shareholder" letter that communicates views from the Big Cheese. The chairperson's letter is designed to put the best possible perspective on the company's operations during the past year. Be aware of this bias. If the company is doing well, the letter will certainly point it out. If the company is having hard times, the letter probably puts a positive spin on the company's difficulties. If the *Titanic* had an annual report, odds are that the letter would have reported, "Great news! A record number of our customers participated in our spontaneous moonlight-swimming program. In addition, we confidently project no operating expenses whatsoever for the subsequent fiscal quarter." You get the point.

To get a good idea of what issues the company's management team feels are important and what goals they want to accomplish, keep the following questions in mind:

- ✔ What does the letter say about changing conditions in the company's business? How about in the industry?

- ✔ If there are difficulties, does the letter communicate a clear and logical action plan (cutting costs, closing money-losing plants, and so on) to get the company back on a positive track?

- ✔ What is being highlighted and why? For example, is the company focusing on research and development for new products or on a new deal with China?

- ✔ Does the letter offer apologies for anything the company did? If, for example, the company fell short of sales expectations, does it offer a reason for the shortcoming?

- ✔ Were there (or will there be) new acquisitions or major developments (selling stuff to China or a new marketing agreement with a very large company)?

The prototype of a great letter to shareholders is the one issued by Warren Buffett. You can access these annual letters at his company's Web site (www.berkshirehathaway.com). His folksy writing style, wit, and lessons for investors make this required reading for all serious stock investors.

What the Company Does

This section of an annual report can have various titles (such as "Sales and Marketing"), but it covers what the company sells. Whatever the company sells — products or services or both — understand what they are and why customers purchase them. If you don't understand what the company offers, then understanding how the company earns money, which is the driving force behind the company's stock, will be difficult. Are the company's core or primary offerings selling well? If earnings for McDonald's are holding steady but earnings strictly from burgers and fries are fizzling, that should be a cause for concern. If a company ceases making money from its specialty, be cautious. Here are some other questions to ask yourself:

✔ How does the company distribute its offerings? Is it through a Web site, malls, representatives, or some other means? Does it sell only to the Canadian market, or is its distribution international in scope? The greater the distribution channels, the greater the sales and, ultimately, the higher the stock price.

✔ Are most of the sales to a definable marketplace? If, for example, most of the company's sales are to Argentina, you should worry — because Argentina has been in dire economic straits since 2001. If the company's customers are not doing well, that will have a direct impact on the company and, eventually, its stock.

✔ How are sales doing versus market standards? In other words, is the company doing better than the industry average? Is the company a market leader in what it offers? The company should be doing better than (or as well as) its peers in the industry. If the company is falling behind its competitors, that doesn't bode well for the stock in the long run.

✔ Does the report include information on the company's competitors and related matters? You should know who the company's competitors are, because they have a direct effect on the company's success. If customers are choosing the competitor over your company, the slumping sales and earnings will ultimately hurt the stock's price.

Financial Statements and Notes — The Beef

Financial statements present a snapshot and summary of a company's financial condition. They are *the* key element of an annual report. Financial statements have three components — the income statement, balance sheet, and cash-flow statement. We delve into each component in Chapter 13, but here we provide an introduction and overview.

Financial statement items

Stock investors read the income statement (or the statement of earnings, or operations) to evaluate a company's profitability. Revenue growth trends and profit margins are just some of the important messages to be gleaned from this financial statement.

Look at the following sections of an income statement:

- ✔ **Revenues:** Are they increasing? If not, why not? By what percentage are sales increasing? Are they at least 10 percent higher than the year before? Sales are, after all, where the money is coming from to pay for the company's activities and future profit.

- ✔ **Expenses:** Are total expenses reported higher than the prior year, and by how much? If an expense item is significantly higher, why? A company with large, rising expenses will see profits suffer, which is not good for the stock price.

- ✔ **Earnings:** This figure reflects the bottom line. Are total earnings higher? How about earnings from operations (leaving out expenses such as taxes and interest)? This is the heart and soul of the income statement and of the company itself. Out of all the numbers in the financial statements, earnings have the greatest single impact on the company's stock price. They begin to reflect a company's ability to generate cash.

The balance sheet (or statement of financial position) is a snapshot of a point in time that shows the state of a company's assets (what it owns), liabilities (what it owes), and what's left over — equity. For a healthy company, assets should always be greater than its liabilities. Equity is one way to measure the value of a company. Among other things, this statement also lets you explore a company's liquidity position, and its debt load in relation to its assets.

Review the following key items found in balance sheets:

- ✔ **Assets:** Have they increased from the prior year? If not, was it due to the sale of an asset or a write-off (uncollectible accounts receivable, for example)?

- ✔ **Inventory:** Is inventory higher or lower than last year? If sales are flat but inventory is growing, that could be a potential problem.

- ✔ **Debts:** These are the biggest weakness on the corporate balance sheet. Make sure that debts aren't a growing item and that they're under control.

- ✔ **Derivatives:** A *derivative* is a speculative and complex financial instrument that does not constitute ownership of an asset (such as a stock, bond, or commodity), but rather a promise to convey ownership. Frequently used to generate income, derivatives carry risks that could increase liabilities. Options and futures are examples of derivatives. If a company has derivatives that are valued higher than the company's net equity, this could cause tremendous problems. (Speculating in derivatives was one of the major reasons behind Enron's bankruptcy.)

✔ **Equity:** Equity is the company's net worth (what is left in the event that all the assets are used to pay off all the company debts). The shareholders' equity should be increasing steadily by at least 10 percent per year. If not, find out why.

Another financial statement — the cash-flow statement — shows where cash is used, and where it comes from. It depicts how well management actually managed the cash. The statement of cash flow helps determine how well a company generates cash. At the end of the day, no company will survive in the long haul if it can't generate cash (after its expenses are paid off).

Statements, messages, and more

When you assess a company for potential investment, look at the messages behind the numbers found in each financial statement, and also in the messages contained in the notes to those statements. These notes put the numbers in a proper and understandable context (and are discussed in the next section). Ask yourself: Is the company doing well? Is it in decline? Is the debt load too high and risky? Several of the chapters that follow show you how to glean and evaluate the many messages found in financial information.

Financial statements show you the recent financial performance of a company. Because financial statements are essentially standardized within industry sectors, you can readily spot changes in a company's numbers, and also make meaningful company-to-company comparisons. Financial statements take the pulse of a business, and are the basis of stock valuation. It is a language that is important to understand at the basic level in order to become an effective stock investor.

Just like the analysts

Analysts of brokerage houses take the information in financial statements one step further — they use the information to assess a company's fundamental strengths and weaknesses, spot important trends, and compare that information to performance in the industry and to the overall economic environment. This book aims to teach you how to apply a few of these principles as well, and Chapters 15, 18, and 19 deal with ratio, business, and industry analyses.

It's not just about numbers

Financial statements are a solid starting point in evaluating a company, representing the numbers side of the business. But stock investors must also obtain additional qualitative information about the company's products and services, technology, research and development focus, intellectual capital, and other things that may set it apart from other companies. The annual report, the main subject of this chapter, contains a lot of this qualitative information. It contains loads of messages.

To recap, every annual report should have (at the very least) a balance sheet and an income statement. Catching the important numbers on a financial statement is not that difficult to do once you know the purpose of each component. It certainly helps all investors to gain some basic accounting knowledge, and Chapter 13 will help you boost yours. With this knowledge, and with other annual report information, evaluating companies you may be invested in will be easier, and you're much more likely to pick winning stocks.

Notes to financial statements

The notes to financial statements are also called footnotes. Carefully read the footnotes, since they tell you what the numbers mean. Sometimes big changes are communicated in very small print. Also, footnotes in annual reports are often longer and more numerous than those found in quarterly reports. It may be useful to obtain the most recent annual report to get a full set of notes, and thus the total picture. The typical categories of footnotes follow.

Significant accounting policies

Important revenue recognition and inventory valuation policies are found here. The way a company depreciates its assets may also be found here. (Depreciation is a downward adjustment made to the value of an asset for wear, tear, and age by allocating its cost over its estimated useful life.) Inventory policy helps you determine the cost of making sales — how much inventory the company started the year with, how much it produced, and what was left over. We discuss how some companies manipulate policies to inflate income and net assets in Chapter 16 and Chapter 17.

Receivables

The receivables footnote tells you how much cash the company can expect to receive from its customers, and the reserve taken to allow for doubtful collections. If the company has only a few large customers, it discloses the details behind this risk.

Debt

In a weak economy, this footnote is critical. It tells you about the amount of debt, its maturity, and how much interest cost is associated with it. If the debt has conditions (covenants) attached to it, determine whether the company is close to breaking those conditions. If it is, the risk of having the company's stock may be great. Having a loan called in is often the first step on the road to insolvency.

Financial instruments

Some companies conduct lots of international business trade in financial vehicles, or instruments, to offset foreign exchange, commodity, and other risks. These complex transactions, while totally legitimate, sometimes go awry, and the losses suffered by investors can be substantial.

Other liabilities

Companies sometimes have extra footnotes for special liabilities common to their business. Oil companies may have environmental liabilities. Drug companies may have settled some patent or health-related lawsuits that are large enough to be disclosed. If the company owes money, and the amount is considered large to the company, the disclosure often appears here.

Extraordinary gains and losses

The company may have experienced a significant windfall, or loss, that is atypical and irregular in nature. It's also usually a once-in-a-while type of event. Examples include significant write-downs of physical assets, or sale of a company property. These types of events are often disclosed in this footnote. While this may affect the bottom line net income figure in a big way, the key thing to remember is that this is not something that will happen over and over, and it has to be considered in that light.

Stock options

Stock options are granted to specified executives and other insiders of a company. They have the right, but not the obligation, to buy a predetermined amount of shares in the company at a set price. This footnote covers details about employee stock ownership and the number of stock options issued. These details are crucial to stock investors, because the more stock a firm issues the more dilution occurs — a bad thing for existing shareholders, who have to share dollar equity in the company with even more shareholders.

Pensions

Pension costs and obligations are detailed in footnotes. The footnote will include information about plan asset values, expected benefits, assumptions behind the numbers, actual benefits paid, and the investment returns of the plan. The amounts can be significant, so careful analysis of this footnote should be a priority to stock investors.

Limitations of footnotes

Although footnotes are required, there are no standards for clarity or brevity. Management is required to tell you nothing beyond the minimum required by accounting standards. Otherwise, they risk being sued. Where this minimum lies is based in most part on management's judgment. A balance must be struck between being as transparent as possible, and disclosing trade secrets and other key information about things that give the company its competitive edge.

Another challenge with footnotes is that sometimes a company will try to confuse you intentionally. Smoke and mirrors, and legal lingo, may mask some unpleasant but important issues. So don't rely on footnotes to get all the beef on the company.

Summary of past financial figures

Although this may not be required by financial accounting standards, some companies provide a summary of past financial figures. This information gives you a motion picture of the company's overall long-term progress. Some reports summarize three years, and some reports go back as far as ten years. It's great to spot trends.

Auditor's Report — Watching the Watchdog

The role of auditors is to independently examine a company's financial information and to make an assessment of its validity and accuracy. Certification by an auditor signals to investors that the company's fiscal statements conform to generally accepted accounting principles (GAAP). In Canada, most large public companies are audited by firms of chartered accountants (CA firms); the U.S. equivalent is firms of certified public accountants (CPA firms).

Annual reports typically include comments from the company's independent accounting firm about the financial statements (not the annual report). The auditor's report should offer an opinion about the fairness of the financial statements presented, and how the statements were prepared. Check to see whether the letter includes any comments regarding changes in certain numbers or how they were reported. For example, a company that wants to report higher earnings may show less depreciation expense by using a less aggressive method of depreciation that spreads (expenses) the cost of an asset over a longer period.

Many investors continue to ask why Enron and Worldcom's financial-statement audits did not expose to shareholders and other interested parties the shady schemes within those companies. What went wrong? What are the shortcomings of auditors' opinions?

One shortcoming of audits is the issue of potential conflicts of interest in the accounting industry:

- ✔ Although auditing firms are charged with protecting investors' interests, they are paid by the companies they audit. This can create an environment that makes it more difficult for firms to perform rigorous audits, because auditors may not wish to criticize management for fear of client loss. The accounting industry regards this fear as groundless, because an audit firm's reputation is at stake with every audit it performs.

- ✔ Throughout the last decade, as revenues from auditing fees declined, accounting firms turned to their consulting practices to generate higher profits. Many auditing firms are still making most of their money performing consulting services for customers, including their audit clients. This is a potential conflict of interest, since if an accounting firm is both auditing and consulting for a client, it loses its independence. It may be reluctant to perform a tough audit for fear of losing the lucrative revenues from consulting work.

- ✔ Some accounting firms have, in the past, tied auditors' compensation to their cross-selling of auditing and consulting services to a client. Many critics of auditors, especially in the U.S., seek a separation of auditing and consulting functions within auditing firms. They also want to see a strong, independent oversight board govern the industry.

- ✔ Another source of potential conflict of interest is that the auditing industry is generally self-policing. Auditing standards are set by Canadian and U.S. auditing bodies that are run by bean counters, and the bodies are funded in part by the industry. Notice something wrong with that picture? Although Canadian and U.S. accounting regulators have disciplinary authority to investigate accounting fraud, they are often slow-moving because they lack the resources necessary to aggressively pursue many investigations.

The other limitation of audits is that they were never meant to guarantee fraud-free companies. The auditor is charged only with providing reasonable assurance as to the fairness of financial statements.

Management Discussion and Analysis (MD&A) of Operations

The MD&A section of an annual report explains results achieved, compares them to expectations and prior results, and describes changes and current trends in the business. This section is where management brings to light operating issues (such as union negotiations), the use of new technologies, and market opportunities. It also provides a glimpse into some of the risks faced by the company, without alarming the reader.

See whether you agree with management's assessment of economic and market conditions that affect the company's prospects. What significant developments in society does management perceive as affecting the company's operations? Does the report include information on the risks it faces?

Where to Get This Stuff

Everything discussed in this chapter can be readily obtained in print, or on the Web.

The serious investor doesn't overlook the wealth of information that you can cull from documents filed with SEDAR, or with the U.S. Securities and Exchange Commission (SEC) through FreeEDGAR. (These document providers are introduced in Chapter 6.) Take the time and effort to review annual-report information, because it offers great insights regarding company activities. Here's how to obtain the main documents that investors should peruse:

- ✔ Drop by the company itself. Investor relations departments keep these publicly available documents on hand and usually give them at no cost to interested parties.

- ✔ Canadian publicly traded companies file annual reports that can be accessed through SEDAR (www.sedar.com). In the U.S., these reports can be accessed at FreeEDGAR (www.freeedgar.com).

- ✔ Use *The Globe and Mail* or the *Wall Street Journal* for their free annual report services. If you read these newspapers' financial pages and see a company name with the club symbol (like the one you see on a playing card), then you can order that company's annual report by calling the number indicated in the legend of the stock table.

When you search the SEDAR and FreeEDGAR databases you can also obtain other filings, such as quarterly financial statements (*10-Q Report* in FreeEDGAR), notices of material changes (*8-K Report* in FreeEDGAR), or a notice of annual or special meetings (*14-A Form* in FreeEDGAR).

Keep in mind that not every company has the same fiscal year. A company with a calendar-year fiscal year (ending December 31) files quarterly reports for each of the first three quarters, and files an annual report for the final quarter. The fourth-quarter data are reported in the annual report along with the statistics for the full year.

Chapter 13

Taking a Statement

· ·

In This Chapter

▶ Inspecting an income statement

▶ Taking a snapshot of assets and liabilities

▶ Assessing cash flows

▶ Staying alert for accounting red flags

· ·

*I*n the previous chapter, we introduce you to financial statements — a key component of the annual report. We discuss the fact that the income statement, balance sheet, cash-flow statement, and notes to financial statements provide you with a big picture of a company's financial health. In this chapter, we dig a little deeper into some of the main "line items" that make up each financial statement. These are the elements or components of financial statements that can have an important story to tell. We admit that accounting is not that exciting, so we will stick only to what you, as an investor, really need to know to be effective.

The Income Statement

It comes as no surprise to you that business and economic activity are undertaken with the idea of generating a *profit*. Because we're not writing an essay on political economy, we don't go into the detail of why that is or isn't a good idea. We'll leave that to others.

Profit is simply the gross revenue of an enterprise, less the cost of producing that income, over a defined period of time. So much is made these days of earnings and earnings reports. Do you hear much about a company's cash balance, accumulated depreciation, or owner's equity on Report on Business TV, MSNBC, and other financial shows? Does everyone salivate four times a year for "asset season"?

Earnings are *the* driving force and key indicator of a company's progress and success. If earnings are growing, the financial press doesn't worry much about the other stuff. Conversely, serve up a couple of double faults on the earnings front, and everybody is all over asset impairment, write-offs, debt, weak cash positions, and the like.

Long-term stock-price appreciation is based on the growth of a company's asset base and owner's equity in that base. If a company is generating cash, and particularly if it earns it at a growing rate, that's a good thing. As Warren Buffett says, "If the business does well, the stock always follows."

There are other earnings measures, such as free cash flow and "EBITDA," which we discuss later in this chapter. The point is that there are many ways to measure income. Each reveals an important aspect of business performance, both for determining the value of the company and for comparing companies.

Revenues — The top line

Revenues are the monies a company is owed for providing goods or services to another party. In large companies revenue recognition can be very complicated, and is one area that unethical managers like to manipulate. Revenue is also referred to as the *top line*.

In smaller companies, sales and revenues are straightforward. They represent accounting dollars generated for business products sold or services performed. (Remember, with accrual accounting it doesn't matter whether the company has been paid yet. If a sale meets accounting tests for recognition, sales can be booked even if cash is received later.)

In many businesses, such as transportation or utilities, the top line may be called *revenues*, but it's the same thing. Occasionally you will see an allowance for returns broken out; if not, you can usually safely assume that they've been factored out, and the sales figure reduced.

Cost of sales

A company's income statement shows how profitable a company's core operations are by indicating the revenue generated from sales of a product or service and deducting the costs associated with the company's products or services. Cost of sales (COS), or cost of goods sold (COGS), are costs that relate directly to the sale of products or services. For manufacturers, this figure includes labour expenses, material costs, and overhead costs (for example, a portion of electricity costs that relate directly to the products sold). COS or COGS for companies selling goods is technically the beginning inventory, plus the cost of goods purchased or manufactured during some period, minus the ending inventory.

When a company uses the terms *costs* and *expenses* in its financial statements, what it may really be trying to say is that costs are incurred to produce products or render services, and expenses are all the other stuff, like paying office rent and support staff.

COS is an important driver of business success. For all but a few companies with high intellectual property or service content, COS is the largest eater of the revenue pie. For example, the physical COS of Microsoft is tiny with respect to revenue, whereas a grocery store like Loblaws or a discount retailer like Zellers may see COS in the 70- or 80-percent range. Apples-to-apples comparisons are critical to effective analysis.

Grossed out on margins

Gross margin, or *gross profit,* is the difference between a company's total sales and its cost of sales. It is the basic economic output of the business before additional overhead, marketing, and financing costs enter the picture. Gross profit takes on added meaning when taken as a percentage. This percentage — and trends in the percentage — speaks volumes for the health and direction of the business.

Selling, general, and administrative (SG&A)

There is a section of every income statement that itemizes a series of expenses called "operating expenses." These are the expenses other than COS, and other than interest and taxes. SG&A expense is one of these operating expenses.

SG&A expenses are operating costs associated with sales, running the business, keeping headquarters, marketing, data processing, and administration. These expenses are "indirect" in nature. No matter the business, any company incurs indirect costs, or costs of doing business not *directly* related to producing and selling individual units of product or service. Some call it overhead; however, it goes a little beyond the traditional definition of overhead, and some overhead items we've seen are usually allocated to direct costs, or COS.

Many investors use SG&A as a barometer of management effectiveness — a solid management team keeps SG&A expenses in check. SG&A can mushroom into a vast slush fund and an internal corporate pork barrel that can easily get out of control. Like gross margin, looking at SG&A as a percentage is best.

Research and development (R&D)

This type of operating expense is common in pharmaceutical and technology companies, which need to make ongoing investments in future products. R&D can be rife with abuse, because if a company wastes money it can easily hide it in the R&D category. Because these investments occur long before products are produced, and because many of them never pan out into saleable products, companies are allowed by accounting rules to expense most research and development (R&D) as a period expense.

Also note that companies without a significant R&D effort may not report it as a separate line. In some financial statements it's called "product development."

Appreciating depreciation and amortization

Depreciation and amortization represent the accountant's assignment of the operating cost of a long-lived asset to specific business periods, or its estimated useful life. *Depreciation* is used when referring to physical fixed assets, and *amortization* is used when referring to intangible assets (such as goodwill, patents, and so forth). Some of you Canadian oil and natural resource investing bugs may run into the term *depletion:* a cost recovery for exhaustion of natural resource assets.

In our experience, depreciation and amortization (operating) expenses show up in a wide variety of ways on the earnings statement. Sometimes you'll see a specific breakout of depreciation expenses, especially for capital-intensive businesses. More often, depreciation expenses are buried in another operating-expense line, often SG&A.

Reserves

Reserves are operating expenses, or charges taken in anticipation of events that are likely to affect financial results. Reserves can be taken for things such as doubtful accounts receivable or other bad debts. Reserves are sometimes taken during the good years, and are used less in unprofitable years to smooth out the earnings numbers and make the company's operations seem more consistent than they really are.

A bit of EBITDA

Some companies and financial analysts like to use EBITDA, or *earnings before interest, taxes, depreciation, and amortization,* as their business-health barometer. EBITDA fans consider it the truest indicator of *operating* success. EBITDA measures operating cash generated before non-operating interest and before taxes and noncash depreciation and amortization. In a sense, EBITDA is operating income before accountants, bankers, and governments. EBITDA is sometimes looked at as a liquidity measure: Positive-EBITDA companies can service their debt, while negative-EBITDA companies must borrow more.

Although the desire for "pure" business measures makes EBITDA compelling, many investors look at EBITDA as a dangerous shell game. Sooner or later, a company must replace assets. A business can't proceed on the assumption that its assets will last forever, which is the

assumption that is made when depreciation and amortization are factored out. Ironically this is especially true for the technology businesses that favour this measure but sit on top of some of the most rapidly depreciating assets! And as for interest and taxes, they're facts of business life. Who are we kidding anyway? Watch out for glowing announcements of positive EBITDA when accompanied by losses on the earnings statement.

In his 2002 letter, Warren Buffett said that there were all too many "tabulations in which managers invariably show 'earnings' far in excess of those allowed by their auditors. In these presentations, the CEO tells his owners 'don't count this, don't count that — just count what makes earnings fat.' Often, a forget-all-this-bad-stuff message is delivered year after year without management so much as blushing."

Interest-ed and taxed

Interest and taxes are the corporate world's equivalent of the proverbial sure things. So, not surprisingly, space is reserved for them on the earnings statement.

Companies invariably have some form of interest income or interest expense, and usually both. Interest income comes primarily from cash and short-term investments reflected on the balance sheet, while interest expense comes, again not surprisingly, from short- and long-term debt balances. Interest reporting is usually done as a net interest — that is, by combining interest income and expense into a net figure.

Taxes are quite complicated, just as they are for individuals, and the details go beyond the scope of this book. There is normally an income-tax provision recorded as a single line item on the earnings statement, although this consists of myriad federal, provincial, and local taxes put together.

You don't need to pay too much attention to these areas, except where interest expenses are disproportionately high and growing. In most situations stock investors treat taxes as a given.

Income from continuing operations — we hope

What results from netting out (deducting) interest and taxes from operating income is *income from continuing operations*. From this figure you can get a good picture of company performance, from not only an operating but also a financial perspective. A close look at interest costs tells you, for instance, whether operating success (operating income) comes at a financial price (high interest expense). If operating income is low or declining while financing cost (interest) is large or increasing, look out below!

Income from continuing operations tells shareholders, in totality, what their investment is returning after everyone, including Canada Customs and Revenue Agency, is paid. Income from continuing operations is a good indicator of total business performance, but be aware of truly extraordinary events driving expenses or income.

Extraordinary items

Extraordinary items on an earnings statement are, according to accounting rules, to be tied to events that are atypical, irregular, and nonrecurring. *Atypical* events aren't related to the usual activities of the business, and occur rarely. *Nonrecurring* events aren't expected to occur again.

Extraordinary items commonly result from business closures ("discontinued operations") or major restatements due to changes in accounting rules. They may result from debt restructurings or other complex financial transactions. They may result from layoffs and other employee transactions. Extraordinary items generally are *not* supposed to include asset write-downs (such as receivables, inventory, or intangibles), foreign currency gains or losses, or divestitures. They are not the elements described in the section "They're such a special item" on the next page.

Our advice to you is to watch for extraordinary expenses that aren't so extraordinary. For example, companies that routinely have some kind of write-off every year or reporting period aren't doing as well as the investing community is being led to believe. If earnings are consistently $1 a share each quarter, with a consistent $4 write-off each year, the true value generated by the business is closer to zero than four.

Also, realized gains or losses on investments are non-recurring items and ought to be segregated on the income statement if significant in amount. Some companies may try to create the impression that these are regular income sources by excluding them from extraordinary, unusual, or special items.

They're such a special item: Impairments, investments, and other write-downs

When the value of an asset changes significantly in the eyes of management, a company can elect to take a write-down recognizing the change. The *write-down* shows up as a decrease in asset value on the balance sheet for the asset category involved, and (usually) as a one-time operating expense somewhere on the earnings statement. The rules for when and how to take these write-downs are, shall we say, flexible. The rules for writing down investment losses, a common theme in the technology arena, are particularly complex and beyond the scope of this book. The good news is that write-downs are normally reported as a separate line and are well documented in the notes.

For you as a stock investor, knowing the detail or amount may not be as important as knowing the pattern. Are these write-downs really one-time adjustments, or does the company continually overinvest in unproductive technology? Is a company quick to recognize mistakes, or does it push the financial impact of mistakes into the financial statements of future periods, towards ultimate fiscal oblivion? Write-down behaviour provides insight into management intentions and effectiveness as well as overall business consistency, and should not be ignored. We discuss how companies may try to manipulate earnings through special items in Chapter 16. Common special items include restructuring charges and discontinued operations, and these are discussed below.

Restructuring charges

Restructuring charges from continuing operations are those expenses, such as employee layoffs, maintenance, or early lease terminations, that are incurred when a company closes down or mothballs facilities, or writes off impaired assets. Since these assets would have been used up in the process of creating operating revenues, charges for restructuring these assets are usually factored into the calculation of net income. Massive employee layoffs and plant closings may indicate that the company does not expect future business activity to support current employee levels or the operation of plants, machinery, and equipment. Restructuring charges include real cash expenses, and not just allocations of expense.

Some companies take what is called the *big bath*. They write off as much as they can now, so that future earnings will look better through higher reported profits. Be mindful of manipulation in this area, one we revisit in Chapter 17.

Discontinued operations

When a company ceases part of its operations it has to report current results, but separately from operating results. This enables investors to make better comparisons from period to period, and creates a fairer representation of results.

Pension tension

After four years of declining stock markets, many large pension plans are underfunded. Companies are now reporting pension losses, instead of the gains they were accustomed to. These losses show up in a variety of forms, including special charges to earnings, cash flow, and equity, depending on the type of plan and the accounting rules involved. Although pension shortfalls may not be an immediate liquidity concern, they are often too large for investors to ignore. Keep an eye on pension expenses.

There you have it: Net income

Sales less COS, less operating expenses, less interest and taxes, less or plus extraordinaries and special items, give you a company's net income, sometimes referred to as *income attributable to common shareholders* or some similar phrase. Net income represents the final net earnings result of the business on an accounting — not necessarily a cash — basis.

Net earnings are usually divided by the number of shares outstanding to arrive at *earnings per share* — the common barometer heard in nearly all financial reports. Most analysts and investors focus on *diluted* earnings per share, which figure in outstanding employee stock options and other equity grants beyond actual shares outstanding.

The Balance Sheet

The balance sheet can be a great indicator of the financial condition of a business. It is a snapshot of assets, liabilities, and what's left over at a point in time. It tells you about where the company has been and how well it did getting there.

Many investors and business analysts look closely for the following in a balance sheet:

- ✔ The absolute and relative size of the numbers
- ✔ The makeup of assets, liabilities, and owner's equity
- ✔ Trends
- ✔ Valuation (assessing whether stated values reflect actual values)

Each of these examinations is done with an eye toward what the figure should be for a company in that line of business. A company such Tim Hortons, which has frequent, small cash sales, shouldn't have a large accounts receivable balance. A retailer like The Bay should have sizeable inventories, but it shouldn't be out of line for the industry and for its category. A semiconductor manufacturer like Tundra has a large amount of capital equipment but should depreciate it aggressively to account for rapid technological change.

To determine whether balance sheet numbers are in line, most analysts apply certain ratios to the numbers. Ratios serve to draw comparisons between companies, and between companies and their industry. By doing so, they detect whether performance is better or worse than industry peers. Ratio analysis is discussed in Chapter 15.

Cash and cash equivalents

For most businesses, cash is the best type of asset to have. With cash, there is no question about its value: Cash is cash! Cash equivalents are essentially cash. They're short-term marketable securities, such as GICs and term deposits, with little to no price risk, that can be converted to cash at a moment's notice.

Value investors in particular like cash. Cash is security and forms the strongest part of the "safety net" that value investors seek. Investors should question a cash balance only if it appears excessive against the needs of the business. Should a company put any extra cash to work in an investment or acquisition that might return more than the 3 or 4 percent it would get in a bank? And why isn't it being returned to shareholders as a dividend? Most companies don't retain that much cash, but occasionally it can become a red flag.

Accounts receivable

Accounts receivable represent funds that are owed to the business, for products delivered or services performed. As individuals, everyone likes to be owed money — until we're owed *too much* money. The same attitude applies to corporations.

Accounts receivable are driven by the type of industry that a company operates in. Obviously a small-sale retailer such as Tim Hortons operates mostly on cash — you don't give them an IOU for those Canadian Maple doughnuts, do you? Most companies that sell directly to consumers have few accounts receivable.

Contrast this to companies that sell to other companies (business-to-business) or to distributors or retailers in the supply chain. Most of this business is done *on account,* meaning that goods or services are delivered and invoices are then sent. The billing process creates an account receivable, which goes away only when the customer pays the bill. So suppliers to other businesses or through distribution and sales channels often have significant accounts receivable.

How much of a company's asset base should be made up of accounts receivable? Current thinking suggests that cash businesses such as Tim Hortons have 5 percent or less of their asset base in accounts receivable. Traditional retailers and other business-to-consumer companies have 20 to 30 percent or more in receivables if they provide credit through their own credit card. Equipment manufacturers and other business-to-business concerns sometimes carry receivables of 50 percent or more of total assets.

For most business-to-business industries, accounts receivable are a part of doing business and, in a sense, a *cost* of doing business (cash is forgone to give the customer time to pay). The question is, "How much commitment to accounts receivable is necessary to support the business?" You should be keenly aware of situations in which companies aren't collecting on their bills or are using accounts receivable to create credit incentives for otherwise questionable customers to buy their product.

To assign value to accounts receivable, pay attention to the following:

- The size of accounts receivable relative to sales and other assets: Is a company extending itself too much to sustain or grow the business? Industry comparisons and common sense dictate the answer.

- Trend: Is the company continuously owed more and more, with potentially greater and greater exposure to nonpayment? Look at historical accounts receivable and compare them to sales.

✔ Quality of accounts receivable: Typically, most companies collect on more than 95 percent of their accounts receivable balances, and thus these are almost as good as cash. But if accounts receivable balances grow, and particularly if large reserves show up on the income statement ("allowance for doubtful accounts" or similar), this is a signal flare that no investor should miss.

Some financial statements show "notes receivable" as a separate balance-sheet item under current assets. Notes receivable are essentially a special form of accounts receivable — a promissory note for a significant amount extended to a specific firm for a specific reason. For the most part, these should be treated like normal accounts receivable, but it might be worth a quick glance at the noteholder and the terms of the note to spot anything unusual.

Inventory

Inventory can be a critical, make-or-break asset and factor in company valuation. Companies live and die by their ability to effectively manage inventory.

Inventory is all valued material procured by a business and resold, with or without added value, to a customer. *Retail inventory* consists of goods bought, warehoused, and sold through stores. *Manufacturing inventory* consists of raw material, work in process, and finished goods inventory awaiting shipment.

For most companies, the key to successfully managing inventory is to match it as closely as possible to sales. That is, the faster that procured inventory can be processed and sold, the better. Money tied up in inventory is money that could not be invested elsewhere in the business. This is referred to as an *opportunity cost* of doing business.

Valuing inventory can be challenging. Companies don't provide much information about their inventories. The most information you'll normally get is a breakdown of how much inventory there was at the beginning of the year, how much inventory was purchased (or manufactured) during the year, and how much was left over at the end of the year. Little else is known about what those inventories really are, or about their real value. A warehouse of outdated Pentium I computer processors probably carries a book inventory value, but they aren't worth much on the market.

Inventory valuation is further affected by accounting methods employed by a firm. The method affects both balance-sheet carrying value and cost recognition on the income statement.

You need to appraise inventory balances for economic value and efficiency of use. Look at the size of the asset in an absolute sense and relative to the size and sales of the business. Look for trends, favourable and unfavourable, in inventory balances. Apply the inventory ratio analyses we discuss in Chapter 15. Look at competitors and industry standards. Where possible, look at inventory quality and past track record for inventory obsolescence and resulting write-offs. And then be conservative. It often makes sense to assign a value of 50 to 75 percent, sometimes less, to inventory values appearing on a balance sheet. The auditors could easily have dropped the ball when they counted and valued a client company's inventory!

Fixed assets

The balance sheet entry called "property, plant, and equipment" (PP&E) is pretty clear from the name. It refers to the fixed assets — land, buildings, machinery, fixtures, office and computer equipment, and similar items — owned by the firm for productive use. Depending on the industry, this item may have a different name. Retail stores, for example, don't have plants.

Valuation of PP&E can vary widely. The key to understanding PP&E value is to understand depreciation. *Depreciation* is an amount subtracted each year by accountants from an asset purchase price for normal wear and tear and technological obsolescence. Depreciation methods are discussed further under the next heading, but for now it's important to note that depreciation can affect underlying asset values substantially. The value of property, plant, and equipment, of course, can vary a lot by what it is, where it is, and how it's used. These in turn vary by industry and things specific to the company itself, such as its location.

Although most PP&E items are subject to depreciation charges, land is not. Is the value of land overstated on the books? Hardly. Land is normally carried at purchase or acquisition value. This affords a unique value-investing opportunity. Land purchased in the 1940s or 1950s is often worth much more today than back then, but it is seldom reflected in the books. There may be some real hidden gems lurking below the balance sheets of forestry, mining, and certain old-line industrial corporations.

There are a variety of accepted methods for assigning depreciation dollars. A detailed discussion of depreciation and depreciation methods is CA stuff that's well beyond the scope of this book. You may find it useful to recognize two major groupings of methods for assigning depreciation dollars: accelerated and straight-line depreciation.

The choice of depreciation methods is important. Accelerated depreciation results in the most conservative PP&E asset valuations. It also results in the most conservative view of earnings and allows more room for future net earnings growth, because you can assume that a greater portion of depreciation is behind you.

But some companies may deliberately prop up current earnings by employing straight-line methods. Watch for companies switching over to straight-line from accelerated methods. Depreciation methods are disclosed in the notes section of the statements.

Depreciation is an accounting — not a cash — expense. No cheque is cut for depreciation. Instead, the cheque is cut when the asset is purchased. Depreciation is the leading difference between stated earnings and cash flows and can mean the difference between survival and failure for a company recording net income losses. Cash flow, unburdened by depreciation, may still be positive. But look out below. Cash consumed to keep a losing business afloat may not be available the next time a key piece of equipment needs to be replaced. Reporting methods that downplay depreciation or ignore it altogether, such as the "pro forma" reporting craze, indicate trouble. For more info on this issue, see Chapter 16.

Investments: Companies are investors, too

Besides more-liquid marketable securities, many companies commit surplus cash to more substantial long-term investments. These investments can serve many purposes: to achieve returns as any other investor would, to participate in the growth of a related or unrelated industry, or to eventually obtain control of the company. Favourable tax treatment of Canadian dividends and gains makes investing in other Canadian companies more attractive still.

There are many ways to value investments, boiling down basically to historical cost or market valuation. Watch out for declining fair values and particularly for large *gross unrealized losses* — future write-offs and asset value impairment loom large. Gauge the size of investments on the balance sheet, look for details, and understand management's intent in making the investments.

Intangible assets

Asset valuation gets *really* fun for Canadian investors, and especially value investors, when the discussion turns to intangibles, also sometimes referred to as "soft" assets. *Intangibles* are non-physical assets that are critical in acquiring and maintaining sales and producing a competitive edge. Intangibles include patents, copyrights, franchises, brand names, and trademarks. Also included is the all-encompassing *goodwill* often acquired when buying (and overpaying for) other companies.

Placing a financial value on these ethereal and nebulous brand-related assets is difficult, but accountants seem to be able to pull it off. If there is a historical cost, accountants may carry the intangible at that cost. This is often the case with goodwill from company acquisitions or mergers.

The key to assessing intangible assets is to understand (1) their carrying value and (2) the amortization technique. Intangible assets should all be amortized, since patents expire, brand value may be diluted, and so forth. Goodwill from acquisitions most certainly — at least for now — must be amortized. Like depreciation, valuation depends heavily on the method of amortization. Basically the same choice is available between straight-line and accelerated amortization, and the chosen method is disclosed somewhere in the financial-statement notes.

Intangibles are subject to a great deal of discretion in their accounting, and their sources and form can be numerous and highly variable from one company to the next. Cast a skeptical eye on large goodwill accounts in particular, especially if a company seems reluctant to write them off. Value investing purists simply deduct intangibles from company valuation altogether. They are considered fluff, and a conservative valuation would remove them completely. In many cases where a company simply overpays to acquire another company, this is still true.

But with the advent of modern technology and marketing, the ideas of intellectual capital and brand equity are part of a company's value and cannot simply be ignored. In fact, for some companies, these intangibles may represent their greatest value. What is the value of the Coca-Cola Company without the brand name? Or the value of Microsoft without its lock on PC operating system design? Such brands and locks often ultimately produce the best profit streams and best value. Contemporary value investors need a clear understanding of intangible assets, and should not just dismiss them in an offhand way.

You can pay me now . . .

Almost everyone, individuals or corporations, has payables, defined as money owed to others for products purchased or services rendered. The liability is created when the service or product arrives; a cash payment follows later to discharge the liability. Nearly all companies maintain a regular balance of current accounts payable, interest payable, and the like.

If payment is received in advance, as with a deposit, the unearned portion is tracked as a liability. Sometimes *contingent liabilities* may be recorded, as in warranty claims expected to be paid but not yet actualized.

There is little for you to do with current liabilities except subtract them from intrinsic company value. But also realize that current liabilities aren't necessarily a bad thing and that they can result in higher effective returns on ownership capital with relatively low cost and risk.

Long-term liabilities

Long-term corporate liabilities are really no different than those in personal finance: They represent contracted commitments to pay back a sum of money over time with interest. For the individual, they come in the form of loans and mortgages; for the corporation, they occur more often in the form of tradable notes and bonds. The result, however, is the same.

As for short-term liabilities, you don't need to look too closely at the amount or quality of these liabilities. Trends can be important, however. Relying increasingly on long-term debt may be a sign of trouble. The company may not be making ends meet, and may be having trouble raising capital from existing or potential owners, which is never a good sign.

In addition, a company that's constantly changing, restructuring, or otherwise tinkering with long-term debt may be sending tacit signals of trouble. The company may be seeking concessions from lenders behind the scenes. In any event, attention paid to this kind of activity diverts attention from the core business, which is not a good thing and should be a warning flag for value investors.

Excessive use of debt signals potential danger if things don't turn out the way a company expects them to. Leverage is good when things are going a company's way. Debt financing can be used to produce more product for more markets — and, thus, more profit and in the end a bigger business. Return to owners is proportionately higher: Their investment stays the same while the returns grow. But as everyone knows, this can work the other way. Stock investors don't like surprises, and a company with uncertain prospects and a lot of debt is very risky.

Again, factor in liabilities as a negative in company and stock valuation and look for unfavourable trends or excessive use of long-term debt. Generally, liabilities don't require the close study that you might give to assets.

And now, meet the owners

Because you're contemplating making an investment in a company, isn't owner's equity (book value) the most important balance-sheet item? You and other investors are, in essence, either directly or indirectly contributing capital, which is in turn converted into an asset *and then* in turn converted into revenue and profit to produce a return to the owner. You're making a decision to allocate capital to a company that for its part tries to do the best job allocating capital to opportunities that produce the best return.

Owner's equity, or book value, is the sum of paid-in capital and retained earnings. It is assets (which can be valued and reported with a degree of latitude) minus liabilities (which occur at face value). Thus, book value reporting is done with a degree of latitude. Value investors talk about three different book value measures:

- Book value as owner's equity, or total book assets less liabilities
- Tangible book value, or total book value less all or part of intangibles
- Book value per share, or the accounting book value divided by the number of common shares outstanding

All three of these measures crop up in value investing discussions and papers; be careful, because sometimes they're used interchangeably.

Like liabilities, the equity portion of the balance sheet is critical to a company's function, but it really requires relatively little scrutiny on your part. We take you on a short tour but avoid the tedious discussions of classes of stock, par value, and the like that befuddle so many readers of financial stories. For this discussion, owner's equity consists of two things: paid-in capital — a fancy word for stock — and retained earnings.

Paid-in capital

Paid-in capital represents the total value paid into the company by its owners — its shareholders. It gets a little complicated with the discussion of par value and "additional" paid-in capital. Total paid-in capital represents capital actually paid into the company at initial or subsequent company stock sales and has nothing to do with market price or market value. You need to pay little attention to this item.

Retained earnings

Retained earnings are profits from past operating periods that are retained or reinvested in the business. Technically speaking, company profits belong to the shareholders, but it becomes management's option to decide whether to actually pay them out. Typically, managers think that they can invest the money more effectively than their shareholders. Stock investors of all stripes are betting that they're right!

So long as a company's business is viable, shareholders probably want to see retained earnings as high as possible, and growing. It's a capital allocation game — the earnings are better suited to that company's purpose than anywhere else. By investing in the company, you've already decided that, so you may as well keep your money on the table.

So generally, more is better, especially if accompanied by a reasonable dividend policy in which management *is* sharing some of the spoils with the owners. On the other hand, watch for rapidly declining or, worse, negative retained-earnings balances. Negative retained earnings are almost a sure sign of trouble, usually brought on by asset values declining faster than expected, excessive debt, an overinflated stock offering price, or a combination of the three. As a value investor, you should view negative retained earnings as another signal flare.

Statement of Cash Flows

Earlier we mentioned the difference in timing between certain accounting transactions and related cash collections and disbursements. Build it and ship it this month and record the revenue, even though cash payments may not arrive until months later. Buy and pay for a million-dollar machine today, but expense it over its production life through depreciation. Amortize a patent and never write a cheque at all.

These transactions and a host of others create differences between accounting earnings and cash measures of business activity. A business needs cash to operate. A business generating positive cash flow is much healthier than one that's bleeding cash and borrowing to stay afloat. Because of noncash items, earnings statements don't give a complete cash picture. So stock investors look for a statement of cash flows as a standard part of the financial-statement package.

Sometimes the statement of cash flows is called "sources and uses of funds" or something similar. Accountants use the terms *funds* and *cash* interchangeably.

The statement of cash flows tracks cash obtained in, or used in, three separate kinds of business activity: operations, investing, and financing. It also tracks dividends paid to shareholders.

Cash flow from operations

Similar to operating income, cash flow from operations tells you what cash is generated from, or *provided by,* normal business operation, and what cash is consumed by, or *used for,* the business. (*Provided by* and *used for* are the terms used on the cash-flow statement.) Net income from continuing operations is thus the starting point.

To that figure add (or subtract) the "adjustments to reconcile net income to operating cash flow." Here is where you *add back* depreciation and amortization dollars; that is, dollars that came out of accounting income but had no corresponding cash payment. So far, so good.

Next comes "cash provided by (used for) current assets and current liabilities." If this is familiar territory, and you understand how increases in current assets and liabilities affect cash, it makes sense to you that an inventory increase consumed some cash. Increases in liabilities *provide* cash. Decreases in liabilities *use* cash. (This concept is easier to grasp: it's a single cash transaction to pay a bill.) Increases in current assets (other than cash) *use* cash. Decreases in assets (as in a net decrease in inventory) *provide* cash.

Cash flow from investing activities

Cash flow from operations tells what cash was generated in the normal course of business and by changes in current asset and liability (working capital) accounts on the balance sheet. But what about cash used to invest in the business? Invest in other businesses? What about cash acquired by selling investments in other businesses? The second section of the statement of cash flow provides this information.

For most growing companies, while cash flow from operations should be positive, cash flow from investing activities is often negative. Why? Is this okay? Yes, because growing companies need more physical investments — property, plant, and equipment (PP&E) — to sustain growth. Generally, negative cash flows in PP&E suggest that the company is satisfied with its growth plan and feels that funds must be invested elsewhere for a maximum investment return.

"Free" cash flow

Free cash flow sounds like what we all want in our lives, eh? Positive cash flow, and it's free! Free cash flow is a good indication of what a company really has left over after meeting obligations, and thus could theoretically return to shareholders. For that reason, free cash flow is sometimes called "owner's earnings."

Free cash flow is defined as net after-tax earnings, plus depreciation and amortization and other noncash items, less annual capital expenditures, less (or plus) changes in working capital (current assets and liabilities).

Earn income, pay for costs of doing business, and what's left over is yours to keep as an owner. Pretty simple. Free cash flow is a much more realistic long-term view of business success and potential owner proceeds than EBITDA (which doesn't factor out as many cash costs) and is used by many investors, especially value investors, as the basis for calculating intrinsic value.

Cash flow from financing activities

Investing activities tell what a firm does with cash to increase or decrease fixed assets and assets not directly related to operations. *Financing activities* tell where a firm has obtained capital in the form of cash to fund the business. Proceeds from the sale of company shares or bonds (long-term debt) are a *source* of cash. If a company pays off a bond issue or buys back its own stock, that is a *use* of cash for financing.

A consistent cash flow from financing activities indicates excessive dependence on credit or equity markets. Typically, this figure oscillates between negative and positive. A big negative spike reflects a big bond issue or stock sale. In such a case, check to see if the resulting cash is used for investments in the business (probably okay), or to make up for a shortfall in operating cash flow (probably not okay). If the generated cash flows straight to the cash balance, you should wonder why a company is selling shares or debt just to increase cash, although often the reasons are difficult to know. Perhaps an acquisition?

Chapter 14

Recognizing Risk

· ·

In This Chapter

▶ Recognizing the types of risks that public companies face

▶ Being alert to certain risks

▶ Getting risk information to prevent investment losses

· ·

*I*n the previous chapter, we showed you the basics of reading financial statements. It's an important skill to have, not least because one of the key reasons that so many investors lost money in the recent bear market was their general disregard for financial performance. Instead of seeing first-hand — and in a very quick way — what companies owned, owed, and had left over, investors relied on analysts who scarcely had investors' best interests foremost in their mind. Others relied on media talking-heads who hyped the next big thing. Still others simply didn't want to perform the due diligence required to get an edge on other investors.

We now turn to a second critical area that was disregarded by investors — risk. While we introduce you to financial and personal risks in Chapter 4, there are more risks that companies face. Many more risks. Any risk a company faces automatically becomes your concern, because risks that come up to bite a company will invariably bite investors with a sharp share price drop.

In the recent bear market, people forgot that technology companies were exposed to piracy of their work, intense competition, and a very cyclical industry. They forgot that when markets go south, companies loaded with obsolete inventory and high debt see the grim reaper all too close to their doorstep. Perhaps investors simply didn't want to face up to risk. Ignorance, after all, was bliss.

This chapter reinforces the importance of understanding risk. Even if the company looked great after you first bought its stock, things change. New risks emerge. Knowing these risks and how to assess them sets the stage for your investment success.

Corporate Governance Risk

Good corporate risk control starts at the top. If the control at the top is poor, you can bet dollars to doughnuts that a culture of poor controls will trickle down to other areas of the company. Poor corporate governance creates a pervasive risk that's referred to as *corporate governance risk*. This risk area merits a deep look from any stock investor. Enron, WorldCom, and even smaller-scale disasters like Livent and Bre-X stemmed from the seeds of poor corporate governance.

The role of the board of directors

To understand what represents good corporate governance, it helps to review the role of the board of directors (BOD) of a public company. The BOD is responsible to the shareholders for overseeing the management of the company, and for the good stewardship and safekeeping of its assets. How does the BOD do this?

The BOD is responsible to set in place the company's systems of internal control, and to arrange for a review of their efficiency and effectiveness. Management control systems are designed to manage, rather than eliminate, the risk of failure to achieve corporate business objectives. These corporate objectives centre around efficient and effective operations, good reporting of results, and compliance to laws, regulations, and policies.

If Dell wants to remain the lowest-cost provider of personal computers, with fast delivery to customers, it will set checks and balances to help it achieve this. These checks may include state-of-the-art production facilities, precise reporting of costs and delivery times, and so on. One thing to remember is that even with reasonably effective management controls, the stock investor can obtain only reasonable, not absolute, assurance that the company will avoid large losses.

How the BOD manages risks

The processes adopted by the BOD to review the efficiency and effectiveness of the systems of management control include reviews of corporate strategy; major projects, investments, or divestments to be undertaken; and the external and internal audit work plans and resulting reports. Many BODs have delegated the oversight of risk to duly created sub-committees of the board, including risk-management committees.

Senior management's role in good governance: Rolling up the sleeves

The BOD manages risks through an *oversight* of corporate governance practices. It sets the tone. It ensures that all the management-control ducks are in a row. But the BOD does not make day-to-day decisions. Its members don't really have to roll up their sleeves — that's the job of senior management.

Since corporate governance is, by definition, a company's strategic response to risk, that response is made through decision makers — senior management. You can tell if management demonstrates basic corporate governance by spotting the following:

- ✔ **Strategic planning.** Does senior management, through press releases, shareholder meetings, or the annual report, demonstrate that it is developing strategic plans and objectives to fulfill the organization's purpose? This purpose may include market leadership, customer-service excellence, and similar high-level objectives.

- ✔ **Leadership.** Has management communicated, via the annual report or other communiqués, the organization's purpose in a *vision statement*? If a company lacks vision, and doesn't know where it is going on its journey, then it is like a rudderless ship. A vision statement is a strong image of a reality made possible by accomplishing the mission. (A *mission statement* tells you why you are beginning a journey.)

- ✔ **Organization design.** Has management established a company structure that makes it run efficiently and effectively? This includes having the right number and location of plants, offices, and staff.

- ✔ **Risk management.** Does management demonstrate an awareness of its risks in its annual report? Is it putting assets at risk to achieve the organization's objectives?

- ✔ **Assurance.** Does management provide feedback to shareholders on the efficiency and effectiveness of its governance and internal control processes? This includes publishing the external auditor's management letter (on internal controls), even if it doesn't have to.

Management's role in controlling risk

Before looking at other risks, it is important to point out that investors should not seek companies that eliminate risk altogether. Risk is an *opportunity* to companies, and companies take advantage of opportunities to make money. Each risk also has a different impact and likelihood, and must be handled and viewed differently. The risk of a flood destroying a plant is remote, but the impact to operations is likely huge. So, transferring this risk to an insurance company is the way to go. The risk of fraud in a company that sells home security systems has to be avoided at all costs. Such a company will make sure that it checks out employees, has good cash control, and has other checks and balances in place to avoid this risk to reputation as much as possible.

As a stock investor, the annual report you get will include a brief discussion of risks. This is likely to be found in the management discussion and analysis (MD&A) section of the annual report. A good discussion of risks will include the steps taken to manage risks. How a company handles its risks will help you better assess whether you've invested in a high-risk company, or one with fewer potential potholes. Look for evidence (in the annual report or even by calling the company's risk executive) of the following risk-management techniques:

- ✔ **Avoid.** Did the company redesign business processes or the physical infrastructure to avoid particular risks? For example, did the last fire result in fire emergency training, new sprinkler systems, and so on?

- ✔ **Diversify.** Did management spread certain risks among numerous assets or processes to reduce the overall risk of loss or impairment? For example, is sensitive and important backup medical data kept in an off-site data storage facility?

- ✔ **Control.** Were activities designed to prevent, detect, or contain adverse events or to promote positive outcomes? For instance, are employees who handle hazardous materials supported by proper prevention training, backup staff, and properly functioning equipment?

- ✔ **Share.** Did management distribute a portion of the risk through a contract with another party, such as an insurance company?

- ✔ **Transfer.** Has management distributed certain risks through contract with another party, such as outsourcing payroll or computer maintenance?

- ✔ **Accept.** Does management allow minor risks to exist to avoid spending more on managing the risks than on the potential damage?

When evaluating overall corporate governance risk, stock investors should also consider *strategic risk,* a risk that exists when bad business decisions are made, implementation of decisions is poor, or a lack of responsiveness to industry changes is apparent. Make sure that when you invest in a company, you understand what it does, why it is doing it, and how it will get it done. Warren Buffett simply avoids any business he does not understand, because he recognizes the importance of a good and well-communicated organizational strategy.

Back to the BOD

In terms of what you should look for in a company's board of directors that represents danger signs for stock investors, observe whether the

- ✔ Board is large (difficult to reach decisions)
- ✔ Chief executive himself appoints outside directors (potential conflicts of interest)
- ✔ Chairperson and chief executive are the same person (potential conflicts of interest)
- ✔ Outside directors have business dealings with the company (potential conflicts of interest)
- ✔ Outside directors are over the age of 70 (stale view of company)
- ✔ Outside directors are busy in that they serve on many other boards (efforts spread too thin)

Ethical Risk

There are several types of risk that can be viewed as stemming from failures in the ethical conduct of a company's management or other employees. Although good corporate governance at the BOD level helps to mitigate ethical problems, the risk of questionable or illegal acts is inherent in all companies.

Fraud

Fraud occurs when there is a lie (deception) and a monetary loss to the company. The lie may be a payroll clerk concealing the fact that there is a fictitious person on payroll, and the monetary loss may be the clerk impersonating that fictitious person to cash the payroll cheque himself. Fraud can also arise from intentional misrepresentation to a company's suppliers and customers. Examples of these fraud risks include theft, bid rigging, bribery, kickback schemes, and customer abuse (overbilling).

If the fraud is significant, you may be able to spot its existence in the notes to the financial statement dealing with litigation. Otherwise, it is usually an internal matter seldom disclosed to the public due to the damage that can be caused to reputation. If a company doesn't have to disclose something like this, it won't. As an investor, just take a quick look at the litigation footnote to see if there is any trend.

Conflict of interest

There may be instances of conflicts of interest where management or employees personally benefit from their positions in the organization. For example, a manager may compel the company he works for to buy goods or services from another company he has a financial interest in. This type of behaviour, if left unchecked, can lead the employee to even worse misdemeanours such as fraud.

In some cases of conflicts of interest — maybe even in the company you invest in — damages have to be paid, and the resultant negative publicity can harm a company's reputation and share price. Again, it is difficult to spot conflicts of interest because they are typically internal and very private matters. But if governance at the top is poor, there is invariably a trickle-down effect throughout the company. E-mail or phone your investor-relations contact to see if the company has a code of conduct that is communicated to all employees. Companies with policies about conflicts of interest have a lower risk of related fraud. As an investor, you may not be able to detect fraud that was already uncovered by the company. But you can see whether the company has policies in place to try to *prevent* fraud from happening in the first place!

Reputational Risk

Reputational risk is what you get when things go really wrong with corporate governance, management controls, and ethical breaches. Reputation is the corporate brand, and it's an extremely important attribute for any company to protect and grow. Reputation is also more than just *image*. Image is the immediate perception of a company; reputation is the stakeholders' collective social memory of the company and its activities.

Negative publicity regarding a company's business practices, whether true or not, will more than likely cause a decline in the customer base, costly lawsuits, and many other headaches. When Martha Stewart was indicted for alleged crimes related to insider trading, her company — Martha Stewart Living Omnimedia — suffered a blow to its reputation. It was guilty by association, and its share price sank.

Any company that fails to deliver on the expectations of its stakeholders — shareholders, customers, regulators, employees, and the larger community — risks experiencing a rapid drop in its share price. It is vital that everyone employed by or associated with the company you invest in (such as a BOD member) acts with the highest level of integrity and professionalism in all that they do.

One way you can spot reputational risk rearing its head is by reading media stories about a company, then following up by checking the press releases the company issues in response. Is a negative article just a case of media sensationalism, or does the story ring true? In other situations, the negative impact of a bad corporate reputation just creeps up on a company, and before you know it the stock is down 30 percent over the course of a year. You never knew that one by one, customers started to exit stage left. The key here is to never underestimate the negative impact of reputational risk.

When a company's reputation gets called into question by the court of public opinion, the punishment — a steep share-price drop — is much worse than the crime. The accused company will have been found guilty well before it had a chance to prove its innocence to shareholders.

Operational Risks

There are certain risks associated with core business operations. These risks don't generally come from the outside (like floods, legislative changes, and so on) but are mainly internal to the company's core business. These are the things that stand in the way of a company meeting its product- and service-related objectives.

Competition

Competitive risks involve marketplace strategy and positioning. They are a by-product of success. For example, increasing market share will provoke competitors to fight back. The only thing a company can do is prepare for the battle by keeping quality high and price low. If the company reports only losses, that may be an indicator to investors that it is not managing competition well.

Companies will respond to competitive threats. Assess those responses to see if they are well thought-out and wise. Be alert to the negative impact of some growth tactics — more advertising and marketing, price cutting, and so on. The boost in sales often does not last long. Be wary of companies that rely only on such strategies.

With many companies experiencing low profitability, mining for new sales can offer decreasing returns on greater effort. Favour companies that promote new products or enter new markets that make sense from a fit perspective. Keep in mind, however, that new markets may not respond the way others did. Look for evidence that the company has tested, or will test, new markets. Competitive risk is also increased if the company is short on expertise with new products or new markets. Big capital outlays may be necessary to hire expertise, so this will eat up cash. A scan of recent press releases and analyst opinions may provide you with this type of information.

Obsolescence

Inventory carries with it a significant risk of obsolescence. Changes in demand patterns, technology, or the nature of the product itself can cause inventory to lose its value quite rapidly. The most extreme example of obsolescence risk is in newspapers, where today's edition becomes almost 100-percent worthless at the stroke of midnight. But almost any other type of inventory has the risk of obsolescence associated with it. Other than jewellery, rare art, land, and similar items, few types of inventory are worth 100 percent of their purchase price, or anywhere near it.

Outsourcing

Many companies outsource parts of their business that are not considered core to their operations. When they do this, there is a risk that external service providers are not providing value for money. There is a loss of oversight and control over the third party and the business process that can lead to undesired losses or other negative outcomes.

Reliance on few customers or suppliers

Relying on single or even a handful of customers or suppliers presents an obvious "all your eggs in one basket" type of risk. You can spot this risk by examining footnotes to financial statements. Accounting standards require that companies disclose significant economic dependence on customers. Reliance on a few suppliers is also usually disclosed either in the footnotes or in the management's discussion and analysis section of the annual report.

Environmental risk

There are various environmental risks that can bite a company you invest in. Be watchful of the following potentially costly environmental risk areas:

- ✔ Air, water, and soil contamination and pollution
- ✔ Noise pollution to the surrounding area
- ✔ Resource wastage, where potentially recyclable materials are instead directed to landfill
- ✔ Deficiencies in protection of human health, cultural properties, endangered species, and sensitive ecosystems

> ✔ Use of dangerous and hazardous substances and materials
>
> ✔ Occupational health and safety issues
>
> ✔ Fire prevention and life safety
>
> ✔ Efficient production, delivery, and use of energy

Any shortfalls in this area invite expensive lawsuits, cleanup costs, fines, penalties, and damage to reputation. Most of us still remember the Exxon *Valdez*. Check out the contingency footnotes in the financial statements for insights into existing or potential environmental liabilities.

Legal

Legal risk arises from the potential for unenforceable contracts, lawsuits, or adverse judgments to disrupt or otherwise negatively affect the operations or condition of a company. Legal issues that are or can become significant are disclosed in the footnotes to the financial statements. These notes are a must to read, since litigation gone bad can destroy a company.

Other operational risks

There are several other operational risks that extend beyond those discussed above. Most of the operational risks we covered, however, are the key ones that apply to most businesses. So we trim our sails here and ease up on further discussion. We don't wish to bore you — just warn you! Just keep in mind that any loss resulting from inadequate or failed business processes, errors made by people, breaches in internal controls, poor reporting of operational results, fraud, or unforeseen significant problems represents an operational risk. Whenever operational problems are indicated, either in press releases or the media, try to identify the underlying causes. Is the cause isolated or recurring? Can it snowball into other problems such as damage to reputation or cash loss?

If the income statement shows recurring unusual or extraordinary losses, that may be an indicator that the company is exposed to undue operational risk. More and more companies are also starting to include management letters from external auditors in their annual reports. These letters discuss management-control weaknesses. If available, scan these letters and assess the significance of the problems. Give credit to any company bold enough to voluntarily disclose the management letter it may get from auditors on internal controls.

Information and Technology Risks

With information technology comes great benefits. Operations speed up, and costs often go down. But technology can also present some risks.

Piracy

Many people are simply unaware that copying software without a valid licence is piracy and therefore against the law, and that by copying software at work they're putting their employer at risk for charges of software piracy. Coming under investigation for software piracy can seriously damage a business's reputation, potentially causing a loss in market share due to poor customer perception.

Piracy of technology can also work the other way, where another company infringes on the patent owned by the company you invested in. You see a lot of this in the technology, biotechnology, and pharmaceutical industries. These are R&D–intensive industries, with lots of ideas floating around ripe for someone else to steal.

Piracy issues like those described above are serious matters. They can make or break a company. Be alert to them by scanning press releases.

Privacy

We can think of few things as destructive to the reputation of a company as when it inadvertently (or intentionally) releases confidential information to a third party. We often hear stories about medical information being hacked and sold to interested parties. Sometimes, sensitive information even gets posted on a Web site! The bottom line is that the e-business boom has created concerns about the security of personal information that is collected and used over the Internet, making privacy risk management a corporate priority.

Businesses must protect the large amounts of personal information exchanged in the transactions that move business. Company stakeholders are concerned about how their information is used, how it is secured, what controls are in place to correct erroneous information, and who this information will be shared with. Such information can include a person's name, contact information, age, occupation, salary, marital status, financial status, religious affiliation, nationality, credit card numbers, identity card numbers, medical records, and employment records. Can you imagine how you would feel if a company lost track of your personal records?

Any semblance of poor controls in this area means that customers may choose to do business elsewhere. Any failure by management to respond to privacy issues and risks can result in adverse consequences that range from loss of market to regulatory sanctions, loss of information flow, costly litigation, and damage to reputation.

As a stock investor, determine if there is a corporate privacy policy. Check out the company Web site for insights. How is privacy managed? What privacy failures have occurred in the industry, and what are consumer protection groups and privacy advocates saying about the issues?

Political Risk

More than any other external influence, politics — along with its sidekick, economics — sets the stage for stock investing success or failure. Politics (especially manifested in taxes, regulations, and legislation) can make or break a company or industry quicker than any other external risk. Economics — how people spend, save, and invest their money in society — also does its share to drive stock prices up and down. Understanding these effects on share prices will either save you a lot or make you a lot of money. (We discuss economics separately, later in this chapter.)

What is political risk?

Political risk is the risk of loss when investing in another country. It is caused by changes in a country's political structure or policies, such as tax laws, tariffs, expropriation of assets, or restriction in repatriation (the "taking back home") of profits. For instance, a company may suffer from such loss in the case of expropriation or nationalization of foreign assets.

A new tax, law, regulation, or government action has a *macro* effect on a stock, an industry, or even an entire economic system, whereas a company has a *micro* effect on an economy. The following gives you a simple snapshot of this trickle-down effect:

Politics → legislation → economy → industry → the company → the stock → the stock investor

If the world of politics produces undesirable legislative and economic policy, negative results will ultimately arise. If it produces positive legislative and economic policy, then positive results occur. A proficient stock investor cannot — *must* not — look at stocks as though they exist in a vacuum. Neither can politics be viewed in a vacuum.

When politics and its impact is considered from a global perspective, it's called geopolitics. *Geopolitical risk* recognizes that societies are integrated, and the action of one nation may create risks that are introduced into another. Stock and other capital markets play a greater role than ever in driving global economies. When the U.S. or another economic powerhouse sneezes, the rest of the world catches a cold.

The new millennium has ushered in an unprecedented series of crises and shocks. First and foremost came the September 11 terrorist attacks, with extreme human, physical, and financial destruction. Then followed chaos in Argentina. Skeletons emerged from the closets of Enron, WorldCom, and Dynegy. Bankruptcy records were set, jobs were lost, and pension savings withered away. The full burst of the technology bubble was complete. All this happened against the backdrop of Asian banks' bad loans, and the crises in Iraq and North Korea. The impact of these events exemplifies how geopolitics touches everyone.

Ascertaining the political climate

You ignore political realities at your own (economic) risk. To stay aware of political risks, ask yourself the following questions about the stock of each company in which you invest:

- What tax or similar laws will directly affect my stock investment adversely?
- Will any laws affect that company's industry?
- Will any current or prospective laws affect the company's sources of revenue?
- Will any current or prospective laws affect the company's expenses or supplies?
- Am I staying informed about political and economic issues that may possibly have a negative impact on my investment?
- Will such things as excessive regulations, price controls, or new taxes have a negative impact on my stock's industry?

Roll down the top

Top-down investing is an approach to investing in which an investor first looks at trends in politics and the general economy and then selects industries and companies that stand poised to benefit from those trends.

Oil and gas service and exploration companies recently benefited from the world need for more energy supplies. But investment opportunities didn't stop there. As oil and gas supplies became costly and problematic, alternative energy sources gained national attention. The debate was rekindled on solar power and exciting new technologies, such as fuel cells. Investors who spotted the trend in alternative energy sought companies that would logically benefit — a good example of this is Canada's Ballard Power Systems, recognized as a leader in fuel-cell technology, which saw its market capitalization quickly rise.

Economic Risk

When people comment about the economy, they make it sound like a giant, amorphous thing in the same way they talk about the stock market and the weather. To put it into perspective, the economy is you and me and millions of others — producers, consumers, entrepreneurs, and workers, all voluntarily trading money for goods and services day in and day out. People and organizations buy, spend, save, and invest billions every hour of every day.

Looking at the economy should be like seeing a huge picture and deciding where on the canvas are the greatest points of interest — investment opportunities. When you look at the economy, you look at the major numbers and trends and judge whether a particular company is well suited to profit from trends and opportunities. You simply rely on your common sense and apply it with the statistics that track the economy in general. If millions of consumers are buying product X, and the market and demand for X are growing, then it stands to reason that the best company offering product X will prosper as well. The reverse can also be true: If more and more people avoid, or just don't spend their money on, a particular product or industry, then the fortunes of those companies will decline as well.

Economic reports are important, because sometimes just one report or statistic is enough to move the stock market. The economic statistics and reports that are the most meaningful to you are the ones that have a direct bearing on your stock or industry. If you invest in real estate or construction stocks, reports that cover housing starts and interest rates are critical to you. If you invest in retail stocks, then information on consumer confidence and debt is important to you.

Industry trade publications and general financial publications, such as *The Globe and Mail* and *Investor's Business Daily,* regularly report on economic data. You can also find it (along with a tremendous database) at www.freelunch.com.

What are some important things in economic data that you should be aware of? Keep reading. The following sections make this information clear.

Grossing you out with GDP

Gross domestic product (GDP), which measures the nation's total output of goods and services for a given quarter, is considered the broadest measure of economic activity. Although it's measured in dollars (the U.S. GDP is currently valued at about $12 trillion, and Canada's is about $1.3 trillion), it is usually quoted as a percentage. You typically hear a news report that says something like, "The economy grew by 2.5 percent last quarter." Because the GDP is an important overall barometer for the economy, it should be a positive number.

You should regularly monitor this macro snapshot along with economic data that relate directly to your stock portfolio. The following list gives some general guidelines for evaluating GDP:

✔ **More than 3 percent:** This number indicates strong growth and bodes well for stocks. At 5 percent or higher, the economy is sizzling!

✔ **1 to 3 percent:** This figure indicates moderate growth and can occur either as the economy is rebounding from a recession or as it is slowing down from a previously strong period.

✔ **0 percent or negative (as low as –3 percent):** This number isn't good and indicates that the economy is either not growing or is actually shrinking a bit. A negative GDP is considered *recessionary* (meaning that the economy's growth is receding).

✔ **Less than –3 percent:** A GDP this low indicates a very difficult period for the economy. A GDP under –3 percent, especially for two or more quarters, indicates a serious recession.

Debt traps

Debt is the general reference for bonds, notes, home mortgages, and any other forms of paper evidencing amounts owed and payable on specified dates or on demand. Corporate debt is a non–government-issued, interest-bearing or discounted debt instrument that obligates the issuing corporation to pay the bondholder a specified sum of money at specific intervals, and to repay the principal amount of the loan at maturity. Consumer debt is similar to corporate debt, except that it involves credit cards, mortgages, and so on.

Debt can be very burdensome and can have a negative impact on economic growth. As an investor, you need to know how much debt is in the economy and whether the debt is growing or shrinking. Debt of all stripes can be a serious risk factor for investors.

A major reason for the economy's recent downturn was overexposure to debt. In fact, during the 1990s virtually every major category of debt hit record levels. The only ways to remove debt are to pay it off or go bankrupt. Because so many individuals and businesses became overextended in debt during that period, bankruptcies hit record levels as well.

Stock investors must monitor debt levels for bear-market potential. Too much debt slows the economy, which in turn can adversely affect the stock market. Overly indebted individuals don't have money to spend or invest. Overly indebted companies may face employee layoffs, cuts in spending, declining profits, and other negative actions. Watch also for corporate problems. If you have stock in a company that has too much debt, or that sells to customers who are overburdened with debt, then that company will suffer. The Bank of Canada and other sources, including such publications as the *National Post,* report consumer and corporate debt levels.

Raising confident consumers

As you often hear on TV, consumer spending accounts for two-thirds of the economy — so consumer behaviour is therefore a risk factor that investors should watch carefully. You can break down consumer activity into two categories:

- ✔ **Consumer income:** If consumer income meets or exceeds the consumer price index, that bodes well for the economy.

- ✔ **Consumer confidence:** This index is measured by prominent surveys that essentially track how the consumer feels about the economy in general and his personal situation in particular. The Conference Board of Canada and the University of Michigan perform the most widely followed surveys. If consumers feel good about the economy and their immediate futures, it bodes well for consumer spending.

Lumping together the data with economic indexes

Because so much economic data is available, many investors prefer to look at indexes that put the data in a nutshell. Indexes try to summarize many economic indicators and put them into a neat, digestible format.

Economic indicators are grouped into categories that try to give a rough idea about the economy's upward and downward cycle. These cyclical indicators are put in three categories that try to time the various phases of the economy's movement:

- ✔ **Leading:** The leading indicators try to be predictive of the economy's path. Stock investors are particularly interested in leading economic indicators, because stock investors usually do not invest because of past or present conditions — investors buy stocks because of expectations for the future.

- ✔ **Coincident:** The coincident indicators essentially tell you where the economy is right now. (For stock investors, most coincident indicators are like the indicator on your car's dashboard blinking "Hot" right about the time you see steam rising from your hood.) The most valuable coincident indicator is the GDP. (See the section "Grossing you out with GDP" earlier in this chapter.)

- ✔ **Lagging:** This type of indicator tells you what just passed in the economy's path (which can be significant because some lagging indicators do precede leading indicators). The unemployment rate is a good example of a lagging indicator.

Of the three categories, the most widely followed is the index of leading economic indicators (LEI). A good example of an indicator that is included in the LEI is the statistic on new construction. If more new construction is being started, that is a positive harbinger of economic growth. The LEI is compiled monthly by the Conference Board (www.conferenceboard.org). In Canada, you can find this information at Statistics Canada (www.statcan.ca).

Key leading indicators

The best indicators of an oncoming recession are not the widely followed data on retail sales, factory output, and employment. Instead, the more valid early-warning signs stem from forward-looking indicators signalled by financial markets and key surveys of business and consumer confidence. The financial market and confidence surveys offer a tremendous amount of early data that gets reflected months later in the higher-profile economic reports.

The National Association of Purchasing Managers index is important for stock investors. If it declines below 50, it indicates a contraction in manufacturing activity. This index is strongly related to GDP growth, and when combined with other leading indicators like business and consumer confidence it has signalled every recession in the past 40 years.

Additional leading indicators include these:

- **Consumer confidence:** Deterioration in consumer confidence is a big signal of an impending economic downturn. Drops of consumer confidence by more than 20 points below its 12-month average (as measured by indexes from Statistics Canada and the U.S. Conference Board) have often heralded the start of recessions. In other words, a sharp difference between expected and actual consumer confidence measures is a reliable signal that has often predicted recessions.

- **A sharp drop in consumer debt growth:** In the latter stages of an economic expansion, growth in product and service demand often outpaces the economy's ability to produce new output. Usually, this growth in demand is powered by credit card and other personal debt. A sharp slowdown in the growth of consumer debt is a key indicator that economic growth is slowing down.

- **Low real interest rates:** Real rates are the difference between the three-month T-bill rate and the rate of inflation. They measure the units of output that will be paid tomorrow, in return for lending one unit of output today. A high real interest rate is a signal that goods are scarce today and are expected to be plentiful tomorrow, and indicates expectations for future economic growth. A low or negative real interest rate is a signal that the market believes that goods are more abundant today than they will be tomorrow, which indicates that the market is predicting a recession.

- **Falling factory capacity utilization:** Declines in capacity utilization from more than 80 percent to below that level have generally pointed to the beginning of recessions.

- **Slowing employment and hours-worked growth:** The unemployment *rate* is a lagging indicator, and should not be used to predict forthcoming economic change. But *slowing growth* in employment and hours worked does in fact tend to accompany the beginning of recessions. For example, when payrolls have grown by less than 1 percent over a one-year period, or less than 0.5 percent over a six-month period, the economy is often at the start of a recession. Beginnings of recessions are also indicated by quarterly declines in total hours worked.

Chapter 15

What the Statements Mean: Ratio Analysis

· ·

In This Chapter

▶ Identifying the strengths and shortcomings of ratio analysis

▶ Examining the different types of ratios

▶ Interpreting specific ratios

· ·

*F*inancial analysts and accountants have developed many business ratios to assist them in evaluating the financial condition of a company. Ratio analysis can help you put things in proper context. Ratios measure the performance and financial condition of a company from year to year, and will help you compare various elements of a company such as profitability, debt load, and operating efficiency.

When a company's ratios differ from those of similar companies, they can serve as early-warning signals of problems — or opportunities. Ratios provide you with a lens to bring into clearer focus the reams of information that come from financial statements. Ratios explain the relationship between two or more numbers, thus providing you with scale and context.

Each ratio provides a clue into some aspect of company performance. Taken together, ratios provide a powerful overall message about the financial condition of a company. This chapter explores the different kinds of ratios and their use in stock investing.

Ratio-nal Analysis

Before delving into ratios, keep some points in mind. First, recognize that not every company or industry is the same. A ratio that seems problematic in one industry may be just fine in another. Second, one solitary ratio is not enough on which to base your investment decision. Look at several ratios covering the significant aspects of a company's finances. Third, look at several years of a company's numbers to judge whether the most recent ratio is better than, worse than, or unchanged from previous years' ratios.

Classes of ratios

There are four general families of ratios: liquidity, operating, leverage, and valuation. When evaluating a company from scratch, you may want to look behind all four of these "doors." When focusing on one aspect — for instance, leverage — you obviously want to focus on ratios that describe that particular aspect of the company.

Although we mention four families of ratios, different financial texts assign different categories and different names; for our purposes, the following four categories of ratios make the most sense:

- **Liquidity:** Measures of the extent to which a company can quickly liquidate assets and cover short-term liabilities. Liquidity ratios are of interest to short-term creditors, such as suppliers and banks. Liquidity is driven by the ability of an asset to be converted into cash quickly and without any price discount.

- **Operating:** Measures of a company's operating efficiency, such as sales to cost of goods sold, net profits to gross income, operating expenses to operating income, and net profit to net worth. Operating ratios also assess how well a company is managing its resources. Does it have too much inventory? Are receivables too high? Situations like these can impair the company's operations.

- **Leverage:** Measures of the degree to which a company is utilizing borrowed money. Companies that are highly leveraged may be at risk of bankruptcy if they are unable to make payments on their debt. They may also be unable to find new lenders in the future. Leverage is not always bad, however; it can increase the shareholders' return on their investment, and often there are tax advantages associated with borrowing.

- **Valuation:** The first three ratio families examine internal business fundamentals, or "intrinsics." When the valuation ratio's curtain opens, stock price makes a glorious and long-awaited entry. Valuation ratios, as the name implies, relate a company's stock price to its performance. The ubiquitous price to earnings (P/E) ratio shows up here, as do its lesser siblings, price-to-sales and price-to-book.

Knowing where to dial in

Anybody with an annual report and a calculator can analyze ratios. Almost all ratios take a pair of numbers from a company's balance sheet, earnings statement, or both.

Ratio analysis can be cumbersome and time-consuming, particularly when you're looking at a group of companies or an industry. Services that "do" the numbers (and particularly the comparisons) for you are hard to find — for free, anyway. A great deal of comparative industry ratio data is available to professional financial and credit analysts, but they pay hefty subscription fees to get it. The challenge is finding it for free (or nearly so). We stock investors like that sort of challenge, don't we?

Here are the best sources of ratio data and comparison we've found:

✔ **Free:** Yahoo!Finance is free. Tricky to find but easy to use, it's a useful resource for cost-conscious value investors. See "Turn On, Tune In: Compare Ratios" at the end of the chapter to learn how to access and use Yahoo!Finance.

✔ **Almost free:** Packagings of financial data from Multex and other financial-data providers sit behind specially constructed screens available from online brokers. Typically, the cost is opening an account. TD Waterhouse, for example, displays a predesigned set of fundamental ratios for different industries and their constituents.

✔ **For a modest fee:** Morningstar Canada (www.morningstar.ca) offers a free window to several key ratios. It doesn't present as many ratios or compare as much as Yahoo!Finance, but it covers Canadian companies better than Yahoo! does. For a fee, you can access Morningstar's PPM (premium portfolio monitor) tool, which offers you objective Morningstar data on more than 15,000 Canadian (and U.S.) stocks and other securities. PPM provides charts and reports of key information, including ratios. Pricing varies and is accessible at their Web site.

Fine-tuning

What does a stock investor look for when doing a ratio analysis?

✔ **Intrinsic meaning:** What does the ratio tell you? If the debt-to-equity ratio is 3 to 1, the company has a lot of debt. If the inventory-to-sales ratio is greater than 1, the company turns its inventory less than once per year. These numbers tell you something without your looking at any comparisons or trends.

✔ **Comparisons:** For many stock investors, and especially stock analysts trying to get a picture of a company's health, comparative analysis is the most important use of ratios. A ratio acquires more meaning when it's compared to direct competitors, the company's industry, or much broader standards like the S&P 500. A profitability measure, such as gross profit margin, reported at 25 percent tells more when direct competitors are at 35 percent plus.

When doing comparisons, be in tune with what you're comparing. Companies can be in many different businesses at once. It's tough to find pure plays in any industry. Realize that both Nortel and JDS Uniphase are both in the telecommunications sectors, yet essentially sell different products. Dell Computer is almost 100-percent in the PC business, while Hewlett-Packard derives only 25 percent of revenues from PCs. Compare apples to apples, compare red apples to green apples with caution, and avoid apples-to-oranges comparisons altogether.

✔ **Consistency:** The hallmark of good management, as well as of an attractive long-term investment, is consistency of results. If profit margins are consistent and changing (hopefully growing) at a consistent rate, the company is predictable — and most likely in control of its markets. Inconsistent ratios reflect inconsistent management, competitive struggles, and cyclical industries, all of which diminish a company's value.

✔ **Trends:** Better than consistency alone is consistency with a favourable trend. Growing profit margins, return on equity, asset utilization, and financial strength are all very desirable, particularly if valuation ratios (P/E and so on) haven't kept pace. A stock investor who studies trends carefully has information that most investors don't.

Enough of the preliminaries. On to the main event. Here, we present some of the key ratios in each category identified in this chapter.

Liquidity Ratios

Liquidity means the ability to quickly turn assets into cash; liquid assets are simply assets that are easier to convert to cash. Real estate, for example, is certainly an asset, but it's not liquid because it could take weeks, months, or even years to convert it to cash. Current assets such as chequing accounts, savings accounts, marketable securities, accounts receivable, and inventory are much easier to sell or convert to cash in a very short period of time. A balance sheet–oriented stock investor looks closely to make sure that the company will be around tomorrow (as many investors did in the 1930s and in the 2000s).

Paying bills or immediate debt takes liquidity. Liquidity ratios help you understand a company's ability to pay its current liabilities. The most common liquidity ratios are the current ratio and the quick ratio; the numbers to calculate them are located on the balance sheet.

Current ratio

The current ratio is the most commonly used liquidity ratio. It answers the question "Does the company have enough financial cushion to meet its current bills?" It is calculated as follows:

Current ratio = Total current assets ÷ Total current liabilities

If Holee Guacamolee Corp. (HGC) has $60,000 in current assets and $20,000 in current liabilities, the current ratio is 3 because the company has $3 of current assets for each $1 of current liabilities. As a general rule, a current ratio of 2 or more is desirable. A current ratio of less than 1 is a red flag that the company may have a cash crunch that could cause financial problems.

Quick ratio

The quick ratio is frequently referred to as the "acid test" ratio. It's a little more stringent than the current ratio in that it is calculated without inventory. I'll use the current-ratio example discussed in the preceding section. What if half of the assets are inventory (in this case, $30,000)? Now what? First, here's the formula for the quick ratio:

Quick ratio = (Current assets less inventory) ÷ Current liabilities

In the example, the quick ratio for HGC is 1.5 ($30,000 divided by $20,000). In other words, the company has $1.50 of "quick" liquid assets for each $1 of current liabilities. This amount is okay. *Quick liquid assets* include any money in the bank, marketable securities, and accounts receivable. If quick liquid assets at the very least equal or exceed total current liabilities, that amount is considered adequate.

The acid test that this ratio reflects is embodied in the question "Can the company pay its bills when times are tough?" In other words, if the company can't sell its goods (inventory), can it still meet its short-term liabilities? Of course, you must watch the accounts receivable as well. If the economy is entering rough times, you want to make sure that the company's customers are paying invoices on a timely basis.

You sometimes see another related ratio: cash to debt. The calculation is self-explanatory. It takes a still-more-conservative view of coverage assets (cash only), and a more pointed view of what needs to be covered (total debt, current and long-term portions).

Cash-flow ratios

Because cash is really the lifeblood of a business, financial strength assessments typically look at cash and cash-flow ratios. But there's a hidden agenda behind these ratios: to assess earnings quality.

Overall cash-flow ratio

This powerful ratio tells whether a business is generating enough cash from its business to sustain itself, grow, and return capital to its owners. Here's the formula:

Overall cash-flow ratio = Cash inflow from operations ÷ (Investing cash outflows + Financing cash outflows)

Operating cash flows represent, as the term implies, cash generated by normal business operations. They should be positive. If not, the company isn't generating enough cash to cover current expenses, let alone replace assets. *Investing* cash flows signify the acquisition or disposal of physical assets and are usually negative, assuming that the company is investing in its business or replacing fixed assets. *Financing* cash flows include proceeds from financing transactions, such as the sale of stock or debt (bonds). They can be either negative or positive, depending on current financing needs and strategy. See Chapter 13 for details.

If the overall cash-flow ratio is greater than 1, the company is generating enough cash internally to cover business needs. If it's less than 1, the company is going to capital markets or is selling assets to keep afloat.

Cash flow and earnings

Now let's talk quality. In Chapters 13, 16, and 17, we introduce the concept that different accounting methods can produce different results on earnings statements. Earnings can be managed up or down, depending on depreciation, amortization, noncash write-offs, revenue recognition, and so on. Comparisons of cash flow with earnings can be used as a quality audit to see how much noncash-accounting stretch went into a report.

You want to see cash flows to accompany earnings. If earnings increase without a corresponding increase in cash flow, earnings quality comes into question. A base measure is the following:

Cash flow to earnings = Cash flow from operations ÷ Net earnings

Because depreciation and other noncash amortizations vary by industry, it's hard to hang a specific goal on this measure. Consistency is good. Favourable industry comparisons also are good. Further, it's good when period-to-period earnings increases are accompanied by corresponding cash-flow increases.

The stock investor's general rule (as with most other ratios): Compare liquidity to industry norms and watch for unhealthy trends. Liquidity ratios don't tell you so much what to buy as what *not* to buy.

Operating Ratios

Operating ratios essentially measure the company's efficiency. "How is the company managing its resources?" is a question commonly answered with operating ratios. If, for example, a company sells products, does it have too much inventory? If it does, that could impair the company's operations. The following sections present common operating ratios. We start with the bigger-picture ratios (that relate bottom-line profits to assets, equity, and sales), and end off with more specific ones (that relate specific balance-sheet or income-statement items to other items of a similar nature).

The return on equity (ROE)

Equity is the amount left from total assets after you account for total liabilities. The net equity (also known as shareholders' equity, stockholders' equity, or net worth) is the bottom line in the company's balance sheet, geographically as well as figuratively. It is calculated as

Return on equity (ROE) = Net income ÷ Net equity

The net income (from the company's income statement) is simply the total income less total expenses. Net income that is not spent or used up increases the company's net equity. Looking at net income is a great way to see whether the company's management is doing a good job growing the business. You can check this out by looking at the net equity from both the most recent balance sheet and the one from a year earlier. Ask yourself whether the current net worth is higher or lower than it was the year before. If it is higher, by what percentage is it higher? Use the ROE in conjunction with the ROA ratio (see the following section) to get a fuller picture of a company's activity.

Return on assets (ROA)

The ROA may seem similar to the ROE, but it actually gives a perspective that completes the picture when coupled with the ROE. The formula for figuring out ROA is

Return on assets = Net income ÷ Total assets

The ROA reflects the relationship between a company's profit and the assets used to generate it. If the company HGC makes a profit of $10,000 and has total assets of $100,000, the ROA is 10 percent. This percentage should be as high as possible, and it should generally be at the same rate as the ROE.

Say that the company has an ROE of 25 percent but an ROA of only 5 percent. Is that good? It sounds okay, but there is a problem. If the ROA is much lower than the ROE, this indicates that the higher ROE may have been generated by something other than total assets — that's right: debt! The use of debt can be a leverage to maximize the ROE, but if the ROA doesn't show a similar percentage of efficiency, then the company may have incurred too much debt. In that case, investors should be aware that it could cause problems down the road.

Return on sales (ROS)

This ratio is just as it sounds:

Return on sales = Net earnings ÷ Sales

Return on sales (ROS) tells you how much profit a firm generated per dollar of sales. This figure is much better known as the *net profit margin.* Closely related is gross margin, which we cover in Chapter 13:

Gross margin = (Sales – Cost of goods sold) ÷ Sales

Obviously, gross margin is a key driver of return on sales and is the driver perhaps most strongly connected to the organization's operational effectiveness. Some analysts also look at operating margin:

Operating margin = (Sales – Cost of goods sold – Operating expenses) ÷ Sales

where SG&A (selling, general, and administrative) expenses, amortizations, and asset recovery are factored in.

Receivables turnover

The accounts receivable turnover ratio gives investors an indication of a company's ability to manage what customers owe it. This ratio uses data from both the income statement (sales) and from the balance sheet (accounts receivable, or AR). The formula is expressed as

AR turnover = Sales ÷ Receivables

Suppose that you have the following data for HGC:

Sales in 2003 are $75,000. On 12/31/03, receivables stood at $25,000.

Sales in 2004 are $80,000. On 12/31/04, receivables stood at $50,000.

Based on these data, you can figure out that sales went up 6.6 percent, but receivables went up 100 percent! In 2003, the AR turnover was 3 ($75,000 divided by $25,000). However, the AR turnover in 2004 sank to 1.6 ($80,000 divided by $50,000), or nearly half. Yes, sales did increase, but the company's ability to collect money due from customers fell dramatically. This information is important to notice for one main reason: What good is selling more when you can't get the money? From a cash-flow point of view, the company's financial situation deteriorated.

A slightly different way of looking at receivables is to show the average number of days that a given receivable dollar lives on the books. To find this number, you divide the AR turnover above into 360 (we round the days down to keep results simple — without too many fractions) to put it on a daily scale:

Average collection period = 360 ÷ AR turnover

You can also apply the same aging concept to inventory turnover, discussed next.

If, based on industry comparisons or stated billing cycles, the collection period is higher than it should be (or growing), watch out. The company may be losing control of its collections, or selling to customers who have questionable credit. This ratio is also sometimes called *days' sales in receivables*.

Inventory turnover

Inventory turnover works like receivables turnover, only you plug in balance-sheet inventory in place of receivables. Here's the formula:

Inventory turnover = Sales ÷ Inventory $

As with receivables turnover, the higher the number the better. High numbers indicate that stuff is flying onto and off of shelves at a rapid rate. Less dust collects on less stuff in fewer warehouses. Also, there's less risk of obsolescence and write-offs and fewer clearance sales — a good thing for any business.

Fixed-asset turnover

This ratio is straightforward:

Fixed-asset turnover = Sales $ ÷ Fixed asset $

Obviously, all else being equal, the company that produces the most sales or revenue per dollar of fixed assets wins.

Total-asset turnover

Again, straightforward:

Total-asset turnover – Sales $ ÷ Total asset $

Here we get a bigger picture of asset productivity as measured by the generation of sales. For the first time, intangible assets are included. Again, industry norms are the benchmark. Comparing a railroad to a software company probably won't make any sense.

Non-financial operating productivity ratios

We find some of these capacity utilization ratios quite interesting, yet inconsistently measured and applied in businesses. Finding the raw data in company statements can be a difficult task — if the numbers are even available. Calculated ratios are even harder to find, although Morningstar Canada and other analysis services make it a point to present certain non-financial operating data. These measures vary by industry, as capacity and operational inputs vary by industry. Here are some examples:

- **Sales per employee:** This ratio tells you how productive a company is in regard to investments in human resources. We think it's worth a look in almost all industries, particularly those that are labour-intensive, such as retail, transportation, and other service industries.

- **Sales per square foot:** This ratio is especially important for retail and similar businesses where occupancy investments are large and sales can be tied directly to them.

> ✔ **Average selling price (ASP):** Many financial reports don't present the number of units sold because they don't have to and they want to keep selling prices secret. But sometimes this information is available (for example, from Boeing and other very-large-ticket manufacturers), and it can be quite revealing as to the direction of a business.

Leverage Ratios

Leverage just means the degree to which a company is using debt financing to operate. Highly leveraged companies risk bankruptcy if they can't meet the payments on their obligations. Leverage (or solvency) ratios have never been more important than now. Leverage ratios look at the relationship between what the company owns and what it owes. Here are a few of the primary leverage-solvency ratios.

Debt-to-equity

The debt to net equity ratio is an indicator of the company's solvency. It answers the question "How dependent is the company on debt?" In other words, it tells you how much the company owes and how much it owns. You calculate it as follows:

> Debt to net equity ratio = Total liabilities ÷ Net equity

If the company HGC has $100,000 in debt and $50,000 in net worth, the debt to net equity ratio is 2. The company has two dollars of debt to every dollar of net worth. In this case, what the company owes is twice the amount of what it owns. Whenever a company's debt to net equity ratio exceeds 1 (as in the example), that isn't good. In fact, the higher the number, the more negative the situation. If the number is too high and the company isn't generating enough income to cover the debt, the company runs the risk of bankruptcy.

Times-interest-earned

Times-interest-earned is a measurement of a company's capacity to pay its debts. It is a multiple by which recurring income from operations provides for payment of interest income. If a company can stay current on its interest payments, the business can usually refinance principal and maintain the confidence of creditors. The formula is:

> Times-interest-earned = Earnings before interest and tax ÷ Interest payments

Working capital

Technically, working capital isn't a ratio, but it does belong to the list of things that serious investors look at. *Working capital* means what the company has in current assets and its relationship to current liabilities. It is a simple equation:

Working capital = Total current assets – Total current liabilities

The point is obvious: Does the company have enough to cover the current bills? If current assets are $25,000 and current liabilities are $25,000, that is a 1 to 1 ratio, which is cutting it close. Current assets should be at least 50-percent higher than current liabilities (say, $1.50 to $1.00) to have enough cushion to pay bills and have some money to finance continuing growth. Preferably the ratio is better, at 2 to 1 or higher.

Financial leverage can be a good thing — to a point, and as long as things are going well. If you put up $1, borrow $9, and invest the $10 total to achieve a 10-percent return, your profit is $1. Your return on equity is 100 percent (your $1 profit divided by the $1 invested). But what if you lose $2? Your creditor still wants his or her $9 back and is entitled to it. You lose your entire investment and then some. On top of that, your creditor demands (and is entitled to) a fixed level of interest payments, which is a constant expense to your enterprise regardless of results. Leverage is thus a double-edged sword.

Valuation Ratios

The ratios presented so far in this chapter are aimed at appraising a company's performance — and thus its intrinsic value. Productivity, financial structure, and profitability are sections in a value investor's orchestra pit. The total sound produced depends on the individual sounds made by individual instruments (ratios) and how they work together.

But as a music buff, how much would you pay to listen to it? That's the question that valuation ratios answer: How much would you pay (and how much are others paying) for tickets to this concert? Here, finally, we introduce *price*. Here, finally, we get to the most popular ratio of all, the one in the newspaper, at parties, on licence plates: the price to earnings (P/E) ratio. Tagging along for the party sophisticates are price to sales, price to book, and a couple of boutique variations on P/E.

Price to earnings

Price to earnings is just as you would expect: the ratio of a price at a point in time to net earnings in a period, usually the trailing 12 months (TTM). Here's the formula:

Price to earnings (P/E) = Stock price ÷ Net earnings per share

A high P/E — say, 20 or higher — indicates a relatively high valuation; a low P/E — say, 15 or less — indicates a relatively low or more conservative one. If you have investing experience, you're probably familiar with P/E, so we won't go into detail or show sample calculations. Rather, we'll share a couple of useful derivatives: earnings to price and price–earnings to growth.

Earnings to price

Earnings to price is simply the reciprocal of P/E, or 1 divided by the P/E. Why do we go here? Earnings-to-price is the functional equivalent of a stock's *yield,* comparable to an interest rate on a fixed-income investment. Because we're talking earnings and not dividends, this yield doesn't usually come your way in the form of a cheque, but it's useful just the same to determine how much return your dollar paid for a share is generating. Many people call this figure *earnings yield.*

Price to sales

Per dollar of shareholder value, how much business does this company generate? Price to sales (P/S) is a straightforward way to answer this question. Here's the formula:

Price to sales = Stock price (total market cap) ÷ Total sales (revenues)

P/S is a common-sense ratio. The lower the better, although there's no specific rule or normalizer like growth. Somewhere around 1.0 usually is considered good. And 2.0 isn't out of hand, but the business had better grow consistently and be prepared to grow into valuation. P/S can be a way to filter out unworthy candidates — such as Cisco, whose P/S once approached 20 (while its P/E approached 100 — already a trouble sign!).

Market cap

When calculating price-to-sales ratios or other valuation measures, it's sometimes easier to look at aggregates rather than per-share amounts. Sales are reported as an aggregate figure, not as a per-share figure. So to compare apples to apples (yes, it's that fruit thing again!), you look at aggregate-share valuation instead of the per-share price. This aggregate figure is known to investors as *market capitalization,* or *market cap* for short. Market cap is simply the number of shares (usually the fully loaded number, including options and equivalents) times the stock price. Divide total market cap by total sales, and you have the price-to-sales ratio.

Price to book

Price to book is getting varying amounts of attention from investors in different sectors. Here's the formula:

Price to book = Stock price (total market cap) ÷ Book value

Recall from Chapter 13 that book value consists of the accounting value of assets less (real) liabilities — sort of an accounting net worth or owner's equity of a corporation. This figure has greater meaning in financial-services industries, where most assets are actual dollars — not factories, inventories, goodwill, and other hard-to-value items. Some book-value measures include intangible assets, and others exclude them.

Stock investors seeking value use price-to-book a bit like price-to-sales: as sort of a smell test for obvious lack of value. A price-to-book ratio of 1.0 is very good — unless the asset base is a bunch of rusty unused railroad tracks. P/B of less than 1.0 signifies a buying opportunity — if book assets are quality assets. A price way out of line with book had better be justified by conservative asset valuation or by the nature of the industry. In the software industry, for example, if R&D (research and development) is properly expensed and intellectual capital intangibles are aggressively amortized, book value and P/B will be low. Trends and especially comparisons are important.

Turn On, Tune In: Compare Ratios

We saved the comparative part of ratio analysis for the end of the chapter on purpose so that you would be more familiar with the ratios involved. This comparative ratio analysis is the only truly free one we know of, as available through Yahoo!Finance. Getting there is a trick in itself:

1. **Get a stock quote for the stock you want to compare to its industry.**

   Simply type the ticker symbol of the company you're looking for and then click "Get Quotes."

2. **In the "More Info" column, click "Profile."**

3. **Scroll down the Profile page until you see the "More from Multex" heading on the left. Click "Ratio Comparisons."**

   The Profile link in Step 2 is also worth a look. It has loads of at-a-glance information that can help you with your investment decisions. We use that link ourselves a lot.

What this ratio comparison tool doesn't do (easily, anyway) is compare one company to another. For side-by-side company comparisons with industry data, Canadian brokers (discount, full service, and online) make company comparisons, usually in a list with industry data included. These lists are handy, but they don't go as deep as the Yahoo!Finance table in that they don't show as many ratios.

Chapter 16

Silly Income-Statement Tricks

In This Chapter

▶ Revealing revenue overstatement

▶ Exposing how companies hide expenses

▶ Exploring how companies use stock options without cost

▶ Understanding how companies smooth income with reserves

▶ Learning about pro forma accounting and disclosure

*N*ow more than ever, stock investors must see beyond the obvious when reviewing financial statements. All too many companies are quick to use aggressive accounting techniques that make their financial statements look better than they really are. Tyco, Enron, and WorldCom quickly come to mind.

It's not enough for stock investors to act as a company watchdog. They should be "forensic investors," acting more like a bloodhound looking for indicators of window dressing (another term that describes aggressive accounting) or even fraud. Stock investors have to look under the hood, at important details in the financial statements. They also have to see how financial-statement messages relate to the broader issues facing the company, to help spot inconsistencies and aggressive accounting.

Most Canadian stock investors are reluctant to review financial statements and related footnotes because of their complexity. It's not fun. This is understandable, since a thorough knowledge of the financial statements of a company of any size can require lots of time and effort. The subject matter can be dry at best. However, using an efficient approach, which we teach you in this chapter, you can quickly glean the key information about a company's financial condition. You can determine its current state and future prospects by focusing on certain indicators of aggressive accounting.

If the message conveyed by financial statements is bad, some companies will be tempted to use creative accounting techniques to hide damaging information, or to provide a twisted and distorted picture of the financial condition of the business. This chapter shows you how companies may try to do this, with a focus on the income statement. It also shows you how to spot aggressive accounting and assess its impact. (Keep in mind that accounting transactions don't affect just the income statement or just the balance sheet. When a transaction affects one financial statement, it eventually impacts the other.) Canadian stock investors should therefore approach financial statements, and the companies they represent, with a healthy skepticism, and be alert to window dressing.

How Did All This Start?

Recent reports of high-profile company failures, such as those noted above, have put the spotlight on aggressive accounting and renewed the call for audited financial statements to show a fair picture of a company's financial performance and position. The main purpose of an audit is to ensure that the financial statements fairly present the company's financial condition, and that they comply with generally accepted accounting principles (GAAP). GAAP is a set of accounting rules and reporting guidelines companies must follow to prepare and present the financial information on the statements.

However, some auditors were not doing their job, which was to provide an opinion on the financial statements. They gave clean bills of health to some very sick companies. Analysts fared no better, as many were too busy giving buy recommendations on those very same troubled companies. The stage was set for a great big fall that even Humpty Dumpty could not duplicate.

Stock investors expect a company to provide meaningful disclosure about where it has been, where it is, and where it is going. Without solid financial statements, the value of the company in investors' eyes may diminish, and they will lose confidence in the company. Companies without solid results are easily tempted into using aggressive accounting.

The problem of creative accounting is not a new one. Even before the bull market of the late 1990s, the market was unforgiving of companies that missed their estimates. It was not uncommon to see a public company failing to meet its so-called "estimate numbers" by one penny, only to watch it lose more than 5 percent of its stock value in one day. The pressures to "make the numbers" often result in earnings manipulation by the company — the subject of this chapter.

How are earnings manipulated? We will present details in this chapter about some of the common methods of window dressing. The following introduces you to several methods that boost current-year earnings or smooth out income, and the details behind these methods are discussed in this chapter:

- ✔ Recording revenue before it is earned

- ✔ Creating fictitious revenue

- ✔ Boosting profits with non-recurring transactions

- ✔ Shifting current expenses to a later period

- ✔ Shifting future expenses to an earlier period

How can you tell from a bird's-eye view that a company may be heading for trouble? Broad indicators include

- ✔ **Earnings trend problems:** One of the most significant indicators of window dressing is a downward trend in earnings. Companies disclose earnings for the last two to three years in the annual report, so do not focus just on one year's net income. Trends in operating income and revenues are also important.

- ✔ **Reduced and inconsistent cash flow:** There are several ways for management to exploit the leeway provided by GAAP to create the illusion of increased earnings. Some key window-dressing approaches are discussed in this chapter. You can use the cash-flow statement to verify the validity of earnings. If net income is moving up while cash flow from operations is falling, something may be out of order.

- ✔ **Excessive debt:** The debt load is a critical factor in determining whether a company can survive difficult times. Companies saddled with too much debt lack the financial flexibility to respond to emergencies, or to take advantage of opportunities. Investors should pay special attention to a company's debt-to-equity ratio, and the total debt-to-shareholders' or -owners' equity. (We discuss ratios in Chapter 15.) The level of shareholders' or owners' equity should exceed the amount of debt by a significant amount; debt payments should be easily serviced. This information can be obtained from the financial statements.

- ✔ **Overstated inventories and receivables:** Accounts receivable and inventory ratios reveal a lot, and are also discussed in Chapter 15. Customers may not be paying their bills, or the company may be stuck with aging merchandise. Liquidity problems will eventually arise. Overstated inventories and receivables are often at the heart of window dressing or even corporate fraud, and can hurt future profits. Trends over time are also important here. Although there may be good reasons for a company to have large or increasing levels of inventory or receivables, it is crucial to determine if the condition is a symptom of ongoing financial difficulty. (Accounts-receivable and inventory issues are discussed in Chapter 17.)

- ✔ **Auditor-switching:** Auditor dismissals and the financial condition of a company can be interdependent. Firms in the midst of financial distress switch auditors more often than do healthy companies.

Revenue Manipulation

Companies sometimes try to boost earnings by manipulating the recognition of revenue. They recognize it before a sale is actually complete, before the product or service is delivered to a customer, or at a time when the customer still has substantial options to terminate, void, or delay the sale. Companies may be tempted to speed revenue recognition — or to simply create it!

Accelerating sales

Companies often negotiate special payment terms and other incentives to entice customers to shift the next fiscal year's first-quarter purchase into the current fiscal year's income statement. The existence of big bonuses for sales staff provides added incentive to meet current-year sales targets. Moving (or "stuffing") large amounts of inventory onto the shoulders of retailers and distributors also avoids having excess inventory in company warehouses, which costs money. Some companies stuff inventories even when they know full well that much of this inventory will not meet end-customer sales targets and will be returned or deeply discounted.

Stock investors need to be mindful that although accelerating revenue in the current year may improve profitability this year, the result is a sales decline showing up on the income statement of the first quarter of the following year. Management may conveniently explain this away as a "seasonal trend."

Stock investors should also be on the lookout for evidence of large changes to inventory levels, especially near year-end. They should also note the magnitude of allowances taken for sales returns of merchandise.

Mortgaging their souls

A number of companies finance their customers to win deals, win new customers, and boost revenues. Although this is common in department-store retailing through store credit cards, it takes on a new scale when billions are lent to single customers to buy telecommunications or pharmaceutical equipment. Nortel is one unhappy victim of this sort of activity, but it is by no means the only one. When customers go bankrupt or otherwise don't meet their obligations, previously recognized revenue vapourizes into thin but stinky air. The related cash is never collected.

This problem is hard to detect until after the fact. Nortel made vague statements in its annual report about "commitments" or "agreements entered into" to extend credit to certain customers. Other than a booking of the revenue into accounts receivable, little is known about whom the money was lent to, in what amounts, or how much is collectible. The quality of the collectible amount relies on the creditworthiness of the debtor.

You know there's a problem when accounts receivable, and particularly bad debt reserves against receivables, start tracking higher as a percentage of revenue. When this happens, it's time to get suspicious. (We discuss accounts receivable in Chapter 17.)

Will that be cash, credit card, or stock?

Beyond the above loan arrangements, it sometimes happens that companies accept a customer's stock as consideration for goods and services sold. Companies occasionally buy stakes in other companies to help influence future product sales or strategic relationships. Technology companies got caught in droves "overinvesting" in their customers. Many continue to take significant investment write-offs.

When some companies accept stock as payment, the value of that stock is booked as revenue despite the fact that the value of those payments was highly volatile. The practice remains legal because, according to GAAP, "consideration" received as payment does not always have to be cash. It has to be measurable. Yet, this is a dangerous signal for stock investors because the value of that sales dollar fluctuates significantly.

Creating revenue out of thin air

Revenues can also be created. Yup. Created — without a bona fide sales transaction. Companies that are audacious enough to do this can artificially swap services and book them as sales. At the same time, the buyer classifies the swap as capital outlays on the balance sheet. In accounting-speak, the income statement gets a revenue credit (good) and the balance sheet gets a debit (also good). Homestore did something like this with AOL.

Similar sleight of hand can be found in the practice of booking as revenues customers' questionable contractual obligations — which may never be collected. This violates the GAAP principle of booking revenues only when collection is likely and the amount of revenue is determinable. Under these scenarios no cash is exchanged or received, but accounting earnings are artificially increased, and assets are inflated.

The practice of revenue creation can result in a real overstatement of cash flow (through an inflated and unadjusted net income figure on the statement of cash flows). There is also a cost in tax payments that would otherwise not have been incurred (higher net income means higher taxes paid to CCRA). So we can see that even when companies practise deceptive accounting their heads are often in the sand regarding future negative impacts that may result.

Moving revenue in mysterious ways

Some companies are so fixated on the top line that they distort the way revenue is presented on the income statement. Analysts and stock investors place a lot of emphasis on revenue growth, so the incentive is there for companies to window dress revenues.

Gross and net

Several companies, especially those in the Internet sector, book revenues that actually belong to someone else! Some Internet travel Web site operators and auction sites have a revenue figure that represents the aggregate value of all products and services sold or brokered, and do not net out the portion of those revenues that belong to the actual service providers.

In many cases, the difference between gross revenue and the company's sales commission was very large. A company's chief financial officer may dismiss such a discrepancy, asserting that it does not impact the company's bottom line. True. But many analysts and investors still value stocks, in part, on the basis of revenue growth. They rely on accurate top lines!

Coupon clipping

Coupon promotions are common techniques used by retailers — especially Internet e-tailers — that wish to promote higher sales volumes. Most companies that engage in window dressing exclude the value of promotional giveaways when booking revenue. They have found a more exciting approach.

Assume for a moment that someone buys a music CD for $30, and uses a $10 coupon to make the purchase. Under GAAP, just $20 of revenue ought to be booked. But some retailers would book $30 in revenue, and charge the $10 in promotional costs to marketing expenses. This may result in artificially higher sales and gross margin, better top-line comments from financial analysts, and an inflated share price. Can you spell "distortion"?

Stock investing for companies

Many companies hold stocks as investments, rather than have cash sit idle or generate small returns. Microsoft, for example, still has investments in scores of small firms. When the technology market was booming, the surging value of those investments boosted Microsoft's bottom line to the tune of more than $2 billion in investment income. In fact, that figure represented most of its total profit during the period. Most public companies don't even have $2 billion in revenues! Microsoft maintained that investing in small start-ups was a key part of the technology business and company growth strategy. That was after the company said it was not anti-competitive! Stock investors need to be mindful of the great distortions in net income — and income-statement presentation — that can occur with investments.

To catch all this, start by being attentive to revenue recognition policies (usually Note 1 or Note 2 of the financial statements) and bizarre increases in sales, receivables, or allowances against receivables.

Hiding Expenses: Capitalizing Costs

You can turn a garden variety of what should be expenses into assets by depreciating and amortizing capital assets (resources that last over one year) more slowly than otherwise required under the principle of reasonableness (in other words, by easing it slowly into expenses). With certain costs incurred, management can judgmentally "over"estimate a period of useful benefit to longer than one year. That would let management justify recording part of it on the balance sheet (as an asset) instead of on the income statement (as an expense).

Small fry

One example of capitalizing expenses is paying for computer peripheral equipment or office supplies and spreading the costs over three or more years. These types of expenses rarely benefit periods longer than a year or two and should probably be expensed when incurred, depending on the circumstances. Another example is advertising, where accounting standards state that advertising expenses should not be capitalized. GAAP is also specific about start-up costs (like store pre-opening costs), and states that these should be expensed instead of capitalized. Be alert to a series of smaller costs that have not been deducted on the income statement and that show up on the balance sheet. It may indicate that management is not shy to use aggressive accounting in more significant areas as well.

Big fry

On a larger scale, some companies set up associated companies to perform R&D work for them. The original company gets to avoid expensing potentially massive research costs by having the associated company assume the R&D costs (and related revenue). After this type of accounting sleight of hand, the cost of R&D essentially disappears from the books. While accounting rules are trying to blow the whistle on this sort of trickery, some companies will continue to practise it until told otherwise.

R&D can also be manipulated the other way, to help a company take a special charge against income. (Special charges to write off assets are discussed in Chapter 17.) Briefly, when assets are acquired in a business combination, they may be assigned their fair values. The acquirer of R&D–related assets accounts for the transaction by judgmentally determining whether there are "future uses" for these assets. If so, R&D assets are capitalized. All others are expensed when the deal closes. So it's somewhat easy to justify expensing these R&D costs.

Now that's a really, really big fry!

WorldCom was the granddaddy of companies classifying operational expenses as capital outlays. It redefined the term "pushing the envelope." Media characterized this chicanery as "overstating cash flow." Actually, WorldCom's cash flow was not really affected by the misclassification, because the cash outlays showed up in the cash-flow statement — only in a different area of it. The only cash impact was the deferred tax deductibility of these capitalized expenses, which instead were depreciated over a number of years. The attempt to inflate reported earnings in effect cost WorldCom some available cash on hand. Oh yes — it also cost thousands of jobs, and massive share-price losses for unsuspecting investors.

Related-party transactions

A "related party" is one that can exercise control or significant influence over the management or operating policies of another party. A problem can arise, for instance, if dealings take place with non-public companies that are controlled by management. In some cases these non-public companies can get saddled with expenses in order for the public company to look great.

Stock investors need to take a closer look at these invisible enterprises that might be propping up the firm. The notes to financial statements disclose the nature, extent, amount, and timing of related-party transactions during the year.

Stock Options

Investors have to be vigilant in assessing the negative effects of stock options. The negative effect happens in the form of dilution of shares, and your stake in the company. When more shares are issued due to someone exercising options, the share of profits and equity that applies to you gets dwindled down.

Alan Greenspan keeps mentioning this issue; Warren Buffett has talked about it for years. Will the economy, investment community, shareholders, and companies themselves be better served with a requirement that the "economic value" of stock options be expensed on financial statements?

Option for what?

An option gives an employee the right, but not the obligation, to buy a share of stock in the future at a predetermined price. The more the price of the stock goes up, the more valuable the right becomes. Options give employees a stake in their company's future. They also give a young (or established) company the chance and ability to grow; the company can use its scarce cash funds for growth, not compensation expense.

What do the stakeholders say?

Current accounting rules provide that the value of an option is not required to be expensed on a company's income statement. A company is, however, required to report its earnings per share on the income statement on a basic and on a "diluted" basis, the latter taking into account the potential reduction in the ownership of existing shareholders due to the granting and exercising of options. Accounting rules also require additional disclosure in the footnotes of the potential impact of options on earnings.

Recent media reports on this hot topic indicated that options were the source of about half of most top executives' compensation, and that this is a very contentious issue for investors and management alike. Alan Greenspan believes that the failure to expense stock options has introduced a significant distortion in reported earnings that has grown with the increasing prevalence of this form of compensation.

While admittedly there is nothing nefarious about encouraging stock owner-ship among employees, those who call for change argue that stock-option compensation has caused company management to focus on actions to drive up the stock price in the short term to provide continuing value for their option programs. These actions are not focused on growth in long-term shareholder wealth. One reason companies have made extensive repurchases of their own company's stock is to keep the stock price up and to absorb newly issued option shares without a significant dilutive effect to existing shareholders (who would no doubt flip out if this happened on a regular basis). Stock purchase, like the grant of options, is not an expense reflected on the income statement — hence the motivation.

So what options do we have?

Those who champion change say that companies should replace option programs with plans that actually encourage and reward stock ownership. Warren Buffett's Berkshire Hathaway rewards employees with cash bonuses, not options.

Accounting standard-setters in Canada and the U.S. are reviewing how to have companies report stock-option costs. However, they have stopped short of requiring all companies to treat options as expenses.

Backers of expensing option costs say that doing so would help present a more accurate picture of a company's financial performance. Several North American surveys found that many companies would have seen reported earnings trimmed by as much as 200 percent had stock-option expenses been recognized on the income statement. It's a big enchilada of an issue!

Reserves

Some companies use unrealistic assumptions to estimate certain liabilities. In doing so, they squirrel away accruals in "cookie jars" during the good times, and reach into them as needed in the bad times. Management can smooth income to show consistency, or a desired trend that investors like to see.

Companies will build up reserves on the balance sheet (as temporary offsets to assets) during highly profitable periods for things such as

- Sales returns and service guarantees
- Loan losses
- Product and service warranty costs
- Insurance losses
- Workers' compensation claims
- Lawsuits

A company builds reserves for these items by booking an expense each period, offsetting the expense by increasing a reserve liability on the balance sheet.

Think of reserve liabilities as the company saying, "I don't know how much in insurance losses and product returns pertains to this year's sales, but I do know that it will be something. So I'll book an expense now on the income statement (in the amount of the estimated liability), and will offset this with a liability on the balance sheet that may occur sometime in the future." When the actual loss occurs, the payment is recorded as a reduction in the balance sheet reserve liability, and doesn't impact the income statement.

The opportunity to manipulate earnings comes in the form of "guessing" how much has to be written off as expenses, regardless of actual write-offs. In other words, reserves are judgmentally determined amounts, so a company wishing to raise profits may manipulate the reserves to accomplish this. It's not too difficult for management to justify a change in reserves to the auditor.

This may simply be based on a change in the business environment. But it could also be a blatant attempt by management to channel profits to the income statement.

Tax Losses

With the economy in the doldrums over the last few years, many companies suffered losses. This often qualified them for tax credits to be received in a future tax period. Many companies recognize this as a special item (revenue) on the income statement in the current year to boost the bottom line. A tax asset is also booked on the balance sheet.

Invariably, after a year or so, window dressers make the tax asset (tax credit receivable) disappear, because the company re-evaluated the likelihood of actually qualifying for the credit and determined that it stood no chance of collecting from CCRA. The tax asset gets written off, a special charge is created (in the year a company would prefer to see a charge), and the investor is left with even more distorted financial statements.

Pro Forma Performance

If "normal" accounting manipulation — the type performed within GAAP rules — wasn't enough to ruin your stock-investing day, consider the latest trend in window dressing: the pro forma earnings statement. Pro forma reports have become almost a public relations alternative to the classic GAAP earnings statement.

Picky, picky

Responding in part to investor and analyst pressure and in part to a fairly loose (to date) compliance environment, companies started using pro forma reporting as a press-friendly reporting alternative. The trend started in 1999 with Yahoo! and has expanded through the technology industry and now beyond.

Actually, pro forma has been in the accounting vocabulary for a long time. Pro forma statements were originally used as "unofficial" statements designed to project — not report — company performance. Companies planning to go public or merge with another company issued a pro forma set of statements to give an investor a clue as to what forward-looking statements might look like. But no more are pro forma statements limited to special situations. Beyond the latitude afforded by GAAP, today's press-friendly financial reporting does an "end run" right around GAAP.

With pro forma reporting, companies can spin their business pretty much as they please. They include certain things but leave out others they consider irrelevant to assessing performance. From your perspective as a stock investor, pro forma reporting not only undermines statement quality but also makes it difficult to compare one company to another.

Pro forma is really an extension of the EBITDA reporting concept made popular in the 1980s (see Chapter 13). Although EBITDA made numbers look better than they were by excluding financing costs and asset recovery, at least the application of EBITDA was consistent from one company to the next.

Companies routinely omit option costs, investment gains and losses, asset impairment or write-downs, goodwill amortization, and other "noncash" items. In that these expenses are noncash, value investors can wink and turn their heads a little — for a while. But we've occasionally seen some very cash-real expenses, such as interest expense, get written out of the pro forma. Bad form!

The good news is . . .

Although companies can release to the public pretty much any pro forma report they please, there is a catch: They must also provide GAAP-compliant numbers in releases and submit full GAAP-compliant reports to regulators. So you have the pro forma reports, good enough for many investors and reflective of how companies want to see themselves. You also have GAAP financial statements. But you must dig deeper to understand the difference between the pro forma and GAAP — and why the company wants to maintain that difference.

From a stock-investing perspective, pro forma reports are obviously dangerous in their concealment of long-term asset recovery and similar expenses. In addition, they make it difficult to compare one company to another, as each company reports different things, and companies may report differently from one period to the next. Sorting out these differences can be very time consuming.

We never said that basing stock investing on financial statements was easy.

Chapter 17

Silly Balance-Sheet Tricks

. . . .

In This Chapter

▶ Exploring asset and liability manipulation

▶ Revealing undiscovered liabilities

▶ Identifying buzzwords that have a sting

▶ Assessing red flags

. . . .

*W*hat with all the media hype about earnings estimates and revenue forecasts, you'd think that the balance sheet was an annoying add-on to the financial statements. However, many in the accounting world believe that it is the balance sheet that ought to be the prime focus for anyone who analyzes financial statements. Perhaps the tide is finally turning.

Think about how most Canadians view their finances. To many, their job is like an income statement — it's the main source of revenue that goes on to pay living expenses. Their bank account is like a balance sheet — it's a reflection of what's been saved and what is owed to others. If someone loses her job, what becomes important at that point in time? The balance sheet, of course. How much is in the savings account until another job comes along? Is the cash in that account enough to meet mortgage and credit card payments?

Clearly, both the income statement and the balance sheet are important. It's just that they paint pictures that are of different importance to different investors. Value investors tend to focus on balance sheets, making sure that they pay less than the intrinsic value of the company. Growth and momentum investors may throw caution to the wind and prioritize those revenue-growing companies that may return 5 percent tomorrow.

Regardless of whether your focus is on the income statement or the balance sheet, the balance sheet is still important. It's also an area that management is tempted to manipulate. The dollars on the balance sheet are often a lot larger than those on the income statement, making financial-statement manipulation easier, and of higher impact.

Accounts-Receivable Allowances

When the values of customer-receivable balances are in doubt — and most to a certain extent are — management sets up a provision called the *allowance for doubtful accounts*. It does this by expensing the amount of the reserve to the income statement, and creating a corresponding liability on the balance sheet. The liability offsets the accounts-receivable balance. Instead of charging accounts-receivable losses to the income statement as they occur, which could cause wild swings in income, the allowance for doubtful accounts is intended to smooth out the income statement impact of bad debts by charging a stable amount of bad-debts expense to the income statement each period. Later, when a specific customer's account is actually identified for write-off, the allowance account gets charged, not the expense account on the income statement. Again, the income statement gets saved from wild fluctuations in bad debts. Okay — that's the theory.

In practice, the allowance for doubtful accounts (a reserve) is an area that involves considerable judgment on management's part, and is susceptible to manipulation. Management looks at past overall write-off history, takes the current status of individual customers into account, and makes some assumptions as to the bad-debts expense amount. At the end of the day, however, the exact amount of actual future bad debts is always unknown. This can be, and is, a popular area used to boost earnings.

Message to auditor: It's the economy, stupid!

A company wishing to squeeze a bit more income into its income-statement earnings may reduce the annual expense slightly to put an upward slant on earnings. This would not be an exorbitant reduction in bad-debt expense, but rather a subtle shift. When the auditors with the green caps and thick glasses come in at the end of the year, the finance people with the Hugo Boss suits will justify their rationale for the allowance account. But that rationale could be a change from reserving 100 percent of doubtful customers' balances to reserving only 40 percent of the doubtful balances. They may come up with and convey a slick reason — like a "recovering economy" — to believe that 60 percent or more of the balances that used to be very doubtful and still are to some extent, will now probably be collected.

Red flags and other signs

Stock investors can spot red flags with the allowance account only if there is enough detailed information available. For example, you can examine the relationship between the allowance for doubtful accounts and gross receivables (adding back the allowance for doubtful accounts to net receivables). Has the allowance as a percentage of gross receivables declined over the years? If so, that could be a sign of manipulation (the company has not maintained adequate allowances). It could also simply mean an improved collectability of receivables. Check out the notes to financial statements, which may provide a breakout of the allowance for doubtful accounts and gross accounts receivable.

If sufficient detail is provided in the income statement, you may be able to spot red flags by analyzing the bad-debt expense (as percentage of sales) trend. Look for significant reduction in the debt-expense percentage from year to year. If there is significant reduction in the bad-debt expense percentage, try to assess the reason for the reduction. While this may be difficult to do, if you spot window dressing elsewhere there's a good chance that it's happening in this area too.

Inventories

Inventory is another area ripe for aggressive accounting. Under GAAP, the LIFO (last-in, first-out) method of accounting for inventory charges the most current prices of inventory to the cost of sales on the income statement. During times of rising prices, the value assigned to the cost of sales will be higher, as pricier inventory sold will be transferred into the cost of sales figure. While we are not really in inflationary times now, there are industries that sell increasingly costly goods. Oil companies, luxury car manufacturers, and some mining companies may still stand to benefit from window dressing their inventories because prices in those sectors never seem to come down or stop rising.

How it's done

If a company wishes to increase its cash flow (by reducing taxes paid due to lower taxable income), it can use the LIFO method of accounting (assuming rising prices) for inventory. It will manage its inventory levels to keep the cost of sales higher. The lower the ending inventory (the less inventory placed in the balance sheet), the lower the net and taxable income. Voila, less taxes to CCRA!

For every company wishing to report lower earnings, there are three that may be tempted to manipulate inventory to increase profits. They reduce the amount of LIFO inventory levels going into the value of cost of sales. They pull this off because goods and products may be grouped into inventory pools (or classes) that they can pick and choose from.

Other companies take the game of establishing many pools of inventory very seriously. Their main objective is to target which inventories get charged to cost of sales. They can use the earlier, lower cost levels of inventory for some pools, with the result of a decrease to cost of goods sold. This means higher profits, but again only when prices are rising.

Another way to increase profits is through the reserve for inventory obsolescence, which can also be manipulated (as we saw in Chapter 16). This reserve account is similar to the allowance for doubtful receivable accounts. It too is used to smooth out the net-income impact of writing off old, mouldy, obsolete inventory. Typically, amounts are properly and gradually written off each quarter (which increases the reserve for inventory obsolescence on the balance sheet), instead of irregularly and suddenly recording the write-down to the income statement when the inventory is deemed obsolete. That's good accounting practice. But any company seeking to boost profits may revisit the account reserved for inventory obsolescence to determine whether they can justify reducing the allowance, and increasing the bottom line.

Auditors will review the validity and reasonableness of inventory pools and reserves to detect any manipulation. But in this area, stock investors will never get close enough to see anything unusual for themselves. This is an example of how much reliance all stock investors place on the work of external auditors.

Creative Acquisition Accounting

In the heyday of the bull market, entire industries were rattled and changed through consolidations, acquisitions, and spin-offs. AOL merged with Time Warner, and Vivendi bought out Seagram-Universal. Some acquirers, particularly those using stock as an acquisition currency, used this crazy environment as an opportunity to engage in very aggressive accounting for acquisitions. What did they do?

In the allocation of the purchase price, they classified a large portion of the acquisition price as "in-process" research and development. *In-process* R&D can be written off as a one-time charge, or "big bath." This has the effect of removing any future earnings drag.

Also be very wary of pre-merger charges. Instead of doing the dirty work of recording those costs on the income statement, some companies compel the acquiree to take a hit, taking as many charges against income as feasible right before the deal closes. This is a clever idea since the target company is poised to be acquired — the terms of the deal are set, so it's not concerned about what its own shareholders will say. The acquiring company gets a head start using a basket of acquired assets that have been written down but that are very productive. There is a reduction in the future amount depreciated each year in the income statement. So be alert to what the acquirer does immediately preceding the merger. Did the acquiree take a charge?

It's been a while since we've seen the type of merger-mania we witnessed in the bull market. So we don't see too much by way of big-bath accounting in the realm of acquisitions. Unfortunately, we do still see a lot of big-bath accounting and special charges. This time, it's because all too many companies are crashing and burning. This scenario is discussed next.

Special Charges and More Big Baths

Many companies that have experienced horrible results choose to take all their lumps at one time. This restructuring, or big-bath accounting, involves claiming massive chunks of losses in the income statement with a corresponding write-down on the balance sheet of an asset, usually an intangible like goodwill.

Canadian investors witnessed this phenomenon with Nortel and other large technology companies. Big-bath accounting even happens in other industries, such as media and pharmaceuticals. At the end of the day, the company is saying that the company it overpaid for in 1999 no longer has much value, and it's writing off the goodwill asset associated with the acquisition on an accelerated basis.

From the viewpoint of an investor there is nothing inherently insidious about big-bath accounting, since doing so does not inflate profits. But it is an embarrassment and a disgrace to the company. So why do companies still do it?

The forward-looking chief financial officer looks into her crystal ball and sees that if more value is written off than should be, then future net income figures will look better. She muses, "Okay, my company looks bad now — but if I run a big bath, income will look great tomorrow. Book it, Danno!" That makes it really, really difficult for stock investors to properly value the company, and to compare it meaningfully with other companies in the same industry. Distortions are large and confusing to unravel. Even Olly would admit to Stan that it's a fine mess they're in. So what can you do in this case?

Where there's smoke . . .

Look for areas where special charges may occur. Restructuring charges can cover lots of expenses, but common categories include the following:

- Closure of physical facilities
- Layoffs and severance costs (treated the same as closing facilities)
- Selling, closing, or exiting a business (discontinued operations)
- Increasing reserves for litigation (if you have a hard time finding facts about litigation, be on the alert for nasty legal surprises)
- Writing off goodwill, or current assets (as described in this chapter)

You have to be alert for instances when a company seizes the opportunity to throw in the kitchen sink as well. Companies may be tempted to write off all too many assets that still have a future economic value to the company.

There are other reasons why companies overstate special charges. Management hopes that analysts will look beyond a one-time loss and focus only on future earnings, as many do.

When a company restructures and takes special charges, company employees, stock investors, creditors, customers, and suppliers all want to understand the impact. It is important that financial reporting provides the information to assess the impact. As a stock investor, always be skeptical about special charges. Try as best you can to assess the impact with the information you have. If it appears that the write-offs are blatant, then be wary of investing in that company. After all, it has already proven that it's capable of making very big mistakes.

Hiding Liabilities: Off-Balance-Sheet Obligations

Some companies hide bad things like excessive debt by transferring it away from the balance sheet. Where does this debt go? Quite often it will be to a special-purpose entity (think Enron), such as an affiliated company or partnership. Companies may push accounting rules to the outer limits and say that their debt does not, by the letter of accounting law, meet the definition of debt to be disclosed as a liability. Instead, these companies disclose complex "agreements" entered into, that not even seasoned analysts can understand without benefit of a flow chart! This lack of full and understandable information challenges the stock investor to find out what the company must pay in order to fulfill its debt and other obligations.

There are four areas, including the type described above, that warrant further mention here. Each has the potential to hide the extent of a company's liabilities, and assets, through complex transactions that may hide the substance of a company's financial position. Let's start with the relatively easy ones!

Leasing transactions

If you rent your home, you don't own it. If you own it, your home is an asset, but any mortgage is a liability. Same with companies. A synthetic lease lets a company consider a purchase of property as a lease, but gives it the tax advantages of ownership. An arm's-length (unrelated) company technically owns the property, usually a financial institution that really doesn't wish to bother operating it. Debt is used to finance the property, and the company has to pay it off. To be able to justify this off-balance-sheet accounting, the lease term has to be short — no more than seven years. If interest rates rise or values drop, the company can land into trouble. Sure, the lease is disclosed in a footnote, but few notice it (and if they did, even fewer can understand it).

To illustrate, take a company that owns aircraft, and finances the planes with debt. You would expect it to report an asset (the aircraft) and a liability (the debt). Under existing GAAP (in most jurisdictions, including Canada and the U.S.), a company that operates assets under a lease that is structured as a short-term operating lease reports neither the asset nor the liability. Imagine a balance sheet that shows an airline without any aircraft. Would you consider that to be a faithful representation of the substance of the transaction? No, neither would we. This matter is now being addressed internationally, and there is a good possibility that these companies will be required to recognize assets and related lease obligations for both capital and operating leases.

Securitization transactions

A company that transfers certain of its assets (like loans or notes receivable) through a securitization transaction may be able to recognize the transaction as a sale of assets, and remove the assets receivable from its balance sheet. Securitization refers to the process of aggregating similar financial instruments, such as loans or mortgages, into a security to be sold on the open market. Companies do this to generate cash more quickly, and to improve their bottom line on the income statement.

Some securitizations are appropriately accounted for as sales. But many others continue to expose the transferring company to significant risks still inherent in the transferred assets, which should not have been removed. Again, management's judgment was allowed to come into play. But was it good judgment?

Commitments and contingencies

A contingent liability is one that is difficult to quantify, or that may or may not come to pass. It's a potential claim for which any liability depends on a future event or circumstance. Examples include outstanding lawsuits, special contract obligations, or debt covenants (terms and conditions that must be upheld).

When evaluating a bank stock, look under the MD&A section of the annual report for discussion about credit risk. In the footnotes, look for discussion about commitments, contingencies, and pledged assets. Determine roughly how big the potential impact can be if some of these commitments turn into reality.

Creation of unconsolidated or special-purpose entities (SPEs)

Under GAAP, a company transferring assets and liabilities to a subsidiary company must consolidate that subsidiary in the parent company's financial statements. However, in some cases, the transferor may be able to elude the requirement to consolidate.

A special purpose entity allows "sponsor/originator" companies bearing most of the SPE's debt risk to keep that debt off the consolidated balance sheet under U.S. GAAP. In Canada and elsewhere, the rules are somewhat similar. The majority of SPEs in the world are perfectly legitimate, and there are also some financing and tax benefits. But keep in mind that the primary motivation of having SPEs is often to achieve off-balance-sheet financing.

Enron wrote the book on SPEs. Then it collapsed. As a result, new U.S. accounting standards require companies to disclose their involvement with an SPE, including the nature and amount of the associated risks. That information must be included in the footnotes of a company's annual report. Canadian GAAP has similar requirements. Read those footnotes carefully if you ever see them. Run a "what if" scenario to see what would happen if those liabilities came to life, sort of the way Frankenstein's monster did.

Pension Plans

Most public companies have pension plans for employees, and corresponding obligations to adequately fund those plans. If there is any deficiency in the amount contributed to the plan, the company ultimately has to fund the shortfall. Cash infusions would dig into the company's cash balances, and could potentially impair its ability to do the things it wants to.

During the heady days of the bull market, companies had little to worry about regarding this rule. In fact, many trimmed their pension contributions, and even offered their employees "contribution holidays," where an employee's share of the pension contribution was nil or very low. Others even increased their assumed annual return on pension assets. Since those surreal days, however, many companies failed to adjust downward the assumptions underpinning their pension plans, such as the returns the plans would generate in upcoming years. Some pension plans are still based on assumptions that their investment funds would grow at a double-digit pace, when in fact recent returns have been closer to nil (and that's if they were lucky!).

Accounting impact, too

In addition to a cash-flow impact, there is also an accounting impact with pension plans. Pension-plan returns are determined for the company annually. If the actual gain on the plan is less than predicted gains, then GAAP requires that a loss be booked on the income statement. To get around reporting the loss, or the full extent of it, companies may pressure actuaries to use favourable assumptions about returns, mortality rates, retirement dates, and so on, in an effort to window dress the impact on the bottom line.

This type of accounting manipulation occurs for companies with *defined-benefit pension plans*. A defined-benefit plan sets required retirement income for a future period, and the employer then funds the plan to ensure that the future pension obligation is met. Management often gets away with this because pension accounting is a nebulous task at best.

For investors, it is very difficult to understand the intricacies of pension plans. But many analysts say that determining the exact impact on earnings, and evaluating how much cash will be spent to prop up ailing plans, is nearly impossible anyway. Pension accounting is based on several estimates and forecasts, and many are not publicly disclosed. But the question has to remain in the back of stock investors' minds: How long will it be before the company has to pay the piper?

Keep in mind, however, that one bad year may not throw pension accounting out of kilter. Bad years tend to offset with good years over the long term. But when you see four consecutive years of poor returns, then problems can't wait to arise.

So, if the bottom line of a company you invest in takes a blow from a pension loss, expect the stock price to suffer. Also keep in mind that companies are not required to disclose actual historical returns on pension-plan assets, or the pension-plan asset mix. All this makes for more confusion and uncertainty.

Oh, and one more thing . . .

Shortfalls and asset returns aren't the only area of manipulation. Discount rates are used by actuaries to calculate the present value of future pension liabilities. They're intended to be based on long-term bond yields. In many cases, however, discount rates remain far too high, and make liabilities look far too low. That implies that companies may not only be overestimating how much money their plans will generate, but also are probably underestimating their liabilities, too.

Smoke and Mirrors

Stock investors who read company financial statements need to be alert to companies that put the spotlight in the annual report on only the great accomplishments. While they duly follow accounting rules and disclose the more nasty items, such as litigation against the company, or dependence on only a few customers, they bury this information behind the good news.

The smoke and mirrors ruse is also prevalent in press releases of quarterly financial results. The spin is almost always positive, despite the fact that the numbers may actually be saying otherwise. Press releases are not currently vetted by audit committees or external auditors, so the stock investor is on his own dissecting the press release for validity.

And Materiality Rabbits, Too

Many accountants started out wanting to be magicians. When they saw that they couldn't do tricks with cards, they went to bean-counting school. Their best trick was the ability to say that one plus one is equal to "anything you want it to be." Even true magicians were impressed.

For the stock investor, accounting manipulation is not entertaining at all. It's more akin to a horror show, really. Be careful when you hear the word "materiality," a concept that many companies misuse. They may intentionally allow accounting errors to slip through within a defined-percentage ceiling. This is actually justified in auditing-speak if, and only if, the effect on profit is too small to matter to a reader of the financial statement.

When auditors question management about these violations of GAAP, they answer dryly, "It doesn't matter. It's immaterial." Often, the auditors will accept this. Materiality is based on considerable judgment. There is no clear-cut line to show where it starts and where it ends. It requires consideration of the potential impact on a stock investor's decision.

Buzzwords

There are several words that may strike fear in stock investors. "Going concern" are two of those words, and they are a biggie. Going concern reflects the idea that a company will continue to operate indefinitely, and will not go out of business and liquidate its assets. This is the basis of most accounting rules. For example, you don't book a receivable if the company is not likely to be around tomorrow. For the going-concern assumption to apply, the company must be able to generate and/or raise enough funds to stay in business. If an auditor suspects a going-concern problem, she is compelled to report it in her auditor's report. If you see this, exit stage left!

"Changing auditors" is another thing you don't want to see happen. Sure, there may be a very good and benign reason for this. But quite frequently, it's because management and the auditor can't agree on a significant accounting issue. If the auditor digs in, he may get fired. Alternatively, if an auditor suspects management fraud and wishes to disassociate herself from the company, she can resign. Either way, it reflects poorly on management. Be very suspicious when this happens, and don't take the word of investor-relations people at face value.

A CEO pursuing "other interests" may be indicative of a captain not wanting to stay behind on a sinking ship. CEOs perched high on their masts have a clear view of the horizon. When they see that big tidal wave coming, they may call in the helicopter and put on their golden parachutes. Alternatively, the captain may have simply faced a mutiny and is walking the gangplank — at night, to save face. If he's lucky, Jonah's whale is lurking below to save him!

Footnotes, oh boring footnotes. But not to management. No siree Bob. This is where management will bury much of the bad stuff! Footnotes are more effective than Sominex in putting you to sleep, or Natural Tears in creating tears of boredom. But ignore these and you risk investment peril. And dealing with the bad stuff in footnotes can be more challenging than a game of I Spy. Just ask the external auditors of Enron. Oops, we forgot, they recently ceased to exist after botching that audit. Enron did, after all, have some fancy footnotes.

Addressing Aggressive Accounting

Recent GAAP changes brought about by regulators and accounting standard setters have improved the transparency of financial statements, and have remedied a handful of the creative accounting techniques discussed in this book. More developments in the world according to GAAP will further curtail manipulative accounting techniques. While tightening GAAP is good for stock investors, it is not the only answer to this problem.

People still question the rigour of audits. Yet, is it possible that too much reliance is placed on the auditors to uncover fraudulent practices of creative accounting? After all, audits provide reasonable assurance, not guarantees, of problem-free accounts. So auditors ought to be considered watchdogs, and not bloodhounds, in the realm of validating financial reporting.

Strengthening the role of the audit committee would be a significant move in the right direction. However, even great audit committees meet only a few times annually. Others meet just before the board of directors meeting, perhaps for a few token minutes to accomplish sign-offs. But if an audit committee meets monthly before each board meeting, and every member has a financial background and is prepared to address tough management and auditor issues, the investor's interest will be served.

There is a clear need for cultural change in the analyst community as well. Earnings estimates should not be a focal point; nor should brokerage houses underwriting revenues. Analysts should penalize those companies that rely on accounting trickery rather than fairness and full disclosure.

The next section provides you with a list of accounting tricks to watch out for.

Checklist for Accounting Manipulation

✔ **Allowance for doubtful accounts.** Are allowances lower than in the past? If so, this can be justified only if the collections process is going exceedingly well, or if the previous allowance was proven to be much too conservative.

✔ **Last in, first out (LIFO) inventory reductions.** Is there evidence that management trimmed inventory layers, so there is no "last in" high cost that in the current period would otherwise lower income?

✔ **Depreciation and amortization.** Although it is difficult for stock investors to access depreciation schedules of various assets, it's important to realize that they are a big part of the earnings equation for many companies. Useful life estimates can be stretched to raise income. Do the key asset lifespans make sense when compared to competitors in the same industry?

✔ **Tax asset valuation accounts.** Many companies record deferred tax assets for the value of business losses. The value is determined based on management's assessment of when the company will generate enough profit to extinguish the asset. Check to see whether a company got an earnings boost due to a sudden optimism about its future earnings prospects, which may actually take longer than estimated to materialize. If so, be on guard.

✔ **Warranty and other reserves.** Many companies offer a warranty for the goods or services they market. Since warranty policies help a firm sell its stuff, warranty-related costs need to be matched with sales revenue from period to period. The estimated warranty expense is based on past experience. Were additions to warranty reserves reduced, perhaps to meet earnings targets? Can reductions like these be justified, or is it just pure income manipulation?

✔ **Pension income.** How does the expected return disclosed in the footnotes mesh with the actual return of pension-plan assets? Expectations of great returns will automatically increase the bottom line without any corresponding increase in cash.

✔ **Capitalization policies.** Can a company justify deferral of expenses (by recording them as assets) when the competition does not? How does a company account for its start-up costs? What voodoo is used to determine the amortization period? What do the accounting policy footnotes say about these things?

✔ **Restructuring charges and special write-downs.** The company blew it. Of course, it will say it's the economy's fault. Is there evidence of big-bath accounting to make future periods look great? Were inventory and fixed assets included in the bath?

✔ **Earnings consistent with cash flow.** Do these two items march to the beat of the same drum? They won't be equal, but they should march side by side. If earnings grow at a pace faster than cash flow, that is a warning sign.

✔ **Understand asset impairments.** Is the rationale for impaired assets, or assets targeted for potential write-downs, clear and valid?

✔ **Extraordinary write-offs.** Are write-offs large or recurring? If so, understand why.

✔ **Accounting policy changes.** Accounting policy notes should be simple and straightforward. Look at depreciation, amortization, and R&D expenses. Are there any complex, unexplained changes? That may spell trouble.

✔ **Big gap between pro forma and GAAP.** Do you understand why? Raise the red flag high if scant company disclosure makes it difficult for you to understand the differences.

✔ **Understand where the revenues come from.** What are the major revenue "segments"? Does the company have a few big customers? Who are they? Are *their* business fundamentals sound? What are the incentives?

Part IV
Investment Strategies and Tactics

The 5th Wave   By Rich Tennant

"SELL".

In this part . . .

Successful stock investing is broader in scope than just selecting individual stocks. It's about seeing the forest and the trees — understanding the environment that the stock market is part of. Just as fish can thrive in good water or die in bad water, the stock market reacts to the general economic tides. This part will explain how, as a successful investor, you won't just pick winners and stop there. You'll also keep up with financial news to understand the type of market you are currently investing in. You'll then look into the industries that particular companies that interest you operate within. This part also shows you how to preserve any gains you make — and minimize losses. Finally, we'll show you what the tax impact of your investment decisions may be, and what you can do to minimize those nasty taxes.

Chapter 18

Taking the Bull (or Bear) by the Horns

In This Chapter

▶ Looking at the bull market

▶ Recognizing the bear market

▶ Deciding what to do in an uncertain market

*U*nderstanding the investment environment may be even more important to your wealth-building success than choosing the right stock. Recent years — and a century of stock-market history — bear (no pun intended) witness to this point.

Bull and bear markets have a tremendous effect on your stock choices. Generally, bull markets tend to precede economic uptrends (also called economic rebound, economic recovery, or economic growth), while bear markets tend to precede economic downtrends (also called recession, deflation, or economic contraction).

The stock market's movement is based on the fact that stock prices go up (or down) based on people's buying or selling behaviour. If more people are buying stock (versus selling), then stock prices will rise. If more people are selling stocks, then stock prices will fall. Why do people buy or sell a stock? It can be explained in one word: *expectations*. People generally buy (or sell) stock in expectation of economic events. If they feel that times are getting bad and the economic stats bear this out (in the form of rising unemployment, shrinking corporate profits, cutbacks in consumer spending, and so on), then they will become more cautious. This can have a couple of results:

✔ They sell stock that they currently own.

✔ They won't buy stock because they believe that stocks will not do well.

Of course, when the economy is doing well, the reverse is true.

Bulling Up

In the beginning, a bull market doesn't look like a bull market at all. It looks like anything but. Maybe that's why so few catch on early. Bull markets are marked by great optimism as the economy roars forward and stocks go skyward. Everyone knows what a bull market should look like, and everyone can recognize it when it has become a mature trend. The saying "I don't know what it is, but I'll know it when I see it" is one that applies to a bull market. But if you can foresee it, you may be able to make a lot of money by getting in just before the crowd sees it.

Because bull markets usually start in the depths of a bear market, do some research regarding bear markets; see the section "Identifying the beast," later in this chapter.

Recognizing the beast

Although in this book we concentrate on the modern era, starting in the early part of the twentieth century, bull markets in stocks have shown themselves many times throughout the past few hundred years — plenty of time to have established some recognizable traits:

- ✔ **Bull markets tend to start at the depths of pessimism — the same way that dawn starts at the edge of darkness.** People have probably just finished being beaten up by a bear market. The phrase "I'm into stock investing" is about as welcome in polite conversation as "I have a contagious disease." If investors are avoiding stocks like the plague (or selling stocks they already have), share prices drop to the point that much of the risk is wrung out of them. Value-oriented investors then can pick up some solid companies at great prices.

- ✔ **The major media mirror this pessimism and amplify it.** Usually, the mainstream media have greater value as a *counterindicator* or *contrarian indicator* — because by the time the major publications find out about the economic trend and report it, the trend has already changed course.

For example, *Time* magazine featured Amazon.com CEO Jeff Bezos as its Man of the Year in 2000, but immediately thereafter Amazon.com's stock price began a long and painful descent, ultimately dropping more than 90 percent from its high in late 1999. Another example is the famous issue of *Business Week* with the pessimistic cover story titled "The Death of Equities," which came out at the tail end of the bear market of the 1970s. What timing — an issue warning investors about the dangers of stock investing just before the greatest bull market in history started.

✔ **Economic statistics have stabilized.** After the economy has hit rock bottom, the economic statistics start to improve. The most-watched set of economic indicators is reported by Statistics Canada and includes information about gross domestic product, inflation, and unemployment. The Bank of Canada's interest rate actions also impact the economy and should be tracked closely. The U.S. has many important indicators that try to foretell economic performance. These are called leading economic indicators and include things such as construction starts and bond yields. Investors review such data to make sure that the North American economy is getting back on its feet before it starts its next move upward. In 1982, the economy was just starting to recover from the 1981 recession. The economic expansion (and accompanying bull market) became the longest in history.

✔ **Economic conditions for individuals and companies are stable and strong.** You'll know that's true if profits are stable or growing for companies in general and if consumers are seeing strong and growing income growth. The logic holds up well: More money being made means more money to eventually spend and invest.

✔ **Industries producing large-ticket items have hit rock bottom and begin their climb.** After consumers and companies have been pummelled by a tough economy, they're not apt to make major financial commitments to items such as new cars, houses, equipment, and so on. Industries that produce these large, expensive items will see sales fall to a low and slowly start to rebound as the economy picks up. In a growing economy, consumers and companies experience greater confidence (both psychologically and financially).

✔ **Demographics appear favourable.** Take a look at the census and government statistics on trends for population growth, as well as the growth in the number of business enterprises. The 1980s and 1990s, for example, saw the rise of the baby boomers, those born during the post–Second World War period of 1946 to 1964. Baby boomers wielded great financial clout, much of it in the stock market. Their investment money played a major role in propelling the stock market to new highs.

✔ **General peace and stability prevail.** A major war or international conflict may have just ended. War is not good for many reasons, and it usually doesn't bode well for the stock market. The recent Iraq war and North Korean arms crisis prove this point.

Believe it or not, a mature bull market poses problems for investors and stock-market experts. In a mature bull market, just about any stock — good, bad, or indifferent — tends to go up. You could be a blind monkey throwing darts and pick a rising stock. When everything goes up and everybody seems to be making a winning pick, human nature kicks in. Both beginning and serious investors believe that their good fortune can be chalked up to superior stock-picking prowess and not simple luck or circumstance. Such overconfidence is a dangerous characteristic for stock investors.

Once investors become convinced of their new-found ability, they grow more daring in their investment approach; they make riskier choices, using less discipline and relying on less diligence and research. Then . . . whammo! They get socked by the market. Overconfidence lures the unsuspecting investor to more dangerous territory, invariably resulting in a very expensive lesson. Overconfidence and money don't mix.

In the 1999–2002 period, this tendency to be foolishly bullish long after the bull was gone was a common phenomenon that we refer to as the Wile E. Coyote effect. Do you remember Wile E. Coyote from those great *Road Runner* cartoons? Of course you do! You know the plot: Mr. Coyote is chasing the Road Runner and seems to be gaining on him. He is confidently ready to pounce on the seemingly unsuspecting bird, but the Road Runner makes a quick turn and watches as Mr. Coyote continues running over a cliff and ultimately plummets down a canyon. A mature bull market does that to investors. Scores of true stories tell of investors lured to a game of easy riches (the dot-com fiasco, for example) only to watch their investment get pulverized. This phenomenon happened not only to beginners but also to experienced investors — including many stock-investing experts who were familiar faces on your TV screen.

No matter how good or bad the economy or stock market is, true financial success comes from work, diligence, and discipline. This advice is especially true when times seem extraordinarily good or resoundingly bad.

Toro! Approaching a bull market

Being fully invested in stocks at the beginning of a bull market makes for spectacular success. But doing so takes some courage. Billionaire business executive J. Paul Getty said that buying low and selling high was the very essence of successful investing. Although most people agree with that advice psychologically, they're very hesitant when it's time to actually take action.

When the bull market is in its infancy, start investing by using the following approach:

- ✔ **Be a bargain hunter.** Frequently, at the tail end of a bear market, stock prices have been sufficiently battered after going through an extended period of low demand and/or disproportionately more selling of the shares by nervous investors. When share prices are lower in value than the book value of companies they represent, there is less risk in acquiring the shares that are generating positive growth in sales and earnings. Chapter 11 can help you better understand concepts such as book value.

✔ **Look for strong fundamentals.** Is the company you're choosing exhibiting solid sales and earnings? Are sales and earnings rising compared to the prior quarter or year? Conduct top-line and bottom-line analyses (which we discuss in Chapter 13) to determine a company's fundamentals. Do the company's products and services make sense to you? In other words, is it selling stuff that the public is starting to demand more of?

✔ **Consider the stock's class.** Remember that some stocks are more aggressive choices than other ones. This choice reflects your risk tolerance as well. Figure out whether you want to invest in a small-cap stock with phenomenal growth prospects (and commensurate risk), or a large-cap stock that is a tried-and-true market leader.

All things being equal, small-cap stocks exhibit the best growth performance in an emerging bull market. Small-cap stocks are more appropriate for investors who have a higher risk tolerance. Of course, most stocks do well in an emerging bull market (actually, that's what makes it a bull market!), so even risk-averse investors who put their money into larger companies will gain.

✔ **Choose appropriate industries.** Look at industries that are poised to rebound as the economy picks up and individuals and organizations begin to spend again. In a rising market, cyclical stocks such as those in the automobile, industrial equipment, and technology industries resume growth. When the economy is doing well, individuals and organizations begin to spend more on items that will meet their needs in an expanding economy. Companies upgrade their technology. Families get a new car or move to a bigger house. Construction firms need more and better equipment as residential and commercial building increases.

✔ **Take stock of your portfolio.** As you start to add stocks to your portfolio, have you first analyzed your situation to make sure that you have diversification not only in stocks and/or stock mutual funds but also in non–stock investments, such as savings bonds and bank accounts? Just because it's a bull market doesn't mean that you should have 100 percent of your investments in stocks; it means that you should consider putting as much as 100 percent of the growth component of your investment money in stocks.

Say that you're investing for the long term. You're not that concerned with risk, and you want maximum growth from your investments. After setting aside money in an emergency fund, you decide that you want to devote your remaining funds of $50,000 to growth stocks. In this case, 100 percent of that sum becomes the *growth component* of your investment portfolio. If you decide to play it safer and split it 50/50 between bonds and stocks, then $25,000 (or 50 percent of your portfolio) would be your growth component. The bonds would then be your *income component.*

✔ **Evaluate your personal goals.** No matter how good the market and the foreseeable prospects for growth, stock investing is a personal matter that should serve your unique needs. For example, how old are you, and how many years away is your retirement? All things being equal, a 35-year-old should have predominantly growth stocks, while a 65-year-old requires more proven, stable performance with large-cap market leaders. The information in Chapter 2 can help you identify appropriate investment goals.

Some investors in a bull market may have very little money in stocks. Why? Maybe they have already reached their financial goals, so wealth preservation is more appropriate than growth. Perhaps they have a million-dollar portfolio and are 70 years old and no longer working. In that case, having, say, 80 percent of their investments in stable, income-producing investments and 20 percent in proven, (yet modestly) growing stocks may make more sense.

The bottom line is that you choose the type of stocks as well as the mix to fit your unique situation and needs.

Bearing Down

Alas, stocks go down as well as up. Some ferocious bear markets have hit stocks on several occasions since the Great Depression. The worst ones were during the periods 1973–1975 and 2000–2003. But a few brief, minor ones occurred during the 1980s and 1990s. You don't need to worry about the occasional dips and short-term bear markets; however, be wary about *secular* (long-term) bear markets, which can last for years. Discipline and a watchful eye can keep you and your money out of trouble.

History in the making

The greatest bear market since the Great Depression started in 1973. The stock market was pummelled as the Dow Jones industrial average (DJIA) fell 45 percent during an 18-month period ending in 1975. The DJIA did not recover to its 1973 high until (you guessed it) 1982. The period from 1973 to 1982 had the hallmarks of tough times, high inflation, high unemployment, war, the energy crisis, and high taxes. The 1970s were a tough decade for most stocks. The 1980s and 1990s were great decades for stock investors. Alas, 2000 to 2003 were rough years for stocks as investors cumulatively lost trillions.

Identifying the beast

Bear markets can be foreseen. When the bear market of 2000 started that spring, observers and advisers had predicted it. However, most advisers and commentators told people to "hang tight," "buy on the dips," and "stay long-term focused." These tips are great when the market is zigzagging upward, but dangerous when it is zigzagging downward. The following sections present some telltale signs of an emerging bear market.

Optimism abounds

Everyone from Main Street to Bay Street feels great. Financial reports declare that the business cycle has been conquered and a new economy or new paradigm has arrived. Good times are here for the foreseeable future! You start to see books with titles such as *The Dow at 100,000* and *Easy Riches in the Stock Market* hit the best-seller lists. The *business cycle* refers to the economy's roller coaster–like behaviour when it expands (growth) and contracts (recession).

Sometimes, the financial experts believe that an economy is doing so well that it can continue to grow indefinitely. Examples of misguided exuberance abound in stock market history. In 1929, Irving Fisher, the best-known financial expert and stock millionaire of his day, made the ill-fated declaration "Stocks have reached a permanent plateau" as he predicted the bull market would continue for the foreseeable future. A few weeks later, the infamous stock market crash occurred. Everyone who had listened to Fisher got clobbered in the greatest bear market of the twentieth century. Even Irving Fisher himself filed for bankruptcy. Gee, not even Irving Fisher should have listened to Irving Fisher! In 1999, an economist boldly stated that the economy will continue growing forever and that "recessions are a thing of the past." Today, that economist is probably in a new job — saying, "Would you like some fries with that?"

Debt levels hit new highs

When optimism is high, people buy things. In 1999, debt levels hit a record high in almost every category: corporate, consumer, mortgage, and margin debt ballooned. This massive debt was mostly ignored by the financial press, yet it was one of the major reasons for the subsequent bear market and recession. When too much debt is accrued, it can be removed in only one of two ways: repayment or bankruptcy.

Excessive speculation, credit, and money supply expand

Whenever a country's money supply grows beyond the economy's needs, massive problems can result. When the money supply expands, more money is circulated into the banking system. (Go to the Bank of Canada [www.bank-banque-canada.ca] and Federal Reserve [www.federalreserve.gov] Web sites to find out more about money supply.) The banks then lend or invest this excess money. The oversupply of money flows into investment projects, such as initial public offerings and bond offerings. When too much money is available for too few worthy projects, invariably a lot of money is invested unwisely. This situation causes massive imbalances in the economic system, ultimately resulting in economic downturns that can take years to rectify.

History proves the truth of this economic situation. It happened to the U.S. and Canadian economies in the late 1920s, and to Japan in the late 1980s. Fortunately, statistics on credit and the money supply are easy to come by and readily available on the Internet. (See the Appendix for resources.)

Government intervention increases

Government has the power to do much good, but when it uses its power improperly it can do a great deal of harm. Every economy throughout history that collapsed ultimately did so because of excessive government intervention. In progressive, free-market economies this intervention usually occurs in the form of taxes, laws, and regulations. Keep a watchful eye on the prime minister and Parliament to monitor federal government intervention. Are they proposing policies that add burdens to the private economy? Are they advocating stringent new laws and regulations? We explain more about this in Chapter 14.

National and/or international conflict arises

Nothing can have a more negative impact on the economy than war, or political or civil unrest. Keep your eye on the news. Ask yourself what effect a particular conflict may have on the economy and the stock market.

Heading into the woods: Approaching a bear market

Sticking to a buy-and-hold strategy (where you buy stock and hold onto it for better or worse) at the onset of a bear market is financial suicide. People have a tough time selling, and financial advisers have an even tougher time telling them to cut their losses — because that's tantamount to saying, "Sorry, I was wrong." Admitting failure is hard for most people.

Understand that investing should be a logical, practical, and unemotional pursuit. You can't be married to stocks — until death do you part — especially because bear markets can divorce you from your money.

In an emerging bear market, keep the following points in mind to maximize your gains (or just to minimize your losses):

- **Review your situation.** Before you consider any move in or out of the market, review your overall financial situation to make sure that your money and financial condition are as secure as possible. Make sure that you have an emergency fund of four to six months' worth of gross living expenses. Keep your debt at a comfortably low level. Review your career, insurance, and so on. Schedule a financial checkup with your financial planner.

- **Remember that cash is king.** When the bear market is coming and economic storm clouds are rolling in, keep the bulk of your money in safe, interest-bearing vehicles such as bank investments, Canadian or other treasury securities, and money market funds. Doing so keeps your money safe. If stocks are falling by 10 to 20 percent or more, you're better off earning a low-percentage interest in a secure, stable investment. In addition, you can do some research while your money is earning interest. Start looking for undervalued stocks with strong fundamentals.

- **Stick to necessities.** In an economic downturn, defensive stocks generally outperform the market. *Defensive stocks* are stocks of companies that sell goods and services that people need no matter how good or bad the economy is doing. Good examples are food and beverage, energy, utilities, and certain healthcare stocks.

- **Use trailing stops.** Trailing stops are our favourite disciplined approach to preserving gains made. See Chapter 20 for the scoop on trailing stops.

Straddling Bear and Bull: Uncertain Markets

Uncertain markets are . . . well . . . uncertain. Markets aren't always up or down. The end of a bear market doesn't automatically mean the beginning of a bull market and vice versa. Sometimes markets move sideways or very little either way until investors and participants in the economy figure out what's what.

Pinpointing uncertainty is tough

Clashing points of view in the media tell you that even the experts are not sure which way the market and the economy will go in the coming months. In uncertain markets, compelling evidence and loads of opinions will evenly line up on both the pro and con side of the economic debate. Bullish and bearish advisers and commentators may both seem persuasive, so you may be left scratching your head, wondering what to do. This is where your patience and diligence pay off.

Sure you want to approach an uncertain market?

The approach to take in uncertain markets is almost simplistic. If you think that a bull market is starting, you want to be 100-percent invested in stocks; if a bear market is starting, you want the percentage to be 0. Therefore, in an uncertain market, 50 percent in stocks and 50 percent in other investments is just right. Of course, these three scenarios should be balanced by many non-stock factors, such as your individual financial situation, age, debt level, career concerns, and so on. However, all things being equal, those allocations aren't far off the mark.

Treat uncertain markets as bear markets until the data prove otherwise. No matter how adventurous you are, the first rule of stock investing is to minimize or avoid losses. If no one can agree on the direction of the market, then you stand a 50-percent chance of being wrong should you take the bullish stance. However, if you take a bearish stance and the market becomes decidedly bullish, no real harm is done except that you may miss a stock-investing opportunity during a brief period of time. Just keep in mind that stock investing is indeed a long-term pursuit. Jumping into a bullish market is easy, but recovering losses isn't always easy.

Chapter 19

Analyzing Industries

. . . .

In This Chapter

▶ Choosing an industry

▶ Understanding different categories of industries

▶ Highlighting some key industries

. . . .

Suppose that you have to bet your entire nest egg on a one-kilometre race. All you need to do is select a winning group. These are your choices:

- ✔ A group of thoroughbred race horses
- ✔ A group of aging Elvis impersonators
- ✔ A group of lethargic snails

This isn't a trick question, and you have one minute to answer. Notice that we didn't ask you to pick a single winner out of a giant mush of horses, Elvii, and snails; we only asked you to pick the winning group in the race. The obvious answer is the thoroughbred racehorses (and, no, they weren't ridden by the aging Elvis impersonators because that would take away from the eloquent point being made). In this example, even the slowest member of group A would easily outdistance the fastest member of either group B or C.

Fortunately, this is where the comparison to stock investing ends. You don't have to choose the absolute winner, because there are lots of winning stocks in second place, too. The basic point is that you increase your odds of winning when you choose a winning industry group as part of your strategy. In the race to build wealth, all you need to do is pick decent stocks in a decent industry (read on) and do so on a long-term basis in a disciplined manner.

A successful long-term investor looks at the industry just as carefully as he looks at the individual stock. Luckily, choosing a winning industry to invest in is *easier* than choosing individual stocks. We know some investors who can pick a winning stock in a losing industry, and I also know investors who have chosen a losing stock in a winning industry (the former is far outnumbered by the latter). Just think how well you would do when you choose a great stock in a great industry! Of course, you would bang your head (or your broker's) against the wall if you chose a bad stock in a bad industry.

Badgering the Witness and Interrogating the Industries

Your common sense is an important tool in choosing industries with winning stocks. The following sections explore some of the most important questions to ask yourself.

Is the industry growing?

The question may seem too obvious, but probably not. The saying "The trend is your friend" applies when choosing an industry in which to invest, as long as the trend is an upward one. If you look at three different stocks that are equal in every significant way, but you find that stock A is in an industry growing 15 percent per year while the other two industries have either little growth or are shrinking, which stock would you choose?

Sometimes, the stock of a financially unsound or poorly run company goes up dramatically because the industry it's in is very exciting to the public. The most obvious example is Internet stocks from 1998 to 2000. Stocks such as Amazon.com shot up to incredible heights because investors thought the Internet was "it." Sooner or later, the measure of a successful company is its ability to be profitable. Serious investors look at the company's fundamentals (see Chapter 9 and Chapter 15 to find out how to do this) and the prospects for the industry's growth before settling on a particular stock.

To judge how well an industry is doing, various information sources monitor all the major industries and measure their progress. The more reliable sources include the following:

- CBS MarketWatch (www.marketwatch.com)
- Adviceforinvestors.com (www.adviceforinvestors.com)
- Standard & Poor's Industry Survey (www.standardpoor.com)
- Hoover's Industry Snapshots (www.hoovers.com)
- Yahoo! Industry News (www.industry.yahoo.com)

The preceding sources generally give you in-depth information about major industries. Visit their Web sites to read their current research and articles along with links to relevant sites for more details.

Are the industry's products or services in demand?

Look at the products and services that an industry provides. Do they look like things that society will continue to want? Are there products and services on the horizon that could replace them? Does the industry face a danger of potential obsolescence?

When evaluating future demand, look for a _sunrise industry,_ which is one that is new or emerging or has promising appeal for the future. Good examples in recent years have been biotech and Internet companies. In contrast, a _sunset industry_ is one that is either declining or has little potential for growth. For example, you probably shouldn't invest in the video cassette manufacturing industry as demand for the new DVD format increases. Owning stock in a strong, profitable company in a sunrise industry is obviously the most desirable choice.

Futurists, trend watchers, and other "seers into the future" predict the following megatrends:

- **The aging of America:** There will be more senior citizens than ever before. Because of this, financial and healthcare services will prosper.
- **Advances in high-tech:** Internet, telecom, medical, and biotechnology innovations will continue.
- **Increasing need for basic materials:** As society advances here and in the rest of the world, building blocks such as metals and other precious commodities will be in demand.

What does the industry's growth rely on?

An industry doesn't exist in a vacuum. External factors weigh heavily on its ability to survive and thrive. Does the industry rely on an established megatrend, in which case it will probably be strong for a while, or on factors that are losing relevance? Technological and demographic changes are other factors that may contribute to an industry's growth.

Perhaps the industry offers great new medical products for senior citizens. What are the prospects for growth? The greying of Canada is an established megatrend. As millions of Canadians climb past age 50, great opportunities await companies that cater to them.

Is this industry dependent on another industry?

This twist on the prior question is a reminder that industries frequently are intertwined and can become codependent. When one industry suffers, you may find it helpful to understand which industries will subsequently suffer. The reverse can also be true — when one industry is doing well, other industries may also reap the benefits.

In either case, if the stock you choose is in an industry that is highly dependent on other industries, you should know about it. If you were considering stocks of resort companies and you saw the headlines blaring "Airlines losing money as public stops flying," what would you do?

Who are the leading companies in the industry?

Once you've chosen the industry, what types of companies do you want to invest in? You can choose from two basic types of companies:

- ✔ **Established leaders:** These companies are considered industry leaders or have a large share of the market. This is the safer way to go; what better investment for novice investors than companies that have already proven themselves?

- ✔ **Innovators:** If the industry is hot and you want to be more aggressive in your approach, why not speculate in companies that offer new products, patents, or technologies? These are probably smaller companies, but they have a greater potential for growth in a proven industry.

Is the industry a target of government action?

You need to know whether the government is targeting an industry, because intervention by politicians and bureaucrats (rightly or wrongly) can have an impact on an industry's economic situation. For example, would you invest in a tobacco company now that the government has issued all of its regulations and warnings?

Investors need to take heed when political "noise" starts coming out about a particular industry. An industry can be hurt either by direct government intervention or by the threat of it. Intervention can take the form of lawsuits, investigations, taxes, regulations, tariffs, or sometimes an outright ban. In any case, there is no greater external threat to a company's survival than being on the wrong end of government intervention.

Sometimes, government action can help an industry. Generally, beneficial action can take two forms:

> ✔ **Deregulation and/or tax decreases:** Government can sometimes reduce burdens on an industry. In the 1990s, the Canadian government deregulated the airlines, an action that in turn caused a boom in travel. The airline industry subsequently experienced solid growth as more Canadians flew than ever before. This increase in travel has declined since then, but likely because of external issues such as war and economic concerns.

> ✔ **Direct funding:** Government has the power to steer taxpayer money toward business as well. In the early 1990s, when Magna was floundering, financing assistance helped the company get back on its feet. Now Magna and its subsidiaries are veritable powerhouses.

Which category does the industry fall into?

Most industries can be placed neatly into several categories, which are discussed next.

Cyclical

Cyclical industries are industries whose fortunes rise and fall with the economy's rise and fall. In other words, if the economy is doing well and the stock market is doing well, cyclical industries tend to do well. When the economy is doing well, consumers and investors are confident and tend to spend and invest more money than usual. Real estate, automobiles, and most technology sub-sectors are great examples of cyclical industries.

Your own situation offers you some common-sense insight into the concept of cyclical industries. Think about your behaviour as a consumer, and you get a great clue into the thinking of millions of Canadian consumers. Think about the times you felt good about your career and your finances. When you (and millions of others) feel good about money and about the future, you have a greater tendency to buy more (and/or more expensive) stuff. When people feel financially strong, they're more apt to buy a new house or car or make some other large financial commitment. Also, people take on more debt because they feel confident that they can pay it back. In light of this, what industries do you think would do well?

The same point also holds for business spending. When businesses think that economic times are good and foresee continuing good times, they tend to spend more money on large purchases such as new equipment or technology. They think that when they're doing well and flush with financial success it's a good idea to reinvest that money to increase future success.

Defensive

Defensive industries are industries that produce goods and services that are needed no matter what's happening in the economy. This is where your common sense kicks in. What will you still buy even if times are tough? Think about what millions of people buy no matter how bad the economy gets. A good example is food. People still need to eat in good times and bad. Other examples of defensive industries are utilities and healthcare.

So how do defensive stocks grow? Their growth generally relies on two factors:

- ✔ **Population growth:** As more and more consumers are born, more people become available to buy.

- ✔ **New markets:** A company can grow by seeking out new groups of consumers who can buy their products and services. Coca-Cola, for example, found new markets in Asia during the 1990s. As communist regimes fell from power and more societies embraced a free market and consumer goods, the company sold more beverages, and its stock soared.

Emerging

Companies in *emerging industries* develop totally new products or services. The biotechnology industry continues to emerge with sub-sectors such as nanotechnology and genetic engineering. These days, change continues to accelerate and presents more investment opportunities than ever before.

Even the beaten-down technology industry continues to innovate. E-commerce and wireless computing and telecommunications continue to grow in new and exciting ways. New materials are being put into chips to make them faster and less power-consuming. The intrinsic value of companies in an emerging industry is based less on traditional benchmarks, and more on the calibre and potential of a new idea.

Growth

Companies making a home in *growth industries* usually have sales and net income that are rising at a faster rate than many other industries. Growth companies tend to increase in market capitalization at above-average rates for several years. They are expected to continue to grow after that too, albeit at a more modest pace.

A sustained rise in stock price, however, does not herald a growth stock. The rise must be based on permanent factors, such as rising sales and sales volumes, solid cash earnings, and productive assets. Growth stocks should exhibit the following:

- ✔ Reinvestment of earnings instead of dividend payouts
- ✔ High rate of return on total assets and equity

> ✔ Tremendous opportunity for growth in cash generation
> ✔ Aggressive, experienced, and competent management

Speculative

There are high-risk, speculative companies operating in — you guessed it — *speculative industries*. There is no guarantee that a company will even survive. In Canada, speculative "penny stocks" can easily be found in oil and gas and mining.

The term *speculative* also refers to the bidding up of a growth company's stock in anticipation of an important discovery or development. If expectations turn out to be nothing but the hot air of hype — something abundantly found in Internet investment site chat rooms — the stock could tank.

Declining

Companies offering products and services in *declining industries* lack potential. Changes in technology or consumer preference force these companies to either change with the times or perish. Often, companies in these industries diversify their products and services through strategic acquisitions, or by adopting new strategies altogether. Steel manufacturing exemplifies a declining industry, where demand for steel has declined because of the existence of alternative materials.

Don't Shoot the Messenger: Key Industries

Not all industries go up and down in tandem. Indeed, at any given time some industry is successful no matter what is happening with the general economy. In fact, investors have made a lot of money simply by choosing an industry that benefits from economic trends. There are several key industries every stock investor should watch.

For sale

Real estate is a key industry because it is a cyclical *bellwether industry* (one that has a great effect on many other industries that may be dependent on it). It is looked at as a key component of economic health because so many other industries, including building materials, mortgages, household appliances, and contract labour services, are tied to it. When the real estate industry is booming, that bodes well for much of the economy.

Housing starts are one way to measure real estate activity. This data is an important leading indicator of health in the industry. Housing starts indicate new construction, which means more business for related industries.

Keep an eye on the real estate industry for negative news that could be bearish for the economy and the stock market. Because real estate is purchased with mortgage money, investors and analysts watch the mortgage market for trouble signs such as rising delinquencies and foreclosures. These statistics serve as a warning for general economic weakness.

Baby, you can drive my car

The auto industry is another business that you should watch very carefully. When cars are selling well, you can generally interpret that as a positive indicator for the economy. People buy new cars when they're doing well. Autos are big-ticket items that are another barometer of people's economic well-being.

Conversely, trouble in the auto industry is a red flag. If auto repossessions and car loan delinquencies are rising, you should view that as a warning about general economic weakness.

Thanking Mr. Roboto

In recent years, technology became very popular with investors. Indeed, it is a great sector, and its impact on the economy's present and future success cannot be underestimated. The shares of technology companies can rise substantially because investors buy them based on expectations — today's untested, unproven companies may become the Microsofts and IBMs of tomorrow. In spite of the sector's potential, companies can still fail if customers don't embrace their products. Even in technology stocks, you still must apply the rules and guidelines about financially successful companies that we discuss throughout this book. Pick the best in a growing industry, and you'll succeed over the long haul.

Banking on it

Banking and financial services are an intrinsic part of any economy. Debt is the most telling sign of this industry for investors. If debt is growing faster than the economy, you need to watch to see how it will impact their stocks and mutual funds. If debt gets out of control, it can be disastrous for the economy.

Chapter 20

Stop! In the Name of Money

- -

In This Chapter

▶ Looking at different types of brokerage orders

▶ Using trailing stops to protect your profits

▶ Trading on margin to maximize profits

▶ Making sense of going short

- -

*I*nvestment success isn't just about picking rising stocks; it's also about how you go about doing it. Frequently, investors think that good stock picking means doing your homework and then executing that purchase or sale. However, you can take it a step further, to maximize profits (or minimize losses). As a stock investor, you can do so by taking advantage of techniques and services available through your garden-variety brokerage account. (See Chapter 8 for more on brokerage accounts, and a bit about fruits and vegetables, too.) This chapter presents some of the best ways you can use these powerful techniques — useful whether you're buying or selling stock. In fact, if you retain nothing more from this chapter than the concept of *trailing stops* (see the section "Trailing stops"), you'll have gotten your money's worth.

Orders you place with your stockbroker neatly fit into two categories:

- ✔ **Time-related orders:** Time-related orders mean just that — the order has a time limit. Typically, these are used in conjunction with conditional orders. (For an example, see the "Limit Orders" section later in this chapter.) The two most common time-related orders are day orders and good-till-cancelled (or GTC) orders, which we explain in their own sections later in this chapter.

- ✔ **Condition-related orders:** A condition-related order is one that should be executed only when a certain condition is met. Conditional orders enhance your ability to buy stocks at a lower price, to sell at a better price, or to minimize potential losses. When stock markets become bearish or uncertain, conditional orders are highly recommended. A good example of a conditional order is a *limit order*. A limit order may say, "Buy SlapShot Company at $45." But if SlapShot Company is not available at $45 (this is the condition), then the order isn't executed.

Get familiar with both kinds of orders, because they're easy to work with and invaluable tools for wealth building and (more importantly) wealth saving!

Using a combination of orders helps you fine-tune your strategy so that you can maintain greater control over your investments. Speak with your broker about the different types of orders you can use to maximize the gains (or minimize the losses) from your stock-investing activities. You also can read the broker's policies on stock orders at the brokerage Web site.

Call It a Day Order

A *day order* (a time-related order) is an order to buy a stock that expires at the end of that particular trading day. If you tell your broker, "Buy BYOB Inc. at $37.50 and make it a day order," you mean that you want to purchase the stock at $37.50. But if the stock doesn't hit that price, your order expires at the end of the trading day unfilled. Why would you place such an order? Maybe BYOB is trading at $39, but you don't want to buy it at that price because you don't believe the stock is worth it. Consequently, you have no problem not getting the stock that day.

When would you use day orders? It depends on your preferences and personal circumstances. We rarely use day orders because there are few events that cause us to say, "Gee, I'll just try to buy or sell between now and the end of today's trading action." However, you may feel that you don't want a specified order to linger beyond today's market action. Perhaps you want to test a price. ("I would like to get rid of stock A at $39 to make a quick profit, but it's currently trading at $37.50. However, I may change my mind tomorrow.") A day order is the perfect strategy to use in this case.

By the way, if you make any trade and don't specify time with the order, most (if not all) brokers automatically treat it as a day order.

Good-till-Cancelled (GTC)

A good-till-cancelled (GTC) order is the most commonly requested order by investors. Although GTC orders are time-related, they are always tied to a condition, such as when the stock achieves a certain price. The GTC order means just what it says: The order stays in effect until it is transacted or until the investor cancels it. Although the order implies that it could run indefinitely, most brokers do set a time limit. The time limit could be 30 days, 60 days, 90 days, or longer. Ask your broker about his particular policy on GTC orders.

A GTC order is usually coupled with conditional or condition-related orders. For example, say that you want to buy ASAP Corp. stock but you don't want to buy it at the current price of $48 per share. You've done your homework on the stock, including looking at the stock's price to earnings ratio, price to book ratio, and so on (see Chapter 15 for more on ratios), and you say, "Hey, this stock isn't worth $48 a share. I would only buy it at $36 per share." You think the stock would make a good addition to your portfolio, but not at the current market price — it's overpriced or overvalued according to your analysis. How should you proceed?

Well, you wouldn't put in a day order to get the stock at $36. To go from $48 to $36 in a day means that the stock would need to fall by 25 percent. The odds are against that happening (unless you know something that we don't). However, the odds that such a decline could happen over a period of a few weeks or a few months are much better. If you want that stock at your price and you are patient, ask your broker to do "a GTC order at $36." This means that your broker will buy the shares if and when they hit the $36 mark (or until you cancel the order). Just make sure that your account has the funds available to complete the transaction.

The bottom line is that GTC orders are very useful, so you should become familiar with your broker's policy on them. While you're at it, ask whether any fees apply. Many brokers don't charge for GTC orders because, if the orders happen to result in a buy (or sell) order, they generate a normal commission just as any stock transaction would. Other brokers may charge a small fee. In many cases, if a fee is charged it's credited against the commission should the transaction occur. Fee or no fee, the GTC order is meant to protect you from further losses or to help you lock in a profit.

When you want to buy

In recent years, people have had a tendency to rush into buying a stock without giving some thought to what they could do to get more for their money. It doesn't occur to some investors that the stock market can be a place for bargain-hunting consumers. If you're ready to buy a quality pair of socks for $16 in a department store but the sales clerk says that those same socks are going on sale tomorrow for only $8, what would you do — assuming that you're a cost-conscious consumer? Unless you're barefoot, you're probably better off waiting. The same point holds true with stocks.

Say that you want to buy SOX Inc. at $26 but it's currently trading at $30. You think that $30 is too expensive, but you're happy to buy the stock at $26 or lower. However, you have no idea whether the stock will move to your desired price today, tomorrow, next week, or even next month. In this case, a GTC order is appropriate.

When you want to sell

Remember the socks you bought? Well, what if you have a hole in your sock (darn it!)? Wouldn't you want to get rid of it? Of course you would. If a stock's price starts to unravel, you want to be able to get rid of it as well.

Perhaps you already own SOX (at $25, for instance) but are concerned that market conditions may drive the price lower. You're not certain which way the stock will move in the coming days and weeks. In this case, a GTC order to sell the stock at a specified price is a suitable strategy. Because the stock price is $25, you may want to place a GTC order to sell it if it falls to $22.50, to prevent further losses. Again, in this example GTC is the time frame, and it accompanies a condition (sell when the stock hits $22.50).

Market Orders

When you buy stock, the simplest type of order is a *market order* — an order to buy or sell a stock at the market's current best available price. It doesn't get any more basic than that.

Here's an example: Beliveau Inc., is available at the market price of $10. When you call up your broker and instruct him to buy 100 shares "at the market," the broker will implement the order for your account, and you pay $1,000 plus commission.

We say "current best available price" because the stock's price is constantly moving, and catching the best price can be a function of the broker's ability to process the stock purchase. For very active stocks, the price change can happen within seconds. It's not unheard of to have three brokers simultaneously place orders for the same stocks and get three different prices because of differences in the broker's capability. (Some computers are faster than others.) The price difference within these seconds usually isn't worth getting concerned about because the difference amounts to pennies. It would matter to day traders and those who buy huge amounts of stock, but it's not a consequential difference to the everyday stock investor.

The advantage of a market order is that the transaction is processed immediately, and you get your stock without worrying about whether it hits a particular price. For example, if you buy Beliveau, Inc. with a market order, you know that by the end of that phone call (or Web site visit), you're assured of getting the stock. The disadvantage of a market order is that you can't control the price that you pay for the stock. Suppose that you learn that Beliveau, Inc. is currently trading at $10 per share. You call your broker to place an order. If the stock jumps to $11 per share before you finish ordering, you end up buying it for $1 more than you figured. Then again, you could get it for $9 if the price moves downward. With a fast-moving stock, you may get it at a significantly higher price than you planned. Conversely, if you're selling a particularly volatile stock, you might lock in a sale price lower (or higher) than you expected if the price changes before you finish your sale.

Market orders get finalized in the chronological order in which they're placed. Your price may change because the orders ahead of you in line caused the stock price to rise or fall based on the latest news.

Stop! I Order You!

A *stop order* (or *stop-loss order,* if you own the stock) is a condition-related order that instructs the broker to sell a particular stock only when the stock reaches a particular price. It acts like a trigger, and the stop order converts to a market order to sell the stock immediately.

The stop-loss order isn't designed to take advantage of small, short-term moves in the stock's price. It's meant to help you protect the bulk of your money when the market turns against your stock investment in a sudden manner.

Say that your Beliveau, Inc. stock rises to $20 per share and you seek to protect your investment against a possible future market decline. A stop-loss order at $18 will trigger your broker to sell the stock immediately if it falls to the $18 mark. In this example, if the stock suddenly drops to $17 it will still trigger the stop-loss order, but the finalized sale price will be $17. In a volatile market, you may not be able to sell at your precise stop-loss price. However, because the order automatically gets converted into a market order, the sale will be done, and you avoid the impact of any further declines in price of the stock.

The main benefit of a stop-loss order is that it prevents a major decline in a stock that you own. It's a form of discipline that is important in investing in order to minimize potential losses. Investors can find it agonizing to sell a stock that has fallen. If they don't sell, however, the stock often continues to plummet as investors continue to hold on while hoping for a rebound in the price.

A stop-loss amount is usually set at about 10 percent below the market value of a stock. This percentage gives the stock some room to fluctuate, which most stocks tend to do on a day-to-day basis.

Trailing stops

Trailing stops are an important technique in wealth preservation for seasoned stock investors and can be one of your key strategies in using stop-loss orders. A *trailing stop* is a stop-loss order that the investor actively manages by moving it up along with the stock's market price. The stop-loss order "trails" the stock price upward. As the stop-loss goes upward, it protects more and more of the stock's value from declining.

To illustrate trailing stops with a real-life example, say that in 1999 you bought ATI Technologies (ATY) at $25 per share. As soon as you finished buying it, you immediately told your broker to put a stop-loss order at $22 and make it a good-till-cancelled (GTC) order. Think of what you did. In effect, you placed an ongoing (GTC) safety net under your stock. The stock can go as high as the sky, but if it should fall the stock's price will trigger a sell order at $22, at which point your stock will automatically be sold, minimizing your loss.

If ATI goes to $50 per share in a few months, you can call your broker and cancel the former stop-loss order at $22 and replace it with a new (higher) stop-loss order. You simply say, "Please put a new stop-loss order at $45 and make it a GTC order." This higher stop-loss price protects not only your original investment of $20, but also a big chunk of your profit. As time goes by and the stock price climbs, you can continue to raise the stop-loss price and add a GTC provision. Now you know why it is called a trailing stop: It trails the stock price upward like a giant tail. All along the way, it protects more and more of your growing investment without limiting its upward movement.

Some investment experts advocate setting a trailing stop of 10 percent below your purchase price. Many investors who invest in very volatile stocks may put in trailing stops of 20 or 25 percent. Is a stop-loss order desirable or advisable in every situation? No. It depends on your level of experience, your investment goals, and the market environment. Still, stop-loss orders are appropriate in most cases, especially if the market seems uncertain (or you do!).

A trailing stop is a stop-loss order that you actively manage. The stop-loss order is good-till-cancelled, and it constantly trails the stock's price as it moves up. To successfully implement trailing stops, keep the following points in mind:

- ✔ **Brokers usually don't place trailing stops for you automatically.** In fact, they won't (or shouldn't) place any type of order without your consent. Deciding on the type of order to place is your responsibility. You can raise, lower, or cancel a trailing stop order at will, but you need to monitor your investment when substantial moves do occur, and to respond to the movement appropriately.

 ✔ **Change the stop-loss order when the stock price moves significantly.** Hopefully, you won't call your broker every time the stock moves 50 cents. Change the stop-loss order when the stock price moves around 10 percent. When you initially purchase the stock (say, at $90 per share), request the broker to place the stop-loss order at $81. When the stock moves to $100, cancel the $81 stop-loss order and replace it at $90. When the stock's price moves to $110, change the stop-loss order to $100, and so on.

 ✔ **Understand your broker's policy on GTC orders.** If your broker usually has a GTC order expire after 30 or 60 days, you should be aware of it. You don't want to risk a sudden drop in your stock's price with the stop-loss order protection. If your broker's time limit is 60 days, note it so that you can renew the order for additional time.

 ✔ **Monitor your stock.** Trailing stops is not a "set it and forget it" technique. Monitoring your investment is critical. Of course, if it falls, the stop-loss order you have will prevent further loss. Should the stock price rise substantially, remember to adjust your trailing stop accordingly. Keep raising the safety net as the stock continues to rise. Part of monitoring the stock is knowing the *beta*, which you can read more about in the next section.

I beta you didn't know this

To be a successful investor, you need to understand the volatility of the particular stock you invest in. In stock market parlance, this is also called the beta of a stock. *Beta* is a quantitative measure of the volatility of a given stock (mutual funds and portfolios, too) relative to the overall market, usually the S&P 500 index. Beta specifically measures the performance movement of the stock as the S&P moves 1 percent up or down. A beta measurement above 1 is more volatile than the overall market, while a beta below 1 is less volatile. Some stocks are relatively stable in their price movements; others jump around.

Because beta measures how volatile or unstable the stock's price is, it tends to be uttered in the same breath as "risk" — more volatility indicates more risk. Similarly, less volatility tends to mean less risk.

Table 21-1 shows some sample betas of well-known companies (as of March 2002):

Table 21-1		Looking at Well-known Betas
Company	*Beta*	*Comments*
Petro Canada	.55	Is less volatile than the market. If the S&P moves $10, Petro-Canada would move only $5.50
Yahoo!	2.63	Is almost three times more volatile than the market
Public Service Enterprise Group	.07	Statistically considered much less volatile than the market

You can find a company's beta at Web sites that usually provide a lot of financial information about the company, such as Yahoo!Finance (`finance.yahoo.com`). Once there, type in your stock ticker symbol, and click the Profile icon. That's where you'll find the beta.

The beta is useful to know because it gives you a general idea of the stock's trading range. If a stock is currently priced at $50 and it typically trades in the $48–$52 range, then a trailing stop at $49 doesn't make sense. Your stock would probably be sold the same day you initiated the stop-loss order. If your stock is a volatile growth stock that could swing up and down by 10 percent, you should more logically set your stop-loss at 15 percent below that day's price.

The stock of a large-cap stock in a mature industry tends to have a low beta — one close to the overall market. Small- and mid-cap stocks in new or emerging industries tend to have greater volatility in their day-to-day price fluctuations; hence, they tend to have a high beta. (You can find an explanation of capitalization in Chapter 1.)

Limit Orders

A *limit order* is a very precise condition-related order, implying that there is a limit either on the buy or the sell side of the transaction. You want to buy (or sell) only at a specified price. Period. Limit orders work better for you if you're buying the stock, but they may not be good for you if you're selling the stock.

Usually there are no special fees for limit orders. Brokers make their money when the order is triggered. At that point, the transaction (buy or sell) would generate a regular commission. However, policies and fees can vary depending on the brokerage. Some Internet brokerages actually charge a small fee for limit orders because they charge low commissions. They may credit the fee against the sell or buy commission if the order is triggered. (This is also true of stop orders, which we discuss earlier in this chapter.)

When you're buying

Just because you like a particular company and you want its stock, doesn't mean that you're willing to pay the current market price. Maybe you want to buy Beliveau, Inc., but the current market price of $20 per share isn't acceptable to you. You prefer to buy it at $16 because you think that price reflects its true market value. What do you do? You tell your broker, "Buy Beliveau with a limit order at $16."

Of course, you don't know exactly when the stock will hit your price of choice. In this example, stock in Beliveau, Inc. may hit $16 by the end of the day or sometime next month or possibly never. You must place an order within a certain time limit. You have to specify whether it is a day order (good for the day) or a GTC order, which we discuss in its own section earlier in this chapter. Unless you know some bad news about the company that the rest of the market doesn't (in which case a day order is advisable), the better option is to make it a GTC limit order. If and when the stock goes to $16 during the time your GTC order is in effect, the order to buy will automatically be performed, and you receive a trade confirmation notice.

What happens if the stock experiences great volatility? What if it drops to $16.01 and then suddenly drops to $15.95 on the next move? Actually, nothing, you may be dismayed to hear. Because your order was limited to $16, it can be transacted only at $16, no more or less. The only way for this particular trade to occur is if the stock rises back to $16. However, if the price keeps dropping, then your limit order won't be transacted and may expire or be cancelled.

When you're buying a stock, many brokers interpret the limit order as "buy at this specific price or better." Presumably, if your limit order is to buy the stock at $10, you'll be just as happy if your broker buys that stock for you at $9.95. This way, if you don't get exactly $10, because the stock's price was volatile, you'll still get the stock at a lower price. Speak to your particular broker to be clear on the meaning of the limit order.

When you're selling

Limit orders are activated only when a stock hits a specific price. If you buy Beliveau, Inc. at $20 and you worry about a decline in the share price, you may decide to put in a limit order at $18. If you watch the news and hear that Beliveau's price is dropping, you may sigh and say, "I sure am glad that I put in that limit order at $18!" However, in a volatile market, the share price may leapfrog over your specified price. It could go from $18.01 to $17.99 and then continue its descent. Because the stock price never hit $18 on the mark, it isn't sold. You may be sitting at home satisfied (mistakenly) that you played it smart, while your stock plummets to $15 or $10 or worse! It's best to have a stop-loss order in place.

Pass the Margin, Please

Margin means buying securities, such as stocks, by using funds you borrow from your broker. Buying stock on margin is similar to buying a house with a mortgage. If you buy a house at the purchase price of $100,000 and put 10 percent down, your equity (the part you own) is $10,000, and you borrow the remaining $90,000 with a mortgage. If the value of the house rises to $120,000 and you sell (for the sake of simplicity, we don't include closing costs in this example), you will make a profit of 100 percent. How is that? The $20,000 gain on the property represents a gain of 20 percent on the purchase price of $100,000, but because your real investment is $10,000 (the down payment), your gain works out to 200 percent (a gain of $20,000 on your initial investment of $10,000).

Buying on margin is an example of using leverage to maximize your gain when prices rise. *Leverage* is simply using borrowed money to increase your profit. This type of leverage is great in a favourable (bull) market, but it works against you in an unfavourable (bear) market. Say that a $100,000 house you purchase with a $90,000 mortgage falls in value to $80,000 (and property values can decrease during economic hard times). Your outstanding debt of $90,000 exceeds the value of the property. Because you owe more than you own, it is negative net worth. Leverage is a double-edged sword.

Marginal outcomes

Suppose that you think that the stock for the company Mergatroid, Inc., currently at $40 per share, will go up in value. You want to buy 100 shares, but you have only $2,000. What can you do? If you're intent on buying 100 shares (versus simply buying the 50 shares that you have cash for), you can borrow the additional $2,000 from your broker on margin. If you do that, what are the potential outcomes?

If the stock price goes up

This is the best outcome for you. If Mergatroid goes to $50 per share, your investment will be worth $5,000, and your outstanding margin loan will be $2,000. If you sell, the total proceeds will pay off the loan and leave you with $3,000. Because your initial investment was $2,000, your profit is a solid

50 percent, because ultimately your $2,000 principal amount generated a $1,000 profit. (For the sake of this example, we leave out any charges, such as commissions and interest paid on the margin loan.) However, if you pay the entire $4,000 upfront — without the margin loan — your $4,000 investment will generate a profit of $1,000, or 25 percent. Using margin, you will double the return on your money.

Leverage, when used properly, is very profitable. However, it is still debt, so understand that you must pay it off eventually.

If the stock price fails to rise

If the stock goes nowhere, you still have to pay interest on that margin loan. If the stock pays dividends, this money can defray some of the cost of the margin loan. In other words, dividends can help you pay off what you borrow from the broker.

Having the stock neither rise nor fall may seem like a neutral situation, but you pay interest on your margin loan with each passing day. For this reason, margin trading can be a good consideration for conservative investors if the stock pays a high dividend. Many times, a high dividend from $5,000 worth of stock can exceed the margin interest you have to pay from the $2,500 (50 percent) you borrow from the broker to buy that stock.

If the stock price goes down, buying on margin can work against you. What if Mergatroid goes to $38 per share? The market value of 100 shares will be $3,800, but your equity will shrink to only $1,800 because you have to pay your $2,000 margin loan. You're not exactly looking at a disaster at this point, but you'd better be careful, because the margin loan exceeds 50 percent of your stock investment. If it goes any lower, you may get the notorious *margin call,* when the broker actually contacts you to ask you to restore the ratio between the margin loan and the value of the securities. See the following section for information about appropriate debt to equity ratios.

Maintaining your balance

When you purchase stock on margin, you must maintain a balanced ratio of margin debt to equity of at least 50 percent. If the debt portion exceeds this limit, then you'll be required to restore that ratio by depositing either more stock or more cash into your brokerage account. The additional stock you deposit can be stock that's transferred from another account.

If, for example, Mergatroid goes to $28 per share, the margin loan portion exceeds 50 percent of the equity value in that stock — in this case, because the market value of your stock is $2,800 but the margin loan is still at $2,000. The margin loan is a worrisome 71 percent of the market value ($2,000 divided by $2,800 = 71 percent). Expect to get a call from your broker to put more securities or cash into the account to restore the 50-percent balance.

If you can't come up with more stock, other securities, or cash, then the next step is to sell stock from the account and use the proceeds to pay off the margin loan. For you, it means realizing a capital loss — you lost money on your investment.

Margin, as you can see, can escalate your profits (on the upside), but magnify your losses (on the downside). If your stock plummets drastically, you can end up with a margin loan that exceeds the market value of the stock you used the loan to purchase. In the emerging bear market of 2000, many people were hurt by stock losses, and a large number of these losses were made worse because people didn't manage the responsibilities involved with margin trading.

If you buy stock on margin, use a disciplined approach. Be extra careful when using leverage, such as a margin loan, because it can backfire. Keep the following points in mind:

- **Have ample reserves of cash or marginable securities in your account.** Try to keep the margin ratio at 40 percent or less to minimize the chance of a margin call.

- **If you're a beginner, consider using margin to buy stock in large companies that have a relatively stable price and pay a good dividend.** Some people buy income stocks that have dividend yields that exceed the margin interest rate, meaning that the stock ends up paying for its own margin loan. Just remember those stop orders.

- **Constantly monitor your stocks.** If the market turns against you, the result will be especially painful if you use margin.

- **Have a payback plan for your margin debt.** Having margin loans against your investments mean that you're paying interest. Your ultimate goal is to make money, and paying interest eats into your profits.

Going Short and Coming Out Ahead

The vast majority of stock investors are familiar with buying stock, holding on to it for a while, and hoping its value goes up. This kind of thinking is called *going long,* and investors who go long are considered to be *long on stocks.* Going long essentially means that you're bullish and seeking your profits from rising prices. However, astute investors also profit in the market when stock prices fall. *Going short* (also called *shorting a stock, selling short,* or *doing a short sale*) on a stock is a common technique for profiting from a stock price decline. Investors have made big profits during bear markets by going short. A short sale is a bet that a particular stock is going down.

To go short, you have to be deemed (by your broker) creditworthy — your account needs to be approved for short selling. When you're approved for margin trading, you're probably set to sell short, too. Speak to your broker (or check for this information on the broker's Web site) about limitations in your account regarding going short.

Because going short on stocks has greater risks than going long, we strongly advise beginning investors to avoid shorting stocks until they become more seasoned.

Most people easily understand making money by going long. It boils down to "buy low and sell high." Piece of cake. Going short means making money by selling high and then buying low. Huh? Thinking in reverse is not a piece of cake. Although thinking of this stock adage in reverse may be challenging, the mechanics of going short are really simple. Consider an example that uses a fictitious company called DOA, Inc. As a stock, DOA ($50 per share) is looking pretty sickly. It has lots of debt and plummeting sales and earnings, and the news is out that DOA's industry will face hard times for the foreseeable future. This situation describes a stock that is an ideal candidate for shorting. The future may be bleak for DOA, but promising for savvy investors.

You must understand brokerage rules before you conduct short selling. The broker must approve you for it, and you must meet the minimum collateral requirement, which is typically 50 percent of the shorted stock's market value. If the stock generates dividends, those are paid to the owner of the stock, not to the person who is borrowing it to go short. (See the next section "Setting up a short sale" to see how this technique works.) Check with your broker for complete details and review the resources in the Appendix.

Setting up a short sale

This section explains how to go short. Say that you believe that DOA is the right stock to short — you're pretty sure its price is going to fall. With DOA at $50, you instruct your broker to "go short 100 shares on DOA." (It doesn't have to be 100 shares; we're just using that as an example.) Now, here's what happens next:

1. **Your broker borrows 100 shares of DOA stock, either from his own inventory or from another client or broker.**

   That's right. The stock can be borrowed from a client, no permission necessary. The broker guarantees the transaction, and the client/owner of the stock never has to be informed about it, because he never loses legal and beneficial right to the stock. You borrow 100 shares, and you'll return 100 shares when it's time to complete the transaction.

2. **Your broker sells the stock and gives you the money.**

   Your account is credited with $5,000 (100 shares × $50) in cash — the money gained from selling the borrowed stock. This cash acts like a loan on which you're going to have to pay interest.

3. **You use the $5,000 for a little while.**

   Your broker has deposited the $5,000 in your account. You can use this money to buy other investments.

4. **You buy the stock back and return it to its rightful owner.**

   When it's time to close or "cover" the transaction (either you want to close it, or the owner of the shares wants to sell them, so you have to give them back), you must return the number of shares you borrowed (in this case, it was 100 shares). If you buy back the 100 shares at $40 per share (remember that you shorted this particular stock because you were sure its price was going to fall) and these 100 shares are returned to their owner, you make a $1,000 profit. (To keep the example tidy, we don't include brokerage commissions.) By selling short, you made money when the stock price fell!

Oops! Going short when prices grow taller

We bet you guessed that there was a flip side to the wonderful profitability of selling short. Presume that you were wrong about DOA and that the stock price rises from the ashes as it goes from $50 to $87. Now what? You still have to return the 100 shares you borrowed. With the stock's price at $87, that means that you have to buy the stock for $8,700 (100 shares at the new, higher price of $87). Ouch! How do you pay for it? Well, you have that original $5,000 in your account from when you initially went short on the stock. But where do you get the other $3,700 ($8,700 less the original $5,000)? You guessed it — your pocket! You have to cough up the difference. If the stock continues to rise, that's a lot of coughing.

How much money do you lose if the stock goes to $100 or more? A heck of a lot. As a matter of fact, there's no limit to how much you can lose. That's why going short can be riskier than going long. With going long, the most you can lose is 100 percent of your money. However, with going short, you can lose more than 100 percent of the money you invest. Yikes!

Because the potential for loss is unlimited when you short a stock, we suggest that you use a stop order (also called a *buy-stop order*) to minimize the damage. Better yet, make it a good-till-cancelled order, which I discuss earlier in this chapter. You can set the stop order at a given price, and if the stock hits that price, you buy the stock back so that you can return it to its owner before the price rises even higher. You still lose money, but you limit your losses.

Watching out for ticks

Short sellers should be aware of the *uptick rule,* which states that you can enter into a short sale only when the stock has just completed an uptick. "Tick" in this case means the actual incremental price movement of the stock you're shorting. For a $10 stock that was just $9.95 a moment ago, the 5-cent difference represents an uptick. If the $10 stock was just $10.10 a moment before, the 10-cent difference is a downtick. The amount of the tick doesn't matter. So, if you short a stock at the price of $40, the immediate prior price must have been $39.99 or lower. The reason for this rule (a Canadian and U.S. securities regulation) is that short selling can aggravate declining stock prices in a rapidly falling market. In practice, going short on a stock whose price is already declining can make the stock price fall even more. Excessive short selling can make the stock more volatile than it would be otherwise.

Chapter 21

'Cause I'm the Tax Man

- -

In This Chapter

▶ Investigating how interest income is taxed

▶ Determining dividend taxes and credits

▶ Considering capital gains and losses

▶ Reviewing which investments to hold in your RRSP

▶ Figuring out strategies to avoid, reduce, split, or defer taxes

▶ Sussing out other types of investment income

- -

*H*ow much tax does investment income draw? Yup, you guessed it — it depends! (We hate it when people say that, too!)

Different forms of income attract different levels of taxation. For example, relative to other types of investment income, interest income draws the most punishing tax. Things get a bit better with dividend income, where Canada Customs and Revenue Agency (CCRA) taxes you, but may also give you a tax credit to cushion the blow. With capital gains, CCRA hits you with only a half-blow — only a fraction of gains or losses are included in, or deducted from, income. And then there's the other investment-related stuff, like real estate investment trusts, which add more murkiness to CCRA's arsenal of rules. We'll explore these and other items in this chapter. Hey, without the smoke and mirrors, tax accountants would starve!

Before cutting into the nitty-gritty stuff, however, we'll set the stage with an overview that will help you deal more easily with the many tax rules that are associated with investment income. Knowing the tax rules for investment income is a critical first step in tax planning, since your objective is to minimize your taxes. We trust that at the end of this chapter you'll realize what we have come to realize — most of the rules, and associated tax planning tips, are more manageable than they look!

Interest Income

Interest income is taxable *in full* in the year in which it is received. There are no deductions or credits associated with interest income. Bank accounts, GICs, term deposits, mortgages receivable, and bonds are some of the financial instruments out there that produce interest income.

CCRA wants your interest income so much that, for interest income on compound-interest obligations obtained after 1989 (for example, Canada Savings Bonds), interest has to be reported on an annual accrual basis. That means you report it as though you have received interest even if you haven't. Investment issuers (like banks) are obliged to send their clients annual information slips (T5s) reporting interest income.

For interest on investments obtained before 1990 and after 1981, interest income can be reported in several ways at the investor's option. If you hold such older investments, a brief refresher on these options never hurts. The options are these:

- ✔ Interest can be accrued and reported annually.

- ✔ Interest can be recognized as received.

- ✔ Interest can be reported as it becomes receivable. This is interest that you fully earned, and you have a legal right to claim it.

- ✔ Interest can be accrued and reported on a triennial basis from the date of acquisition. This means that interest on compounding investments needs to be reported only once every three years, starting at the year of acquisition. If you don't elect one of the other ways, then this is the method that CCRA applies.

You can use different options for different investments, but you have to apply your choices consistently from year to year. Of course, if an interest-bearing investment is held within your RRSP, the tax on the interest earned is deferred until the time you withdraw it. We'll discuss RRSP strategy later in this chapter.

CCRA holds that investments of a similar nature must report their income in a similar manner. For instance, if you report interest on a Canada Savings Bond on an annual accrual basis, you should report all your government bonds in like manner.

Some interest-bearing investments have their own unique reporting methods. These investments include annuity contracts, investments bought at a discount to face value, stripped bonds, Canada Savings Bonds, and indexed debt obligations. Consider these nuances when making investment and tax planning decisions: they can have a major impact on your taxes payable. Check out these and other tax law requirements at CCRA's Web site (www.ccra-adrc.gc.ca).

Dividend Income

Compared to interest income, any dividends you receive from a Canadian corporation are subject to preferential tax rates. Dividends received are taxed at a lower rate because of the availability of a dividend tax credit. This dividend tax credit is available to taxpayers because the corporation has already paid tax on the earnings that it distributed as dividends to its investors. In this way, CCRA provides against double taxation.

Dividend income received from foreign companies — before any withholding tax was held back — is taxed at the same full tax rates as interest income. There is no gross-up and dividend tax credit treatment. Amounts included in your tax return are converted to Canadian dollars, of course. However, a foreign tax credit is available for any foreign taxes withheld. So foreign dividends are taxed more like interest, instead of like dividends from Canadian companies.

If dividends from Canadian and foreign corporations were received inside your RRSP, tax on this income is deferred. When you finally withdraw money from your RRSP, it will be fully taxable as regular income. That's because inside RRSPs investment income loses its nature and comes in only one flavour — high-tax vanilla. Inside RRSPs, you also lose the tax advantage of applying the dividend or the foreign tax credit. Again, we'll deal with RRSP strategy later in this chapter.

Grossed out

Taxpayers who received dividends from a taxable Canadian corporation must gross the dividends up by one-quarter (that is, multiply them by 1.25) and include that grossed-up amount in taxable income. Hey! That's not fair! But wait — the federal dividend tax credit we mentioned previously, equal to two-thirds of the gross-up amount, or 13.33 percent of the grossed-up dividend, reduces your federal income tax payable. Provincial tax credits are available, too. Okay, that's better. Again, while dividends from foreign corporations must be included in taxable income, they are not eligible for the gross-up and dividend tax credit treatment.

Provinces now have their own dividend tax credit similar to the federal credit. Previously, the provincial tax was calculated as a simple percentage of the federal tax after the federal dividend tax credit was applied.

Stock dividends and splits

A *stock dividend* is a dividend that a corporation pays by issuing shares instead of cash. Stock dividends are generally considered to be ordinary taxable dividends, and are treated as such. The amount of the dividend you include in taxable income — your share of the increase in paid-up capital — also represents the cost of your new shares for future sales, and capital gain or loss calculations.

Stock splits, where you get more shares but without any change in total dollar value of those shares, are not taxable. You gained or lost nothing from an economic or tax standpoint.

When you get your T3 or T5 tax slip showing your annual dividend income (including any stock dividend values), you'll see that there are boxes that contain both actual dividends and the taxable amount of dividends paid. Be careful to include only the taxable amount of dividends on your tax return.

If your spouse has low income and you are claiming him or her as a dependant, and he or she earns dividends eligible for the gross-up and dividend tax credit, consider transferring those dividends to yourself and including them in your income. The tax benefits associated with dividends are more valuable in your hands (in your higher tax bracket) than in your spouse's hands.

Capital Gains and Losses

A *capital gain* occurs when you sell or otherwise dispose of a capital property for more than what you paid for it — technically, CCRA refers to this cost as the "adjusted cost base," since CCRA may sometimes require you to adjust your original cost. However, we'll keep things simple and leave special rules about costs out of the picture for now. Just keep in mind that capital gains are reduced by any disposition costs incurred, such as brokers' commissions.

Unlike ordinary income such as salary or interest, only 50 percent of the capital gain that you make outside of your RRSP is included in your taxable income. This is called a "taxable capital gain," and this portion of the total capital gain is taxed in the year of the sale. If you suffer a capital loss, where your cost exceeds your proceeds, the 50-percent "allowable" portion must first be used to offset any taxable capital gains that may exist in the same year. Any unused allowable capital allowance amount can be carried back up to three years, or carried forward indefinitely, but only to reduce any future taxable capital gains.

The capital gain and loss inclusion rate was not always 50 percent. A few years ago, the inclusion rate was lowered twice — from 75 percent to 66.67 percent, and then to 50 percent. This complicated the calculation of capital gains quite a bit, especially if you had to apply capital losses of one year against capital gains of another. Now, things should be simpler. Phew.

Keep in mind that just because you did not receive any proceeds from a sale, that doesn't always mean that you have no capital gain or loss to report. A special scenario can play out when you gift shares or other capital property to family members. In such cases, CCRA may "deem" you to have received fair-market-value consideration at the time of the gift (or a sale for less than fair market value). The amount of cash actually changing hands is irrelevant to CCRA.

Capital-gains deduction

Capital gains from dispositions of small-business-corporation (SBC) shares may be eligible for a deduction of up to $500,000. At a 50-percent inclusion rate, this translates into a $250,000 taxable amount (or benefit, depending on how you view it). But your claim of this special deduction may be reduced by past capital gains deduction claims, or allowable business investment losses and other adjustments. A detailed discussion of this area is beyond the scope of this book. If you have SBC shares, we recommend that you seek professional advice from a tax adviser when you're ready to sell or transfer them.

Superficial losses

CCRA has certain rules concerning superficial losses. A superficial loss occurs when a taxpayer executes a transaction (like a sale or other transfer of investments) that creates a loss while they, or a related person, keep or quickly regain control of the same or identical property that created the loss in the first place. CCRA applies the superficial loss provision beginning 30 days before and ending 30 days after the disposition of a property. In other words, no fancy footwork (such as manipulation of the timing or ownership of losses) is permitted a month before or after the sale.

Reserves

If the sale of a property results in a capital gain, and a portion of the sales proceeds are not due until subsequent to the year-end, you may claim a "reasonable reserve" for the unrealized part of that gain. However, you can't wait forever. At least one-fifth of the capital gain must be included in taxable income every year, unless it stems from the sale of shares in an SBC to any children you may have. In that case, a minimum one-tenth of the capital gain must be included in your income each year. We recommend that you seek professional tax advice whenever dealing with complex areas such as SBC shares, and even reserves.

Deferred-Income Tax Shelters and Plans

Deferred-income plans like RRSPs are designed to let you earn investment income and at the same time *defer* paying tax as long as the investments and income stay inside the plan. RRSPs even go a step further and provide a tax deduction, within CCRA limits, for contributions you make. The following sections explore RRSPs and other deferred income plans. You'll learn how you can use these plans strategically to maximize your investment returns. But before you can implement tax strategy and planning in this area, you first have to understand how these plans actually work.

Registered Retirement Savings Plans (RRSPs)

A Registered Retirement Savings Plan is a registered savings plan that lets you contribute cash or eligible investments for future use — usually for retirement. You can open several different RRSP accounts, and passively or actively invest in each one in different ways with different investments, such as GICs, stocks, or mutual funds.

Because RRSP contributions lower your taxable income, you save tax immediately. Keep in mind, however, that RRSP withdrawals trigger an income inclusion for the year — even if the full amount withdrawn is reinstated into the plan later that same year. Also bear in mind that while you can pay RRSP-related administrative fees outside of your plan, they are not tax-deductible.

RRSP contribution limits

Your RRSP contribution limit is 18 percent of your prior year's *earned income*, less the prior year's pension adjustment reported on your annual T4. If you have any additional past-service pension adjustments, they are also deducted. The contribution limit is also adjusted for total pension adjustment reversals (PARs) made. PARs reinstate lost contribution room if you left your employer's registered pension plan and/or deferred profit sharing plan before retirement.

Earned income limits

Earned income includes employment earnings (net of union dues and eligible employment expenses); net income from self-employment and partnerships; net rental income; royalties; research grants (net of related expenses); disability pensions under the CPP or QPP; alimony or separation allowances received; employee profit-sharing-plan allocations; and supplementary unemployment benefit plan payments (not Employment Insurance, or EI) — *less* current year's loss from self-employment or an active partnership; deductible alimony and maintenance payments; and current-year rental losses.

 There is only one significant disadvantage of dividends, compared to fully-taxed salary or interest income. In the context of the earned income calculation that determines your RRSP contribution room, dividends are not deemed by CCRA to be earned income. Therefore, they don't create RRSP contribution room for you.

Dollar limits

Annual RRSP contributions cannot be greater than $13,500 in 2003. That limit rises to $14,500 in 2004 and $15,500 in 2005. After that time, the allowable limits are scheduled to be indexed to the average rate of wage inflation.

Check out the notice of assessment you receive from CCRA after filing your prior year's tax return. There you can find your RRSP contribution limits for the current tax year. Contributions have to be made within 60 days of the calendar year-end for them to be deductible for the previous tax year. Bear in mind that unused RRSP limits that have accumulated since 1991 can be carried forward. Also remember that contributions to your RRSP can be made until the end of the calendar year in which you turn 69.

 The government presented its 2003 budget on February 18, 2003. Few substantive tax changes were made. However, one key change is an expected increase to RRSP contribution levels. The proposed contribution limits, still subject to Royal assent at the time of writing, are $14,500 for 2003, $15,500 for 2004, and $16,500 for 2005. In 2006 and thereafter, the limit will be capped at $18,000. In 2007, the $18,000 limit will be indexed for inflation. Check with your bank to see if and when these proposed limits kick in.

Spousal Registered Retirement Savings Plans

Many investors have their own RRSP and also open a spouse or common-law partner's RRSP, subject to limits of deductible amounts. Spousal contributions are deemed by CCRA to be the recipient spouse/common-law partner's property. Spousal contributions reduce the contributor's RRSP limit, but they don't impact the recipient spouse's contribution limits for their own RRSP.

Your spousal RRSP contribution has no immediate added tax benefit over and above contributing toward your personal RRSP. But your tax savings could be large in the future, since spousal RRSP contributions can provide you and your spouse with the opportunity to balance out retirement income and reduce your combined future taxes. Withdrawals by a spouse in retirement could be non-taxable, or taxed at much lower rates than if all the savings were being drawn by only one spouse. Be mindful, however, that withdrawals from a spousal plan might be taxable in your hands if spousal contributions were made in either the year of the withdrawal or the two preceding years. Spousal RRSP contributions can be made until the end of the year in which the spouse or common-law partner turns 69.

Self-directed RRSPs

Self-directed RRSPs are popular with Canadians who wish to hold and manage individual stocks in their RRSP. Another reason many stock investors set up a self-directed RRSP is to capitalize on the 30-percent foreign-content limit (the same as for non–self-directed RRSPs) by exploring stocks traded on stock exchanges outside of Canada and still get a tax deduction.

A self-directed RRSP provides a greater selection of investment options than regular RRSPs. That's the key difference between the two choices. They are available through discount and full-service brokerage firms. These plans are designed for Canadians who wish to personally control and manage the assets residing in the plan. As for non–self-directed RRSPs, the annual administration fee and commissions you pay are not tax deductible.

The list of what you can throw into a self-directed RRSP plan, over and above stocks, includes rights and warrants of corporations listed on Canadian stock exchanges; mortgages and mortgage-backed securities; mutual funds; bank deposit accounts and investment certificates; treasury bills; savings bonds; and federal, provincial, and municipal bonds and debentures.

Also keep in mind that the 30-percent foreign-content limit is based on the aggregate book value of each RRSP. This book value includes things like cost plus any distributions, interest, or dividends received, minus any amount withdrawn from the plan. If you hold several RRSPs, each plan would be allowed its own 30-percent foreign-content limitation.

Retirement allowances

You can transfer *retiring allowances* (like severance packages and accumulated attendance credits) directly into your RRSP, subject to certain limits and rules. For years of service from 1989 to 1995 inclusive, the contribution limit is $2,000 per year of service. For those years before 1989, an additional $1,500 can be contributed (for a potential total of $3,500 per year) for each year of service that you did not have a pension plan. For years of service from 1996 and on, no additional "bump" contributions are permitted. Also, you can't carry forward these unused RRSP contributions to future periods.

Locked-in RRSPs

When employees leave their workplace, they may have a choice of either receiving a pension at retirement or transferring the commuted value of their pension to another plan. Under strict Canadian law, the commuted value cannot be immediately paid out directly to the individual. Instead, the transferred commuted (actuarially calculated) value is either placed directly into another company pension plan or placed in a locked-in retirement account (LIRA), also referred to as a "locked-in RRSP." Both are essentially the same thing.

With a regular RRSP, you can make a withdrawal at any time. With a locked-in RRSP, early withdrawals typically cannot be made. Furthermore, when you retire as early as age 55, or as late as age 69, the locked-in RRSP cash can be applied to purchase a life annuity or a life income fund (ask your tax adviser if one of these is a route you should consider). You may not be able to transfer funds into a RRIF (discussed below). However, Ontario and other residents are now an exception, and may be able to transfer proceeds of locked-in RRSPs into a locked-in RRIF. This is another complex area beyond the scope of this book, which you should discuss with your tax adviser when appropriate.

Registered Retirement Income Funds (RRIFs)

When the time comes, you have to terminate your RRSP(s) by the end of the year in which you turn 69. You have three options to choose from when you terminate your RRSP:

- Withdraw the RRSP funds, where the total lump-sum cash withdrawn is included in your annual income.

- Transfer your RRSP into a RRIF. A RRIF is like an RRSP since the RRIF's funds and income earned stay untaxed until they are withdrawn. You can exercise management control over investment decisions. With a RRIF, however, you must withdraw a minimum amount from the plan each year, based on your age, or that of a younger spouse or common-law partner. The minimum amount to be withdrawn increases each year until age 94. At that time amounts become set at 20 percent annually until such time that the plan is depleted.

- Buy an annuity providing a regular income for a set period of time. This may include your lifetime, the combined lifetime of both you and your spouse or common-law partner, a set period, or a combination of these. The choices are wide open. No part of the RRSP will be taxed immediately on this type of transfer. The tax comes in when the annuity payments begin to be received.

Take note that you can withdraw amounts over and above the minimum, although any excess amounts withdrawn will also become taxable in that year.

If you have an RRSP or other tax shelter, you have a few obligations. You are required to identify any tax-sheltered investment deductions, and disclose the shelter identification number on your tax return. The folks that sold you their tax shelter products should provide you with the required filing forms and associated details, like the amount of the deduction.

Also be aware of the fact that you face a number of special rules regarding tax-shelter deductions, which can result in alternative minimum tax (AMT), or be exposed to "at-risk rules," where you are not allowed to write off more than the cost base of your investment.

Apart from this, your deductions for interest expense will also be restricted if certain loans are deemed by CCRA to be "limited-recourse debt." Limited-recourse rules require that funds must be borrowed with bona fide arrangements in place to repay the principal back within ten years. It can't be a phantom loan, where there is no intention to repay it within a reasonable time period. Interest must be payable on a regular basis, at interest rates greater

---

Invest inside or outside your RRSP?

The money you make on your investments draws different effective rates of tax, depending on the type of income you receive from the investment. Income you generate from your investments held outside of your RRSP will be taxed differently if it is interest income, dividends, or capital gains. But the variables and choices don't end there.

You can choose to earn investment income either inside or outside of an RRSP — each option has different tax and other consequences. This is where it pays to know a little about the tax treatment of various sources of investment income. This will make it easier to decide which of your investments should be in a tax-advantaged plan such as an RRSP, and which investments should be held outside of an RRSP. There is no "one-size-fits-all" formula to apply here, only rules that can be carefully plugged into your personal financial objectives.

---

than or equal to those prescribed by CCRA. You have to be at full risk for the loan. Also, if you have limited-recourse debt, it's not included in the cost base of your investment. This can potentially set the stage for high taxable capital gains.

A Recap

You may recall that, in general, fixed-income investments such as GICs and bonds generate regular interest income, while stocks may generate capital gains and, in certain cases, dividends. You may also recall that a capital gain is the profit realized when a capital property like a stock is sold. For example, if you purchase a stock for $30 and sell it for $45, your capital gain is $15.

To contrast again, interest income is taxable even if it has not been paid out. Also, capital gains are taxed at a more merciful 50 percent. Dividends, an altogether different kind of animal, entitle you to a dividend tax credit that lowers your effective tax on dividends. Interest income is taxable at relatively high rates of tax, but if a GIC or bond is held inside your RRSP, any tax on interest earned is deferred until the time you withdraw it. Keep these principles in mind.

Capital gains are the key focus of most stock investors, so the taxation of capital gains and treatment of capital losses are important considerations. The current capital gains inclusion rate is 50 percent, so only one-half of any capital gains you generate outside your RRSP will be subject to tax in the year of the sale. For instance, if you invested $15,000 in stocks outside your RRSP and later sold the stocks for $25,000, only $5,000 of this income (50 percent of the

$10,000 capital gain) would be taxable in the year of sale. But if you realized that capital gain inside your RRSP, the full amount of the capital gain would be taxable when you withdraw it from your RRSP. You lose the tax benefit of the 50-percent exclusion from taxable income. However, you would defer the tax up until the time you withdrew monies from your plan. Also bear in mind that you'll likely be in a lower tax bracket in your retirement years than you are in currently. As you can see, there is no clear solution.

Things to consider

Following is a recap of issues, some conflicting, that you should consider for application to your personal situation:

- Deferring tax through an RRSP is great, but many Canadians value the immediate tax deductions a lot more. Sure, tax-smart investing outside of an RRSP may not defer tax, but it can help you reduce it.

- RRSP withdrawals are fully taxable. Withdrawals from your non-RRSP account may be taxed at preferential rates, saving you money.

- Consider your current tax deduction available where you have contribution room. Your immediate tax savings can be invested. Investing outside an RRSP does not afford you this instant benefit.

- Income splitting, or shifting taxable income from the hands of one family member who pays tax at a high rate to another who pays at a lower rate, can be accomplished with spousal RRSPs. Income splitting outside an RRSP is administratively more tedious.

- Non-RRSP accounts provide a bit more selection in what you can hold as investments. However, you can hold a lot in an RRSP too. Although RRSPs cap your foreign content at 30 percent of the book value of assets, you can sidestep this in a number of ways, including the use of RRSP derivative funds.

- An RRSP instills disciplined investing. The annual contribution deadline compels many Canadians to contribute at least something to the plan.

The great RRSP debate

A popular view holds that, since interest income is more heavily taxed, it may not be best to keep investments that generate interest income outside of your RRSP. If you hold them inside your RRSP, your interest returns will be higher, since your income is temporarily sheltered from tax. Capital gains and dividends, on the other hand, are taxed at preferential rates. You may want to hold investments generating capital gains and dividends outside of your RRSP.

A somewhat opposing view that focuses less on the various types of investment income and more on the big picture is contained in a report available online at www.rbc.com/economics/market/pdf/rrsp03.pdf. It concludes in a sweeping way that Canadian investors are better off going the RRSP route. Period.

There is no one right answer, since everyone has different personal and financial objectives. But seeking the advice of a financial or tax planner will likely help you arrive at the best decision.

Mutual Funds

If you hold stocks indirectly through mutual funds outside of an RRSP, taxation depends on whether you acquire a share of a mutual fund corporation or a unit of a mutual fund trust (like a REIT). With both, you may receive distributions during the year. With a mutual fund corporation, these distributions are either capital gains dividends — which are treated the same as capital gains, with only 50 percent included in income — or taxable dividends. A mutual fund trust allocates its income to the unitholders, who then report the income as capital gains, dividends, foreign income, or other income. Regardless of source, when you sell units of mutual fund trusts or shares of mutual fund corporations you may realize a capital gain on the disposition. Again, the beneficial tax treatment of capital gains and dividends is lost if they are received within an RRSP.

Funds often reinvest distributions to fund unitholders as new shares of the fund. Here, while you don't see the cash, you'll still be taxed on the income distributed. That's why you may have received a tax slip even though you saw no cash. Track the reinvestments well, since they will increase your adjusted cost base and therefore reduce any capital gains when you sell the investment.

The Tax-wise REIT

A *real estate investment trust* (REIT) is essentially a closed-end mutual fund trust. The number of investors is limited. Each year the trust earns rental income, and sometimes capital gains. However, these items are taxed at the unitholder level, and most of the cash generated by the REIT is distributed to the unitholder. Since REITs can deduct depreciation, a noncash expense, the REIT's income passed on to and taxed at the unitholder level is less than the cash that the unitholder actually receives.

The bottom line from a tax perspective is that a certain percentage of distributions you get from a REIT will escape from being included in your current year's taxable income. All you do in the current year is reduce your REIT's tax cost base by a simply calculated amount. You realize a capital gain (on a lower adjusted cost base) when the units are sold. Tax deferral is a key benefit of REITs. Another tax benefit is that when you do sell your REIT units, only 50 percent of any capital gain is included in your taxable income.

Here are a couple of other ways to look at the taxation of REITs:

✔ **In light of the distributions you received:** On a quarterly or monthly basis you will be paid an actual cash distribution based on your REIT's income. At the end of every calendar year, you will get a further distribution of cash representing any realized capital gains and other income.

✔ **In light of the income allocated to you:** After the end of the year, you will also receive a T3 Supplementary Form. (You get a T3 instead of a T5 because a REIT is a mutual fund trust for the purposes of the Income Tax Act.) The T3 Supplementary shows you, among other things, your allocation of taxable income and taxable capital gains for the year. These figures are the ones to include as part of your taxable income for the year. If you sell your units before the end of the calendar year, you'll still get a T3 from your formerly held REIT representing the part of the year when you received distributions.

✔ **In light of the ACB (Adjusted-cost base) reduction:** To the extent that the sum total of *distributions* received exceeds your *taxable income* allocation for the year, your REIT unit ACB is reduced.

Labour-Sponsored Venture Capital Corporation (LSVCC)

Labour-sponsored venture capital corporations are investment funds created by a group of shareholders. Their motivation to invest is encouraged by the federal and provincial governments. They provide tax credits in exchange for investors committing capital for a long period of time to risky small-business ventures. LSVCCs are similar in a few ways to mutual funds, yet they are not mutual funds. LSVCC portfolios include companies that are not publicly traded.

The federal government, Ontario, and other selected provinces each provide a maximum credit of 15 percent on a $5,000 investment. In effect, they provide a combined federal and provincial tax credit of $1,500. Some LSVCCs even qualify for an extra 5-percent Ontario credit, to a maximum of $250.

An LSVCC credit does not reduce the cost base of your shares. Rather, it will reduce any capital loss realized on its disposition. To avoid a tax credit claw-back, where the government takes back money previously credited to you, LSVCC investments usually have to be held for at least eight years. As a bonus, LSVCC purchases are RRSP-eligible. This allows you to get the regular RRSP tax deduction, as well as the federal and provincial tax credits. LSVCC investments undertaken in the first 60 days of the year qualify as contributions for either the previous or current tax year, just as for regular RRSPs.

Oil, Gas, and Mineral Stock Investments

CCRA offers tax incentives to encourage Canadians to invest capital for the exploration and development of oil, gas, and minerals. These incentives are provided through limited partnerships, flow-through shares, joint ventures, and royalty trust units. By going through these risky avenues, stock investors may be able to deduct certain exploration expenses.

Joint ventures and limited partnerships are a lot alike, except for the fact that "at-risk" rules do not apply to the former. Flow-through shares enable companies to forgo certain deductions they could have claimed and pass them on to investors. Flow-through-share investor deductions typically lower the cost base of the shares to nil. This can ultimately result in a tax-preferential capital gain when the shares are sold.

Also take note that (as of 2000) CCRA permits a temporary non-refundable investment tax credit to be claimed. The rate is 15 percent, to cover certain Canadian mineral exploration expenses further to a flow-through share structure. The flow-through agreement must have been executed on or subsequent to October 18, 2000. It must also be applicable to eligible expenses incurred by a corporation on or after that date and prior to the year 2004.

Furthermore, as of 2002 the government also provides tax incentives regarding the availability of flow-through shares for Canadian investors in certain renewable-energy and energy-conservation projects. This applies to eligible Canadian conservation expenses incurred after 2002 regarding flow-through share agreements entered into after July 26, 2002.

Check out the suitability of these tax-advantaged but risky mechanisms with your investment and tax adviser before proceeding. As you can see, the rules are tight and complex.

As an added incentive to seek professional advice when your tax situation gets complicated, you can deduct fees (but not commissions) for advice you get regarding the purchase, sale, and administration of shares and certain other securities. But those fees have to be paid to professionals whose main business is managing such investments. Check out Chapter 7 to help you weed out the hucksters from the pros!

Although we always recommend that you seek professional tax advice, some Canadians — like our national mascot, the beaver — are habitual do-it-yourselfers. If you're one of those, check out some of the available software packages designed to help you with your taxes. In fact, some software companies, like QuickTax (`www.quicktax.ca`), offer special software specifically for investment or RRSP planning.

Part V
The Part of Tens

The 5th Wave — By Rich Tennant

IN A BIZARRE MIX-UP, KEN BALANCES A BUS SCHEDULE INSTEAD OF HIS CHECKBOOK, AND THEN CONTINUES BY BOOKING A SEAT FOR HE AND LAVERNE IN THE LOCAL BANK'S SAFE DEPOSIT BOX.*

* From that time forward, Laverne handled their financial affairs.

In this part . . .

This wouldn't be a ...*For Dummies* book if we didn't include a Part of Tens. Here you find quick reference lists to many of the most basic stock-investing concepts and practices. Check the information in this part when you don't have time to read the denser parts of the book, or when you just need a quick refresher on what to do before, after, and even during your stock-investing pursuits.

Chapter 22

Ten Things to Think about Before You Invest

· ·

*T*hrough the years, we've seen the good, the bad, and some of the ugly of investing, so we're aware of some common mistakes and oversights by investors. Many people start investing before they're really ready. These same people would probably never leave on vacation without filling up the gas tank or shutting off the oven. Yet these people often don't prepare as thoroughly when they're investing thousands of their hard-earned dollars. The following sections offer specific ways to get your house in order before you begin investing.

Have Adequate Insurance

Do you have proper coverage for potential problems, such as disability or the death of a breadwinner in your family? Many stock portfolios get liquidated pretty fast when the dependants of the deceased need money for daily living expenses. You may work a lifetime to build your stock portfolio. If you don't have appropriate insurance, it could be wiped out very quickly and need-lessly. See an insurance professional to guarantee that you and your family are protected.

Update Your Career Skills

Do you keep your skills and expertise up-to-date so that you can continue to be employable regardless of how uncertain the economy is? No matter how secure your job or company is, you should periodically update your résumé and job skills to maintain your employability. At least once every two years, take your most current résumé to an employment agency and ask, "How quickly can you get me a job?" If your question is met with hesitation or a grimace, update your skills and expertise as soon as possible, while you're still employed.

Take Care of Estate Planning

In case of death, do you have a will, trust, or other vehicle that will take care of your estate for the benefit of your family? Even if you already have a will or trust in place, ask an estate planning specialist to make sure that it complies with changing Canadian laws.

Establish an Emergency Fund

An emergency fund is a critical component of your financial well-being. Investors make a huge mistake by not having one. They assume that their stock portfolio and/or mutual fund investment will do, but they're wrong. Your stocks and mutual funds are meant for long-term growth, not short-term cash needs. Set up an emergency fund by putting at least three to six months' worth of gross living expenses in a safe, interest-bearing bank account or money market mutual fund.

Set Up a Budget

Budgeting is a crucial part of your financial foundation. Budgeting is the act of regularly monitoring and controlling what you make (income) and what you spend (expenses). Are you keeping your spending under control? Does income meet or exceed your expenses? The bottom line is that if you can't (or won't) budget, then you're less likely to succeed as an investor. Fortunately, budgeting is easy, and many resources are available to help you set up a budget that suits your needs and goals. See the Appendix for resources that include budgeting help.

Understand Basic Economics

The average citizen is incredibly ill-informed about economics. Yet a knowledge of economics is extremely important to everyone's investment goals. In fact, plenty of financial advisers and stock experts have lost a lot of money for themselves and their clients because they were woefully uninformed about basic economics. Concepts such as supply and demand aren't distant, arcane abstractions; they affect your money and financial success every day. If you do read up on economics, look for authors who are well versed in free-market principles, which lie at the heart of sound investment decisions. Economics based on socialist or communist reasoning will do more harm than good. In other words, if you're going to read Marx, make sure that it's Groucho and not Karl. We discuss economics in Chapter 14.

Learn the Lingo

If you move to Italy, it would behoove you to learn Italian. Sure, you probably could function in that society without knowing the language, but you would be at a great disadvantage. The same advice applies to the language of stock investing. Because stock investing means putting your money into businesses, you need to have a basic knowledge of accounting and business terminology. For example, you should know what words such as "earnings," "debt," and "equity" mean, and you also should become familiar with documents such as balance sheets and income statements. Check out the Appendix for resources and Web sites that help you quickly and easily become acquainted with financial and investment jargon.

Read about Investing

If we had to mention only one behaviour that separates successful investors from unsuccessful ones, it would be reading. Just as in almost every discipline, people who read more learn more and benefit. Become an avid reader of stock investing publications and books. Browse investment newspapers, such as *Investor's Digest of Canada* and *Investor's Business Daily*. Read books written by (and on) the great investors in history and the strategies they employed. Read commentaries from financial writers and advisers that present both bullish and bearish opinions on the market. Look for different points of view on the stock market to develop and challenge your ability to be a logical and independent financial thinker.

Don't Follow the Herd

When the legendary billionaire J. Paul Getty was asked about successful investing, he said that "buy low and sell high" was more than just a catchy phrase; it was the essence of successful investing. If you look deeper into this almost too-simple advice, you come away with the greater point: Do the opposite of what the crowd is doing. More often than not, the herd mentality is wrong. Think like a contrarian investor. Contrarians often make a lot of money on the simple premise of buying when others are selling and vice versa. Contrarians look for stocks that are generally ignored by the market at large. They look for hidden values that the public hasn't yet discovered. If the contrarian hears a dozen high-profile stock experts say "Buy Quagmire Inc.," he won't buy it — because the public has already bought up the stock and there's usually little growth left in it.

However, if you do your own research (which is what this book is about), you can find great stocks before the market does and then watch the stock price rise when experts and the public start to notice your stock. As the public bids up the price of your shares, look for great opportunities to sell and lock in a handsome profit.

Discipline Yourself

Successful investors do their homework on a stock, stick to their principles, and use a disciplined approach to stock buying (and selling). At the very least, they invest by using disciplined techniques that will help ensure a profit or limit loss. (Techniques such as trailing stops are a great example of a disciplined approach. See Chapter 20 for more information.) Discipline is your ally in stock investing. Frequently, investors lose money or destroy their wealth as they let their emotions rule. Fear and greed are emotions that have driven bad investment decisions throughout history. Develop a rational and disciplined approach, and your long-term investment success will be more assured.

Chapter 23

Ten Things to Remember After You Invest

$\bullet$ $\bullet$

*Y*ou did the research and planning, and you finally bought your stock. Can you sit back and relax? Of course not! Successful investing involves actively monitoring your stocks for as long as you have them. Your house is an investment, and you didn't stop your due diligence on the closing date. If anything, the work increased; the chores are never done! For stock investors, the same type of diligence applies.

Diversify Your Portfolio

Diversify your investments. That doesn't mean that you simply purchase a batch of different stocks, although we do hope that you have a batch of different stocks. Diversification for the successful investor happens at more than one level. An investor with five different stocks is, all things being equal, more diversified (hence safer) than an investor with all her money in a single stock. Strong diversification also means spreading your money among the following places:

✔ **Stocks in different industries:** What if you have five stocks but all of them are with companies in the same industry? Well, if that industry gets into trouble, then your stock portfolio will suffer.

✔ **Stocks in different segments of the economy:** Owning stocks in different industries doesn't necessarily mean that you're diversified. Sometimes different industries are dependent on each other and can affect each other. As a good example, consider airlines, cruises, and resorts. Each may be considered a different industry, but all of them are in the same segment or sector of the economy.

✔ **Other types of financial investments:** Besides investing in stocks, consider other investments that help you minimize your risks and maximize the return on your money. Examples include mutual funds, bonds, and real estate.

Recognize that You're in for the Long Haul

Stocks are most appropriate for long-term considerations. If you jump into a stock but then jump out of it in a few days or weeks, you're not investing, you're speculating. Short-term price movements always seem to act irrationally and actually work against you. However, the longer the time frame, the greater the chance of success. Now don't get us wrong; we're not automatic "buy and hold" or "get it and forget it" aficionados. "Buy and hold" can be financial suicide at the start of a long-term bear market. However, studies have shown that stocks are the top-performing category of financial investments (as opposed to bank accounts and bonds, for example) when compared over long periods of time, such as ten years or more.

Know the Business

Always ask yourself, "What kind of business am I investing in?" What does the company really do? A stock is a representative piece of a company and its future prospects. The stock is ultimately only as good as the company you invest in. Because you invest in a stock for the long term, you should consider yourself a business owner. Make an effort to understand the company, its management, and its products and services. What does the company sell? Does it consistently earn a profit? Does it offer new, innovative products or technologies? Is it among the leaders in its industry?

Know the Industry

What industry is your stock in? The more you know about what's happening in the industry and its prospects for future growth, the more money you'll make with that particular company. If an industry is doing well, that bodes well for your stock. You can see that the saying "A rising tide lifts all boats" certainly applies to stock investing. Judging the strength and growth of an industry is easier than judging an individual company. Therefore, you increase your chances of success by investing in the best companies at the forefront of healthy, growing industries.

Plan for Taxes

Are you planning your stock investing and general finances with tax planning in mind? According to the Canadian Tax Foundation, taxes take a bigger bite out of the average consumer's budget than food, clothing, and shelter combined. You will pay more in taxes in your working lifetime than you would for a mortgage or an automobile. If the average taxpayer reduced his taxes by even a few percentage points over his career, this money could easily add up to $100,000 to $250,000. If this extra money were properly invested, even a low-salaried individual could accumulate wealth exceeding a million dollars. Do tax reduction and tax deferral strategies make a significant difference to your wealth-building program? Absolutely. If you're seeking to build wealth through stock investing, this is especially important. After you make some profitable stock investment purchases, check with a tax adviser about the implications of your investment decisions before you make a sale. Maximizing your success means more than making money; it also means keeping more of it. Stay informed about the ongoing changes in Canadian tax legislation. Investors should keep a watchful eye on capital gains tax rates. Keep track of your expenses, because many investment-related expenses are tax deductible. Also check with your tax adviser about the latest rules on RRSPs and other tax-advantaged programs. The name of the game is to keep more of the fruits of your labour. We discuss the taxation of investment income in Chapter 21.

Stay Informed

Are you an avid reader about current events and do you understand how they affect your stock portfolio? Do you watch the evening news with a critical eye for investment opportunities? Staying informed helps you see how your company and/or industry may suffer or benefit from current or pending laws, regulations, and societal trends. Whether the news media are warning about SARS across the globe, mad cow disease in Alberta, or stringent environmental regulations affecting Newfoundland's off-shore oil rigs and the companies behind them, astute Canadian investors always look for the ripple effects. When you watch the news or read newspapers, make it second nature to ask yourself the following questions:

- Will any stocks be impacted, either positively or negatively, by this piece of news?
- If a particular country or region of the world is experiencing problems, will the company you plan to invest in be affected adversely?
- If a major event has caused my company's stock price to fall, should I sell it, or view it as a chance to buy more stock at a bargain price?

✔ If the media report the passage of a new law or the enactment of a tough government policy, will that news be good or bad for my stock?

Alert investors know that stocks don't exist in a vacuum. All types of events can affect your portfolio and its future prospects for success.

Know What's New with the Company

Stock investors have an obligation to stay informed about the companies in which they invest. Doing so can protect you against losses and may even help you reap some profits. Here are some points to keep in mind:

✔ Check to see whether the company is making major purchases and how it is paying for them. Is it buying new equipment or taking a sizable stake in another company? Is it using cash or debt?

✔ Watch the management of the company. Are difficulties with the company forcing the CEO to resign? Are the company's earnings strong and growing? Are the company's insiders, as a group, buying or selling the company's stock in recent months?

✔ Is the company being investigated by a domestic or foreign securities regulator for fraud or malfeasance? Have any class-action shareholder lawsuits been launched against the company?

Even in the best of times, a company's stock can suffer because of negative events happening within the company.

Compare and Profit

When anyone asked comedian Henny Youngman, "How is your wife?" his typical response was, "Compared to what?" Stock investors need to regularly see how are their stocks are doing compared to some objective benchmark. The fancy term for this process is *comparative analysis*. Ask yourself the following questions regarding the company's progress:

✔ How is the company doing this year compared to last year?

✔ What are the expectations for the company next year compared to this year?

✔ How is the company doing compared to its industry peers?

✔ Is the company doing well compared to popular indexes, such as the S&P/TSX composite index?

Employ Investing Techniques

Investment success depends not only on what you invest in but also on how you invest. Use investing techniques that will maximize your financial progress. Here are some points to keep in mind:

- ✔ Use trailing stops (which we describe in Chapter 20) and other stock orders where available and appropriate. If you bought a stock at $10 a few years ago and it's now $65, be protective about your gain. Put that stop-loss order in and give yourself peace of mind by knowing that if the market goes against you, the worst that happens is that you're forced to take a profit instead of watching your gains (or worse, your original principal) get wiped out in a bear market.

- ✔ Are you using dollar-cost averaging (DCA) to purchase your stock over an extended period of time? Dollar-cost averaging helps you get the stock at various prices so that ultimately you can buy your stock at a lower average cost, and it reduces volatility too. Under DCA, securities are purchased in fixed dollar amounts at regular intervals, regardless of what direction the market is moving. As prices of securities rise, fewer units are bought; as prices fall, more units are bought.

- ✔ Are you using limit orders to buy stocks at a good price? Perhaps you think that a particular stock would be a great addition to your portfolio, but it's too expensive. If the stock is at $50 and you want to buy it at $45 or lower, put in a limit order with your broker. (For more on limit orders and other orders, see Chapter 20.)

The bottom line is that certain investment techniques can make your stock investing more profitable and less risky.

Stay Focused

Are you staying focused on your short-term and long-term goals? A stock, like any investment, is simply a tool to help you achieve a particular result, such as funding a post-secondary education or reaching financial independence. In other words, stock investing should be seen as a means to an end and not an end in itself. As you approach your retirement years, the long-term focus on stocks should start to change. Once you get into your 60s and 70s, a greater portion of your investable funds should shift away from stocks and into more stable, income-producing investments, such as bonds, GICs, and certificates of deposit. Until you get there, stay focused on your stocks and continuously ask yourself the following questions:

✔ Are my stocks continuing to perform satisfactorily to help me achieve my financial goals? If, for example, your target goal is to accrue enough assets to reach a million dollars in net worth, are you tracking your total portfolio value and performance to expedite your progress toward that target amount?

✔ Am I getting too attached to a particular stock and losing focus on why I have that stock at all? Perhaps you had a winning stock for years and now that stock is losing steam. Will you continue to hold on to it as a sentimental favourite, or will you be disciplined enough to get rid of it?

Chapter 24

Ten Warning Signs of a Stock's Decline

• •

*H*ave you ever watched a movie and noticed that one of the characters coughs excessively throughout the entire film? To us, that's a dead giveaway that the character is a goner. Or maybe you've seen a movie in which a bit character annoys a crime boss, so right away you know that it's time for him to "sleep with the fishes." Stocks are not that different. If you're alert, you can recognize some definite signs that your investment may be ready to kick the bucket. Let the tips in this chapter serve as an "insurance policy" on your stock investment, and help you avoid — or at least minimize — costly losses.

Earnings Slow Down or Head South

Profit is the lifeblood of a company. Of course, the opposite is true as well. The lack of profit is a sign of a company's poor financial health. Watch the earnings. Are they increasing or not? If they aren't, find out why. If the general economy is experiencing a recession, stagnant earnings are still better than robust losses — everything is relative. Earnings slowdowns for a company may very well be a temporary phenomenon. If a company's earnings are holding up better than its competitors and/or the market in general, you don't need to be alarmed.

Nonetheless, a company's earnings are its most important measure of success. Keep an eye on the company's P/E ratio. It could change negatively (go up) because of one of two basic scenarios:

- ✔ The stock price goes up as earnings barely budge.
- ✔ The stock price doesn't move, yet earnings drop.

Both of these scenarios will result in a rising P/E ratio that will ultimately have a negative effect on the stock price.

A P/E ratio that is lower than industry competitors' P/E ratios makes a company's stock a favourable investment.

Don't buy the argument "Although the company has losses, its sales are exploding." This is a variation of "The company may be losing money, but it'll make it up on volume." For example, say that Sweet Patootee, Inc. (SPI), had sales of $1 billion in 2001/2002 and that sales are expected to be $1.5 billion in 2002/2003, projecting an increase at SPI by 50 percent. But what if SPI's earnings were $200 million in 2001/2002 and the company was actually expecting a loss for 2002/2003? The company wouldn't succeed, because sales without earnings isn't enough — the company needs to make a profit.

Sales Slow Down

Before you invest in a company, make sure that sales are strong and rising. If sales start to decline, that downward motion will ultimately affect earnings. (See the previous section, "Earnings Slow Down or Head South.") Although the earnings of a company may safely go up and down, sales should consistently rise. If they cease to rise, a variety of reasons may be to blame. Perhaps the company is having marketing problems, or a competitor is eating away at its market share. Maybe a new technology is replacing its products and services. In any case, falling sales raise a red flag you shouldn't ignore.

Exuberant Analysts Despite Logic

Too often, stocks that any logical person with some modest financial acumen would avoid like the plague receive glowing praise from analysts. Why is this? In many instances, there is, alas, a dark motive. Analysts are, after all, employed by companies that earn hefty investment-banking fees from the very companies the analysts tout. Can you smell a rat? Conflict of interest was a primary factor in a recent U.S. Securities and Exchange Commission (SEC) survey showing that brokers overwhelmingly gave glowing recommendations on stocks ("strong buy," "buy," and "market outperform"). The SEC noticed only an outright "sell" recommendation in less than 1 percent of all the recommendations that it reviewed, even though 2000 witnessed crashing stock prices in most of the popular stocks that were analyzed.

Analysts, no matter how objective they may sound, are still employees of companies that make money from the same companies that the analysts analyze. In fact, you should always be wary of the views of analysts, especially those who make positive recommendations even when the company in question has worrisome features, such as no income and tremendous debt. It seems like a paradox: Sell a stock when all the pros say to buy it? How can that be? Remember, the merits of any stock should speak for themselves.

When a company is losing money, all the great recommendations in the world will not reverse its fortunes. Also, keep in mind that if everybody is buying a particular stock — the current analysts' favourite — who's left to buy it? When it turns out to be a dud, you won't be able to sell it off because all the other suckers already own it (thanks to analysts' recommendations). And, if they already own it, they're probably already aware of the company's flaws. What happens then? You got it: More and more people will end up selling it. When more people are selling rather than buying a stock, its price declines.

Insider Selling

Heavy insider selling is to a stock what garlic, sunsets, and crosses are to vampires: an almost certain sign of doom! If you notice that increasing numbers of insiders (such as the president of the company, the treasurer, and the vice-president of finance, for instance) are selling their stock holdings, you can consider it a red flag. In recent years, massive insider selling has become a telltale sign of a company's imminent fall from grace. After all, who better to know the company's prospects for success (or lack of) than the company's high-level management? What management does (selling stock, for example) speaks louder than what management says. For more information on insider trading, see Chapter 14.

Dividend Cuts

For investors who own income stock, dividends are the primary consideration. But, income stock or not, dividend cuts are a negative sign. Of course, if a company is having modest financial difficulty, perhaps a dividend cut is a good thing for the overall health of the company. However, usually a dividend cut is seen as a sign that a company is having trouble with its cash flow. In either case, a dividend cut is a warning sign that trouble may be brewing for the firm as it becomes . . . uh . . . less firm. If your stock announces a dividend cut, find out why. The cut may be simply a temporary measure to help the company out of some minor financial difficulty, or it may be a sign of deeper trouble. Check the company's fundamentals and then decide. (Refer to Chapter 12 and Chapter 13 to find out how to read and interpret company financial documents.)

Increased Negative Coverage

You may easily recognize unfavourable reports of a company's stock as a sign to unload that stock. Or you may be a contrarian and see bad press as an opportunity to scoop up some shares of a company victimized by negative reporting. In any case, take the negative reports as a signal to further investigate the merits of holding on to the stock or to sell it so that you can make room in your portfolio for a more promising stock choice.

Industry Problems

Sometimes being a strong company doesn't matter if that company's industry is having problems; if the industry is in trouble, the company's decline is probably not that far behind. Tighten up those trailing stops. (See Chapter 20 to find out how.)

Political Problems

Political considerations are always a factor in investing. Be it taxes, regulations, or other government actions, politics can easily break a company and send its stock plummeting. If your company's stock is sensitive to political developments, be aware of potential political pitfalls for your stock (or industry) of choice. Reading *The Globe and Mail* or the *Wall Street Journal* and regularly viewing major financial Web sites can help you stay informed. (We give you lists of sources in the Appendix.) In recent years, drug and tobacco stocks in general suffered because of prevailing political attitudes. Also, certain stocks in particular (Microsoft and ATI Technologies, for example) have seen their stock prices drop drastically because they were targets of government actions for reasons ranging from antitrust concerns to alleged insider trading.

Debt Is Too High or Unsustainable

Excessive debt is the kiss of death for a struggling company. From 2000 to 2003, many companies that experts thought were untouchable went bankrupt. A good example is U.S.–based 360 Networks, which once filed for Chapter 11 bankruptcy protection from creditors. Most analysts gave positive recommendations on the stock ("Buy it!"), but the company's financial data showed billions of dollars of debt. Chapter 13 and the Appendix can help you read and understand a company's financial data clearly so that you can make an informed decision about buying or selling its stock.

Funny Accounting: No Laughing Here!

Throughout this book, we discuss the topic of aggressive accounting as an important way to see how well (or how poorly) a company is doing. Understanding a company's balance sheet and income statement and making a simple comparison of these documents over a period of several years can give you great insights into the company's prospects. You don't have to be an accountant to grasp key concepts. Enron is a perfect example of how you can avoid a stock-investing disaster with some rudimentary knowledge of accounting. Despite the fact that Enron hid many of its financial problems from public view, the information that was available made the message clear: "Big problems coming! Stay away!" If investors had done their homework, they would have plainly seen the following revealing points in 2000, beginning more than a year and a half before the collapse:

- **Enron's price to earnings (P/E) ratio hit 90 in 2000.** This stratospheric P/E kept most stock investors (including ourselves) away.

- **Its price to book (P/B) ratio hit 12.** For investors, this meant that the market value of the company, compared to the company's book value (also called "accounting value"), was 12 to 1 — for every $12 of market value, investors were getting only $1 in book value. When you consider that a P/B ratio of 3 or 4 is considered nosebleed territory for value investors, you can see that Enron's P/B ratio was screaming, "Watch out!"

- **The price to sales (P/S) ratio hit an incredible 221.** This means that investors paid $221 in market value for every $1 of sales the company generated. When a P/S of 5 or 10 is considered too high, 221 is astronomical!

We culled the information in the preceding list from Enron's public filings, which anyone could have seen. To understand these points more fully (along with other equally incisive and lucid accounting and financial cues), and to know how to use the information to avoid similar mistakes in the future, see Chapters 16 and 17.

Appendix

Resources for Stock Investors

• •

Getting and staying informed is an ongoing priority for stock investors. The lists in this appendix represent some of the best information resources available.

Basics of Investing

These resources will help you learn about the basics of stock investing, and your rights.

Canadian Securities Institute
www.csi.ca

National Association of Securities Dealers
www.nasd.org

SmartMoney
www.smartmoney.com

The Investment FAQ
www.invest-faq.com

The Motley Fool
www.fool.com

Financial-planning Sources

To find a financial planner to help you with your general financial needs, contact the following organizations:

Canadian Association of Financial Planning
www.cafp.org

Canadian MoneySaver
www.canadianmoneysaver.ca

Financial Advisor Pages
www.fapages.com

RRSP.org
www.rrsp.org

General Investor Supersites

These are one-stop investor supermarkets, and have everything but the kitchen sink. Most investor supersites have comprehensive stock-investor services including stock quotes, charts, portfolio tracking, stock screening, investment articles, discussion forums, company profiles, company press releases, stock market statistics, economic data, and more.

Adviceforinvestors.com
www.adviceforinvestors.com

Bloomberg
www.bloomberg.com

CBS MarketWatch
cbs.marketwatch.com

CNN Money
money.cnn.com

Invest$Link
www.wwfn.com/links.html

InvestorLinks
www.investorlinks.com

MSN Money
moneycentral.msn.com

Silicon Investor
www.siliconinvestor.com

Stockhouse
www.stockhouse.ca

Thomson Financial Network
www.thomsonfn.com

Yahoo!Finance
finance.yahoo.com

Stock-investing Web Sites

Many of these are also supersites, but have a sharp focus on stock investing.

Allstocks.com
www.allstocks.com

Buy Sell or Hold
www.buysellorhold.com

FinancialWeb
www.financialweb.com

Markethistory.com
www.markethistory.com

Multex Investor Network
www.multexinvestor.com

RagingBull.com
www.ragingbull.com

Simply Stocks
www.simplystocks.com

Standard & Poor's
www.standardandpoors.com

Stocks.com
www.stocks.com

StockSites.net
www.stocksites.net

Stock Exchanges

These are the homes of Canadian and U.S. stocks, where they are traded.

American Stock Exchange
www.amex.com

Chicago Stock Exchange
www.chicagostockex.com

Instinet
www.instinet.com

Island ECN
www.island.com

Nasdaq
www.nasdaq.com

New York Stock Exchange
www.nyse.com

OTC Bulletin Board
www.otcbb.com

TSX
www.tse.com

Periodicals and Magazines

These are classic investment publications.

Barron's
www.barrons.com

Canadian MoneySaver
www.canadianmoneysaver.ca

Forbes magazine
www.forbes.com

Investor's Business Daily
www.ibd.com

Investor's Digest of Canada
(no Web site, but award winning publication nonetheless)

Kiplinger's Personal Finance magazine
www.kiplinger.com

SmartMoney
www.smartmoney.com

Wall Street Journal
www.wsj.com

Investor Associations and Organizations

These organizations have, first and foremost, your educational and other interests in mind.

American Association of Individual Investors (AAII)
ww.aaii.org

Canadian Society of Technical Analysts
www.csta.org

Investment Funds Institute of Canada
www.ific.ca

National Association of Investors Corp. (NAIC)
www.better-investing.org

Stock Screens

Stock screens are online tools that help you find stocks that meet your specific criteria.

FinanCenter
www.financenter.com

Hoover's
www.hoovers.com

SmartMoney
www.smartmoney.com/tools

Zacks Advisor
www.zacksadvisor.com

Company Research and Analyst Evaluations

These sites feature and focus on investment analysis, advice, and research about stocks.

The Financial Center
www.tfc.com

Hulbert Financial Digest
www.hulbertdigest.com

Moody's
www.moodys.com

Morningstar
www.morningstar.com

Morningstar Canada
www.morningstar.ca

Richard Russell's Dow Theory Letters

www.dowtheoryletters.com

Value Line Investment Survey

www.valueline.com

Quotes

Plain and simple quotes can be readily found here. Okay — even not so simple ones, too!

Freerealtime.com

www.freerealtime.com

Quote.com

finance.lycos.com

Stockhouse

www.stockhouse.ca

Stockwatch

new.stockwatch.com

Webfin (Canoe)

www.webfin.com/en

Yahoo!Finance

finance.yahoo.com

Charts

See where your stock has been, and guess where it may be going with these resources.

BigCharts

bigcharts.marketwatch.com

ChartSmart

www.chartsmart.com

ClearStation
clearstation.etrade.com

Equis (Reuters)
www.equis.com

Tradingcharts.com
www.tradingcharts.com

Earnings and Earnings Estimates

These professional sites track analysts' earnings estimates for major companies. Some of these record more than 15,000 such changes, made by more than 3,500 analysts at 210 brokerage firms covering 5,000 companies across North America.

Briefing.com
www.briefing.com

First Call
www1.firstcall.com

Reuters BridgeChannel
channel.bridge.com/bc

Zacks
my.zacks.com

Industry Analysis

These sites have great content about the big picture, including economic, political, and geopolitical analysis.

CBS MarketWatch
cbs.marketwatch.com

Hoover's
www.hoovers.com

Standard & Poor's
www2.standardandpoors.com

Stockhouse Canada
www.stockhouse.ca

External Factors that Affect Market Value

These statistics about the economy and industry come right from the horse's mouth.

American Institute of Economic Research (AIER)
www.aier.org

Department of Finance of Canada
www.fin.gc.ca

Economy.com, Inc.
www.economy.com

Federal Reserve Board
www.federalreserve.gov

FreeLunch.com
www.freelunch.com

U.S. Securities and Exchange Commission (SEC)
www.sec.gov

Technical Analysis

Tools of the technical analysis trade can be found here, as well as commentary about trading strategy.

BigCharts
bigcharts.marketwatch.com

Elliott Wave International
www.elliottwave.com

StockCharts.com, Inc.
www.stockcharts.com

Insider Trading

See what company insiders are doing with their own company stock at these tracking sites.

SEDI
www.sedi.ca

U.S. Securities and Exchange Commission (SEC)
www.sec.gov

Street Insider
www.streetinsider.com

Taxes

Calculate and minimize your taxes with these resources.

Canada Customs and Revenue Agency
www.ccra-adrc.gc.ca

Cantax
www.cantax.com

H & R Block
www.handrblock.com/tax/canada

Intuit Canada
www.intuit.ca

Quicken Financial Network — Canada
www.quicken.ca

Tax and Accounting Sites Directory
www.taxsites.com

Fraud

These investor advocacy sites offer fraud-related advice and referrals.

National Association of Securities Dealers
www.nasdr.com

U.S. Securities and Exchange Commission (SEC)
www.sec.gov

The Canadian Investor Protection Fund
www.cipf.ca

The National Fraud Center
www.fraud.org

Investment News

These are online "investment newspapers and shows" that talk stock shop.

China Online
www.chinaonline.com

Market Reporter
www.marketreporter.com

News Alert
www.newsalert.com

ON24
www.on24.com

Online Investor
www.theonlineinvestor.com

UK Invest

www.uk-invest.com

Public Filings

Check out the latest company press releases and statutory filings here.

EDGAR Online

www.edgar-online.com

FreeEDGAR

www.freeedgar.com

SEDAR

www.sedar.com

10k Wizard

www.10kwizard.com

Press Releases

Business Wire

www.businesswire.com

Canada NewsWire

www.newswire.ca

PR Newswire

www.prnewswire.com

IPOs

Not yet extinct, IPOs may one day rise like the phoenix!

IPO Monitor

www.ipomonitor.com

Index

• A •

acceleration of sales, 242
account executive, 117–118
accounting
  accounting policies, 179
  aggressive accounting.
    See creative accounting
    techniques
  big-bath accounting,
    255–256
  generally accepted
    accounting principles
    (GAAP), 240
  research on, 87–88
accounting policy
  changes, 263
accounts receivable,
  194–195, 242–243
accumulate recommenda-
  tions, 130
acid test ratio, 227–228
adjusted-cost base, 314
Adviceforinvestors.com,
  92, 278
AGAP principles, 166–168
aggressive accounting. See
  creative accounting
  techniques
aggressive investing, 43–45
aging of America, 279
Air Canada, 157
Alcoa, 69
allowance for doubtful
  accounts, 252–253, 262
alternative minimum tax
  (AMT), 310
Altria Group, 69
Amazon.com, 268
American Express Co., 69

American Stock Exchange
  (AMEX), 81, 86, 87
amortization, 188, 262
analysts
  attention, 141
  recommendations, 129–131
Anderson-Tully, 77
annual report
  auditor's report, 181–182
  described, 173–174
  financial statements and
    notes, 176–181
  letter from the chair, 175
  MD&A section, 182–183
  products and services, 176
AOL, 243, 254
appraisal, 163
appreciating asset, 28
appreciation, 39, 188
approval of stock sale, 14
Argentina, 78
asset allocation, 64
asset impairments, 263
asset valuation, 197
assets
  annual growth rate, 24–25
  appreciating asset, 28
  on balance sheet, 22–25
  current asset, 24
  depreciating asset, 28
  fixed assets, 196–197
  liquidity of, 22–23
  long-term assets, 25
  pledged assets, 258
  reallocation of, 29
  typical list of, 24
Association for Investment
  Management and
  Research (AIMR), 110
"at-risk rules," 310, 315
ATI Technologies Inc., 14, 290

AT&T, 69
atypical events, 190
auditor-switching, 241, 261
auditors, 260
auditor's report, 181–182
audits, 182, 262
auto industry, 284
average, 68
average selling price
  (ASP), 233

• B •

balance sheet
  accounts receivable,
    194–195
  analysis of, 28–29
  assets, 22–25
  cash and cash
    equivalents, 193
  company's, 87, 143
  contingent liabilities, 198
  current liabilities, 198
  defined, 22
  fixed assets, 196–197
  intangible assets, 197–198
  inventory, 195–196
  investments, 197
  key items, 177–178
  liabilities, 25–27
  long-term liabilities, 199
  net worth, 27
  notes receivable, 195
  owner's equity, 199–201
  paid-in capital, 200
  retained earnings, 200–201
  use of, 192–193
balance sheet manipulation
  allowance for doubtful
    accounts, 252–253

big-bath accounting, 255–256
checklist, 262–263
creative acquisition accounting, 254–255
inventories, 253–254
off-balance-sheet obligations, 256–258
pre-merger charges, 255
special charges, 255–256
Bank of Canada, 269, 273
banking industry, 284
Bankruptcy Canada, 26
Barron's, 102, 131
basic materials, 279
BBX system, 76
BCE, 157
bear market
in 1973, 272
approach at onset of, 274–275
identifying, 273–274
in late 1990s, 9, 41
and optimism, 273
REITs during, 159
waiting out, 149
worse, 272
bellwether industry, 283
Berkshire Hathaway, 175, 247
beta, 291–292
Bezos, Jeff, 268
Bid.com, 146
big-bath accounting, 255–256
biotechnology industry, 147
Biovail, 141, 146
Bloomberg, 92
board of directors
danger signs, 209
risk-management, 206
role of, 206
stock dividend declaration, 16
Boeing, 69
bond rating, 157
book value, 139
book value per share, 42
broad-based index, 68, 70

brokerage accounts
cash accounts, 128
margin accounts, 128–129
option accounts, 129
brokerage commissions, 116
brokerage orders
buying on margin, 294–296
condition-related orders, 285
day orders, 285, 286
good-till-cancelled (GTC) orders, 285, 286–287, 291, 298
limit orders, 292–294
margin. *See* margin
market orders, 288–289
short sales, 296–299
stop-loss order, 289, 290
stop order, 289, 298
time-related orders, 285
trailing stops, 290–291
brokerage reports, 132–133
brokers
churning, 118
commission structures, 124–126
discount, 118–119
fees, 116
vs. financial planners, 104
finding, 122
full-service, 117–118
interviewing, 121
online brokerage services, 119, 123–124, 127
and personal investing style, 121
personal *vs.* institutional, 116
primary task, 116
recommendations, evaluation of, 129–131
role of, 115–116
selection of, 120–122
self-regulatory organiza-tions (SROs), 120
special features, 124–127
budgeting, 320

Buffett, Warren, 43, 164, 175, 189, 208, 246, 247
bull market
approach during infancy of, 270–272
in late 1990s, 37
pessimism, 268–269
recognizable traits, 268–270
Wile E. Coyote effect, 270
business cycle, 273
business deals, 99
Business Week, 268
buy recommendation, 129
buy-stop order. *See* stop order
buying stocks, 287
buzzwords, 261

• *C* •

CAC-40 (France), 78
Canada Bond Rating Service, 157
Canada Customs and Revenue (CCRA), 26, 152, 302
Canada Deposit Insurance Corporation (CDIC), 23, 122
Canadian Association of Financial Planners (CAFP), 110
Canadian Association of Insurance and Financial Advisers (CAIFA), 110
Canadian Business, 102
Canadian Institute of Financial Planning, 110
Canadian Investment Manager (CIM), 109
Canadian Investor Protection Fund (CIPF), 122
Canadian National Railway, 146

Canadian Securities
    Administrators (CSA),
    13, 120
Canadian Securities Institute
    (CSI), 109, 110, 121
capital gains and losses, 39,
    304–306
capitalizing expenses,
    245–246, 263
career skills, 319
cash, 23, 193, 275
cash accounts, 128
cash equivalents, 193
cash flow, 29, 32–34, 56,
    228–229, 241, 263
cash flow from financing
    activities, 203
cash flow from investing
    activities, 202
cash flow from operations,
    201–202
cash-flow ratios, 228–229
cash-flow statement, 30–34,
    201–203
Caterpillar, 69
cause and effect, 89–90
CBS MarketWatch. *See*
    MarketWatch.com
CDNX exchange, 70–71
CEOs, and "other
    interests," 261
Certified Financial Planner
    (CFP), 109
Certified General
    Accountant (CGA), 109
Certified Management
    Accountant (CMA), 109
Chartered Accountant
    (CA), 110
Chartered Financial Analyst
    (CFA), 110
Chartered Financial
    Consultant (CH.F.C.), 110
Chartered Financial
    Planner, 110
charts, 341–342
churning, 118

CIBC World Markets, 12
Cisco Systems, 53–54
Citigroup, 69, 70
closing date, 101
co-owners, 15
Coca-Cola, 69, 140, 282
coincident indicators, 220
commitments, 258
commodities, 39
"Communications," in
    company name, 47
company information
    accounting information,
        87–88
    annual report. *See* annual
        report
    balance sheet, 87, 143
    bond rating, 157
    comparative financial
        analysis, 88
    debt, 145
    earnings, 145
    earnings growth, 144
    equity growth, 144
    history, lessons from, 142
    income statement, 143
    insider buying, 144
    know the business, 324
    management, evaluation
        of, 142–144
    net income, 88
    new information, 326
    sales, 145
    SEDAR, 183
    staying on top of, 92–93
    vital signs, 137
company research and
    analyst evaluations,
    340–341
comparative analysis,
    226, 326
comparative financial
    analysis, 88
competitive risk, 211
composite index, 68
concept stock investing,
    46–47

condition-related orders, 285
conflict of interest, 210
conservative investing,
    43–45, 149
consistency, 168, 226
consumer
    bankruptcies, 26–27
    confidence, 219, 221
    debt growth, 221
    income, 219
    publications, 142
Consumer Reports, 142
contingent liabilities,
    198, 258
contrarian indicator, 268
contrarian investors, 321
corporate governance risk,
    206–209
corporate malfeasance, 13
cost of goods sold (COGS),
    186–187
cost of sales (COS), 186–187
counterindicator, 268
coupon promotions, 244
creative accounting
    techniques
    balance sheet manipula-
        tion. *See* balance sheet
        manipulation
    broad indicators of, 241
    capitalizing expenses,
        245–246
    checklist, 262–263
    and declining stocks, 333
    pro forma earnings
        statement, 249–250
    recent regulations, 261–262
    related-party transactions,
        246
    reserves, 248–249
    revenue manipulation,
        242–245
    stock options, 246–248
    tax asset valuation
        accounts, 262
    tax losses, 249

creative acquisition accounting, 254–255
credentials, 109–110
credit card interest, 26
culture, trends in, 95
currency hedging, 58
currency risk, 57–58
current asset, 24
current ratio, 227
cyclical industries, 281

• *D* •

DAX (Germany), 78
"Day Last" column, 100
day orders, 285, 286
day traders, 46
debt. *See* liabilities
debt-to-equity, 233
debt traps, 218–219
declining industries, 283
declining stock, warning signs of, 329–333
defence stocks, 150
defensive industries, 282
defensive stocks, 150, 275
deferred-income tax shelters and plans, 306
defined-benefit pension plans, 259
Dell Computers, 146
demographics, 269
depletion, 188
depreciating asset, 28
depreciation, 188, 197, 262
deregulation, 281
derivatives, 177–178
Diamonds (Down Jones Industrial Average Depository Receipts), 80–81
diluted earnings per share, 192
discipline, 170, 322
discontinued operations, 192
discount brokers, 118–119

Disney, 69
diversification, 62–63, 64, 81, 156–157, 170, 323
dividend tax credit, 152, 303
dividends
dates, 101
declaration of, 15
defined, 37
described, 15–17, 150
grossed-up amount, 303
high-dividend stocks, 150
importance of, 43
increases, history of, 150
inflation, effect of, 151–152
vs. interest, 37, 40, 152
life of quarterly dividend, 16
payout ratio, 156, 158
record date, 15
and RRSP contribution room, 307
stock dividend, 304
in stock tables, 97–98
tax implications, 303–304
value of, 42–43
Dodge, David, 23
doing a short sale. *See* short sale
dollar-cost averaging (DCA), 327
Dominion Bond Rating Service, 157
dot-com companies, 30, 47, 60, 140, 146
Dow, Charles, 67
Dow Jones industrial average, 67, 68–70, 72
Dow Jones Industrial Average Depository Receipts (Diamonds), 80–81
DrKoop.com, 30, 51
due diligence, 170
DuPont, 69

• *E* •

earned income, 306, 307
earnings, 177, 186, 228–229, 263, 342
earnings estimates, 342
earnings growth, 144
earnings manipulation. *See* creative accounting techniques
earnings multiple, 100
earnings per share, 192
earnings reports, 98, 99
earnings to price ratio, 235
earnings trend problems, 241
Eastman Kodak, 69
EBITDA (earnings before interest, taxes, depreciation, and amortization), 189, 250
economic risk
coincident indicators, 220
confident consumers, 219
debt traps, 218–219
economic indexes, 219–220
gross domestic product (GDP), 218
lagging indicators, 220
leading indicators, 220
statistics and reports, 217
economic statistics, 217, 269, 343
economics
cause and effect, 89–90
supply and demand, 88–89
understandings, 320
the economy, 93–94, 252
emergency fund, 23, 28, 59, 62, 320
emerging industries, 282
emotional risk
emotions, importance of, 59

falling in love with
stock, 60
fear, role of, 60
greed, 60
EnCanada Corporation, 157
Enron, 181, 239, 256, 333
entertainment, trends in, 95
environmental risk, 212–213
equity, 178, 229
equity growth, 144
established companies, 280
estate planning, 320
ethical risk, 209–210
eToys.com, 30, 51, 146
E*Trade Canada, 115, 119
ex-dividend, 16
excessive debt, 241, 332
exchange-traded funds
(ETFs)
in Canada, 79–80
choice of, 79–81
described, 78–79
Diamonds (Down Jones
Industrial Average
Depository Receipts),
80–81
diversification, 81
HOLDRS (Holding
Company Depositary
Receipts), 81
management fees, 80
QQQ, 81
SPDRs (Spiders), 81
tax implications, 80
exchangetradedfunds.com,
80
expectations, 267
expenses, 177
extraordinary items,
190–191, 263
Exxon Mobil, 69

● *F* ●

factory capacity
utilization, 221

fair market value, 139
fear, role of, 60
Federal Reserve ("the Fed"),
90, 273
fees
brokerage
commissions, 116
brokers, 116
discount brokers, 119
financial planners, 106
limit orders, 292–293
management fees, and
Diamonds, 80
margin interest
charges, 116
online brokerage
services, 123
services charges, 116
Fellow of the Canadian
Securities Institute
(FCSI), 110
financial consultant, 117–118
financial goals, 64
Financial Management
Advisor (FMA), 110
financial news
company information,
92–93
the economy, 93–94
government actions, 94
industry news, 93
public officials, activities
of, 94
purpose of reading, 92
resources, 345–346
trends, identification of, 95
financial plan, 113–114
financial planners
vs. brokers, 104
changes, keeping track
of, 106
credentials, 109–110
credibility, 109–110
fees, 106
guidelines for
choosing, 107

vs. investment
advisers, 104
licensing, 105
qualifications, 109–110
questions to ask
prospective advisers,
108–109
reasons to consult, 105
role of, 110–111
services, 104–105
Financial Planners Standards
Council (FPSC), 109
financial planning
clarification of current
financial situation and
problems, 113
clarification of roles and
responsibilities, 112
financial plan, 113–114
goals and expectations,
determination of, 112
information gathering, 112
resources, 335–336
search for and find a
planner, 111–112
financial position
cash flow, 29, 32–34
cash-flow statement, 30–34
emergency fund, 23, 28,
59, 62
funding your stock
program, 29–34
income, 30–31
income statement, 30
outflow, 31–32
personal balance sheet,
22–29
and risk minimization,
61–62
tax savings as investment
money, 34
financial problems, 99
financial risk, 51–52
financial services
industry, 284

financial statements
    balance sheet. *See* balance
        sheet
    components of, 176
    creative accounting
        techniques. *See* creative
        accounting techniques
    income statement. *See*
        income statement
    items, 177–178
    messages behind the
        numbers, 178–179
    notes to, 179–181
    summary of past
        figures, 181
Fisher, Irving, 273
fixed-asset turnover, 232
fixed assets, 196–197
focus on goals, 327–328
footnotes. *See* notes to
    financial statements
"footsie," 78
foreign-exchange risk, 57–58
fraud, 209, 345
free cash flow, 202
FreeEDGAR, 148, 183
freelunch.com, 217
FTSE-100 (Great Britain), 78
full-service brokers, 117–118
fundamental analysis, 130,
    137–138
fundamental investing, 45
funding your stock program,
    29–34

● *G* ●

GAAP. *See* generally
    accepted accounting
    principles (GAAP)
GAAP violations, 260
gas investments, 315–316
General Electric, 69, 70
General Motors, 69
generally accepted
    accounting principles
    (GAAP), 240, 243, 245,
    249, 250, 253, 257, 258,
    259, 261–262

geopolitical risk, 50, 216
Getty, J. Paul, 321
The Globe and Mail, 10, 92,
    95, 183, 217
going concern, 261
going long, 296
going public, 10–12
going short. *See* short sale
good-till-cancelled (GTC)
    orders, 285, 286–287,
    291, 298
goodwill, 198
government action, 280–281
government actions,
    89–90, 94
government intervention,
    274
governmental problems, 99
Great Depression, 38, 272
greed, 60
Greenspan, Alan, 246, 247
gross domestic product
    (GDP), 93, 218
gross margin or profit, 187
growth, 39
growth industries, 282–283
growth investing
    described, 39
    earnings growth, 144
    equity growth, 144
    fundamental analysis,
        137–138
    insider buying, 144
    lessons from history, 142
    management, evaluation of,
        142–144
    recommendations, source
        of, 141–142
    return on equity (ROE), 143
    vs. value investing, 41
    value-oriented approach,
        138, 139
growth stocks
    described, 136–137
    great selections, 144
    leaders, 140
    megatrends, 140
    niche companies, 140–141
    profitability numbers, 145

selection of, 136
small cap stocks, 145–148
value, determination of,
    138–139
vs. value stocks, 138–139
who's buying, 141–142

● *H* ●

head and shoulders, 46
healthy companies, 137–138
Hewlett-Packard, 69
high-interest debt, 26
high-tech advances, 279
history, lessons from, 142
hold recommendations, 130
HOLDRS (Holding Company
    Depositary Receipts), 81
Home Depot, 69, 70, 146
home equity financing, 27
Homestore, 243
Honeywell International
    Inc., 69
Hoover's Industry
    Snapshots, 278
housing starts, 94, 284

● *I* ●

IBM (International Business
    Machines), 69
illiquid investments, 23
in-process R&D, 254
income, 30–31
income and expense
    statement. *See* income
    statement
income from continuing
    operations, 190
income investing
    described, 39–41, 149
    and diversification,
        156–157
    dividends *vs.* interest, 40
    financial needs and,
        155–156
    stock selection tips,
        154–157

vs. value investing, 41
yield, importance of, 40–41
income statement
  amortization, 188
  vs. cash-flow statement, 30
  cost of goods sold (COGS), 186–187
  cost of sales (COS), 186–187
  creative accounting techniques. *See* creative accounting techniques
  depreciation, 188
  described, 143
  extraordinary items, 190–191
  gross margin or profit, 187
  income from continuing operations, 190
  interest income or expense, 189–190
  net income, 192
  research and development (R&D), 188
  reserves, 188
  revenues, 177, 186
  sections of, 177
  selling, general, and administrative (SG&A), 187–188
  tax expense, 189
  write-downs, 191–192
income stocks
  advantages of, 150–151
  analysis of, 152–153
  bond rating, 157
  defensive stocks, 150
  disadvantages, 151–152
  dividends, 150
  interest-rate sensitivity, 151
  investors, suitable, 149
  payout ratio, 156
  real estate investment trusts (REITs), 159–160
  selection tips, 154–157
  utilities, 158
independent financial publications, 102

index of leading economic indicators (LEI), 94
indexes
  vs. average, 68
  broad-based index, 68, 70
  calculation of, 68
  composite index, 68
  defined, 67
  Dow Jones industrial average, 67, 68–70, 72
  economic, 219–220
  exchange-traded funds (ETFs), 78–81
  how they work, 67–68
  industry indexes, 70
  international, 77–78
  investing in, 78–81
  market-value weighted index, 68
  Nasdaq 100 index, 73
  Nasdaq composite index, 73
  other U.S. indexes, 74–75
  price-weighted index, 68
  Russell 3000 index, 74–75
  sector indexes, 70
  S&P/TSX 60 index, 71–72
  Standard & Poor's 500, 73–74
  weighting, 68
  Wilshire Total Market Index (Wilshire 5000 index), 75
indirect benefits, 99
industry analysis
  dependence on another industry, 280
  government action, 280–281
  growth, 278, 279
  industrial categories, 281–283
  key industries, 283–284
  know the industry, 324
  leading companies, 280
  products or services, demand for, 279
  resources, 342–343
industry indexes, 70

industry news, 93
inflation, 57, 151–152
inflation risk, 57
information and technology risks, 214–215
information gathering. *See* research
initial public offering (IPO), 10–11, 146, 346
innovation, 44
innovators, 280
insider trading, 144, 344
Institute of Canadian Bankers, 110
institutional buying, 141
insurance coverage, 319
intangible assets, 197–198
intangibles, 168
Intel, 69
interest
  defined, 37
  vs. dividends, 37, 40, 152
  expense, 189
  income, 189, 302
  low rates, impact of, 221
interest-rate risk
  company's customers, effect on, 53–54
  company's financial position, 53
  described, 52–53
  income stocks, 151
  investment decision-making considerations, 54
  stock prices, impact on, 54–55
intermediate-term investment, 37
international conflicts, 274
International Paper, 69
Internet brokers. *See* online brokerage services
intrinsic value, 139, 163
inventory, 195–196, 241, 253–254
inventory turnover, 231–232
inventory valuation, 195
investing activities, 203

investing basics, resources
for, 335
investment advisers, 104
investment approaches
guidelines, 35–36
intermediate-term
investment, 37
long term investment, 38
short term investment,
36–37
style. *See* investment styles
time frame, 36–38
Investment Dealers Association (IDA), 13, 120
investment news. *See*
financial news
investment risk. *See* risk
investment skills, 19
investment styles
see also specific styles
aggressive investing, 43–45
and brokers, choice of, 121
concept stock investing,
46–47
conservative investing,
43–45
differences between,
164–165
fundamental investing, 45
growth investing, 39
income investing, 39–41
momentum investing,
41, 47
and small cap stocks, 147
story stock investing,
46–47
technical analysis-based
investing, 45–46
value investing, 41–43
investment tips, evaluation
of, 101–102
investments
on balance sheet, 197
reallocation of, 29
investor advocacy sites, 345
investor associations and
organizations, 339–340

investor profile, 64
investor psychology, 59–60
investor supersites, 336–337
Investor's Business Daily, 92,
217, 321
Investor's Digest of Canada,
131, 321

• J •

JDS Uniphase, 90
job security, 62
Johnson & Johnson, 69
joint ventures, 315
J.P. Morgan Chase, 69, 70
junk bonds, 157

• K •

know thyself, 91
knowledge, and risk
minimization, 61

• L •

labour-sponsored venture
capital corporation
(LSUCC), 314–315
lagging indicators, 220
language of stock
investing, 321
large cap, 18, 36, 44
large-cap stocks, 147
large-ticket items, 269
leaders, 140
leading economic indicators
(LEI), 94, 220–221, 269
leasing transactions, 257
legal risk, 213
letter to shareholders, 175
leverage, 294
leverage ratios, 224
liabilities
common liabilities, 25–26
contingent liabilities,
198, 258

current, 198
defined, 25
excessive debt, 241
high-interest debt, 26
long-term, 199
off-balance-sheet
obligations, 256–258
reduction of debt, 62
unsecured debt, 26
liability issues, 99
LIFO (last-in, first-out)
method, 253–254, 262
limit orders, 292–294, 327
limited partnerships, 315
Lipschitz & Farquar, 146
liquidation value, 139
liquidity, 22–23
"liquidity crisis," 23
liquidity ratios, 224, 226–229
liquidity risk, 55
locked-in RRSPs, 309
long on stocks, 296
long-term assets, 25
long term investment, 20,
38, 164, 324
long-term liabilities, 199

• M •

magazines, 339
management
and corporate governance
risk, 207
evaluation of, 142–144
risk-management, 207–208
management discussion
and analysis (MD&A),
182–183, 208
margin
accounts, 128–129
defined, 294
interest charges, 116
maintaining balance,
295–296
potential outcomes,
294–295
trading on margin, 121

the market. *See* stock market
market capitalization, 17–18, 36, 236
market makers, 75, 76
market orders, 288–289
market perform recommendations, 130
market risk, 55–56
market-value weighted index, 68
MarketWatch.com, 92, 131, 278
materiality, 260
McCain, 140
McDonald's, 69
megatrends, 140, 279
Merck, 69, 141
Merrill Lynch, 81
Merrill Lynch HSBC Canada, 115, 118
micro cap, 18
Microsoft Corporation, 69, 70, 140, 187, 244
mid cap, 18, 36
mineral investments, 315–316
momentum investing, 41, 47
Morningstar Canada, 225
mortgage refinancing, 27
Multex, 225
multiple, 100
Mutual Fund Dealers Association (MFDA), 13
mutual funds, 313

● *N* ●

Nasdaq, 12, 73, 86, 87
Nasdaq 100 index, 73
Nasdaq composite index, 73
Nasdaq National Market, 81
National Association of Purchasing Managers index, 220
National Association of Securities Dealers Automated Quote, 73

National Post, 10, 92, 95
NEPA Foundation, 131
Nestlé, 77
net-change column, 100
net income, 88, 192
net worth, 27
"Network," in company name, 47
neutral recommendations, 130
new markets, 282
new products, 99
New York Stock Exchange, 12, 86
New York Stock Exchange composite index, 68
newsletter recommendations, 141
niche companies, 140–141
Nikkei (Japan), 77
non-financial operating productivity ratios, 232–233
nonrecurring events, 190
Nortel, 70, 90, 144, 168, 242
notes receivable, 195
notes to financial statements
  accounting policies, 179
  burial of bad things in, 261
  debt, 179
  extraordinary gains and losses, 180
  financial instruments, 180
  limitations of, 180–181
  pensions, 180
  receivables, 179
  special liabilities, 180
  stock options, 180
novice investors, 149
NYSE resources, 86

● *O* ●

obsolescence, 212
off-balance-sheet obligations
  commitments, 258
  contingent liabilities, 258

leasing transactions, 257
  pension plans, 258–260
  pledged assets, 258
  securitization transactions, 257
  special-purpose entities, 258
  special-purpose entities (SPEs), 256, 258
oil investments, 315–316
online brokerage account, 127
online brokerage services, 119, 123–124
Ontario Securities Commission, 131
operating ratios, 224, 229–233
operational risk, 211–213
opportunity cost of doing business, 195
option accounts, 129
options, 39
outgo, 23
outsourcing, 212
Over the Counter Bulletin Board (OTCBB), 75–77
over-the-counter (OTC) stocks, 75–77
overstated inventories and receivables, 241
owner's equity, 199–201

● *P* ●

P/E ratio, 42, 100, 235
paid-in capital, 200
payout ratio, 156, 158
payroll taxes, 32
"penny stocks," 283
pension adjustment reversals (PARs), 306
pension income, 263
pensions, 192, 258–260
periodicals, 339
personal bankruptcies, 26–27

Personal Financial Planner (PFP), 110
personal risk, 58–59
Petro-Canada, 141, 292
Pets.com, 30
Pink Sheets, 76–77
piracy issues, 214
pledged assets, 258
political considerations, 94, 332
political risk, 215–217
population growth, 282
pre-merger charges, 255
press releases, 260, 346
price, 234
price to book ratio, 236
price-to-earnings ratio, 42, 100, 235
price to sale ratio, 235
price-weighted index, 68
primary underwriter, 11
privacy issues, 214–215
private companies, 10
pro forma reports, 249–250, 263
Procter & Gamble, 69
profit, 185, 326
profit and loss statement, 30
property, plant, and equipment (PP&E), 196
prospectus, 12–13
public filings, 346
Public Service Enterprise Group, 292
purchasing-power risk, 57

• **Q** •

QQQ ("the Qube"), 81
quick ratio, 227–228
QuickTax, 316
quotes, 341

• **R** •

rainy-day fund. *See* emergency fund

ratio analysis
classes of ratios, 224
comparisons, 226, 236–237
consistency, 226
intrinsic meaning, 225
sources of ratio data and comparison, 225
trends, 226
ratios
acid test ratio, 227–228
average selling price (ASP), 233
cash-flow ratios, 228–229
current ratio, 227
debt-to-equity, 233
earnings to price, 235
fixed-asset turnover, 232
inventory turnover, 231–232
leverage ratios, 224, 233–234
liquidity ratios, 224, 226–229
operating ratios, 224, 229–233
P/E ratio, 235
price to book ratio, 236
price to sale ratio, 235
quick ratio, 227–228
receivables turnover, 231
return on assets (ROA), 230
return on equity (ROE), 229
return on sales (ROS), 230
sales per employee, 232
sales per square foot, 232
times-interest-earned, 233
total-asset turnover, 232
valuation ratios, 224, 234–236
working capital, 234
RBC Dominion Securities, 118
real estate corporations, 159–160
real estate industry, 283–284

real estate investment trusts (REITs), 58, 150–151, 159–160, 313–314
real estate risks, 160
reallocation of investments and assets, 29
receivables, 241
receivables turnover, 231
recommendations
evaluation of, 130–131
source of, 141–142
types of, 129–130
reduced and inconsistent cash flow, 241
Registered Financial Planner (R.F.P.), 110
registered rep, 117–118
registered retirement savings plans. *See* RRSPs (registered retirement savings plan)
regulations
creative accounting techniques, 261–262
effectiveness in Canada, 13
provincial and territorial securities commissions, 13
securities acts, 13
Securities and Exchange Commission (SEC), 12–13
self-regulation, 13
REITs. *See* real estate investment trusts (REITs)
related-party transactions, 246
reputational risk, 210–211
research
accounting information, 87–88
closing date, 101
companies, 87–91, 92–93
company research and analyst evaluations, 340–341

comparative financial analysis, 88
dividend date, 101
economics, 88–91
the economy, 93–94
financial news, 92–95
government actions, 94
industry news, 93
investment tips, evaluation of, 101–102
know thyself, 91
NYSE resources, 86
public officials, activities of, 94
reading about investing, 321
staying informed, 325–326
stock tables, 95–100
trends, identification of, 95
TSX educational resources, 86
what you need to know, 85–91
research and development (R&D), 141, 188, 245–246, 254
Research in Motion, 146
reserves, 188, 248–249, 263, 305–306
resources
  basics of investing, 335
  charts, 341–342
  company research and analyst evaluations, 340–341
  earnings and earnings estimates, 342
  external factors affecting market value, 343
  financial planning sources, 335–336
  fraud, 345
  industry analysis, 342–343
  initial public offerings, 346
  insider trading, 344
  investment news, 345–346
  investor associations and organizations, 339–340

investor supersites, 336–337
periodicals and magazines, 339
press releases, 346
public filings, 346
quotes, 341
stock exchanges, 338
stock-investing Web sites, 337–338
stock screens, 340
taxes, 344–345
technical analysis (TA), 343–344
restructuring charges, 191–192, 263
retained earnings, 200–201
retirees, 149
retiring allowances, 309
return on assets (ROA), 230
return on equity (ROE), 143, 229
return on sales (ROS), 230
return *vs.* risk, 49, 63–64
revenue manipulation
  acceleration of sales, 242
  customer's stock as consideration, 243
  distorted presentation, 244
  gross *vs.* net revenue, 244
  loan arrangements, 242–243
  revenue creation, 243
  stocks as investments, 244–245
revenues, 177, 263
risk
  and beta, 291
  Canada *vs.* U.S., 13
  competitive risk, 211
  corporate governance risk, 206–209
  currency risk, 57–58
  economic risk, 217–221
  emotional risk, 59–60
  environmental risk, 212–213
  ethical risk, 209–210

financial risk, 51–52
foreign-exchange risk, 57–58
geopolitical risk, 50, 216
of going short, 297
inflation, 57
information and technology risks, 214–215
interest-rate risk, 52–55
and knowledge, 65
legal risk, 213
liquidity risk, 55
market risk, 55–56
of obsolescence, 212
operational risk, 211–213
outsourcing, 212
personal risk, 58–59
political risk, 215–217
purchasing-power, 57
real estate, 160
reliance on few customers or suppliers, 212
reputational risk, 210–211
vs. return, 49, 63–64
risk tolerance, 36
risk *vs.* return, 49
speculating, 56
strategic risk, 208
tax risk, 58
types of, 50
risk-management techniques, 208
risk minimization
  diversification, 62–63
  finances, preparation of, 61–62
  knowledge, 61
risk tolerance, 36, 149
Rogers Communications, 141
RRIFs (registered retirement income fund), 58, 310–311
RRSPs (registered retirement savings plan)
  contribution limits, 306, 307
  debate, 312–313

dividend income, 303
earned income limits, 307
and ETFs, 80
foreign-content limit, 309
locked-in, 309
pension adjustment
    reversals (PARs), 306
retiring allowances, 309
rule changes, 106
self-directed, 308–309
spousal, 308
as tax strategy, 34, 58, 306
transfer to RRIF, 310
Russell 3000 index, 74–75

• *S* •

sales per employee, 232
sales per square foot, 232
SBC Communications, 69
Scotia McLeod Direct
    Investing, 119
Seagram Universal, 254
secondary market, 12
securities acts, 13
Securities and Exchange
    Commission (SEC),
    12–13, 183
securities commissions, 13
securitization
    transactions, 257
SEDAR, 147–148, 183
self-directed RRSPs, 308–309
self-regulatory organizations
    (SROs), 13, 120
sell recommendations, 130
selling, general, and
    administrative (SG&A),
    187–188
selling stocks, 288
September 11, 2
services charges, 116
shareholder
    dividends, 15–17
    as owner, 15
    rights, 15

role of, 14–15
shareholders' report. *See*
    annual report
short sale
    defined, 296
    how to go short, 297–298
    risks, 297
    stock price increases, 298
    uptick rule, 299
short term investment, 20,
    36–37
shorting a stock. *See* short
    sale
slowing growth in
    employment, 221
small cap, 18, 36, 44–45
small cap stocks, 145–148
SmartMoney, 102
society, trends in, 95
S&P/TSX 60 index, 71
S&P/TSX composite, 68
SPDRs (Spiders), 81
special-purpose entities
    (SPEs), 256, 258
speculating, 56
speculative industries, 283
speculative stocks, 145–148
spousal RRSPs, 308
SROs. *See* self-regulatory
    organizations (SROs)
Standard & Poor's, 157
Standard & Poor's 500, 73–74
Standard & Poor's
    Depository Receipts, 81
Standard & Poor's Industry
    Survey, 278
start-up companies, 10
statement of cash flows.
    See cash-flow statement
Statistics Canada, 269
stock certificate, 14
stock dividend, 16, 304
stock exchanges, 338
stock-investing Web sites,
    336–338
stock market

described, 10
risk, 55–56
secondary market, 12
volatility, 20
Stock Market Place, 86
stock offerings, 11
stock options, and creative
    accounting, 246–248
stock prices
    determination of, 167
    and interest-rate risk, 54–55
    long-term appreciation, 186
stock screens, 340
stock splits, 304
stock symbol, 97
stock tables
    "Day Last" column, 100
    dividend column, 97–98
    52-week high, 96
    52-week low, 97
    name and symbol, 97
    net-change column, 100
    P/E ratio, 100
    volume, 98–99
    yield, 99
stock value
    book value per share, 42
    determining, 17–18
    dividend value, 42–43
    growth stocks, 138–139
    measurement of, 41–43
    price-earnings ratio, 42
stockholder. *See* shareholder
stockhouse.ca, 154
stocks
    vs. the company, 14
    decline, warning signs of,
        329–333
    defence, 150
    defensive, 150, 275
    definition of, 14
    growth stocks. *See* growth
        stocks
    head and shoulders, 46
    income stocks. *See*
        income stocks

issuance of stock, 10–11
over-the-counter (OTC), 75–77
Pink Sheet, 76–77
price-earnings ratio, 42
small cap, 145–148
yield, 40–41
stop-loss order, 289, 290
stop order, 289, 298
story stock investing, 46–47
strategic risk, 208
strong buy recommendation, 129
subsidiary underwriter, 11
supply and demand, 88–89
syndicate, 11

• *T* •

TA investor, 45–46
tax asset valuation accounts, 262
tax decreases, 281
tax implications
  capital gains and losses, 304–306
  and creative accounting, 249
  deferred-income tax shelters and plans, 306
  see also RRIFs (registered retirement income fund); RRSPs (registered retirement savings plan)
  dividend income, 303–304
  dividend tax credit, 152, 303
  Dow Jones Industrial Average Depository Receipts (Diamonds), 80
  interest income, 302
  labour-sponsored venture capital corporation (LSUCC), 314–315
  mutual funds, 313

oil, gas and minerals investments, 315–316
  REITs, 160, 313–314
  resources, 344–345
  review of tax issues, 311–312
  stock dividend, 304
  stock splits, 304
  superficial losses, 305
  tax planning, 325
tax losses, 249
tax risk, 58
tax savings, 34
TD Waterhouse, 115, 119, 225
TD Waterhouse Investment Advice, 118
technical analysis (TA), 45–46, 130, 343–344
technology companies, 284
360 Networks, 332
3M, 69
time frame of investment
  intermediate-term investment, 37
  long term investment, 38
  short term investment, 36–37
Time magazine, 268
time-related orders, 285
Time Warner, 254
times-interest-earned, 233
top-down investing, 216
Toronto Stock Exchange (TSX)
  exchanges, 70–73
  public market, 12
  Web site, 86, 120
total-asset turnover, 232
trading on margin, 121
  see also margin
trailing stops, 275, 290–291, 327
trends, 95, 226
TSX. *See* Toronto Stock Exchange (TSX)

TSX educational resources, 86
TSX Group, 70
TSX Markets, 70
TSX Venture Exchange, 70
Tyco, 239

• *U* •

ultra cap, 18
uncertain markets, 275–276
unconsolidated entities, 256, 258
underwriters, 11–12
unemployment rate, 221
Union Carbide, 70
United Technologies, 69
unsecured debt, 26
uptick rule, 299
utilities, 158

• *V* •

valuation ratios, 224, 234–236
value, 139
value investing
  AGAP principles, 166–168
  appraisal of business, 163
  book value per share, 42
  consistency, 45
  defined, 162–163
  described, 41, 162–166
  discipline, 170
  diversification, 170
  dividend value, 42–43
  due diligence, 170
  vs. growth investing, 41
  ignore the market, 164–165
  vs. income investing, 41
  long-term focus, 164
  no magic formula, 169
  not all or nothing, 170
  vs. other styles, 165–167
  price-earnings ratio, 42

your own investment
analyst, 164
value investments, types
of, 169
Value Line, 148
value-oriented-growth
investors, 138, 139
value stocks, *vs.* growth
stocks, 138–139
Vancouver and Alberta
Stock Exchanges, 70–71
Vick, Timothy, 139
Vivendi, 254
volatility
in short term, 37

stock market, 20
volume, 98–99

● *W* ●

Wal-Mart Stores, 69
Wall Street Journal, 10,
92, 183
Wall Street on Sale
(Vick), 139
war, 50, 274
warranties, 263
Webfin.com, 131
weighting, 68
Wile E. Coyote effect, 270

Wilshire Total Market
Index (Wilshire 5000
index), 75
working capital, 234
WorldCom, 181, 239, 246
write-down, 191–192, 263

● *Y* ●

Yahoo!, 136–137, 154, 292
Yahoo! Industry News, 278
Yahoo!Finance, 225, 292
yield, 40–41, 99